THE END OF VICTORY CULTURE

THE END OF VICTORY CULTURE

Cold War America and the Disillusioning of a Generation

TOM ENGELHARDT

BasicBooks
A Division of HarperCollins*Publishers*

"Producing War" in part IV was originally published in a somewhat different form in *The Nation* as "The Gulf War as Total Television." *The Nation*, May 11, 1992, p. 1.

Library of Congress Cataloging-in-Publication Data
Engelhardt, Tom 1944–
        The end of victory culture / by Tom Engelhardt.
            p.   cm.
        Includes bibliographical references and index.
        ISBN 0–465–01984–6 (cloth)
        ISBN 0–465–01985–4 (paper)
        1. Popular culture—United States—History—20th century.
2. Sociology, Military—United States.   3. War and society.
4. United States—Social life and customs—1945–1970.
5. United States—Social life and customs—1970–   I. Title.
E169.04.E64   1994
973.9—dc20   94–22732
                                                  CIP

96 97 98 99 ♦/RRD 9 8 7 6 5 4 3 2 1

For Nancy

CONTENTS

I. WAR STORY

II. CONTAINMENTS (1945–1962)

III. THE ERA OF REVERSALS (1962–1975)

IV. AFTERLIFE (1975–1994)

THE END OF VICTORY CULTURE

PART I

WAR STORY

I

Triumphalist Despair

ON DECEMBER 8, 1941, the morning after Japan's "unprovoked and dastardly attack" on Pearl Harbor, that "date which will live in infamy," President Franklin Delano Roosevelt addressed a joint session of Congress. Speaking of "severe damage to American naval and military forces" and "very many American lives . . . lost," he offered up a litany of defeat and disaster. "Last night Japanese forces attacked Guam. Last night Japanese forces attacked the Philippine Islands. Last night the Japanese attacked Wake Island. And this morning the Japanese attacked Midway Island." Yet he also offered the American people one certainty in the face of "this premeditated invasion." He promised that they, "in their righteous might, will win through to absolute victory," to "inevitable triumph."

The press followed the president's lead. *Life* magazine, in its first report on Pearl Harbor, spoke of Japan's attack as potential "national hara-kiri," and of the future possibility of "strangl[ing] the island empire by blockade. . . . It will take not only all-out U.S. military might but great persistence and great courage to hurl back attack and to win the final victory." But victory was not to be doubted. It was "the ultimate goal," the magazine commented the following week, one that already had in place "its battle cry . . . a fine fighting slogan . . . 'Remember Pearl Harbor.'" [1]

Almost immediately, Hollywood's film studios began producing war movies in which, from Wake Island to the Philippines, a savage, nonwhite enemy ambushed and overwhelmed small groups of outnumbered American soldiers. In these films, too, however, defeat was only a springboard for victory. Such triumphalism in a moment of despair was not just a propaganda ploy to mobilize a shocked nation. Triumphalism was in the American grain. From the president to ordinary citizens, it seemed second nature to call on an American culture of victory hundreds of years in the making to explain such an event.

After all, hadn't American history been a processional of progress from the moment European explorers and settlers first set foot on the continent? Weren't defeats, from the Alamo to Custer's Last Stand, just mobilizing preludes to victory? Ultimate triumph out where the boundary lines were still being drawn was a given; and victory, when it came, was guaranteed to bathe all preceding American acts in a purifying glow.

As every child learned in school, our history was an inclusive saga of expanding liberties and rights that started in a vast, fertile, nearly empty land whose native inhabitants more or less faded away after that first Thanksgiving. From its oversized flocks of birds and herds of buffalo to the massive, ancient bones its early naturalists dug up, size seemed to embody the promise of America. The largeness of its mission—whether imagined in terms of a wilderness to be tamed, a continent to be populated, freedoms to be granted, immigrants to be welcomed, a destiny to be made manifest, or a needy world to be supplied with goods—was seldom in doubt. If occasional wrongs were committed or mistakes made, these were correctable; if unfreedom existed within America's borders, it was only so that—as with slavery—it might be wiped away forever. In this land, whites had fought each other reluctantly, with great heroism, and for the highest principles, whether in rebellion against a British king or in a civil war of "brother against brother."

This was, you might say, the free story of America, given away to millions of children who could not wait to be let out of school to pay for a second, recess version found especially at the movies. This second version—a sanguinary tale of warfare against savage lesser peoples—anchored the first in American consciousness, expanding the boundaries of that space within which freedom might "ring." In this tale, embodied in countless westerns, the land was not empty but to-be-emptied, and pleasure came out of the barrel of a gun.

As the enemy bore down without warning from the peripheries of human existence, whooping and screeching, burning and killing, the viewer, inside a defensive circle of wagons, found himself behind the sights of a rifle. It was, then, with finger pressing on trigger that American children received an unforgettable history of their country's westward progress to dominance. In this tale, you had no choice. Either you pulled the trigger or you died, for war was invariably portrayed as a series of reactive incidents rather than organized and invasive campaigns. When the savages fell in countless numbers in a spectacle of slaughter, it was instantly made innocent—and thrilling—by the cleansing powers of the just victory certain to come.

At the heart of this story—what I will call the American war story—lay the nearly 250 years of Indian wars that "cleared" the continent for settlement. From its origins, this war story was essentially defensive in nature, and the justness of American acts was certified not only by how many of *them* died, but by how few of *us* there were to begin with. The band of brothers, the small patrol, or, classically, the lone white frontiersman gained the right to destroy through a sacramental rite of initiation in the wilderness. In this trial by nature, it was the Indians who, by the ambush, the atrocity, and the capture of the white woman (or even of the frontiersman himself)—by, in fact, their very numbers—became the aggressors and so sealed their own fate. Assimilating the Indians' most useful traits, including their love for the wilderness, the individual or the small group earned the moral right to kill, and kill again, in a defensive, if orgiastic, manner.

Whether those lone figures were forced to turn themselves into killing machines or the collectivity arrived in time to destroy the savages, inferior American numbers were invariably translated into a numerology of Indian destruction. When the frontiersman merged into a larger war scenario, he ensured that help would arrive just in time to dispatch the savages who held the white woman captive or encircled the wagon train, settler's cabin, or fort. From the seventeenth century on, Americans were repeatedly shown the slaughter of Indians as a form of reassurance and entertainment; and audiences almost invariably cheered, or were cheered, by what they read, heard, or saw. In this war story, the statistics of slaughter were prized and emphasized.

The American war story was especially effective as a builder of national consciousness because it seemed so natural, so innocent, so nearly childlike and was so little contradicted by the realities of invasion or defeat. Although a racially grounded tale, it deflected attention from the racial horror story most central to the country's development—that of the African-American—and onto more satisfying borderlands of the imagination. In a country uninvaded since 1812 and, after 1865, opposed at home only by small populations of native peoples, most Americans encountered war as a print, theater, screen, or playtime experience.

The Japanese attack on Pearl Harbor fit the lineaments of this story well. At the country's periphery, a savage, nonwhite enemy had launched a barbaric attack on Americans going about their lives early one Sunday morning, and that enemy would be repaid in brutal combat on distant jungle islands in a modern version of "Indian fighting." A mobilized nation's armed forces would embark on an island-hopping campaign of revenge leading to total victory, while, for most Americans, war would still be a distant experience.

On the home front—despite the rationing of some consumer items and the absence of others—the war had a dreamy, unwarlike quality. Between Pearl Harbor and V-J Day, Americans who had lived the previous "peace" decade in the desperation of the Great Depression found themselves with jobs, cash, and prospects. Resorts and hotels operated at capacity despite gas rationing; nightclubs were packed; racetracks were mobbed (until closed in 1945); movie theaters overflowed; book sales leaped; and the greatest fear of the American public, according to pollsters, was not defeat abroad but the possibility that peace might bring another economic collapse.[2]

On August 6, 1945, all that changed in a blinding flash over the city of Hiroshima that left Americans more bereft than they could then have imagined. In the afterglow of Japan's surrender, Americans would experience an ambush that could not be contained on distant frontiers; and their postwar culture would be transformed in bewildering ways, as the story that had helped order their sense of history for almost 300 years proved no longer sustainable. The atomic bomb that leveled Hiroshima also blasted openings into a netherworld of consciousness where victory and defeat, enemy and self, threatened to merge. Shadowed by the bomb, victory became conceivable only under the most limited of conditions, and an enemy too diffuse to be comfortably located beyond national borders had to be confronted in an un-American spirit of doubt.

From the rubble of war rose communism, a "hydra-headed" super-enemy, where previously the triple nationalisms of fascism—German, Italian, Japanese—had stood. A shape-shifting adversary, its forms proliferated in the American imagination. It was "monolithic godless communism," "the Communist conspiracy," "the Communist menace," "international communism"; or regionally, "Asian communism," "Chinese communism," "the puppets of Moscow and Peking"; or more grandiosely, a "Red blueprint to conquer the world"; or domestically, "internal subversion" or "twenty years of treason." Although the enemy was often identified with one super-nation, the Soviet Union, it seemed to mock all national boundaries and stories.

In a sense, communism had never existed in the same world with the United States and its story of national exceptionalism. Its founding father, Karl Marx, had imagined it as a burrowing "old mole," respectful of no national borders. It was at home only in opposition to those boundless twins, capitalism and imperialism, and long before World War II it had become identified in the United States with labor strife and oppressed ethnic or racial groups, exactly the sorts of phenomena that the frontier story of the suppression of the Indian so successfully avoided. If what could be universalized in the American experience—the promise of freedom and abundance—came out of a providential national tale, what was national in the Communist story seemed a happenstance of history. The United States could only be the United States, while communism was the Soviet Union only by the luck of the historical draw.[3]

Being everywhere and nowhere, inside and out, the postwar enemy seemed omnipresent yet impossible to target. A nightmarish search for enemy-ness became the defining, even obsessive domestic act of the Cold War years, while strategic planning for future victory abroad led "prudent" men, familiar with the triumphant lessons of World War II, toward the charnel house of history. American policy makers soon found themselves writing obsessively, not for public consumption but for each other, about a possible "global war of annihilation." In their new combat scenarios, the United States could either forswear meaningful victory or strike first, taking on an uncivilized and treacherous role long reserved for the enemy. In secret directives, these men began to plan for the possibility that 100 atomic bombs landing on targets in the United States would kill or injure 22 million Americans, or that an American "blow" might result in the "complete destruction" of the Soviet Union.[4]

The question of whether or not to use triumphal weapons of a suicidal nature to accomplish national ends proved deeply unsettling not just for adults planning global strategy, but also for children experiencing both the pride of parents returning victorious from the world war and the fear that that war's most wondrous weapon engendered. As one young man told sociologist Kenneth Keniston in 1967:

> I remember the end of World War II, and leading a parade of kids around our summer house, me with a potato masher . . . [and] I remember a guy came to our summer house, it must have been '48 or '49—and sold my mother . . . the first A [volume] of an encyclopedia. . . . I remember reading it and seeing a picture of an atomic bomb and a tank going over some rubble. And I think I became hysterical.[5]

If the story of victory in World War II was for a time endlessly replayed in the movies, in comics, and on television, other cultural vistas were also opening up for the young, ones that led directly into whatever terrified grownups. To escape not into the war story but into places where that story was dissolving held unexpected pleasures, not the least of which was the visible horror of adults at what you were doing. In fears, there turned out to be thrills. Many children instinctively grasped the corrosiveness of the postwar transformation, gravitating toward new forms of storytelling that seemed to rise unbidden from alien worlds: horror comics and science fiction films that drew on the horrors of the bomb, the Holocaust, and the Communist menace; juvenile delinquency movies and fashions that drew on fears of a missing underclass; rock and roll and hipsterism, which fed off fears of racial and sexual otherness; and *MAD* magazine, which drew on a mocking, dismantling voice lodged deep in the culture. In those years, some children embraced with gusto the secret despair of adults who claimed to be living happily in the freest, richest, most generous country on Earth.

From that world of haunting pleasures, I have one personal document—a map of Chinese world conquest I drew in 1959 on a piece of paper hidden inside my American history textbook. While our teacher discussed the Constitution, I took the cartographical look of the island-hopping campaign in the Pacific, globalized it, and set it in an unimaginable future nine years distant. (The map is labeled "War Ends Oct. 6, 1968.") In an otherwise blank mid-Pacific, I drew a crude mushroom cloud captioned, "Atom blast destroys Pacific Isles & U.S. missile supply," an indication of how difficult it was to imagine World War II–style scenarios in a nuclear age. With atomic weapons in place, after all, one might have had the more daunting task of visualizing extinction. My approach to the fighting was otherwise traditional—hundreds of tiny arrows winging their way over every land mass from Greenland to Australia. To reach the United States, the Chinese invaders crossed the Bering Strait, met up with another army routed through Greenland, and swept down on my home. I would have been twenty-four when I became a "Red Chinese" subject.

It seems unsurprising that in those years when fantasies of enemy invasions and takeovers sprouted unchecked, an adolescent, even from a liberal New York City family, would have absorbed the mind-set of his society. My map, in fact, traced a horror story that would soon obsess Kennedy-era officials like Secretary of State Dean Rusk and military adviser General Maxwell Taylor, who believed Chinese "aggression" and "expansionism" presented dangers not just for Asia but for the world. Yet this map was something more than a child's version of Cold War fantasies and fears. To make that map in a class presenting an ideal view of state and citizen, to make it inside a textbook whose dedicatory page held an ode to the American car ("In our great country can be found factories with parking lots full of automobiles. . . . They are symbols, too, that their owners are free . . . free to move on to other work, free to seek other ways of life, free in body and spirit") constituted a half-conscious oppositional act. It is not simply that the map amuses me now but that I found secret pleasure and entertainment then in playing with the worst nightmare the anti-Communist mind could produce.[6]

Like so many other adolescent acts in those years, that map was a corrosive gesture. With every arrow, a bit of another country fell not to victory culture but to a darker culture of defeat. Representing horror *and* yearning, that map said: This is what it would be like if *your* vision proved true, and wouldn't it be something! Part of the secret world of my childhood, that map prefigured a far more unnerving future I could hardly have imagined. Only a few years from the moment I sat in that classroom, some young radical students, recently made aware of an American war in a country called South Vietnam, were producing a map that went far beyond my ambiguous product, but was related to it. In that 1965 map, which appeared in the *National Vietnam Newsletter*, "enemy-occupied areas" of Vietnam turn out to be those occupied by the United States and its South Vietnamese allies.[7]

Yet the boys who fled into the haunted landscapes of the Cold War held another sort of flight close to their hearts as well. They were the last generation to celebrate the national war story with generic toy soldiers on the floors of their rooms, or with toy guns in streets or parks; the last to enact or cheer the moment when the enemy dropped in his tens, hundreds, thousands before our blazing guns, proof of American triumph.

Scenarios of ambush and slaughter, of their savagery and our civilization, of their deceit and our revenge, so essential to victory culture, were still basic to boyhood in the 1950s. This escape into a triumphal past—for generally, children were less likely to shoot down Chicoms or Ruskies or Reds than Indians or Japs or Nazis—held little of the dark or frightening. Children of the 1950s would later remember with genuine fondness these sunny moments of play out of sight of grownups and deeply involved in a story draining from adult culture. Men, and sometimes women, even those who identified themselves as antiwar during the Vietnam years, often recall the war play, war scenarios, and war toys of their childhood with a special fondness.

So those children of the 1950s grasped the pleasures of victory culture as an act of faith, and the horrors of nuclear culture as an act of faithless mockery, and held both the triumph and the mocking horror close without necessarily experiencing them as contraries. In this way, they caught the essence of the adult culture of that time, which—despite America's dominant economic and military position in the world—was one not of triumph, but of triumphalist despair.

Triumphalist despair proved a unique and unstable mix. Without the possibility of total victory, without the ballast of the war story, "freedom" came unanchored as the "freest country on earth" presided over a

"Free World," many of whose members from Franco's Spain to Diem's Vietnam embodied unfreedom. Though the political rhetoric of freedom grew ever thicker, within a decade American freedom, like the Free World, would seem a sham to young people horrified by a war fought in freedom's name that had the look of an atrocity.

It is now practically a cliché that, with the end of the Cold War and the "loss of the enemy," American culture has entered a period of crisis that raises profound questions about national purpose and identity. This book, however, views that loss of enemy as part of a crisis that began with the atomic explosion over Hiroshima—at the moment of total victory in World War II. How Americans have dealt (or failed to deal) with the implications of the global dominance to which their history had brought them in 1945, and how they have (or have not) come to terms with the slow-motion collapse of a heroic war ethos thereafter, are central themes underlying American popular culture from 1945 on.

Between 1945 and 1975, victory culture ended in America. This book traces its decomposition through those years of generational loss and societal disillusionment to Vietnam, which was its graveyard for all to see. It was a bare two decades from the beaches of Normandy to the beachfronts of Danang, from Overlord to Operation Hades, from GIs as liberators to grunts as perpetrators, from home front mobilization to anti-war demonstrations organized by the "Mobe." The shortness of the span seemed surrealistic. The answers of 1945 dissolved so quickly into the questions of 1965. How could a great imperial presence have come to doubt itself so? Nothing was more puzzling than this—than the question mark itself—except the fact that one of the least significant nations on earth seemed responsible for bringing it to public attention.

Indicative of this stunning transformation were the official propaganda films the government produced for each war. Soon after World War II began, at the request of Army Chief of Staff George C. Marshall, Hollywood director Frank Capra (*Mr. Deeds Goes to Town, Mr. Smith Goes to Washington*) embarked on the production of a series of documentaries. Their purpose was to orient American troops to the nature of the enemy they were fighting and to the postwar world they were fighting for. These movies relied on enemy film clips, according to Capra, to "let the enemy prove to our soldiers the enormity of his cause—and the justness of ours." They appeared under the general title *Why We Fight.* The "why" was purely informative in nature. It had no interrogative force whatsoever. In it lurked not the faintest hint of a question, only of a powerful answer.

With their stark vision of "a free world" versus "a slave world," of "civilization against barbarism" and "good against evil," backed up by dramatic Disney-produced animated sequences, these films exuded the clarity and confidence of a country that knew its place in history. The last of them, *Know Your Enemy—Japan*, was released on the day of the atomic bombing of Nagasaki. The first, *Prelude to War*, was considered so powerful that President Roosevelt urged it be put into commercial distribution. As one trailer touted it, "55 minutes of Democracy's Dynamite! . . . the greatest gangster movie ever filmed . . . the inside story of how the mobsters plotted to grab the world! . . . [M]ore diabolical . . . than any horror-movie you ever saw!"[8]

Prelude to War vividly depicted enemy atrocities ranging from the real (Nazi desecrations of churches, a Chinese baby killed in a Japanese air raid) to the imagined (the "conquering Jap army" superimposed on the White House—"You will see what they did to the men and women of Nanking, Hong Kong, and Manila. Imagine the field day they'd enjoy if they marched through the streets of Washington"). Behind these atrocities—the acts of "a savage with a machine gun"—lay a mobilizing vision of an "us or them" struggle. Faced with two animated globes, one white, one black, a daylight world and a world of endless night, what question could there be? "Two worlds stand against each other," intoned the narrator. "One must die, one must live. One hundred and seventy years of freedom decrees our answer."[9]

In 1965, the government released its first film about the war in Vietnam. Modeled on the *Why We Fight* series, it was framed by images of Hitler and Mussolini arriving in Munich in 1938, and of British Prime Minister Neville Chamberlain declaring peace-in-our-time while Nazi flags flapped and *Sieg Heils* were offered up ("Peace in our time," comments an ominous voice-over, "a shortcut to disaster"). This was expectable framing material; for the immediate war story within which Americans, from the president on down, still generally cared to live was that of World War II, and Hanoi was imagined to exist somewhere just south of Munich.

There was, however, another, more alien frame for this film, scripted by the State Department to rally support for President Lyndon B. Johnson's already embattled Vietnam policy. The film opens on the president at a press conference reading aloud a letter from "a woman in the Midwest who wanted to know why her son was in Vietnam."

"In my humble way," the president recites slowly in his homey, nasal twang, "I am writing to you about the crisis in Vietnam. I have a son who is now in Vietnam. My husband served in World War II. Our country was at war, but now, this time, it is just something that I don't understand. Why?"

Johnson's voice picks up the question, "Why Vietnam?" as if it were his, not the woman's, and the phrase resonates three times as the film's title, *Why Viet-nam*, flashes on the screen. Though the written title lacks the question mark, a question mark seems to tremble behind every clip of the film. "Why," the president soon asks, "must young Americans, born into a land exultant with hope and with golden promise, toil and suffer and sometimes die in such a remote and distant place? The answer, like the war itself, is not an easy one." In fact, no answer, only an endless question, is forthcoming.

In the inability of government propaganda to evade this question mark lay an unnerving change in consciousness. Despite an unrestrained desire to present the government's point of view, the film's producers could find no stance beyond a defensive one. Every statement was essentially a response to a question that would not go away. Doubt, not confidence, was where you now had to begin.

In 1965, the time had already passed when the enemy could prove themselves monstrous to Americans. It is the president who has to claim in their name that the war is "guided by North Vietnam and . . . spurred by Communist China. Its goal is to conquer the south and to extend the Asiatic dominion of communism." It is Secretary of State Dean Rusk who has to claim in their name that "the declared doctrine and purpose of the Chinese Communists remain clear, the domination of all of Southeast Asia, and indeed if we listened to what they're saying to us, the domination of the great world beyond." When one of their film clips is used, North Vietnamese leader Ho Chi Minh, shown surrounded by enthralled children, seems to have the spontaneous charm of a Charlie Chaplin. ("Behind the smile is a mind which is planning a reign of terror," claims the narrational voice-over defensively.)

For most of the film, however, while the enemy's atrocities are enumerated, the enemy remains strangely absent—as vague and frustrating to pinpoint as an explanation for the war itself. Over shots of a wounded American being helicoptered out of battle, the narrator explains that "even with superior equipment, this is a different war to prosecute. There are no front lines here. The war is everywhere, against an enemy that is seldom clearly seen."

Much of the rest of the film involves little more than scenes of victimization—destroyed U.S. military equipment, wounded or dead American soldiers and civilian personnel—scenes in which no enemy is ever in sight. Against this backdrop, the alternating voices of president and narrator can be heard awkwardly fending off questions the film never directly acknowledges, swearing that "we will not surrender," "not retreat," not abandon our "commitment," not "dishonor our word." It is as if the film had remained at that news conference, answering increasingly hostile questions from a public as present yet invisible as the enemy.

The film's final scenes are set against flag-draped coffins being unloaded from a plane for burial in the United States, scenes unimaginably distant from the triumphal certainty of World War II. It is in the presence of what could not help but look like defeat that the president almost plaintively pleads his case: "I do not find it easy to send the flower of our youth, our finest young men into battle. . . . We did not choose to be the guardians at the gate, but there is no one else. Nor would surrender in Vietnam bring peace, because we learned from Hitler in Munich that success only feeds the appetite of aggression."

Despite the framing shots of Hitler, next to nothing of the ethos of World War II or the war story remained in *Why Viet-Nam*. No longer was it a simple matter of fleshing out the nature of an aggressive and savage enemy, assuring the public of a victory to come, or laying out postwar goals. While these propaganda films were released into high schools and colleges, their theatrical release was evidently not considered. Then again, mobilizing the public was never part of the Vietnam agenda. Something stranger was going on. The public was to be shored up, TV event by TV event, to offer support only in the form of "opinion" to pollsters. In fact, the public's most important act of support was simply to remain inert. It was to be mobilized to do exactly nothing. Its task was not to act, because action, in the context of Vietnam, meant opposing the president's war. The president needed the support of abstract "opinion" to ward off the question mark, and an absence of live oppositional bodies to ensure that the invisible enemy be held at bay.

"If freedom is to survive in any American hometown," declares the narrator of *Why Viet-Nam*, "it must be preserved in such nations as Vietnam." Yet the continental United States was under attack only in the sense that the memory of World War II was being slowly picked apart, and just circling the wagons wasn't protection enough. *Why Viet-Nam* conveniently located American doubt in those simple people out there— mothers in the Midwest who wanted to be convinced that this was indeed World War II. The question mark, however, had lodged itself, first and foremost, within official Washington. Doubt grew like some subversive foreign entity right inside the president's head. It was certainly no fluke that the question mark was lodged so deeply in, yet not officially on *Why Viet-Nam*. Thanks to an article by James Thomson, Jr., a State Department East Asian specialist in the Kennedy and Johnson administrations, we know that the issue of acknowledging the question mark was argued out in the most literal way within at least one part of the

Johnson administration. "[M]y most discouraging assignment in the realm of public relations," Thomson recalled, "was the preparation of a White House pamphlet entitled *Why Vietnam*, in September, 1965; in a gesture toward my conscience, I fought—and lost—a battle to have the title followed by a question mark."[10]

But the question mark could not be evaded by technical means, for it was already there. In that year of massive escalation, the defensive stance of the government's first significant propaganda film about the war only confirmed its existence. The no-name director of *Why Viet-Nam* faced a problem Frank Capra could not have imagined. It was not the enemy but Americans who were now required to deny the "enormity" and prove the "justness" of their cause, and their cause, when examined, did not look so great.

The strain of doing this made for propaganda that looked exactly like what it was. The growing oppositional movement took it as such. The historian Henry Steele Commager, for instance, denounced the film for its "fabrications." "When Communists sponsor such propaganda," he wrote in the *Saturday Review*, "we call it brainwashing." Some in the antiwar movement found such films useful organizing tools: "The U.S. Army and the Department of Defense have made numerous and expensively produced films arguing their case for Vietnam and wars of counterinsurgency in general. Made with your tax money, they are available for 'educational' showings (free) and should be used with films made by the Vietnamese showing why they are fighting," suggested the May 1969 issue of *Liberation* magazine. To them, the government's defensive lies and evasions were instantly visible, even laughable, when set against the Capraesque mobilizing emotions of enemy propaganda films.[11]

Already in shreds in 1965, the film's response to the question, Why Vietnam? has long since dematerialized, but the question mark is still with us. In this, the film was in good company. There was no American narrative form that could long have contained the story of a slow-motion defeat inflicted by a nonwhite people in a frontier war in which the statistics of American victory seemed everywhere evident. Instead, the forms that might once have contained such a war dematerialized as well. By the early 1970s, the war story was even being swept out of childhood, along with the war films, westerns, comics, war toys, and TV shows that had been its vessels. The very word *war* had fallen into disrepute as an attraction for the child audience, and the United States had been shorn of a version of its history that was close to a secular religion.

Certainly, Vietnam marked a definitive exit point in American history and the 1960s, a sharp break with the past. There, the war story finally lost its ability to mobilize young people under "freedom's banner" except

in opposition to itself, a loss experienced by a generation as both a confusing "liberation" and a wrenching betrayal. There, the war story's
codes were jumbled, its roles redistributed, its certitudes dismantled, and
new kinds of potential space opened up that proved, finally, less liberating than frightening. Americans had lived with and within victory culture for so long that no one left its precincts voluntarily. Even the assault
on that culture by the young in those years was hardly as oppositional as
then imagined. In part, it too was a playing out of aspects of victory culture, and as that culture collapsed, those who had opposed it, being
caught up in a symbiotic relationship with it, collapsed as a force as well.

The loss of boundaries beyond which conflict could be projected and of
an enemy suitable for defeat in those borderlands meant a collapse of
story. The post–Vietnam War years have so far represented only the afterlife of this societal crisis, the playing out of storylessness. It is hardly surprising that, after 1975, the basic impulse of America's political and military leaders (as well as of many other Americans) was not to forge a new
relationship to the world but to reconstruct a lost identity of triumph.
After all, the ruins of the war story are all around us, as are the ghostly
fragments of what was once repressed from that story. But in a world that
has moved far beyond triumphalist despair, the war story cannot be simply reconstituted.

Experts in "Communist studies" used to say that Communist states
could not exist without external enemies. Ironically, this very issue has
proved central to American national identity. Is there an imaginable
"America" without enemies and without the story of their slaughter and
our triumph? Can there be a new story Americans will tell about and to
themselves, no less to the world, that might sustain them as citizens and
selves? So far only warring fragments of race, gender, religion, and ethnicity have risen to fill the space emptied of victory culture. Whether those
fragments of "identity" presage some longer-term collapse or something
new remains unknown.

2

Story Time

Just before dawn Mason stormed one entrance of the fort and Underhill the other. The sounds themselves must have been terrifying, with Pequot shouts of alarm, "Owanux! Owanux!" ("Englishmen! Englishmen!"), mixed with war whoops, screams of women and children, musket shots, barked orders. Warriors within the wigwams pelted the English with their arrows so effectively they made "the fort too hot for us," Underhill admitted: "Most courageously these Pequeats behaved themselves." Mason, reaching the same conclusion, declared to his men, "We must Burn them." Immediately stepping into a wigwam he "brought out a firebrand, and putting it into the Matts with which they were covered, set the Wigwams on Fire." Underhill from his side started a fire with powder, "both meeting in the centre of the fort, blazed most terribly, and burnt all in the space of half an hour." The stench of frying flesh, the flames, and the heat drove the English outside the walls: Many of the Pequots "were burnt in the fort, both men, women, and children. Others [who were] forced out . . . our soldiers received and entertained with the point of the sword. Down fell men, women, and children."[1]

The date was June 5, 1637; the fort, a native stockade; the assault, a surprise attack on sleeping Pequots; the results, four hundred men, women, and children killed. The sneak attack, the assault on the fort, the use of fire, the savagery of the killing—all of these were later to be transformed into specific "Indian" traits in the American war story. In fact, of the elements that made up the initial accounts of the Pequot massacre, only the statistics of death generally did not change hands. Those "four hundred" were to die over and over again for audience satisfaction and

pleasure, a slaughter justified by their treacherous ambushes, their torture of captives, their savage use of fire and other hellish modes of
killing, and their attack on the fort (settler's cabin, or wagon train).[2]

Impulsive cruelty became the essence of Indianness. Benjamin
Franklin denounced "barbarous tribes of savages that delight in war and
take pride in murder"; and the earliest nineteenth century schoolbooks
graphically displayed a well-established iconography of Indian cruelty.
The primal pleasure Indians took in "the cries of their victims," their
"diabolical thirst for blood," and their "lust of murderous deeds" were
detailed with an emphasis on their mistreatment of white captives. "It
was a favorite amusement among the Indians of New York to burn the
soles of the feet of the faithful missionaries, whose sole object was to
save their souls," read one text. "[They] cast an infirm old man into the
flames, here, they dashed against the trees children snatched away from
the breasts of their dying mothers," went another.

According to historian Ruth Miller Elson, children in early nineteenth-century America were exceedingly familiar through these texts
with "the details of the major Indian massacres" and with individual
Indian cruelties. Most such books, for instance, had at least one illustration of an Indian, tomahawk raised, about to murder and presumably
scalp a helpless white mother holding an infant in her arms.[3]

At the beginning, however, "their" traits and "ours," their acts and
ours, had not yet been fully distributed. The disentangling of traits and
acts—who inherited which—would be the narrative spoils of victory. To
the winners would go engineering rights to the story; to the losers, the
traits and acts which would ensure that the story unfolded as the winners
said it had.

Later that June of 1637, most remaining Pequots either surrendered or,
in flight and starving, were pursued some sixty miles by the Europeans
and then killed or captured. Some captives were indentured to families in
the Massachusetts Bay Colony; some sold into slavery in the West Indies;
and about twenty were given over to a Skipper John Gallop who "threw
them bound into the sea or, as a Puritan historian exulted, fed 'the fishes
with 'em.'" The dogged, merciless pursuit was to remain a white possession, an understandable trait of revenge; the capture and mistreatment of
hostages, however, was to become an Indian one.

Of those Pequots harried and chased near to present-day New Haven,
Connecticut, Governor John Winthrop wrote at the time: "Hard by a
most hideous swamp, so thick with bushes and so quagmiry, as men
could hardly crowd into it, they were all gotten." Three hundred Pequots,
historian Richard Drinnon tells us, "were literally run to ground. Many
of those killed were tramped into the mud or buried in swamp mire." In

this way did the "quagmire" first enter American history, as a burial place not for white hopes but for Indian bodies as worthless as the land into which they sank.[4]

From massacres, atrocities, and captivities on all sides, the earliest narrative fruits of victory began to appear in the form of "Indian" acts— the bloody scalp trophy, the baby whose brains had been smashed out against a tree, the white mother hatcheted in her bed, the captives burned or roasted to death, or slit open, or murdered in the stealth of night, their bodies mutilated in unheard of ways.

Well into the nineteenth century, from the white–Indian conflict in certain regions of the country came a striking cautionary tale. As T. L. McKenney, chief administrator of Indian affairs, 1816–1830, recalled in his memoirs:

> Which of us has not listened with sensations of horror to nursery stories that are told of the Indian and his cruelties? In our infant mind he stood for the Moloch of our country. We have been made to hear his yell; and to our eyes have been presented his tall, gaunt form with the skins of beasts dangling around his limbs, and his eyes like fire, eager to find some new victim on which to fasten himself, and glut his appetite for blood. . . . We have been startled by the shriek of the dying mother; and hushed that we might hear the last sigh of the expiring infant.

The horrors of the New World, particularly of what that world let loose in its European newcomers, were indeed monstrous enough that they needed much taming to fit the proportions of a tale suitable not so much to frighten as to thrill a child.

At the beginning, there had been an armed horror that was not yet a story, a bloody hell of torture, dismemberment, and enslavement, of desperate retribution against the less-than-human, and of helplessness and captivity at the hands of peoples referred to as "the devil's instruments" or "barbarians," as "wolves" or "mad dogs," as vermin to be exterminated.[5]†

---

†No more decisive boundary could have been drawn between those who deserved the land and those who deserved nothing than this verbal transformation of the Indian into an animal. George Washington, for instance, wrote of the difficulty of driving Indians off their land by force of arms rather than by treaties. It was "like driving the wild beasts of ye forests, which will return as soon as the pursuit is at an end, and fall, perhaps upon those that are left there; when the gradual extension of our settlements will as certainly cause the savage, as the wolf, to retire; both being beasts of prey tho' they differ in shape."[6]

In the beginning, the New World was boundaryless and overwhelming for most Europeans. No clear distinction existed between frontier and settled areas. The land, vast beyond imagining, extended ever westward into the unknown.

A waste and howling wilderness
Where none inhabited
But hellish fiends, and brutish men
That devils worshiped,

as Michael Wigglesworth wrote in 1662. That boundless wilderness might threaten to crush the settler, or alternately as a landscape of strange and sensual pleasures to seduce the settler. In either case, where no external boundaries existed, internal boundaries threatened to collapse, releasing into the world of the civilized, into God's world, either an unrestrained savagery or an unfettered sensuality.[7]

Every society has ways of dealing with and reducing the Other. Crucial to those first Europeans, however, was the desperate closeness of those Others. Native Americans were already on the land. They had staked out their claims to be at the heart of the story before it could even begin and did not seem to grasp that God had granted the newcomers settlement rights. For them, the land was already a cherished centrality.

The need to displace these darker-skinned Others was urgent, although the virulent new diseases that preceded the arrival of large numbers of Europeans eased the task considerably. In the three years before first landing at Cape Cod, for instance, a plague wiped out 90 percent or more of the native inhabitants of southern New England. Such plagues were hailed as "miraculous." "God hath hereby cleared our title to this place," Governor Winthrop wrote a friend in 1634.[8]

At stake in the story as it first developed was who was peripheral to whom. After all, the initial European invaders of North America were outnumbered by their "savage" neighbors, just as in some areas of the South whites would soon be outnumbered by the African slaves they were importing to work their lands. Historian Peter Wood has estimated that a black majority was established in South Carolina as early as 1708, and only grew thereafter. (The fastest growing part of South Carolina's population, however, was enslaved Indian war captives.) If anything, this majority was vastly overestimated by anxious whites, fearing Indian attacks and black uprisings. In 1734, a Captain Von Reck typically claimed that there were "five Negroes to one White" in the colony. As an Anglican minister commented, "[W]e make use of a wile for our present security to make the Indians and negros a check upon each other lest by

their vastly superior numbers we should be crushed by one or the other."
The fear of being overwhelmed and slaughtered was undoubtedly intense,
although this sense of insecurity would someday be carried into the story
as a glorious sign of innate superiority. Americans entering battle ever
after would be portrayed as an outnumbered force.[9]

The problems that Europeans faced in constructing a life and a narrative about that life in the New World had not been issues to those they
left behind. Unlike the European imperial stories in which the dark-
skinned Other, separated by the vastness of oceans, was an exotic or
romantic creature as strange as the parrot or the rhinoceros, in the New
World it was the Europeans who were initially "out there." They were
the marginal ones in something close to exile in a land beyond all civilized bounds.

As a result, theirs was originally a tale of loss, of violent uprooting and
disorientation, hence all the towns longingly named after their imagined
European counterparts, those places of origin, with only a "new" ap-
pended to them. Europeans at home indulged in fantasies about the
Edenic quality of life in North America, as did a small number of arriving
Europeans. Thomas Morton, for instance, wrote in *New English Canaan*,
published in 1637, of the "millions of Turtledoves [on] the greene
boughes, which sate pecking of the full ripe pleasant grapes that were
supported by the lusty trees, whose fruitfull loade did cause the armes to
bend . . . which made the Land to me seeme paradice," and of the "very
ingenious and very subtile" peoples who lived there.

Most arriving settlers, however, indulged in a different style of fantasy.
The Puritans, William Bradford feared, would be

> in continual danger of the savage people, who are cruel, barbarous,
> and most treacherous, being most furious in their rage and merciless
> where they overcome; not being content only to take away life, but
> delight to torment men in the most bloody manner that may be, flay-
> ing some alive with the shells of fishes, cutting off the members and
> joints of others by piecemeal and broiling on the coals, eat the collops
> of their flesh in their sight whilst they live, with other cruelties horri-
> ble to be related.[10]

How a profound tale of loss of cultural bearings was to be turned into a
story of eternal gain, how that periphery was to be transformed into this
heartland, how this chosen people was to occupy their chosen land and
create a true new England or new Jerusalem—this was the problem.
None of this would be possible as long as a pagan people occupied what
the Puritans in particular had envisioned as an uninhabited wilderness,

America Deserta, a great emptiness in which they, the new Israelites, would construct a City of God. For the land to be emptied, its native inhabitants would have to be left in the condition in which the Puritans arrived. They would have to be transformed into exiles, their existence made peripheral to that of the Europeans, their lands turned into living exhibits of marginality.

The Indian reservation, already imagined by the Puritans and called a "praying town," would someday prove a perfect way to display this marginality. The reservation's land would be least representative of The Land, for the most marginal of lands were naturally to be given to the most peripheral of peoples. It might be established on a small, unattractive shard of former tribal land or on a vast unattractive expanse like the Great Plains to which tens of thousands of Eastern Indians were forcibly "removed" in the 1830s, when it was thought of as the Great American Desert, a "barrens" fit only for "mongrel races" and "uninhabitable by Anglo-Americans." Whether desert or swamp, the main attribute of their land would be its worthlessness in white eyes.[11]

The successful emptying of the land opened necessary space for the intense idealism with which the United States became associated, with its emphasis on liberty for and the inclusion of all. Yet for such idealism to thrive, that emptying had to be seen as something other than a succession of horrors. It was important that the arrival of the Europeans be a matter of "settlement" not "invasion," and the move across the continent "expansion" not "conquest" (in the style of the Spanish whose "black legend" of cruelty stood as a scorned example of what had not been done in the land of the free). The presentation of this emptying took two often interrelated forms. In the first of these, the land was basically "vacant" to begin with, ready to be peopled in all its primal glory. In this version of the story, war was, at best, a subtheme in a larger tale of the nobility of the idea of freedom—the freedom of tough bodies, tough minds, and expansive new ideas to move across the emptiness of a great continent.

As George Bancroft summed up this vision in the introduction to volume one of his ground-breaking *History of the United States*, published in 1834:

[O]ur constitution, fixed in the affections of the people, from whose choice it has sprung . . . fearlessly opens an asylum to the virtuous, the unfortunate, and the oppressed of every nation. And yet it is but little more than two centuries, since the oldest of our states received its first permanent colony. Before that time the whole territory was an unproductive waste. Throughout its wide extent the arts had not erected a monument. Its only inhabitants were a few scattered tribes of feeble barbarians, destitute of commerce and of political connection. The axe and the ploughshare were unknown. The soil, which had been gathering fertility from the repose of centuries, was lavishing its strength in magnificent but useless vegetation. In the view of civilization the immense domain was a solitude. It is the object of the present work . . . to follow the steps by which a favoring Providence, calling our institutions into being, has conducted the country to its present happiness and glory.[12]

This version of the story depended for its particular brand of sunniness on the innocent disappearance of the Other from history. Where the Other had hardly been, a great, challenging wilderness stretched from sea to sea, a fertile blankness, a "virgin soil" on which a story of freedom could be writ large for all the world to see. In this New World, time began with the arrival of European settlers, whose main challenge was the timeless land. The history that preceded American history stretched back through Europe to Greece and Rome. The native peoples of the Americas were part of a prior natural history (as in an aptly titled 1953 textbook, *America Before Man*, which took its reader from the dinosaur through the Indian in a cataloging of species that preceded first landfall).

Without the conquest of the Native American, with the enslavement of the African as an aberrant sideshow in the progress of liberty, against the blank of a continent where population simply "spread," disagreements among whites were what had to be overcome—even, as in the Civil War, by force of arms. This was history as a success story, an ennobling tale of the growth of a powerhouse of goods and ideas, a land of natural abundance open to the emigration of "free men" everywhere.

If this first version was a bowdlerized fairy tale, the second was a far more thrilling and bloody story in which an embattled, chosen-people-in-formation cleared the land in person. Emptiness lay at the sunny end of this story, not at its beginning. There were no invasions or conquests here either, however, for by the time the telling began, "we" were already at home on the continent.

CAPTIVITIES

The earliest popular texts to attempt to make narrative sense of and establish certain boundaries around not-yet-American experience were Puritan sermons of armed retribution and accounts of captivity, especially the captivity experiences of white women. More than five hundred of these had been published by the nineteenth century, and some proved to be the earliest American best sellers. The first of them was Mary Rowlandson's "narrative" of her captivity. Published in 1682, it was in its fifteenth edition by 1800. Such accounts, initially pious recitals of God's fearful judgments in a sinful world, later became "simple blood-and-thunder shockers." As a form, captivity narratives did far more than simply emphasize native savagery and depredations. They were the origin myths of the war story, for by putting the Indians in the position of invaders, violently intruding on a settled world, they made the need for certain types of explanations unnecessary.[13]

In a sense, then, history in North America begins with the capture of white women and the idea of white victimization. Without necessarily straying far from the often horrific facts of any given experience—the autobiographical nature of these accounts, even if sometimes fraudulently produced, was crucial—captivity narratives instantly turned the invader into the invaded and created the foundation for any act of retribution that might follow.

It was only in this primal American scene that women were individually celebrated for taking on warlike roles. Only as captives or potential captives could they also become warriors, armed mothers defending home, children, or purity. Hannah Dustan of Haverhill, Massachusetts, was the first to gain such renown. Taken by "Formidable Salvages" in 1697, just after delivering her eighth child, she and her attending nurse were marched 150 miles through the wilderness by their captors. As described by the Puritan minister Cotton Mather, she was forced to watch as they "dash'd out the Brains of [her] Infant against a Tree." Later, with help, she took up a hatchet, murdering ten of the twelve members of an Indian family, before escaping with her captors' scalps. For the scalps she received "a bounty of fifty pounds from the General Assembly along with 'presents of Congratulation' from friends and much press from Mather." Only in this way could women be hailed as "amazons" for accomplishing murderous deeds in the wilderness.[14]†

---

†Mary Ludwig (Molly Pitcher), who in 1778 accompanied her husband into the Battle of Monmouth as his water carrier and replaced him at his cannon when he fell, was honored with a sergeant's commission by George Washington himself. But hers was a singular fate. Otherwise, except as famous captives, women played almost no individualized parts in the cast of characters that was to inhabit the war story well into the twentieth century. There were neither the female sachems of Native American tradition, nor figures like Joan of Arc and Catherine the Great of feudal Europe, nor the Harriet Tubmans and Sojourner Truths of a very different freedom story. Even as captives, according to historian June Namias, their

In the meeting of Europeans, Africans, and Native Americans in the New World, the experience of fear and terror was hardly confined to one group. Captivity—and captivity narratives—might have provided a framework for the history of all peoples on the North American continent. After all, Indian captivity experiences were commonplace. From the first Pequots sold into Caribbean slavery to the children forcibly placed in Indian schools in the nineteenth and twentieth centuries, much of Native American history involved a series of captivities. Certainly, the reservation system was a form of captivity, in conception somewhere between prison and zoo.

The greatest captivity, of course, was that of the half-million or more Africans brought to North America as slaves. Yet the captivity "story" was a captive of the victor's culture. There may have been no theme more commonly invoked from 1682 to the present in newspapers, penny dreadfuls, medicine shows, Wild West shows, paintings, sculptures, dime novels, plays, and films than that of the white, female captive victimized by a horrifying enemy, with its concomitant themes of rescue and retribution. Three hundred-plus years of invocation to mobilize or thrill testify to a powerful urge for an image of victimization at the heart of the war story.

Historian Bernard Bailyn has written: "American culture in th[e] early period becomes most fully comprehensible when seen as the exotic far western periphery, a marchland, of the metropolitan European culture system." For the European released into this periphery, the first American "freedom" was from captivity to certain civilized norms. It was the freedom to organize a bloodletting that could be justified only in a land of invasive savages and threatening subhumans.

It was not just in relation to those already occupying the land—the pregnant Indians who had their children ripped from their bellies and "hung upon trees," or those burned alive, or whose bodies were fed to dogs—that this savagery was played out. At an extreme, Bailyn cites the letters

of the South Carolina missionary Le Jau, with their tales of slave women being "scalloped" and left to die in the woods or burnt alive on suspicion of arson; of masters who "hamstring, mai[m], & unlimb"

---

portrayal generally moved from strength to weakness, from "amazon" to, by the nineteenth century, "frail flower." The female patriot had no significant place— except as the mother of future patriots—in a story so tied to war; nor did the frontierswoman, except in a few novels or dime novels in which white women like Calamity Jane appeared in men's clothing and took up the gun.[15]

their slaves "for small faults," or for falling asleep at work "scourge" them twice a day, then "muffle" them so that they could not eat, and at night bind them into a "hellish machine . . . [in] the shape of a coffin where [they] could not stirr"; of laws, no longer even remarked on, that required the castration of Negro runaways.

This embracing of savagery, amid boundless feelings of terror, as a strange form of pleasure was an essential aspect of the American experience.[16]

So an armed haunting preceded the national story into existence, while a special ferocity accompanied the push "westward" and gave a particularly savage quality to warfare, even among white Europeans in North America. This horror story shadowed a national story that did not fully solidify until the 1830s. What began to dissipate, however, was the visceral terror that the wilderness and its inhabitants would engulf the tenuous coastal colonies, that the new settlers might be pushed into the sea. In a series of attacks in 1622, after all, the Powhatan Confederacy had killed about a third of the settlers in Virginia, nearly eradicating the Jamestown colony; and, as late as 1676, Indians not only attacked towns all along the Massachusetts frontier, overrunning Lancaster, where Mary Rowlandson was captured, but struck within ten miles of Boston.[17]

Once the revolutionary separation from England had taken place, however, disparities in weapons technology and population mass began to give the push across the continent an inexorable quality, and fear of defeat became localized in passing moments on ever more distant frontiers. Fear of European intervention remained alive through the Civil War; but after 1848 nothing seriously obstructed increasingly expansive visions of an American nation, not the tribal peoples of North America, or the defeated Mexicans, or the Filipinos, who would at century's end experience the savagery of "Injun fighting" firsthand, or the Puerto Ricans, who were to become U.S. property, or the Cubans, who would endure a protectorate, or other peoples of the Caribbean and Central America, who would experience military interventions.

Largely forgotten would be the War of 1812, because there was no place in the story for a defeat that was not a birthing moment for the culture of triumph or for a war that ended well short of victory. The only acceptable defeats or last stands would be those that were the end of the beginning for us and the beginning of the end for them.

Other than the War of 1812, Pancho Villa's 1915 raid on Columbus, New Mexico, and the Japanese attack on Pearl Harbor, landings in the Aleutian Islands, and scattered balloon bombings of the West Coast, Americans never experienced an armed foreign threat, no less an invasion; nor did they have to account for defeat in war. U.S. history would be a tale of unparalleled success against peoples who, until World War I, were generally categorized as inferior (and nonwhite), hence doomed to submission. The ease of victory in these martial events that spread the promise (though seldom the actuality) of "freedom" to lesser peoples meant that Americans would remain free to organize their national story to their own specifications, largely around the unbalanced conflict between white settler and Indian, while the centrality of that conflict to the story could be maintained long after Native Americans had been relegated to the reservation.

Reimagined as unpossessed, everything on the continent could be discovered and named for the first time. An unknown land awaited an inventory. The measuring, mapping, and cataloging of places, species, and peoples proceeded at a frenetic pace. In 1804, when President Thomas Jefferson dispatched the country's first great transcontinental military expedition under Captain Meriwether Lewis and Lieutenant William Clark of the U.S. Army to find a route to "Cathay," he made sure that its scientific observations would be of an all-encompassing nature.

Lewis and Clark departed with detailed instructions to study the "soil and face of the country." They were to fix their position by astronomical observations for mapping purposes and to closely observe Indian population size and "their language, dress, and monuments." They were to survey, in the words of historian William H. Goetzmann, the land's "vegetable production, its animals, its fossils, the existing minerals, including metals, limestone, coal, salts, mineral waters, and saltpeter . . . take note of volcanic action and . . . keep statistics on the weather."

Throughout most of the nineteenth century, naturalists, zoologists, geologists, botanists, ethnologists, and artists accompanied the many surveying expeditions, military and civilian, intent on capturing the land in all its aspects, as did paleontologists and archeologists intent on making the past, whether "ancient Silurian mollusks or sun-bleached Comanche skulls," part of the national patrimony. As specimens of every sort flowed back from the West, scientists began to organize this booty into a hierarchy of possessed flora and fauna in the Smithsonian Institution (founded in 1846) and other repositories. There, the image of the New Land would be captured for all time. Native American arts and artifacts would become part of this natural history, not of human history, whose artifacts from Sumerian seals to Peale portraits would be found in the separate art museum.[18]

As with the land's topography and boundaries, so, too, the topography and boundaries of the story and the naming of its elements seemed under control. Who was inside, who out; where "we" belonged and where the "enemy" belonged, we alone would determine. This power to organize narrative boundaries without fear of contradiction gave the war story its extraordinary simplifying and unifying presence; and the threat of resistance from peoples beyond (or still temporarily within) those boundaries, while no longer imperiling, gave it a continuing sense of tension. Simply by circling the "wagons," Americans could now create a sense of home anywhere they were; and since they were always potentially at home, any act against an American automatically put all Americans in the position of having their boundaries violated.

Because of this aggressively mobile sense of home, captivities, ambushes, and last stands came to take the place, in miniature, of the absent enemy invasion, and the sense of violation these engendered became an empowering force for the enemy's annihilation. Whether or not an actual annihilation followed, in the war story an annihilation invariably occurred, one that lay not just in commonplace scenes of retributive slaughter, but in taking on the roles of victor and victim, leaving next to nothing to the Other.

The "noble savage" might seem an exception to this, but from James Fenimore Cooper's novels to Edward Curtis's nostalgia-tinged photos, he proved a self-annihilating victim. Invariably the "last" of his kind, the "vanishing" native's destiny was to perform a removal on himself, and his nobility lay, reassuringly, in his willingness to make way. Such a figure was helping to create the "vacant" land, leaving behind only a memory of himself and a frisson of emotion. "Very soon not one will be living. How sad to think of a whole nation gone forever!" went a nineteenth-century children's text that suggested one "drop a tear" for the Indians.[19]

In the emptiness where the Other had once been, "America" was born as a land of inclusion and hope, offering the expansive possibilities of life, liberty, and the pursuit of happiness. The intensity with which freedom was promised (as Americans pitched "the tents of liberty farther westward, farther southward") and with which imperial "greatness" was pursued by making "alien" and "savage" peoples "wards" of Washington seldom seemed problematic to white Americans. As his biographer Timothy Flint wrote in 1833, frontiersman Daniel Boone delighted in the thought that "the rich and boundless valleys of the great west—the garden of the earth—and the paradise of hunters, had been won from the dominion of the savage tribes, and opened as an asylum for the oppressed, the enterprising, and the free of every land." With various conquered peoples deemed unready for or congenitally incapable of self-government, the extension of the promise of freedom only made exclusion ever more imperative.[20]

Under the pressure of these two yoked yet contradictory impulses—
toward a liberty that promised inclusiveness and a greatness that was
exclusionary—someday the story would begin to unravel; and central to
that unraveling would be pressure for inclusion from a people whose
presence in North America challenged the very idea of boundaries. Held
in a tyrannical embrace within a democratic society, African-Americans
could neither be incorporated into the inclusive narrative nor thrust
beyond the geographic boundaries of the nation. Feared yet not an
enemy, excluded yet close by, demeaned yet needed, they presented
whites with an insoluble dilemma.

"WE KNOW NO MASTER BUT OURSELVES"

On February 18, 1865, singing "John Brown's Body," the black 54th
Massachusetts Infantry marched into Charleston, South Carolina, where
the first shot of the Civil War had been fired on Fort Sumter almost four
years earlier. "Five weeks later, the city witnessed a 'grand jubilee' of
freedom, a vast outpouring of celebration and pride by the city's black
community," recounts historian Eric Foner. "Four thousand blacks took
part in a massive parade—soldiers, fire companies, members of the various trades with their respective tools, schoolchildren carrying a banner
with the inscription 'We Know No Master but Ourselves.'" On April 14,
the Union flag was raised over Fort Sumter. "One white army officer was
moved to tears by the raising of the standard 'that now for the first time
is the black man's as well as the white man's flag.'"[21]

Here, then, was a narrative of battle in America that had the possibility of underpinning a true freedom story, one with African-Americans as
its central characters, as their condition of bondage had been its central
causation. A wrenching four-year struggle in the country's heartland,
involving the deaths of more than 620,000 soldiers and uncounted civilians, the American Civil War ended slavery and, in the most literal sense,
resulted in total victory for the nation, for the "Union." ("Before 1861,"
historian James McPherson has written, "the two words 'United States'
were generally rendered as a plural noun: 'the United States are a republic.' The war marked a transition of the United States to a singular
noun.")[22]

That war has fascinated, even obsessed generations of Americans. Yet
it was also a conflict in which only the losers, the forces of unfreedom (to
Unionists), could be portrayed as outnumbered American underdogs. In

fact, the Civil War proved unincorporable into victory culture because there was no triumphant interpretation on which whites could agree.

Did it begin with a defensive attack on Fort Sumter, as Southerners insisted, or as Northerners would have it, with a dishonorable sneak attack that brought out the populace in "one great Eagle-scream" for the flag? Was the "swath" General William Tecumseh Sherman's army "cut through to the sea" a barbaric act of burning, looting, and destruction or a war-ending feat of military genius? Were the Kansas killings committed by John Brown's prewar band of abolitionists and William Clarke Quantrill's rebel raiders the cold-blooded atrocities of barbarians or the understandable acts of heroic partisans? Was the mistreatment of captive Union soldiers in prisons like Andersonville all one could expect of slaveholders "born to tyranny and reared to cruelty," as the *New York Times* suggested, or was it a consequence of the vise the North had placed on the Southern economy?[23]

The war that ended in total victory for Northern whites ended in bitterness and humiliating conquest for Southern ones. Yet even for Northerners, victory celebrations had barely ended when President Abraham Lincoln was vengefully assassinated and millions of mourning citizens found themselves lining the route of his funeral train on its slow progress from Washington, D.C., to Springfield, Illinois. In this epic tale, in which every heroic act seemed a horror in someone else's eyes, whites could least unite around the war as a freedom narrative. Well into the war, most Northerners, including the president, would have accepted a Southern return to the Union without emancipation, as later, Union troops would be enjoined to deal with blacks crossing into their lines as "contraband"—that is, "the confiscated property of the enemy"—rather than liberated humanity. If black slaves "voted with their feet," massively insisting on their own freedom from the South's "peculiar institution," what most whites were willing to free them into was another matter. Certainly, few whites, North or South, could imagine releasing the black—hence, a history of racial horror—into the heart of the national tale.

From such material it proved impossible to fashion a narrative of triumph that might fascinate, thrill, and cheer all audiences. There was, however, another, more minimalist path of interpretation available from the moment victorious Union soldiers and vanquished rebels exchanged a "salute of honor" at surrender ceremonies near Appomatox Courthouse. This was to treat the war as a white family "tragedy" to be followed by rites of "reconciliation" rather than ceremonies of victory, a path from which the freed slaves, like the blacks, slave or free, who joined the Union army, would be excluded.[24]

It was this interpretation that, with the passage of time, white Northerners and Southerners found they could generally agree upon, one that mobilized both groups in "tacit forgetfulness" (as historian Edward Linenthal has written) to exclude all that was unpleasant from a new Civil War narrative. For this to happen, the conflict had to be abstracted from history and restricted to a tale of battle strategy, highlighting the bravery and nobility of opposing armies, the skills of their generals, and a sense that losers and winners alike had fought for high, if vague, principles ("divergent views of [the] Constitution," as Virginia's governor put it in 1917).

Much of this new narrative would be worked out on the former battlefields of the war in rites of reconciliation between veterans that grew more elaborate with each passing decade. Not surprisingly, these developed only after the war's animosities had begun to burn down and the South's "criminal responsibility" for the war was less emphasized in the North; only after Reconstruction ended with the withdrawal of federal troops from Southern politics, the reimposition of white-rule regimes, and a partial reinslavement of blacks.

Northern veterans, for instance, returned to the Gettysburg battlefield to memorialize the Union victory there years before the first Southern veterans appeared. The first Southern memorial—that of the 2nd Maryland Confederate Infantry—was erected there in 1886; and the first reenactment of Pickett's charge, the final Confederate assault, took place in 1887. ("The [Southern veterans] marched up to the right of the Northern column and halted," reported Colonel John B. Bachelder at the time, "and above the explosion of . . . roman candles, sky rockets and the blare of red lights . . . by a common impulse of American Humanity. . . the two commands moved forward and spontaneously grasped each other's hands.") From such ceremonies black veterans were generally excluded. They had no place on a reconciled battlefield where visions of "immortal Anglo-Saxon bravery" and a "golden mist of American valor" would descend over the war's memory. It was not that an American commitment to freedom would be less honored, but that it would have less and less to do with those the war had freed.[25]

If blacks had no place in the familial battle narratives of a post-Reconstruction "American Humanity"—despite the 200,000 blacks who had served in the Union army and navy—then how much less could they be freed to enter the war story where they comfortably fit the roles of neither ally nor enemy. In the years to come, they would be found neither in dime novels nor in cowboy films. Though in real life they would fight with both redskins and bluecoats, they would be absent from the stories created about the West for the nation's delectation. Though many would migrate westward to Kansas and elsewhere in search of a world beyond the boundaries of white rule, when the story left the environs of the Civil War and fled once again into the West, it would be a West without them.[26]

How, then, was this "alien" presence to be dealt with? As it happened, no cultural form proved capable of containing and shaping the black presence into entertainment that would not haunt the white viewer. Only in the minstrel show had blackness proved assimilable. There, whites put on blackface, took on the persona of a Jim Crow or a Zip Coon, and haunted themselves. Vast painted lips and ravenous mouths, an unquenchable lust for the watermelon, the licentious discontrol of dancing bodies, an exaggerated oratorical foolishness, and ludicrous, imitative dress styles—it was only in this singularly hysterical, derisive, and fantastic form that, from the early nineteenth century to *Amos 'n' Andy*, whites could successfully visualize blackness.

Yet the absence of African-Americans from the rest of the narrative was an intensely awkward one. Too threatening to be culturally visible, they had long made their presence felt, in novelist Toni Morrison's phrase, by "silence and evasion." Unseen, they shaped what could be seen. "For a people who made much of their 'newness'—their potential, freedom, and innocence—it is striking how dour, how troubled, how frightened and haunted our early and founding literature truly is."[27]

Intimate with American history as atrocity, blacks haunted that story by their absence and were the most haunted by it. For them, there would be no discrete set of reservations or any boundaries they could be pushed beyond. They were as necessary to the Southern agricultural system as Irish, Italian, and Eastern European immigrants would be to the Northern urban industrial one. To contain this now "free" population, whites created a system of segregation that offered a solution to the problem of how to marginalize a people at the heart of a society. In the post-Reconstruction era, wherever blacks were, however intimately that place might be linked to the world of whiteness, it was designated marginal. The boundaries of such a system were, however, inherently unstable. No matter how violently policed, they had to be constantly redrawn in one's head in every moment of daily life.

This was hardly material for the creation of triumphant scenarios of innocence and entertainment, which was undoubtedly why the fantasy scenario basic to white-black relations, the kidnapping and rape of the white woman by the black man, was so useless for entertainment purposes. Similar as it was to the capture-rescue scenario of the frontier, its threat lay too close to home. The white woman would have to be carried back heroically not from a distant wilderness but from down the street, from as close, in fact, as a penis could get to a vagina in a nearby house or back yard on any block.

Similarly, white rituals of extralegal violence against blacks could only be viewed close up and untransformed. Unlike the distant, mythologized simplicity of the spectacle of slaughter, the striking aspect of these rituals was their grotesque overelaboration. A community of whites—men, women, and children—would turn out to participate in or watch a lynching, whose time and place might be advertised in local newspapers. The atmosphere, according to the psychiatrist James P. Comer, would be "drunken [and] orgy-like." The black man (or rarely woman) would often be beaten, mutilated, castrated, "roasted alive," hung, and "riddled" by bullets as if no single act of terror, no single method of killing, could compensate for the shakiness that had been revealed at the borders of the system of caste separation.

Take a Vicksburg, Mississippi, *Evening Post* report on a turn-of-the-century lynching of a black man and woman who had killed a white intruder in their home.

[C]aptured, they were tied to trees and while the funeral pyres were being prepared they were forced to suffer the most fiendish tortures. The blacks were forced to hold out their hands while one finger at a time was chopped off. The fingers were distributed as souvenirs. The ears of the murderers were cut off. [The man] was beaten severely, his skull was fractured, and one of his eyes, knocked out with a stick, hung by a shred from the socket. . . . The most excruciating form of punishment consisted in the use of a large corkscrew in the hands of some of the mob. This instrument was bored into the flesh of the man and woman in the arms, legs and body, and then pulled out, the spirals tearing out big pieces of raw, quivering flesh every time it was withdrawn.

Such "brutal vigilante tactics," writes historian George Frederickson, "reflected a persistent insecurity about the effectiveness of white dominance and a lack of faith in the full adequacy of legal or institutional controls over blacks."[28]

The atrocity that accompanied a reservation system with ghostly boundaries could not be sanitized. No matter how explained, such acts of white terror inevitably failed to carry the look of innocence and so did not lend themselves to the war story's cleansed contours. There was as well no space available for an African-American "warrior" to occupy, either as a noble savage (whose vanishing was, of course, out of the question) or as a savage enemy. Unlike the Indian, the black was known to be

cowardly and not of a martial nature, and this was not to be contradicted—even by the service of black soldiers in war.

As with director D. W. Griffith's epic film *The Birth of a Nation*
(1915), any formulations that placed blacks in the story proved momentary. Griffith's substitution of the black man's rape of the white woman
for the red man's capture of the white woman, his appropriation of the
ride-to-the-rescue for the Ku Klux Klan, and his placing of the destruction
of a rabble of black soldiers at the heart of his spectacle of the Civil War
and after lasted only one film before being returned to the war story's
more comfortable landscapes. While the quarter-century from Civil
War's end to the Wounded Knee massacre in the West provided the material for thousands of westerns, those same years in the South—Reconstruction and the resurgence of white-supremacy regimes—led to only a
handful of films.†

Only in a state of minstrel showlike abasement, as servants, maids, or
the ignorant butts of unpleasant jokes, only playing blacks as whites had
played them, could the black be "seen." Even when movies, in a liberal
spirit, began to explore themes of victimization linked to black-white
relations, blacks were generally left out. Lynching, for instance, could be
portrayed as a crime against whites in the West (*The Ox-Bow Incident*,
1943), a small town (*Fury*, 1936), or even New England (*Talk of the
Town*, 1942), just not in the South, and not against blacks. In the same
way, the unsettled nature of post–World War II race relations could be
more readily enacted with Jews (*Gentleman's Agreement*, 1947) or Indians (*Broken Arrow*, 1950), even though they were clearly stalking horses
for blacks. When, for instance, Gregory Peck, playing a WASP journalist
masquerading as a Jew to expose anti-Semitism, finally bursts into an
angry tirade in *Gentleman's Agreement*, he blasts not "Christian America," but "white Christian America."

From the first, the way of absence had been central to the treatment of
blacks in the American historical record. As historian Nathan Huggins
has written:

> [I]n no official document of [the Founding Fathers'] creation did they
> address, frankly and openly, the conspicuous fact of racial slavery. . . .

---

†What was unassimilable to the war story, however, proved central to the stories
blacks told or wrote. For over one hundred years, as literary critic Trudier Harris
has suggested, "Black writers from Charles Waddell Chesnutt to . . . Ralph Ellison
[have] all presented the tragic consequences, usually death by lynching and burning, which frequently awaited black men who found themselves accidentally or
voluntarily in 'questionable' circumstances with white women."[29]

[The] master narrative [of U.S. history], like the Constitution itself, could find no place at its center for racial slavery, or the racial caste system that followed Emancipation. . . . Black historians aside, American history, almost universally, was written as if blacks did not exist and their experience was of no consequence.

Even in the writing about slavery, where blacks might logically be considered the principal subject, the habit was to write about it as an abstract social or economic institution, to see it as provocative of sectionalism and as a contributing cause of the Civil War. The slave's testimony was never sought and never recorded by historians. It was quite audacious for Kenneth Stampp to conclude his 1956 study of slavery with a former slave voicing a "simple and chastening truth for those who would try to understand the meaning of bondage": "'Tisn't he who has stood and looked on, that can tell you what slavery is—'tis he who has endured. . . . I was black . . . but I had the feelings of a man as well as any man."[30]

"SO FOUGHT THE HEROES OF BATAAN"

In 1945, black soldiers came home from a war to liberate others and from a segregated military—so much so that even blood plasma supplies for the wounded were not mixed—with a new sense of militancy, ready to demand a new deal. Unlike whites, they had fought the war for the "Double V"—victory at home as well as overseas. Now, many were to insist that their country fulfill its inclusionary promise—and being included meant gaining equality not just in combat but in the combative story of the spread of American greatness. If Hollywood first began tentatively creating a space for the black soldier in its wartime combat films and the armed forces were officially integrated in 1948, such changes barely touched the movie genre of choice for the war story, the western.

The western had leaped from the dime novel and the Wild West show onto the screen with its iconic scenes, many over two hundred years old, intact: the attack on the settler's cabin or the fort, the capture and rescue, the Indian ambush, the last stand, the spectacle of slaughter. Between 1910 and 1960, film critic J. Hoberman estimates, one-quarter of all films made were westerns; and the western, which in the 1950s achieved a dominant position on the small screen at home as well, remained a particularly white genre (even though one-quarter or more of all late-nineteenth-century cowboys had been black).

The first commercially successful western, *The Great Train Robbery*

(1903), was followed so quickly by others that, by 1908, film distributors' catalogs "listed their products under the headings 'Drama,' 'Comic,' and 'Western'"; and soon after, reviewers began complaining that westerns were a boring "thing of the past," filled with hoary clichés ("sheriffs, outlaws, bad Indians, good Indians, Mexican villains, heroic outlaws, desperate halfbreeds, etc.").[31]

Long a basic form that the pursuit of entertainment happiness had taken, the emptying tale of frontiersman and savage, bluecoat and redskin, cowboy and Indian, would prove a staple for generations of movie viewers from its first screenings in peephole machine parlors and nickelodeons in turn-of-the-century urban slum neighborhoods. There, American businessmen and then immigrant entrepreneurs pursued their own commercial happiness by offering immigrants the inclusionary pleasures of an American "education" through such familiar historical visions as *Rescue of the Child from Indians*, *Brush Between Cowboys and Indians*, and *The Indian's Revenge or Osceola, the Last of the Seminoles*.[32]

Film came too late to produce anything but versions of a victory already won in the Indian wars or of a mythology already perfected in other entertainment forms, though not too late to use some of the participants from those wars. Buffalo Bill Cody appeared with his Wild West Show in 1894 in one of Edison's earliest Kinetoscope "peepshow" machines and later made a film of "the last Indian battles" in which cavalry and Sioux veterans of Wounded Knee reenacted the event. Those who had not been participants could still create biographies that said they had. Early silent film star Tom Mix, "a Pennsylvania farm boy, army deserter, and rodeo performer . . . invented a biography which included a claim that he was part-Cherokee . . . that his father was a captain in Custer's 7th Cavalry, and that he himself . . . had been a Rough Rider, a veteran of the Filipino Insurrection and the Boxer Rebellion, a marshall [and] a Texas Ranger."[33]

On the other hand, modern war and war films were contemporaneous events. While they had the older form to draw on for iconic inspiration, war films had to be created almost from scratch and in a hurry. It took Hollywood only nine months after Pearl Harbor to get the first images of a cunning, savage, murderous Japanese enemy into movie theaters in films so closely tied to events that they were invariably accompanied by breathless prefatory or end scrolls meant to bring the relatively clumsy movie production process into line with the increasingly swift pace of war production. ("So fought the heroes of Bataan," went a typical coda from the film of the same name. "Their sacrifices made possible our victories in the Coral and Bismarck Seas, at Midway, on New Guinea and Guadalcanal.")

In the post–World War II years, a new generation was to absorb victory culture, first and foremost, on screen through the western and the war film, not just in local movie theaters but, after the Hollywood studios began to sell off their film libraries, on television. In the darkness of living room, den, or bedroom, after school and late into the night, an endless past looped by in which savage enemies of every sort from lands close and far, times recent and long ago, leaped from ambush and fell by the hundreds before blazing American guns.

3

Ambush at Kamikaze Pass

ONCE, ANY MOVIEGOER knew that out there somewhere, behind those rocks or up those trees, down that valley or on the ledges above that mountain pass, *they* waited patiently for the moment when their ambush would be sprung and the whites would fall like leaves. As the canvas-covered wagons of civilization rolled forward, who could blame the settlers for looking apprehensively toward the heights, hostile and distant, or at sunset circling the wagons. It was from within that secure yet fragile circle at the center of the plains, a circle enclosing pioneer mothers and children, that the white men (and cameras) stared out. There, at dawn or dusk, naked, painted, intent on burning and killing, the savages would come. With good cover and better technology, what choice did the whites have but to mow down the enemy, wipe them out?

From silent films to "hip" westerns like *Butch Cassidy and the Sundance Kid* (1969), there may have been no more common or less commented upon scene; none more generically thrilling or less considered by either audiences or critics than the spectacle of the slaughter of the non-white. Featured in thousands of movies, its prototype was certainly the band of Indians, whooping and circling the wagon train, but "they" could be Arabs charging the North African fort (*Beau Geste*), Chinese rushing the foreign legations (*55 Days in Peking*), Mexicans rushing the Alamo (*The Alamo*), Japanese banzai-ing American foxholes (*Bataan*), or Chinese human-waving American lines (*Retreat, Hell!*).

This was not simply a matter of fantasy or wish fulfillment. Countless times since the eighteenth century, Western powers, their militaries armed and trained in ways appropriate to an industrial age, had taken on non-Western (and nonwhite) powers and brought them down in battles or short wars of predictably one-sided carnage. At the heart of Western–non-Western relations, then, there came to exist increasingly ritualized scenes of slaughter. Again and again, the technology, tactics, and discipline involved in industrially organized warfare had led to casualty figures so lopsided as to seem proof of the innate superiority of "white civilization" in the face of the savagery of the nonwhite world.

This slaughter was a spectacle meant to be seen. It gave Western–non-Western power relations—and the colonized world that followed from them—a sense of the foreordained. Only when reversed, as with the massacre of British general Charles Gordon's forces at Khartoum or George Armstrong Custer's at the Little Big Horn, was it denounced as a horror and an outrage to humanity. Otherwise the sight of such carnage and the production of such casualty figures were considered in the nature of things, visible evidence of a hierarchic order, racially (later, genetically) coded into humanity. From the collapse of Chinese defenses in the face of British attacks during the Opium War of 1842 ("On the 18th of May the offensive operations were extended to Chapu, which was captured with the loss of nine killed and fifty wounded. Here again the Chinese losses must have been very heavy, as the British buried from 1,200 to 1,500 of their dead"), to the Battle of Omdurman in the Sudan, where the British, using Maxim machine guns, killed 11,000 Dervishes at a cost of 48 British casualties ("It was not a battle but an execution. . . . The bodies were . . . spread evenly over acres and acres"), the inequality essential to such "wars" was manifest.[1]

All these murderous battles—whether the charge of Afghan warriors across a mile of open ground into British guns in 1880, with 132 British casualties and 3,000 Afghan ones, or the 1,000 Hehe tribesmen killed in East Africa by a single German officer commanding native troops armed with two machine guns—only reinforced the irrational quality of the Other. To oppose the foregone conclusion of such a war seemed so lacking in sanity that a resistant enemy leader was often considered quite mad (as in the various "mad mullahs" the British fought in Northern Africa). Even on those rare occasions when victory went to the Other, the statistics of death seemed to deny the result. At Adowa in 1896, Ethiopian troops under the Emperor Menelik routed an Italian army, killing six thousand and wounding or capturing four thousand. The victorious Ethiopians, however, lost an estimated seventeen thousand troops.[2]

This record of slaughters, which might in another context have seemed like an unbroken tale of horrors, had long proved closer to a fairy tale, a popular folk spectacle for the entertainment and reassurance of Western societies. It was a story that did not suffer but gained in the retelling (or rewriting, or rebroadcasting, or perhaps most crucially,

refilming). In its repetition it proved deeply comforting just as the hun-
dredth rereading of a bedtime story reassures a child of the predictable
rightness, safeness, and sameness of the world.

The statistics of slaughter, which in the American context escalated in
impressiveness from Puritan encounters with the Narraganset Indians to
the firebombing and atomic destruction of Japan, were facts of the historical record. It *had* happened out there as it was to happen on screen, and
in both places the numbers seemed to confirm not just the success but
the essential rightness and goodness of the country. Until 1945, so regular was this record of slaughter that it was seen as nothing less than the
natural order of the universe. Those rare instances when slaughter visibly
tilted in the other direction—like the Alamo and Pearl Harbor—were
inversely immortalized as illustrations of the enemy's incomprehensible
infamy and deceit. Their aberrant nature ingrained them in the national
memory as proof of the righteousness of subsequent acts of vengeance.

Only profound treachery or the help of renegades from the superior
culture could conceivably have made such events possible. In the wake
of the battle of the Little Big Horn, spurious explanations involving
"white" aid to the victors sprang to life. After all, how could an "unedu-
cated savage" have defeated a West Point–educated officer like George
Armstrong Custer unless, as rumored, Sitting Bull was a "half-breed"
whose French, learned at St. John's College in Canada, had given him
access to Napoleon's military tactics; or had the Sioux actually been led
into battle by a "swarthy" white renegade graduate of West Point nicknamed Bison? Similarly, when General Douglas MacArthur learned that
the Japanese had wiped out his air force on the ground in the Philippines
on December 8, 1941, he "refused to believe that the pilots could have
been Japanese. He insisted they must have been white mercenaries."[3]

At the heart of the war story lay the ambush, extraordinary evidence
of the enemy's treacherous behavior. While all ambushes involved deceit,
none was more heinous than the "sneak attack," that surprise assault on
a peaceful, unsuspecting people. Pearl Harbor stood at the end of a long
line of sneak attacks that helped explain any success a nonwhite enemy
might have against American forces. (Prominent among Indian traits portrayed in early nineteenth-century textbooks, for instance, was "making
war without declaring it.") The ultimate ambush was the "last stand,"
for it offered up in miniature a vision of the fate the enemy had in store
for all Americans, a fate implicit in every unsuccessful ambush, in any
sneak attack. In their hearts, *they* desired our total annihilation. The last
stand was simply that, reduced to a local event, one that could expand to
its rightful dimensions in the imagination. In a last-stand movie, where
the ambush became the film's climax, each white death had to be repaid

in advance by untold enemy ones; and so the slaughter of the enemy and the normal justification for it (the massacre of whites) had to be reversed.[4]

The ambush had long been essential to the adventure film, the historical drama, and especially the western. It came in countless variations, but whether it was a cabin, wagon train, stage coach, way station, fort, or even town that was attacked, the whites were forever inside and at home, while outside was a hell that might someday become a home. "We" were a defined set of individuals or at least human types; "they," an undefined mass of inhumanity. The wagon train/stagecoach/fort was the locus of civilized life. Stationary or mobile, it was home.

Like the captivity narrative, the ambush scenario flipped history on its head, making the intruder exchange places with the intruded upon. It was the Indians, in these films, who had to break in upon the circle. Naturally, the viewer identified with those inside whom the movie certified as human, not those left enigmatically lurking on the overlooking bluffs. Little wonder that he had no feelings for a treacherous and aggressive enemy who fell before his withering fire. Within that cinematic structure, the opportunity for empathy ceased to exist.

"We" were not always right. There were stupid commanders, greedy bankers, mean-spirited street toughs, and tight-lipped temperance harridans, but even our mistakes, our evils, confirmed our humanity. We represented a range of human types and values—the courageous and the cowardly, the altruistic and the greedy, the democratic and the aristocratic. Our variety only emphasized their sameness and their threatening sameness made us bury our differences. The whites portrayed in westerns or adventure films were the romanticized flotsam and jetsam of Western society—mercenaries, prostitutes, con artists, opportunists, thieves, and killers. Yet no matter what their characters, proclivities, or hostilities toward one another, in relation to the enemy, they stood as one.

For the nonwhite, annihilation was built not just into the on-screen Hollywood spectacle but into its casting structures. Available to the Other were only four roles: the invisible, the evil, the dependent, and the expendable. Nonwhites were often simply a backdrop for all-white drama, an element of exoticism against which to play out the tensions of the white world. Even the distant locales in which they lived were often indistinguishable and, on studio back lots, interchangeable, as were the details of "native" dress and custom, speech and behavior—never more so than when a film trumpeted its "authenticity."[5]

When the inhabitants of these borderlands emerged from their oases, ravines, huts, or tepees, they found that there was but one role in which a nonwhite (usually played by a white actor) was likely to come out on top, and that was the villain with his fanatical speeches and propensity for odd tortures. Only as a repository for evil could the nonwhite momentarily triumph. Whether an Indian chief, a Mexican bandit leader, or an Oriental despot, his pre–World War II essence was the same. Set against his shiny pate or silken voice, his hard eyes or false laugh, no white could look anything but good.

The alternative was to join "our" side in a state of helplessness and dependence. This meant for women the roles of barmaid, geisha, nurse's aid, missionary convert, harem girl, or Indian princess; for children, adorable wards or orphans. In each case, a grateful nonwhite face would be there to reflect back to the audience American (or Western) generosity and humanity. Such children (or childlike women) were proof that the American story was inclusive for those not resistant to it. The ultimate nonwhite, of course, was the sidekick, whose major attribute was his willingness to sacrifice his life for his white companion. In this lay a characteristic implicit in all nonwhite roles—expendability. For movie-makers and audiences alike, friendly nonwhites merely mirrored aspects of white humanity, as in a dream in which all characters turn out to be you. Such movies added up to a vast minstrel show in which the Other was represented by a limited set of red-, black-, brown-, or yellow-face masks created by, and if important enough, worn by whites—as in *The Birth of a Nation*, where white actors costumed as white-sheeted Klansmen chased white actors in blackface through history. From Don Ameche to Sal Mineo, Cyd Charisse to Loretta Young, the list of white actors and actresses "in redskin" alone is stunning.[6]

Of course, the role of choice for the nonwhite was the corpse, and no scene has been less examined than the one that produced most of them. If war was hell, killing them wasn't. The irony of this cinematic slaughter was that it combined a certain historical reality with a powerful flight into fantasy. As a start, the scene of carnage was portrayed bloodlessly. It had a look of ease, and so of harmlessness. The enemy fell from cliffs, trees, or horses, dead certainly, but without obvious injury. In fact, nonwhites invariably died in a generic manner whose familiarity only emphasized their sameness and their inability to experience pain.

They died at a distance, while "we" were hurt close up and in individualized ways. Despite the initial shock of the ambush, once they swooped to the attack, they tended to fight with inconceivable stupidity. Indians circled endlessly, shooting gallery–like targets for our guns; Africans or Himalayan hill peoples charged blindly into our positions.

Their impulse was quite literally to throw their lives away. When fighting such people, there was no alternative to slaughter. It was in their nature to wish to be exterminated.

Nothing illuminated more vividly the frontier between them and us than the issue of how life was to be valued in battle. On our side, each life threatened (man, woman, child, or dog) was a tragedy-in-the-making. Each life lost was to be emblazoned in our minds (hence, those end-of-movie moments when our ghostly dead reappeared marching proudly into memory). On the other hand, even when wounded, they did not value their lives enough to save themselves. At the orders of evil and fanatic leaders, they threw themselves at rifles or machine guns without regard for the predictable results. All of this they did without explanation, for beyond the boundaries of the American story (or the British or French imperial dramas that sometimes stood in its stead), there was no other; no family to cherish, no cause that gave meaning to life.

From the acceptance of such a framework, from the placement of the camera, flowed the pleasure of watching the slaughter of the nonwhite; tens, hundreds, thousands to a film in a scene that normally preceded the positive resolution of relationships among the whites. This represented a triumphant taming of what might have been unbearable. As such, it was the least noted, yet most impressive accomplishment of the war story—this settling and ordering of a wilderness of human horrors into a celebratory tale of progress through devastation. Generations grew up thrilling to a rising on-screen body count, as others had once thrilled to a dime novel hero who, according to historian Henry Nash Smith, killed Indians in their thousands "with one hand tied behind [him]."[7]

Whatever the film, the sorting out of the human from the inhuman was crucial to the organization of the spectacle of slaughter. Take the path-breaking John Ford western *Stagecoach* (1939), a film neither particularly warlike nor faintly about Indians. Except for the passing comment—"Geronimo . . . nice name for a butcher"—and a certain feeling of threat that hangs over a movie in which a stagecoach travels without cavalry escort through Apache territory, Indians play no part in most of the film.

Ford concentrates on melding a crew, a unit, out of disparate white wanderers and outcasts. The stagecoach becomes their idealized home, far more so than the grim town from which it departs or the dark and deadly one toward which it heads. It is a place where whites can sort out, even fight out, their disagreements and form new, more lasting relationships. It is even a place where new life (a baby) can come into being. Its passengers are doubly recognizable to the audience, as types and as actors, for Hollywood's industrial system of filmmaking had its own carefully melded and reshufflable crews to offer audiences. John Wayne playing the Ringo Kid, for instance, authenticates his character exactly because he was already so recognizable from earlier B westerns. Even the scenery—this was director Ford's first trip into the stunning and bizarre landscape of Monument Valley—is individualized. Only the Indians, painted, armed, implacable, and massed on bluffs overlooking the flatlands through which the stage must pass, are not individualized. They are recognizable only as a force of (cinematic) nature preparing to sweep down on the coach.

The journey is almost over; the passengers have no hint that danger awaits, that like the precious new life they carry with them, they are immeasurably vulnerable in their clumsy vehicle, which cannot possibly outrun Geronimo's fleet, mounted warriors. Here, then, is the ambush, and with it comes the peculiar unreality that deprives the spectacle of its horror. The Indians seem to have no scouts, no advance warning of the stage's approach, so instead of cutting it off, they find themselves chasing it from the rear as the male passengers pour fire out at them. It never occurs to the tribesmen to shoot the stage's horses (though an Indian does leap on one); nor are they accurate with gun or arrow. Of the nine outnumbered whites inside (two of whom, as women, are helpless noncombatants), they manage to kill only the least differentiated, most expendable one, while wounding another.

For the whites in the jouncing coach, on the other hand, every shot hits home. At least sixteen Indians are shown biting the dust, so the body count of *Stagecoach* could be considered an impressive sixteen to one and a half. (All Indians who fall are assumed dead in such films.) However, since the whites never miss and we see them shoot many times more, the implied body count is far higher. Despite this, by sheer force of numbers the savages seem about to overpower the stage, when the new mother, a cavalry wife, cries out, "Can you hear it? Can you hear it? The bugle. They're blowing the charge!"

Here begins the ride-to-the-rescue, and it is magnificent. Flags fluttering, sabers pointing, the cavalry sweeps across the plain, leaving in its wake a smaller but closer unit inside the stagecoach. They unify us, making our outsiders into insiders. At no moment in the spectacle of slaughter does the camera eye ever waver from our point of view to theirs. We always look outward at the outrage of their savage aggression.

The more successful their ambush, the more in the long run they doom themselves. The last stand, being anything but a "last" event, seals that doom. As Pearl Harbor combined the sneak attack ("a stab-in-the-back on Sunday morning") and the last stand, it proved a singularly mobilizing event. It was the First Stand of a renewed cult of victory. Not surprisingly, then, in the momentary shock of defeat in 1941, Hollywood turned to ambush culture and to the last stand, in particular, to organize a renewed version of the war story.

THE EXTERMINATORY IMPULSE

The year is 1759; the place, colonial America. Major Robert Rogers assembles his rangers. He plans to lead them through the swamps to take the Abenaki Indians and their French mentors by surprise at the town of St. Francis.

The year is 1940; the place, a movie theater where director King Vidor has assembled his "troops" on screen in *Northwest Passage*. In Asia and Europe, much of the world is already at war, and fear of war is growing in America. Vidor's movie is one of a series of frontier epics including *Santa Fe Trail*, *Geronimo*, and *They Died with Their Boots On* that will, in these years of encroaching danger, recapture screen time from the down-and-dirty, Depression-inspired gangster film. These large-scale studio productions are succeeding in reinvigorating the western genre, while ransacking frontier history for clues to American survival in a mean and dangerous world. It is a time for marshaling explanations and spelling out justifications that might otherwise never need be spoken.[8]

For the role of Major Rogers, MGM gives Vidor the redoubtable Spencer Tracy, while Rogers' Rangers are a variegated crew of white character actors representing a cross-section of human attitudes. As Rogers lines his men up to brief them on their mission, so the film lines up its justifications for that mission. Rogers first addresses the hesitant British General Amhearst: "Those red hellions up there came down and hacked and murdered us, burned our homes, stole women, brained babies, scalped stragglers, and roasted officers over slow fires for five years. If you were in our place, what would you do?"

Then he exhorts his troops (as well as movie audiences aware of atrocities being committed by other savages on more up-to-date frontiers): "Most of you have lost folks and friends in Indian raids since fifty-seven. You'll find their scalps at St. Francis." He calls on a ranger to detail the way the Abenakis tortured captured officers after a previous battle. ("Phillips had a strip of skin torn upward from his stomach. They hung him from a tree by it while he was still alive.") "But *they* were soldiers," Rogers continues.

As soldiers, they had to take their chances. But your folks on the border farms, they weren't fighting anybody. They were clearing woods
and plowing and raising children, trying to make a home of it. And
then one night Abenaki tomahawks hit the door. If it was over quick
they were lucky. Now, if there's any man here who doesn't want to
follow me against these Indians he can step out now and nothing will
be said at home.

None do.

Because movies like *Northwest Passage* reflected not only themes
reaching deep into American history but the industrial organization of
film, some eerie resonances exist. Through their back lots and across the
"centuries," the studios recycled writers, directors, actors, plots, and
script lines, not to speak of costumes, music, sets, and clips from previous films. So in 1944, only four years later, Spencer Tracy could be found
playing another military figure bent on a murderous, retaliatory mission.
As Lieutenant Colonel James H. Doolittle in *Thirty Seconds Over Tokyo*,
he too is planning to take his men through a "back door" into enemy territory; and he too contemplates the atrocity-ridden nature of that enemy.
("I was assistant naval attaché at our embassy in Japan long enough to
learn a few things about the Orient," one officer tells him. "My advice is,
see that you're not forced down over Japan.")

Three times, Doolittle too offers his rangers of the air a way out. "If
any of you have any moral feelings about this necessary killing, if you
feel that you might think of yourself afterward as a murderer, I want you
to drop out. We'll find someone to take your place. I promise you no one
will blame you for your feelings."

After various ordeals, the rangers of both films gather for a final set of
instructions: "Now," begins Tracy as Rogers, "we're under orders to wipe
out this town, so see that you do it. Kill every fighting Indian, kill 'em
quick and kill 'em dead . . . fire the village." ("Shoot down the dogs that
tortured my brother!" exclaims a soldier.) "Now," begins Tracy as
Doolittle, "let me repeat something I've said previously. You are to bomb
the military targets assigned to you and nothing else. Of course, in an
operation of this kind you cannot avoid killing civilians." Both then proceed to "fire the village."

The spelling out of a framework for the annihilation of a savage enemy
was the essence of *Northwest Passage* as it was of *Thirty Seconds Over
Tokyo*. No chance was missed to make the necessary points, in words ("I
don't pretend to like the idea of killing a bunch of people," says a pilot to
the strains of "Red River Valley," "but it's a case of drop a bomb on them

or pretty soon they'll be dropping one on Ellen [his pregnant wife]") or in pictures (the camera pauses to survey the gargantuan wooden frame at St. Francis where white scalps are hung in the style of shrunken heads in a South Seas Island film). At the triumphant core of each film was the suffering of the American soldier, not of the surprised enemy falling under a rain of bullets or bombs. It would be the victor—whether starving on a trek back from St. Francis or losing a leg after crashing a B-25 in China—who would also be the victim.

The fierce overexplication in *Northwest Passage*, rare in frontier films, indicated that a new cinematic genre was just beyond the horizon, a genre only awaiting a horrific ambush to be called into existence. For exterminatory language was picked up wholesale in the new war film that arose from the post–Pearl Harbor shock of defeat, when the Japanese became a nation of "monkeys," little better than vermin to be eradicated.

The war film that would be experienced by the children of the 1950s was largely a creation of the Pacific front. Although films about modern warfare had been made after World War I, they had had an antiwar thrust to them. The most famous, *All Quiet on the Western Front* (1930), even allowed the audience to experience the war empathetically, through enemy eyes. Whether showing "duels" among "knights" of the air or more horrifying encounters between a riven (white) humanity, these films had a distinctly nonexterminatory tone. They were, in fact, continuations of Civil War rites of reconciliation, those acts of kindness between enemies on memorialized battlefields, or in nineteenth-century school texts that showed Northern and Southern soldiers "dying together and recognizing their common humanity."

A moving convention of films set on the western front (perhaps first seen in King Vidor's silent movie, *The Big Parade* [1925]) went something like this: An American soldier finds himself caught in a foxhole (trench, farmhouse) in no man's land with a wounded German. He is about to shoot when the begrimed young man makes a V with his fingers, indicating a desire for a cigarette. Though speaking different languages, the two enemies share a smoke and the American succors the poor German boy until he dies. No matter how vile the German, whether Hun or later Nazi, he was distinctly a human type, even if often "perverse . . . , cold, diagrammatic, pedantic, unimaginative, and thoroughly sinister."[9]

Although in World War II the European front was given priority, on screen those priorities were decisively reversed. Whether in the air, under the sea, or on the ground, World War II was initially largely a one-front screen war against the Japanese. For the Hollywood studios, in those months of fear and rage, the choice between a tradition of pacifistic combat films set in the European heartland and a *Northwest Passage* was obvious, and in this, Hollywood reflected more general war feelings. It was in the Pacific that the forms and boundaries of victory culture seemed most recognizable, even in defeat.

Because war had since 1865 been such a distant, mythologized event, the shock of an attack on U.S. territory and of defeat by an enemy previously believed inferior in every way was remarkably powerful. Diplomatic treachery of the basest sort, the most monstrous sneak attack in history, a catastrophic string of ambushes and last stands at Guam and Wake Island, on the Bataan Peninsula and at Corregidor, in the Aleutians and possibly soon on the West Coast—this was how Americans absorbed the coming of war. "For most Americans," as Paul Fussell has written, "the war was about revenge against the Japanese, and the reason the European part had to be finished first was so that maximum attention could be devoted to the real business, the absolute torment and destruction of the Japanese. The slogan was conspicuously *Remember Pearl Harbor*. No one ever shouted or sang *Remember Poland*."[10]

So wartime brought the war story back to consciousness in a visceral way, but it needed to be modernized to account for a series of defeats as well as for the potentially exterminatory victory to come. The War Department, for instance, enlisted director John Ford to produce *December 7* (1943), a documentary re-creation of the attack on Pearl Harbor. Known for his westerns, Ford drew on last-stand imagery to display a fleet (and a nation) caught in the oceanic equivalent of a box canyon and nearly wiped out, but at the center of the film was something new, scenes of a slaughter of Americans without significant offsetting enemy deaths. Minute after minute, with bugles sounding the cavalry charge in the background, U.S. ships blow up and Americans are gunned down. The enemy deaths that should have preceded this orgy of destruction remain largely a matter for the future. "Well, you may crow, Mister Tojo," announces Ford's narrator. "You've done a good job of stabbing in the back. You've darkened our cities, you've destroyed our property, you've spilled our blood. Our faith tells us that to all this treachery there can be but one answer, a time-honored answer, for all they that take up the sword shall perish with the sword."

At the same time, the war against the Nazis was being organized as a screen narrative of "liberation" of former allies like the French or even of enemies like the Italians. On the European front, Hollywood concentrated on films of resistance like *Casablanca* (1942) or *The Moon Is Down* (1943). Even Germany held out liberatory possibilities, for it was assumed that individual Germans continued to resist the grip of Nazism and that there were still honorable men in the German military. In the

Pacific, however, against an enemy who fought a give-no-quarter war, refused to surrender, and lacked individuality, there would be no Japanese to liberate. The on-screen war there focused instead on exalting sacrificial American deaths in preparation for an exterminatory victory.

In portraying the Japanese, Hollywood's moviemakers resisted the desire of liberal government officials in the Office of War Information (OWI) to give the war an ideological rather than a racial cast. Despite OWI warnings to the studios not to show the enemy as "a little buck-toothed treacherous Jap" and to develop "antifascist" Japanese characters, the Eastern enemy was uniformly shown as brutal, treacherous, and subhuman. In this, the movie industry reflected popular attitudes. A poll of servicemen revealed that 38–48 percent of soldiers agreed with the statement "I would really like to kill a Japanese soldier"; only 5–9 percent when it came to Germans. "In the European theater," writes historian Ronald Spector, "54 percent of combat infantrymen interviewed said that seeing Axis POWs had given them the feeling 'they are men just like us; it's too bad we have to be fighting them.' In contrast, only 20 percent had such a reaction in the Pacific after seeing Japanese prisoners; 42 percent 'felt all the more like killing them.' Only 18 percent felt more like killing the German POWs."[11]

Despite the massive air campaign against Germany, wartime airpower movies like *Bombardier* (1943), *Thirty Seconds over Tokyo*, and *The Purple Heart* (1944) concentrated on the bombing of Japan. Even in cartoons, the antics of Bugs Bunny or Daffy Duck outwitting dopey Germans bore little relation to the scenes in Looney Tunes' "Tokio Jokio" of the incineration of a country. Similarly, as war began, it was still possible in *To Be or Not to Be* (1942) to imagine Hitler as a fool and his treatment of the Jews as a comic opera event (with Jack Benny's refrain, "So they call me Concentration Camp Erhardt!" a running gag line). From the start, no comedies were imaginable when it came to the Japanese.[12]

In return for Pearl Harbor, the United States was about to pick up the torch. A dirty job had been turned over to Americans and it had to be explained in such a way that no one should feel embarrassed, shamed, or dirtied by it. The war's earliest films, like *Wake Island* (1942) and *Bataan* (1943), borrowed from earlier war movies and from the western but spelled out the essential impulses of the war story in a way that had long been unnecessary.

Guadalcanal Diary (1943) was typical. The Japanese, faceless "monkeys," "apes," "gooks," cruel and treacherous slaughterers, must be given "a dose of [their] own medicine." They must be bayoneted, massacred, burned out, driven into the sea, "blasted from the earth that hides them." Like animals, they must be hunted down, flushed out of cover with a turkey call, and shot. They "ain't people." In *The Purple Heart*, about the "war crimes" trial of downed American fliers in Japan, the leader of the imprisoned fliers tells the Japanese judge: "We'll come by night and we'll come by day. We'll blacken your skies and burn your cities to the ground until you get down on your knees and beg for mercy. . . . This was war. You asked for it. You started it . . . and now we won't stop until your crummy little empire is wiped off the face of the earth."

In *Objective Burma* (1945), an American journalist who has just seen the hideously mutilated bodies of American prisoners exclaims, "This was done in cold blood by a people who claim to be civilized. . . . Stinking little savages! Wipe 'em off the face of the earth, I say. Wipe 'em off the face of the earth!"

If the enunciation of annihilation in *Northwest Passage* was to become common on screen in the war years, the same would be true of the rangers' torching of St. Francis. What made such scenes so unlike atrocities to movie audiences was the way in which, even when ambushing the enemy, Americans always ended up in defensive positions. Whether entrenched around St. Francis or seated within the fragile husk of a B-26, it was not they who went to slaughter, but the enemy who gave himself up to be slaughtered.

Films about World War II in the Pacific made during the war used the banzai charge (and after the war the kamikaze attack) to modernize the imagery of encirclement common in westerns: from the deck of the flagship amid the fleet corralled off Okinawa, we peer apprehensively through our binoculars. The horizon is empty, yet the radar has picked up unidentified flying objects. At their guns, the men look grimly toward the empty sky. A speck on the horizon! Faces tense, jokes fall away. It's the kamikaze, the human torpedo, leading an airborne banzai charge. He carries within him an inexplicable urge for death, disorder, and the annihilation of the forces of democracy. Throwing himself on the American fleet, bomb in portal, he acts out of no desire to defend home or country. Inside that machine can be no boy terrified or browbeaten into an act beyond imagining. As an episode in the 1952–1953 TV documentary series *Victory at Sea* described the essential encounter, Americans "pit courage and skill against the self-destroying frenzy of the Japanese . . . a duel between gunners who want to live and pilots who want to die."

Similarly, creeping directly into American gun sights ridiculously camouflaged as a tree or bush in *Bataan*, the Japanese soldier exhibits no bravery, for his acts lack a human dimension. Even in those brief moments when you "meet" him, "he" is a faceless blur—strange, barbarous, deadly, and lacking all regard for his own existence. When he speaks English, he explains this himself. Whether or not he uses some regional variant of the "ugh" language invented for the Hollywood Indian, his thought process is always fractured, for he mutilates language and thought in the same way he mutilates bodies. Unlike foreigners the audience is to care for, who speak in charmingly accented English, the racial enemy speaks in a horrifying version of pig Latin, or creates a pig thought out of the normal processes of expression.

Take the captured Japanese officer in *Halls of Montezuma* (1950). On an island in the Pacific, hours before the big attack, the marines are pinned down by Japanese mortars. If the Americans do not locate the enemy position, their attack will fail. The officer obstinately refuses to help. An American (Richard Widmark) pleads with him. "You have a future—to rebuild Japan—to live for." "Captain," the Japanese replies, "you seem to have forgotten, my people for centuries have thought not of living well but dying well. Have you not studied our Judo, our science. . . . We always take the obvious and reverse it. Death is the basis of our strength."

Suddenly, a mortar shell explodes above the bunker. Everyone ducks. Rafters fall, dust billows. Slowly, the air clears. A shocked voice calls out, "My God, the Jap's committed hara-kiri!" Fortunately, he had already given the game away by reminding the Americans of the quirks of the nonwhite mind. As any schoolboy should have known, Orientals not only write but think backwards. The Japanese had placed their rockets on the front slope of the mountain, not (as logic would have dictated) the protected rear slope. To the welling up of the Marine Hymn, the attack moves forward, preparing to wipe the enemy off the rocky face of this particular patch of planet Earth.

In the backwards world of the racial enemy, Americans could be betrayed by their own generous natures. Given the innate treachery of the Japanese, the sneak attack became a problem not just for the group but for each individual. At any time, a wounded or "dead" enemy soldier might rise like a monster from hell to stab an unsuspecting American in the back. In *Bataan*, a "monkey" playing "possum" levitates from a field of corpses, samurai sword in hand, to do the deed. In *Destination Tokyo* (1943), a warm-hearted Irish noncom on a sub, reaching out to help a downed Japanese pilot from the water ("Looks like the war's over for you, son"), is knifed in the back. So when Sergeant Dane in *Bataan* sprays all Japanese bodies, dead or wounded, with bullets or the machine gunner in *Destination Tokyo* riddles the pilot, who can blame them?

If humanitarian gestures on the Western front confirmed the brotherhood of man, the exterminatory impulse was the only sensible one in the East. Reconciliation there took place not with the enemy but within the

American patrol, which began to integrate on screen. In *Bataan*, for instance, a black demolition man (and singing minister) and a Tommy Dorsey–loving chicano from Los Angeles show that they can die almost as well as their white compatriots. While in Korean War films, from *Steel Helmet* (1951) to *Pork Chop Hill* (1959), blacks or even Japanese-Americans would begin openly considering the racial problems of American society. ("What do I care about this stinkin' hill. You ought to see where I live back home. I sure ain't sure I'd die for that.")

If the kamikaze headed toward us only as an inexplicable and malevolent force, Americans were incapable of kamikaze acts not because they did not commit them but because, when done by someone known to us in the name of a cause we cherish or to save us from being overrun by them, such acts were no longer unrecognizable. Each then represented a profound gift of life to those left behind. In the desperate early days of 1942 in the Pacific, there were a number of reported cases in which American pilots tried to dive their planes into Japanese ships. Captain Richard E. Fleming, the only recipient of the Congressional Medal of Honor for the Battle of Midway, was leading his dive bomber squadron in an attack on the disabled cruiser *Mikuma* when his plane was hit by anti-aircraft fire. It "rocked wildly . . . but . . . soon righted itself and continued down under control. At an altitude of only 350 feet, Fleming released his bomb. Then he followed it straight down to the Japanese carrier." St. Paul, his hometown, later named its airport in his honor. In the same way, "Colin" became a popular first name for boys because of war hero Captain Colin P. Kelly, Jr., who was generally (if incorrectly) believed to have won the Medal of Honor for plunging his B-17 into the smokestack of the Japanese battleship *Haruna* in the first days of the war.[13]†

This sort of heroism was highlighted in war films like *Bataan*, where a desperately wounded flier was shown diving his plane into a bridge the Japanese were rebuilding. There was even kamikaze sex. In *So Proudly We Hail* (1943), nurse Veronica Lake, trapped on Bataan, "places a hand grenade inside her blouse . . . and walks slowly toward the enemy in her combat fatigues. As she nears them, she takes off her helmet, and releases her long, very blonde hair over her shoulders. When they come near her, in obvious delight, she pulls the pin on her grenade and everybody blows up."

In fact, many of the war films of this period, from *Wake Island* (1942)

---

†Kelly actually received a posthumous Distinguished Service Cross for sinking the *Haruna* and making sure his crew bailed out before his plane crashed. The *Haruna*, however, was nowhere nearby at the time, and Kelly seems either to have hit a minesweeper or no ship at all.

to *They Were Expendable* (1945), had a kamikaze feeling to them. But as "we" were defending "home" and knew ourselves for the individuals we were, the act of diving a plane into a bridge or refusing to leave a platoon certain to be wiped out bore no relation to suicidal enemy acts.[14]

Where the western and the new war film differed was in their portrayal of American suffering. In the western it was common, early in a film, to view the results of Indian savagery. A burnt out wagon or homestead and a body or two shot full of arrows were evidence enough of Indian behavior. White suffering could be left, in part, to the imagination; and except in replays of the Custer story, heroic figures of white authority were guaranteed to survive Indian attacks, while secondary characters were handed over to death with visible reluctance. Part of the reason for this was that the camera had not witnessed the seventeenth- or eighteenth-century sense that victory might not be the only result of engagement with the Indian. The camera arrived only to "record" triumph—and the already embroidered myths of a victorious culture.

Unlike the western, the war film, leaping off from the shock of the Greatest Ambush of All and the taste of defeat, incorporated a cult of heroic death into its early series of last-stand films. Generally focused on "expendable" single units or patrols, these films portrayed the slow death of the group as the sacrifice that would ensure the return of victory culture. As in John Ford's *December 7*, where a plane paints a final vast "V" in the sky, Americans were able from the first moments of the war to appropriate defeat as a stance for triumph, to portray Pearl Harbor, Bataan, and Wake Island as the mega- and mini-Alamos from which the largest victory in human history would flow.

In the immediate postwar period, pride in on-screen western and war culture was any boy's inheritance. After a brief hiatus, a new cycle of westerns and World War II films like John Wayne's box office hit *The Sands of Iwo Jima* (1949) began to appear in movie theaters. In addition, by the mid-1950s the older cinematic versions of the war story had started their endless rounds through television's off-hours. But if children could still retreat into victory culture and politicians invoke it, the ambush had nonetheless taken on a new meaning. Victory culture had been built on an ambush that could touch all but the imagination in only the most limited of ways. Now, for the first time since the earliest days of the European invasion of North America, the ambush threatened actual extermination.

As a military-industrial complex grew to monstrous proportions in those years, the ambush grew with it. Each step up the ladder of military "preparedness" ensured that against a nuclear Pearl Harbor there could be no defense. Planning for and fear of such a sneak attack was at the heart of nuclear strategy, of all those thoughts about "the unthinkable." With the possibility of a nuclear first strike, the ambush had escaped its familiar boundaries. Writ so large, it obliterated victory and sapped the last stand of all symbolic meaning. The president could no longer address the people *after* a "day of infamy"; he would have to do so beforehand.

On October 22, 1962, President Kennedy appeared on nationwide television. "Unmistakable evidence has established the fact that a series of offensive missile sites is now in preparation on [the] imprisoned island [of Cuba]," he warned, informing Americans of a confrontation between the Soviet Union and the United States, the earth's two nuclear superpowers, whose unthinkable possibilities were then being considered. "We will not prematurely or unnecessarily risk the costs of worldwide nuclear war in which even the fruits of victory would be ashes in our mouth," he said grimly, "but neither will we shrink from the risk at any time it must be faced."[15]

Nothing could rally Americans for such a war. The mobilizing last stand had been replaced by a demobilizing one. After this Alamo, there would be no Texas; after this Little Big Horn, no Montana; after this Pearl Harbor, no Hawaii.

4

Premonitions: The Asian Death of Victory Culture

IN THE IMMEDIATE postwar years, American policy planners—like most historians today—saw the Cold War as largely a Europe-centered affair. Although the importance of securing and rebuilding Japan and of stanching the nationalist and revolutionary aspirations of previously colonized peoples in Asia, Africa, and Latin America was apparent to them, the rest of the world was imagined as something of a sideshow. Whatever happened elsewhere, it was in Europe that the fate of humanity would be settled.[1]

After 1948, however, Europe entered an era of armed stasis. For the next forty years, the United States and the Soviet Union faced off across increasingly fortified Central European dividing lines, behind which massive armies conducted mock maneuvers and each side's nuclear weapons threatened to obliterate the other's version of Europe. The Berlin blockade of 1948, the Hungarian rebellion of 1956, and the Berlin crisis of 1958–1961 reinforced a sense that global peril, even the possibility of nuclear extermination, lay there. If the rest of the world—from Indonesia and the Congo to Cuba—experienced its Cold War moments in the sun, these were seen as episodes whose significance lay elsewhere.

From 1965 on, a small country in Asia called Vietnam slowly filled American consciousness, shoving aside all other places and issues. This seemed almost unbearably puzzling, for the historical linkages registered in that consciousness in no way seemed to lead to Vietnam. Although many explanations would be offered for the years of war there, something deeply puzzling remained for which no American explanation could adequately account.

To begin to understand why events in Vietnam proved so central to the world's great superpower, a history of American doubt in Asia, a history of the question mark, would have to—and remains to—be written. For victory culture was lost in Asia, that extended westward frontier where the enemy should have been easiest to identify and triumph doubly assured. Only in Asia did war still prove possible for the United States; and there in three crucial events—the use of the atomic bomb on Japan, the "loss" of China, and the Korean War—the way was prepared for Vietnam.

Between 1945 and 1975, the U.S. military reduced first Japan, then Korea, and finally Indochina to ruin. In each case, however, the end result proved disconcertingly unlike the one that the war story assured Americans would come. In each, that narrative began to suffer statistical breakdown as the link between the spectacle of slaughter and its predictable results, between dead bodies recorded and mastery over the Other, was called into question. In that period of "gaps"—whether of missiles, generations, or credibility—the earliest gap appeared between the statistics of victory and victory itself, a puzzling, unnerving space that only widened with the years, and in that space appeared doubt.

In the case of Japan, victory was not lacking, it was just too resoundingly achieved: two flashes resulting in the highest instant body count in the history of warfare. Despite a national consensus justifying the use of any weapon to avenge Pearl Harbor, the implications of that body count were unnerving enough that U.S. forces occupying Japan sealed off not just the Japanese but the American public as well from all but the most limited information about the nature of atomic death and, in particular, the effects of radiation at Hiroshima and Nagasaki. Photos and film of the event, eyewitness and journalistic accounts, as well as medical studies were locked away in Occupation files. Similarly, the government would attempt throughout the 1950s to minimize or cover up evidence of the deleterious effects of domestic atomic testing, for those two moments of blinding light had revealed in victory perils almost as terrifying as in defeat, holding out not the promise of an American Earth, but of no Earth at all.[2]

Unexpectedly, then, the first challenge to a Pax Americana came not from defeat but from the totality of victory, not from Communists threatening a Europe in ruins but from an American victory weapon that threatened someday to make national triumph and international annihilation indistinguishable. As of August 6, 1945, there was such a thing as too much power for the safety of humanity. This gave an eerie twist to the otherwise triumphal American feeling that its story had proved to be *the* story, that history might be reaching its culmination in "the American way of life," that swords might be beaten into refrigerators, and that the erstwhile "arsenal of democracy," the "super" power with the "super" weapon, might also become a supermarket dispensing goods to the whole planet.

· Here was a victory in no sense previously imagined, for it was victory as atrocity, and its dismayingly apocalyptic implications were felt within minutes of the midday announcement of the Hiroshima bomb. By evening, H. V. Kaltenborn, "the dean of radio news commentators," was saying over the air, "For all we know, we have created a Frankenstein! We must assume that with the passage of only a little time, an improved form of the new weapon we use today can be turned against us." By the next morning, a *St. Louis Post-Dispatch* editorial was speculating on whether science had "signed the mammalian world's death warrant, and deeded an earth in ruins to the ants," or whether, as a *Milwaukee Journal* editorial asked, "a self-perpetuating chain of atomic destruction" could, like "a forest fire sweeping before high winds," destroy the planet. (Similarly, some of the scientists awaiting the first atomic test at Los Alamos had shared a fear that "the explosion might escape its apparent bounds." Enrico Fermi had half-jokingly "invite[d] bets . . . against first the destruction of all human life and second just that of human life in New Mexico.")[3]

Despite triumphal feelings about the impending victory over Japan, many Americans might privately have described their reaction to the announcement as did John Haynes Holmes, minister of the Community Church of New York City: "Everything else seemed suddenly to become insignificant. I seemed to grow cold, as though I had been transported to the waste spaces of the moon . . . for I knew that the final crisis in human history had come. What that atomic bomb had done to Japan, it could do to us." As cultural historian Paul Boyer has written of American reactions at the dawn of the atomic age, "All the major elements of our contemporary engagement with the nuclear reality took shape literally within days of Hiroshima."

The "great fear" that "we," not "they," might be the next victims of nuclear extermination was to chase Americans through the coming decades. Almost immediately, newspapers, then magazines, then radio, and throughout the 1950s television began to picture in graphic and terrifying detail an America reduced to a vaporized wasteland. On August 8, 1945, the *Milwaukee Journal* published the first such image—"a large map of [Milwaukee] overlaid by concentric circles of destruction." Within months, such scenarios had been fully fleshed out. In November 1945, *Life* magazine published "The 36-Hour War," in which an unnamed enemy in "equatorial Africa" launched a surprise atomic attack on thirteen sites ranging from Boulder Dam to Washington, D.C., resulting in 10 million instant deaths. Although the United States "wins" the war, the final dramatic illustration was of two pockmarked stone lions standing guard over New York City's obliterated main public library, while heavily shielded technicians "test the rubble of the shattered city for radioactivity."[4]

Such articles were to become commonplace, as were mind-numbing projected casualty figures. A 1951 issue of *Colliers* magazine, for instance, was devoted to a "Preview of the War We Do Not Want." In its imagined World War III, before the Soviet Union is rescued from communism through a United Nations occupation, Alaska suffers an invasion and A-bombs fall on Detroit, New York (twice), Chicago, Philadelphia, and Washington, D.C., while "Red submarines fire atomic-headed missiles into Boston, Los Angeles, San Francisco, Norfolk (Virginia), and Bremerton (Washington)." Among the issue's many futuristic articles, Edward R. Murrow "reported" on his ride in a B-36 that obliterated Moscow ("We felt nothing. It was the most professional, nerveless military operation I have ever seen"), and Associated Press columnist Hal Boyle "covered" the destruction of Washington, D.C.: "The American capital is missing in action. A single enemy atom bomb has destroyed the heart of the city. The rest is rapidly becoming a fire-washed memory. . . . Uncounted thousands are dead. More thousands of injured lie . . . on hospital lawns and parks or walk unheeded until they fall."

On television, actual bomb tests as well as simulated atomic attacks on major American cities were viewed by millions. "CBS was particularly fond of this genre," according to media critic J. Fred MacDonald. "As early as June 29, 1952, Edward R. Murrow on 'See It Now' covered a mock attack upon New York City. The premiere of 'Air Power' in November 1956 simulated a Russian bombardment of Los Angeles, Chicago, New York City, and other American metropolitan centers. The network returned to the theme on December 8, 1957, when 'The Day Called "X"' surveyed Portland, Oregon, under thermonuclear attack."[5]

The bomb, product of American scientific wizardry, final weapon in the war of good over evil, had flashed triumphantly over Hiroshima, sending its invisible destructive force through time to ensure a future filled with lingering death. Its destructive power had also reached beyond Japan to the American imagination. There, it threatened to undermine the war story in its moment of glory by joining an American act to that other atrocity revealed in 1945—the Holocaust.†

---

†That other end-of-story was long walled off from the American-produced one. No fantasies of Nazi death camps in America or of genocidal acts in Midwestern cities haunted the period; nor in the writings of any but a few critics like Lewis

From then on, American triumphalism was forced to coexist with something that looked, even to Americans, like an embarrassing slaughter of ungraspable dimensions.

Within this unsettling context, between 1946 and 1953, the United States found itself in China and Korea unable to apply its nuclear might to secure a world either in its image or to its liking. In addition, on September 24, 1949, a brief announcement from Washington informed the public that the Russians had tested their first atomic bomb, and done so some years ahead of official (if not scientific) predictions.

For several years, Americans had projected acts of which only they were capable onto Russia, and levels of destruction that could only have been visited elsewhere onto the United States. Now, facing an actual (though as yet undeliverable) Russian bomb, reaction to official pronouncements and media predictions of doom and disaster proved remarkably mild. Perhaps the public was unwilling to play out the implications in real time or perhaps it was a relief to discover that projection had not proved so far from reality, that a possibility of future American victimhood genuinely existed.[6]

A HISTORY OF THE QUESTION MARK

With remarkable speed in the immediate postwar years, three enemy nations, Germany, Japan, and Italy, became "Free World" allies and two major allies, the Soviet Union and China, became paramount enemies. As Soviet dictator Joseph Stalin took on the Hitlerian mantle in opinion polls, the Chinese, admired during the war as hardworking, honest, brave, religious, and intelligent, gained the wartime "Japanese" traits of being ignorant, warlike, sly, treacherous, and cruel.[7]

If this transformation was unsettling, nothing proved more literally dis-orienting than the event that accompanied it—the Communist victory in the Chinese civil war in 1949. In combination with news of the first Soviet atomic test and the signing of a thirty-year Sino–Soviet

---

Mumford and Dwight Macdonald was a link made between the two great industrial processes of death that emerged from twentieth-century war. Until Robert J. Lifton, author of *Death in Life: Survivors of Hiroshima*, published his study of Nazi doctors in 1986, those who studied the bomb did not study the death camps, and vice versa. For many years, the two events were unlikely even to appear, however innocently, in the same sentence, the unspoken barrier between them reflecting a fear that the bomb had the power to destroy the distinction not only between victory and defeat, but between good and evil nations.

mutual assistance pact as well as later Chinese military successes in the Korean War, the event released new, potentially unbounded fears into society. As a high official of the Eisenhower administration commented, "In practically everything one ever read . . . the Asiatic is always plowing with his fingernails and the European is handling the machine. Now the Chinese is flying a jet! Disturbing, especially since you have several hundred million of them teamed up with the USSR. I always thought the Yellow Peril business was nonsense. . . . Now I can visualize that Asiatics teamed up with the Slavs could indeed conquer the world!"

Nothing in the record of events known to the public had pointed to this unexpected verdict of history. As Japan became an enemy in the Pacific in the 1930s, China had gained a special place in American consciousness. Although the Chinese had been the first people legally barred from entry to the United States and there were fifteen anti-Chinese exclusion laws on the books at the time of Pearl Harbor, China was increasingly assumed to be America's junior partner in Asia. Awesome in weight of numbers, ancient in civilization, besieged by Japanese invaders, the Chinese people came to be seen as democratically inclined and desirous of, even dependent upon, the promise of an American-style future.[8]

China was a "republic" run by the Kuomintang or Nationalist Party. Its Christian leader Chiang Kai-shek was a living reminder of the long-standing American missionary effort there, and his Wellesley-educated wife symbolized China's natural affinity for things American. (The couple were *Time* magazine's man and wife of the year in 1938.) Even before the United States entered the war and Roosevelt declared China one of the "Big Four" nations who were to determine the shape of the postwar world, American volunteer pilots were fighting the Japanese from Chinese territory.

In wartime propaganda, China's place in the American Century was a given. As Nebraska's Republican senator Kenneth Wherry put it, "We will lift Shanghai up and up, ever up, until it is just like Kansas City." The Office of War Information in its manual for the movie industry emphasized that Hollywood should portray China as "a great nation, cultured and liberal, with whom, inevitably, we will be closely bound in the world that is to come." The OWI bureaucrats need not have worried. According to a poll they conducted in 1942, 82 percent of Americans believed China could be counted on after the war, as opposed to only 72 percent who felt the same vis-à-vis Great Britain.[9]

In newspapers, in magazines, and on film, shifty Japanese eyes gleamed cruelly behind thick-lensed glasses, while handsome Chinese faces beamed radiantly at Americans. In the 1944 film *Thirty Seconds*

Over Tokyo, a bomber pilot, downed on the Chinese coast, is rescued by a Chinese guerrilla and his wounds tended by a father-and-son team of Chinese doctors. When the pilot bids the son goodbye, he exclaims, "You saved my life, Doc." "I hope someday you'll come back to us," the young doctor replies fervently. "We'll be back," the flier assures him. "Maybe not us ourselves but a lot of guys like us and I'd like to be with them, cause you're our kind of people."

However, in the civil war that followed the world war, Chiang Kai-shek's American-armed and trained forces suffered a series of crushing defeats at the hands of Communist guerrilla armies and were driven off the Asian mainland onto the island of Taiwan. On October 1, 1949, a new Chinese leader, Mao Zedong, reviewed his troops from Tiananmen Square in the heart of the former imperial capital Beijing and proclaimed to the world that the Chinese people had "stood up." What they had stood up against, it seemed, were the values and economic visions of the United States. In the blinking of a historical eye, Japan, that enemy country of death-loving, emperor-worshiping fanatics had become a democratically oriented protégé in the Pacific, while the vast land of oppressed peasant individualists, immortalized in Pearl Buck's 1931 novel *The Good Earth*, had been transformed into a terrifying red blot on the map. "Our kind of people" had become a nation of "blue ants."

Chiang Kai-shek's powerful supporters in the United States were unprepared for such an end. The loss of the land that former Congresswoman Clare Booth Luce, wife of the man who coined the phrase the "American Century," had once called "the greatest country in the world in terms of what counts most—individual human souls" was terrifying because inconceivable. How could primitive peasant armies have wrested the prize of Asia from the dominant power on earth and turned it into, in Assistant Secretary of State Dean Rusk's phrase, "a colonial Russian government, a Slavic Manchukuo on a large scale"? One only had to add up the economic and military ledgers of power to recognize the absurdity of the situation. As a "choice" of the Chinese people, it was beyond consideration.[10]

This transformation of assured victory into shocking defeat in Asia called out for an explanation, and there was one at hand. It had first been developed by Chiang Kai-shek's American supporters (sometimes known as the China Lobby) and was later adopted by Republicans, assorted conservatives, and right-wingers eager for an issue on which to attack the Democratic administration of President Harry Truman. This explanation—or rather this fantasy that passed for an explanation—released the enemy from beyond the bounds of civilization and relocated him at the center of the American story. There, he began to lose his identifying racial characteristics, taking on instead the invisible, penetrative power associated with the bomb.

Offered first for the loss of China and then for a whole range of perceived setbacks, this explanation suggested that in a "carefully planned retreat from victory," a clique of Asian experts in the State Department associated with various Communist-influenced institutes and publica tions had purposely "lost" a whole country that was otherwise America's. They had "given" it away, "sold it down the Amur." This "conspiracy" to "betray" was part of an even larger betrayal—"twenty years of treason" in the pungent words of Senator Joseph McCarthy—by a "secret, invisible government" within the government who held the president and his highest advisers "captive."

What the public had unknowingly experienced in two decades of Democratic misrule was "stupidity at the top—treason just below." After all, looked at objectively, how else could the United States have been defeated? From "giveaway" at Yalta to "betrayal" in China, from the deceived states of Eastern Europe to the stolen "secret" of the atomic bomb, no horrific or duplicitous act of the enemy could not be traced back to Americans! Hundreds of millions of people had been turned into "slave labor" due to traitors at the highest levels of government and in the most sensitive cultural institutions. This treason had been covered up by a monstrous conspiracy. As a result, according to Senator McCarthy, "the Communists within our borders have been more responsible for the success of Communism abroad than Soviet Russia."[11]

The loss of China was a particularly painful blow because, without the basest treachery, there was no way to account for it; and this manipulation of millions had been organized, it was claimed, by amazingly small numbers of people—205 or 81 or 57 State Department officials, or a few scholars, journalists, and officials associated with the Institute of Pacific Relations, or *Amerasia* magazine, or by a Communist Party with, at best, a few thousand members.

It was in Korea, though, that victory culture suffered its most severe, because inexplicable, ambush; for there, the statistics of slaughter lost their predictive quality—and slaughter without victory had a less than pleasing look to it. In 1951, Senator Joseph McCarthy, ever sensitive to an exploitable issue, attacked the Truman administration for a strategy in Korea that "turned that war into a pointless slaughter, reversing the dictum of Von Clausewitz and every military theorist after him that the object of a war is not merely to kill but to impose your will on the enemy." What made Korea so unnerving was that the stigmata of a frontier war—whether measured in disequilibriums of casualties, ordnance expended, or technological destruction—were all impressively present.

For much of the war, the ratio of Communist to UN casualties stood somewhere between 20:1 and 14:1. Only in the final months of fierce trench warfare did it briefly fall to just over 2:1. Yet the war refused to conclude in a predictable fashion.[12]

Even today, Korea is referred to as the "forgotten" war, and the desire to repress it from memory was understandable. Relatively small, under-industrialized North Korea, a half-power occupying a half-peninsula, sup-ported by the Russians and newly Communist China, faced the U.S.-backed, agrarian South in a war of unification. In that war, out of a population of 30 million Koreans, as many as 4 million died, as did at least a million Chinese, 54,000 Americans, and several thousand troops from fifteen nations allied with the United States and fighting under the United Nations' flag.

Many aspects of the war would have seemed familiar in the Vietnam era: the burning of villages suspected of harboring guerrillas; the use of napalm against "gooks"; the question of whether to bomb the dam sys-tem in the North; the unpopularity of the war among soldiers and civil-ians; the belief that the military was "leashed" and kept from victory by politicians; and an inability to separate the enemy from the civilian pop-ulation. Take this conversation among GIs searching Korean refugees for hidden weapons in Samuel Fuller's wartime film Steel Helmet (1951):

OFFICER: They're hiding behind them white pajamas and wearing them women's clothes. . . . These guys are smart.

SECOND OFFICER: We're wasting our time.

SERGEANT: Look. . . . I don't want to turn my back and have some old lady shoot my head off.

SOLDIER SEARCHING A KOREAN: They all look alike to me.

SERGEANT: Don't you know how to tell the difference? . . . He's a South Korean when he's running with you and he's a North Korean when he's running after you.

But no aspect of that war would later seem more Vietnam-like than the inability of the military to translate its enormous power advantage into victory. Its capacity to inflict largely uncontested damage on Korea was almost without parallel. From 1950 to 1953, the air force dropped World War II levels of explosives on the peninsula, leaving hardly a build-ing standing in the northern and central parts of the country, and driving much of the population quite literally underground. The desolation in the North was far more extreme than that later experienced in North Vietnam. Meanwhile, naval ships prowled the waters off North Korea, untouchable, bombarding coastal areas with unprecedented levels of ordnance. The city of Wosun, for example, was bombarded round-the-clock from the sea for forty-one days and nights, "the longest sustained naval or air bombardment of a city in history," according to Rear Admiral Allan F. Smith.[13]

At rear bases in Japan, atomic bombs were readied, the president spoke publicly of their use, and the government seriously weighed various plans for their employment. According to historians Bruce Cumings and Jon Halliday, the nearest the United States came to using them was "in early spring 1951. On 10 March, MacArthur asked for something he called a 'D' Day atomic capability.'... On 5 April the Joint Chiefs ordered immediate atomic retaliation against Manchurian bases if large numbers of new [Chinese] troops came into the fighting . . . and on 6 April Truman issued an order approving the Joint Chiefs' request and the transfer of a limited number of complete atomic weapons 'to military custody.'"

China, as well as Korea, was publicly and privately threatened with atomic attack. Lone B-29s were even sent on Hiroshima-like bombing runs over the North to drop dummy bombs in simulations of the real thing. In January 1953, a new artillery piece, the 280mm atomic cannon, was given a noticeable place in Dwight D. Eisenhower's inaugural parade, and subsequently a battery of the guns was sent to Korea. Yet North Korea, twice "defeated" and threatened with obliteration, did not surrender. Conventional military power, no matter in what quantities applied, seemed too little for victory; nuclear power remained too monstrous to be used on the puny targets that presented themselves after conventional air attacks had taken their toll.[14]

On the other hand, to launch surprise atomic attacks on China or Russia as logic might have dictated (since the North Koreans were seen as no more than their "pawns" or "puppets") meant committing acts that admirals, embittered at loss of funds to a nuclearizing air force, had already called "immoral" in the private councils of the Truman administration, and that Paul Nitze in NSC 68, the guiding secret document of the Cold War, had more politely termed "morally corrosive" to the American people. ("An immoral weapon," replied an air force general, "is one too big for your service to deliver.") Although "general" or "global" war, which meant a massive atomic attack on the Soviet Union, was constantly on the minds of civilian and military planners, it seemed that a limit had been reached from which, on a frontierless horizon, could be seen not impending victory but limitless horror.[15]

This was an unprecedented situation. It was not that, as with Japan, victory held unexpected surprises, but that, despite the presence of triumphal statistics, the outcome was proving a barely disguised defeat.

Twice, American troops were sent into terrifying retreat, not simply in individual battles but in full-scale campaigns—once by the North Koreans, once due to Chinese intervention. ("The worst defeat of U.S. forces since Bull Run," commented Secretary of State Dean Acheson.) Unbelievably, the army that had defeated the Japanese and the Nazis had been put to flight twice in a year by poorly equipped peasant troops. How could this have happened to a country industrialized at levels, armed in a fashion, and technologically advanced in ways never before seen, a country that should have had history in its grasp?[16]†

Only two strategic choices seemed available. The first was to take the war to China (and possibly the Soviet Union), an escalation that would undoubtedly have involved the use of nuclear weapons as General Douglas MacArthur and others, possibly including the Joint Chiefs of Staff, urged.

In interviews published posthumously [MacArthur] said he had a plan that would have won the war in ten days: "I would have dropped between thirty and fifty atomic bombs . . . strung across the neck of Manchuria." Then he would have introduced half a million Chinese Nationalist troops at the Yalu and then "spread behind us—from the Sea of Japan to the Yellow Sea—a belt of radioactive cobalt . . . it has an active life of between sixty and 120 years. . . . My plan was a cinch."

Though the Truman administration never backed (and possibly never heard of) such a plan, "global war" was never far from the mind of administration strategists, and by November 1951 a Gallup Poll found 51 percent of a frustrated public ready to embrace the dropping of atomic bombs on "military targets" (a precipitous rise from 23 percent in August 1950).

The second option was to limit the war to Korea and settle for a vicious stalemate that, to a public for which war and victory had become synonymous, seemed a violation. Public opinion had recoiled remarkably quickly from this frontier war that so little accorded with an American script. By February 1951, eight months into the conflict, only 39 percent of Americans polled supported the war effort—and the figure kept drop-

---

†It has been argued that this was, in part, an illusion, that the demobilization of the military after World War II left an ill-equipped and ill-trained shell of an army available for duty in 1950. Certainly, it was the Korean War that spurred the first full-scale militarization of American society that did not end with war's end. This does not change the way Americans then perceived the war, however.[17]

ping. In 1952, Dwight D. Eisenhower was voted into the presidency at least partially on the slogan, "Let it be Asians against Asians," and on a vague promise to deal with the situation ("I will go to Korea").[18]

With the signing of an armistice at Panmunjom in 1953, the war was noisily "forgotten" amid recriminations over the actions of American prisoners of war, for an unprecedented "wholesale breakdown of morale" within enemy prison camps had proved as puzzling and un-American as the war itself. Seventy percent of POWs, according to one study, had "collapsed" under the pressure of captivity and collaborated in some fashion with the enemy. Some had issued statements in language redolent of the other side, accusing their own government of, among other things, engaging in "germ warfare." Captured Air Force First Lieutenant John Quinn's long "confession" of his supposed role in dropping "germ bombs" on North Korea ended in this way: "I was forced to be the tool of these war mongers and made to . . . do this awful crime against the people of Korea and the Chinese Volunteers. Because I am a soldier I must follow orders and these orders came from those imperialists on Wall Street." Twenty-one POWs committed an even more unlikely act. They defected to the enemy, choosing voluntarily to live in China after the war.[19]

How could this have happened? Two explanations were offered. The POWs were seen alternately as "brainwashed" victims of secret Communist—and Asian—mind control techniques ("menticide"); or as symbols of a weakening of the national will, "a new failure," as one officer put it, "in the childhood and adolescent training of our young men—a new softness." This debate reflected confusion over the location of the real enemy. Was the enemy out there, or was it some aspect of the American self? Disbelief that the United States could be stalemated by Asian peasants led to a provisional postwar victory for an invisible, internal enemy. In 1955, a Code of Conduct for prisoners was introduced that would restrict the future actions of that enemy within.[20]

The enemy, wherever located, had not been vanquished despite three years of hellish destruction, and so Korean War veterans came home to no parades in an era when formal military displays of all sorts were on the rise. Though the shock the Korean War caused to American confidence was not given a name like the "Korean Syndrome," the war raised a dreadful, and dread-filled, question mark in the Asian heart of the American Century, one that would plaintively attach itself to a coming conflict in Vietnam.[21]

PART II

CONTAINMENTS
(1945—1962)

1

War Games

"Record Day Raid on Berlin, 2500 Tons of Bombs Dropped on Capitol" is the New York Sun's front-page headline for April 29, 1944. Just under incomplete box scores for the Dodgers–Giants, Yankees–Senators games (4–0, top of the seventh; 2–1, bottom of the fourth) is a photo of my father, standing beside his commanding officer, grinning. Its caption reads, "Lieut.-Col. Philip George Cochran (right) of Erie, Pa., and Major Charles L. Engelhardt of New York, leaders of American air commando operations in Burma, chat at an air station in Burma."

The first panel of the Terry and the Pirates comic strip shows a U.S. transport plane flying under heavy cloud cover. A balloon voice says, "Maybe they're running a different kind of war down here! If that guy above the overcast says he's a major Englewillie—and ordered us to change course." A second balloon answers, "If it's a nip trick—why don't they attack us? I'm not breaking silence until he gives us the code of the day." In panel two, a fighter plane with a rising sun emblem is shown above the clouds, its pilot saying, "Don't pretend you can't hear me in that transport! This is Major Englewillie—" In the background, three planes swoop toward the Japanese fighter while a voice exclaims, "Why, Major Englewillie, how you've changed!" In the final panel below the words, "People can get hurt doing this," the Japanese plane is shown exploding into flames.

"Englewillie" was my father's nickname. Cartoonist Milton Caniff gave the artwork for this May 26, 1944, strip to him in 1967 inscribed:

"For 'Major ENGLEWILLIE' himself . . . with a nostalgic backward nod toward the Big Adventure."

The film *Rocky Mountain* opened in New York in 1950. I was six years old. Errol Flynn was forty-one, nine years from death and already on a downward slide into scandal and ridicule when he played Captain Lafe Barstow in a style so minimalist he hardly existed on screen. Barstow is being sent west by Robert E. Lee with "six rattleheaded kids and an old man" in a last, desperate attempt to save California for the Confederacy. His patrol of Johnny Rebs includes Jimmy Weeks, "a little red-necked cropper who could fight like a wildcat with hydrophobia and carried a useless dog two thousand miles."

Spot, the dog, a tiny white mutt with dark ears, is a whirlwind of energy in this Civil War pastiche of tired western motifs: Indians attack a stagecoach; Flynn rides to the rescue, saves a blond woman on her way to meet her fiancé, a Union officer, then captures his bluecoat patrol. Grays and blues find themselves trapped on a mountainside surrounded by hostile reds. To the incessant beating of tom-toms, they unite. The Rebs unfurl a Confederate flag and ride heroically off the mountain diverting the savages, while the Union soldiers escape with the woman and Jimmy's dog. The whooping Indians chase the Rebs; bluecoated cavalry, summoned by the lieutenant, race to save them. Spot escapes the woman's arms to chase after Jimmy. Flynn's men, trapped in a box canyon, turn on their pursuers ("They've seen our backs, let's show 'em our faces!").

All this proved riveting to me in a way impossible to imagine today. I already knew how such stories turned out, for I had practiced them many times with my friends, my six-guns strapped to my waist, or alone with toy soldiers in my room. So I never doubted the fates of Captain Barstow or Jimmy and his little dog. *Of course,* they were surrounded. *Of course,* they were outnumbered. *Of course,* the cavalry would arrive in time.

But in the case of *Rocky Mountain*, a rare Custer-less last-stand film, Flynn's body was transformed into a pincushion of arrows and every Reb wiped out before help (or Spot) arrived. Consolation lay only in the reverent way the bluecoats later lined up and drew their sabers, in the sound of taps being played, in the welling up of "Dixie," in the sight of Spot in the arms of the lieutenant's fiancé. Consolation lay only in a reaffirmation of the unity of blue and gray, of white and white when faced with red savagery.

At six, however, I couldn't believe my eyes. I had cried before at the movies—when, for instance, the Wicked Witch of the West in *The Wizard of Oz* had driven me under my seat. But these were tears of a different sort, for this massacre threatened my vision of how the world worked. These were tears beyond consolation, the kind a child weeps on first confronting injustice, and they were only possible in a woman's company, for already, at six, to cry in the presence of my father would have been unthinkable.

That my mother took me to *Rocky Mountain* seems, in retrospect, somewhat odd, for westerns like war and adventure movies were my father's domain. Women in films of this sort were a drag, either distracting dance hall girls or simpering schoolteachers from that dreary place (experience would soon confirm the truth of this) "back East."

Sitting close to my mother that day in stunned silence, I did not immediately begin to cry. Only later, in the street, when I had accepted the unacceptable—that the wrong side had won—did the tears flow. Unstanchable by my puzzled mother, they reflected my sense that the order of the universe had been violated. That the cavalry might not arrive, that the surrounded, embattled self might not be saved, that the Other might storm and retake history's central staging ground, that we might lose and be eradicated from the earth had not previously been imagined. This was a haunting moment for me, and *Rocky Mountain* my first unintended horror film.

The unquestioned world of the war story was already embedded in that tearful boy. A child of the children of Jewish runaways and immigrants whose grandfather had arrived in the United States the year after the Wounded Knee massacre, I identified fully with the disparate squad/crew/patrol of bluecoats/cowboys/adventurers/GIs who made the war story such a unifying experience. For me, *Rocky Mountain* was horrifying exactly because that story was already the organizing principle for so many autonomous moments when, with friends in some park or field or a warren of rooms or in private reverie, beyond the gaze or interest of adults, I took up the various thrilling rites of war play.

Imagine me now, an eight-year-old, running through the potato fields behind a friend's house in Long Island. The year is 1952. America is enmeshed in its second Asian war of the century, this time against—to a child—a horrific but blurry enemy. From photos of begrimed GIs with hollow eyes I've seen in a magazine, I know the enemy is frightening, but whether what's frightening is communism or the Russians or the Reds or maybe the Chinese I'm not so sure. Anyway, the fighting that goes on and on in a faraway land called Korea is unimaginably distant from this moment.

My friend and I crouch down, furrowed dirt and leafy potato plants as far as the eye can see. The two of us scan the horizon. Somewhere out there the enemy is approaching—not the one in Korea, but a real enemy, the Japs or Nazis ("Japanazis," as World War II comic books sometimes called them) or maybe the Indians. The choice is ours. No parents are nearby to tell us what to do, no teachers to instruct us, and we're armed. I grip a stick. I can feel the curve where it fits into my palm, and what more do I need than a good eye, the ability to make battle sounds—the sharp rat-a-tat of a machine gun, the budda-budda of ack-ack fire, or the long whistle of incoming artillery—and a sense of available possibilities?

We've been at this for an hour already, beating back attack after attack, then diving for our "foxholes" between the rows of plants. "Watch out!" my friend shouts as loud as he wants, because no one cares that we and the invisible but palpable enemy are here at war in these fields. Yes, I notice it now, too: the faint motion of leaves that might pass for the wind. It's them! A banzai charge! We leap up, firing madly, but with deadly accuracy. The enemy begins to fall.

As they had for generations, such war games in the 1950s meant hours of open-ended play outdoors with only minimal equipment needed, or solitary dream play at home with generic ragtag fighting figures—a bag or two of olive green soldiers, some U.S. Navy "frogmen" redeemable with a dime and a cereal box top from Kellogg's in Battle Creek, Michigan, a motley crew of cowboys and Indians, cavalry and knights, and if you were lucky, some metal "Brittains." In parks and woods, on sidewalks and floors nationwide, boys (and some girls) were left alone, without apparent instruction, to develop endless war play scenarios with no-name toys.†

Adults could leave such war play to the invention of children because all that was needed was still in the air. Who was good and who bad; who the aggressor and who the defender; who could be killed and under what conditions were accepted facts of a childhood world that drew strength from a World War II adult culture still in the home. A boy's ritualistic association of war, war films, and westerns with father may seem obvious, but in those years it had a special, visceral quality to it. After all, the

---

†Although elsewhere in this book I often use "child" and "boy" interchangeably because the war story was so distinctly a boy's and man's story, this hardly meant that only boys took part in, enjoyed, or were affected by war scenarios and war play. Girls participated, sometimes in quite traditional ways, as was true with my wife, who remembers creating elaborate, romantic scenarios in El Paso, Texas, in the early 1950s, in which her Toni doll awaited the return of her husband from "war." But in addition to waiting for the soldiers to come home or being tied to trees until rescued from neighborhood Indians, girls also played at war in recognizably boylike ways; and those who did so in the post–World War II years seem often to have strikingly happy recollections of the experience, though these remain largely unrecorded.[1]

fathers of millions of baby boom children had, only a few years earlier, returned triumphant from that greatest of all wars; and as that generation was coming to consciousness, the war film returned to the screen, glorifying World War II as *the* American war (in almost every case supported by and with script oversight from the Pentagon).[2]

My father (when employed) often worked six days a week, leaving as I awoke and returning at dinnertime. So Sunday afternoons at movie houses along New York City's 42nd Street, seeing double-feature "grind" westerns or war movies, was our special time together. My association of my father with war movies was fiercely felt. For me, the war John Wayne and my dad fought together (one loaned out from the frontier; the other on leave from normal life), that global war against the Japanese ("I studied in your University of Southern California") and the Nazis ("You lie, Sweinhund!") was part and parcel of fatherhood. Like millions of other dads, mine was a living representative of war, American style.

Just after Pearl Harbor, my father, a thirty-five-year-old Jew from Brooklyn with a small insurance business, had volunteered for the army air corps. He joined to fight Hitler but was sent to Burma as operations officer for the 1st Air Commando Group. He was "Pops" to the men in his unit, a glider outfit that dropped behind Japanese lines. ("In a world where anyone over twenty-seven or twenty-eight was likely to be called 'Dad,' thirty was dangerously old and thirty-five close to senile.")[3]

Returning to the United States just before my birth in July 1944, he was assigned to the Pentagon and demobilized late in 1945. But the war clung to him, a frightening if intangible presence in our household, for it had somehow collapsed his postwar life. Years after his return, years of anticlimax and failure, he still liked his friends to call him Major; yet he generally refused to discuss his war experiences.

On rare occasions, unbidden, he would offer up an unexpected anecdote about the ineptness of Indian laborers or the bravery of the Gurkhas, a mountain people with whom his unit had fought. They went armed, he said, with *kukris*, curved knives sharp enough to slit a man in two. Less frequently, he would make some sudden, fierce reference to the unnameable things the "Japs" had done to friends of his. Even years later, to suggest buying a Japanese (or German) product was to risk a terrifying explosion of anger.

My father's more general silence on the war reflected bitterness not just about its brutal realities, but about the loss of career his service entailed. For those who had "profiteered" at home he had many words, though he would never address a civil word to any of them. Our family was not to buy anything at the grocery store conveniently located several doors from our apartment building, for instance, because its owner had been a war profiteer. For me, it was a place to be passed quickly each day, for who knew what horrors lurked behind those mundane signs announcing the price of meat and vegetables?

What my father had done in the war and what the war had done to him, what of the war (including respect) he had been unable to bring back to civilian life—this I could sense. There were stories here to be told, and my father's silence told them in a way words could not. The citizen-warrior had no need to speak, for silence was a heroic virtue, a frontier trait (as anyone who visited a movie theater in those days knew). In any case, nothing need be said when the glory-filled nature of that war, of all American wars, was apparent in movies, toys, and comics, on TV, and even in alluring artifacts hidden in our apartment.

In the recesses of the closet in the "guest room" (which doubled as "the bar") sat a faded green duffle bag, bunched at the top and locked. Opened only twice in my presence, it held a cornucopia of war documents—surveillance shots of airfields and airplanes, letters headed "War Department, Headquarters of the Army Air Forces," and photos of my father in uniform, unrecognizably young and slim, his face glistening like a movie star's (and so unlike the red-faced bull of a man who roamed the house each night). In that fabulous bag lay layers of war booty—an old mess kit, dog tags, insignia, two-sided silk maps of Burma that could be wadded in the fist, safe passes for surrendering Japanese, a Presidential Appointment to the rank of Major, and underneath it all, a gun, a black revolver with which, perhaps, my father had once shot real Japs, and in a box, a handful of bullets.

High in my parents' bedroom closet lay an ornate *kukri* in a plain wooden box, a war treasure fit for the Arabian nights. Held in a black velvet sheath, inscribed "From 3rd BN 6th Gurkha Rifles Burma Chindits 1944" on a silver field above two peacocks, its black curved handle awaited a savage hand strong enough to slit a throat. Nearby, reachable on tiptoe from a chair was my father's air force dress hat. A golden eagle spread its wings above the brim. In the mirror, that hat lent me the look of a warrior. Gun, *kukri*, hat—with such artifacts, who knew what feats my silent, angry father had performed for his country?

WAR AS PEACE

Such domestic dreams of war were well suited to the unique form of militarization American society was experiencing. After 1945, the country had undergone a brief and partial demobilization, on and off screen. However, from 1950 on, unprecedented funds began to flow into military coffers. Pentagon expenditures more than quadrupled, from $10.9 billion in 1948 to $49.6 billion in 1953, and the foundations of a new national security state were constructed amid promises of militarized prosperity. For the first time in three quarters of a century, the country was led by a retired general. Known for his serenity and love of golf, President Dwight D. Eisenhower was symbolic of a military gaining in stature as it suburbanized.[4]

Like some rising tide, soaring Pentagon budgets seemed to lift the armed forces out of the realm of actual warfare and into a new, sacral realm of armed fantasy and entertainment. In homes across the country, for instance, a reverent populace shut down on Sunday afternoons during the 1952–1953 television season to watch the TV series *Victory at Sea*. "For twenty-six Sundays last year," wrote *Harper's Magazine* editor Bernard DeVoto, "neither the telephone nor the doorbell was answered at my house between 3 and 3:30 P.M."

Produced "in cooperation with the U.S. Navy," illustrated by archival clips "from all sides" of the world war, driven by the voice of a single narrator, rushed forward by an overpowering, unending score composed by Richard Rogers, *Victory at Sea* urged its viewers along a single path from defeat to victory, from slavery to freedom, from global collapse and barbarism to a triumphant American world. The bombs, American bombs, fell to a light but dramatic cadence. "From island to island, continent to continent, the children of free peoples move the forces of tyranny from the face of the earth . . . it is, it *will* be so, until the forces of tyranny are no more."[5]

Victory at Sea was not alone. Documentary series like *Crusade in Europe* and *Crusade in the Pacific* had preceded it on television, and others like *Air Power* would be inspired by its success. There would be dramatic series like *The West Point Story*, combat series like *The Silent Service* (about submarine warfare), military comedies like *The Phil Silvers Show*, and army-sponsored shows like *Talent Patrol*, which highlighted the entertainment skills of service men and women. Certain of these began as propaganda for (and all were considered useful to) military recruitment drives. To such shows, the services extended offers of help of every imaginable sort—from the loan of a military campus or base as a set to specially shot footage of subs diving or missiles being launched.

Then there were shows produced by the Defense Department for the networks or for independent stations: *The Armed Forces Hour* with its service documentaries like the navy's *Take 'Er Down* or the air force's *Air Defense*; military sports broadcasts; even films of atomic tests. Finally, there was the popular documentary series, *The Big Picture*.

("From Korea to Germany, from Alaska to Puerto Rico, all over the world the United States Army is on the alert to defend our country—you, the American people—against aggression. This is 'The Big Picture,' an official television report to the nation from the United States Army.")

Military experts were loaned out to shows with military themes, weaponry and soldiers were on call for battle reenactments, and special help was offered to network news programs. Take the aid the services gave NBC's *Wide Wide World* for a 1957 show: "Courtesy of the Pentagon, viewers for 90 minutes saw an array of live military maneuvers— precision bombing drills from Luke Air Force Base near Phoenix . . . an amphibious assault conducted at Marine Corps installations at Quantico, Virginia . . . and demonstrations by the U.S. Army of its latest equipment at Fort Sill, Oklahoma."[6]

This was more than military oversight, censorship, or propaganda (though it was all of those). The marriage of the military way of life to the television set (owned by half of all American families by 1953) and the movie screen was part of a larger transformation of the military's role in the years after the Korean War. War was being replaced by increasingly elaborate war games. Garrisoning bases over much of the globe, facing the Communist enemy at potential flash points from Berlin to the straits of Taiwan, the Pentagon focused on the production of war spectacles and spectaculars.

Whether played out in the heads of strategists in war rooms and Pentagon-related think tanks, or with massed armies acting out scenarios of aggression and defense in Europe and the United States, the military production process came closer to movie making than war making. Military men had entered a fantasy universe in which they found themselves writing "scripts" for apocalyptic future nuclear exchanges that could only be fought in the imagination. In a sense, the armed forces had nowhere to go but on screen. (It was fitting, then, that Elvis Presley's drafting in 1958 became the biggest "military" story of the decade.)

Like millions of other children, I reveled in the forms of militarized entertainment then available. I waited impatiently for my father to drive me up the Hudson River to West Point to watch the Long Gray Line of cadets drill. Behind ack-ack guns or torpedo sights in penny arcades, I raced against time to shoot Zeroes from the heavens or blast U-boats to the depths. (It would take advances in technology and the collapse of victory culture before arcade games ended in a player's destruction. In the 1950s, they could not get you; you could only run out of time to get them.) I avidly went to war films, read war comics, and amassed toy soldiers. On the appropriate holidays, my father took me to parades, glorious affairs in which massed troops marched down Fifth Avenue to the upbeat cadences of military bands followed by awesome processionals of jeeps and artillery pieces, tanks and the occasional missile amid whirling drill teams and endless salutes.[7]

Yet what I so often played at being, I never dreamt of becoming. As a middle-class boy, it did not occur to me that I might grow up to be a soldier. I often imagined myself as an army kid, however, because in the early 1950s my father owned a gas station on Governor's Island, a military base in New York Harbor. For me, the ferry trip to the island on a Saturday morning seemed edenic. To cross the harbor was to enter a world in which father, war, entertainment, and the previously unexperienced wonders of suburbia fused. Drilling soldiers, buzzing jeeps, grassy parade grounds, pick-up baseball games, a vast swimming pool, and a movie theater showing old Buck Rogers serials and Republic westerns— this was a vision of the good life, military style, of "war" without pain. To me, it was life sunnyside up.[8]

The worlds of the warrior and of abundance were, to my gaze, no more antithetical than they were to the corporate executives, university research scientists, and military officers who were using a rising military budget and the fear of communism to create a new national security economy. An alliance between big industry, big science, and the military had been forged during World War II. This alliance had blurred the boundaries between the military and civilian by fusing a double set of desires: for technological breakthroughs leading to ever more instant weapons of destruction and to ever easier living.

The arms race and the race for the good life were now to be put on the same "war" footing. In the war years, in the context of a full-employment economy, large numbers of Americans had for the first time begun to dream of buying their way into the future. In June 1944, the Office of Civilian Requirements released a list of the most desired items in civilian postwar buying plans. Nine practical yet fantastic appliances stood atop it: the washing machine, electric iron, refrigerator, stove, toaster, radio, vacuum cleaner, electric fan, and hot water heater.[9]

The companies developing the new technologies of war were already advertising the coming technologies of peace that would make wondrous household objects available to all. "[I]n these days of tired bodies and troubled minds it's good . . . to think about . . . the new kind of a home you will have after victory," began a 1944 ad from General Electric. The "pioneering" war production work of its researchers, wrote an ad man for General Motors ("Victory is our business"), "will provide more and better things for more people in the coming years of peace." The Farnsworth

Television and Radio Corporation, then making "radar and military electronic weapons," touted the upcoming "miracle of television." "Each second, 30 *complete pictures* are thrown on the television screen."

"Look . . . that's what I'm going to have!" exclaims the stylishly dressed woman in a November 1945 "every house needs Westinghouse" ad. She is admiring a scale model "combination kitchen and laundry . . . a dream come true" with a "new electric range so automatic you can put a meal in to cook and then forget it," an "electric refrigerator with ample space for everything, frozen foods included," a "laundromat," and even a "new automatic clothes dryer." All were to be made available "as soon as possible."[10]

In the 1950s, all did become available as a "military Keynesianism" drove the U.S. economy toward a consumerism in which desire for the ever larger car and missile, electric range and tank, television console and submarine, was wedded in single corporate entities. The companies— General Electric, General Motors, and Westinghouse, among others— producing the large objects for the American home were also major contractors developing the weapons systems ushering the Pentagon into its own age of abundance. As cultural historian Stephen J. Whitfield has written, "What enhanced the home was not unrelated to what protected the homeland."

It seemed natural for Charles Wilson, president of General Motors, to become secretary of defense in the Eisenhower administration, just as retiring generals and admirals found it natural to move into the employ of corporations they had only recently employed on the government's behalf. Meanwhile, personnel from the Pentagon spread throughout the civilian government. By 1957, 200 generals and admirals as well as 1,300 colonels or naval officers of similar rank, retired or on leave, worked for civilian agencies; and military funding spilled over into a Congress that redirected its largess to districts nationwide.[11]

Washington, according to historian Ernest May, became a "military headquarters." The Pentagon was "the dominant consumer of the federal government's discretionary funds [and] defense and defense-related agencies accounted steadily for 60 to 70 percent of all federal personnel. . . . [T]he main business of the U.S. government had become the development, maintenance, positioning, exploitation, and regulation of military forces." Globally, the military's presence was unavoidable. Former wartime Chief of Staff General George C. Marshall, appointed secretary of state, had saved Europe for the Free World with an economic plan named after himself; while General Douglas MacArthur ruled Japan and Lieutenant General Lucius D. Clay a large chunk of Germany as American-style proconsuls. By the end of the 1950s, a new acronymic landscape of DEW lines, SAC bases, NORAD defense systems, and missiles named after Greek or Norse gods was being constructed in North America; while U.S. troops were stationed on hundreds of military bases worldwide.[12]

The military and its corporate contractors—by 1961, 20,000 principal firms and 100,000 subcontractors—represented the era's unassailable growth industry. No one dared cross them. Even Senator Joseph McCarthy, who could with impunity attack presidents and presidential candidates alike ("Alger . . . I mean Adlai" was his famous "slip" during the 1952 presidential campaign) made his fatal political mistake in attacking the military.

If the peaceable giants of consumer production were also the militarized giants of weapons production, the armed forces with its ability to obliterate any nation was also a measure of abundance. Between 1953 and 1963, the army was effectively demilitarized. The most overarmed force in history scored its final military success of the decade with a seaborne landing at Inchon, Korea, in 1950. Army funds, particularly for the development of new weaponry, were curtailed, and monies flowed instead to the air force, especially into the Strategic Air Command's airborne nuclear forces. In Secretary of State John Foster Dulles's phrase, "massive retaliation" would be the military doctrine of the day.

The war that would never be fought—the imagined Soviet assault on the Western European heartland—became of overriding importance to the Joint Chiefs of Staff. The army's wartime role would be to hold the line in Europe until the air force could turn Russia into "a smoking, radiating ruin." In a situation where conflict promised cataclysm, and in the words of Army Chief of Staff Maxwell Taylor, "there could be no real victory," a military paralysis set in. In the wake of the Korean armistice, war was loosed from the military's grasp. In the world's nether regions and "peripheral" lands from the Caribbean to the Mideast, Africa to Southeast Asia, the United States would engage in a new style of armed combat led by a new group of armed Americans.[13]

Against Communist enemies believed to be "masters of special warfare" and experts in unseen terror, another kind of battle was deemed necessary. Americans would have to descend into the "pit" and "fight fire with fire." Everywhere on earth, the Communists would have to be "countered" with a new kind of warfare in which assassination, hostage taking, intimidation, and torture would be sanctioned activities. As General James Doolittle, famed raider of Tokyo, wrote in a review of Central Intelligence Agency (CIA) activities ordered by President Eisenhower,

"There are no rules in such a game. Hitherto acceptable norms of human conduct do not apply. If the United States is to survive, long-standing American concepts of 'fair play' must be reconsidered."[14]

From President Eisenhower on down, American leaders felt that the public could not be mobilized to support such wars. The military, too, proved reluctant to publicly redefine its troops as tricksters, torturers, and assassins. All of this lay beyond the "rules" of war, which was, in any case, descending into a conceptual hell. At the nuclear level, it could be planned but not acted upon; while in Third World lands, it could be acted upon but not acknowledged. In its new, dirtied form, it was becoming an embarrassment.

As a result, the battlefield was inherited by "covert" organizations, whose quasi-wars in Guatemala, Iran, Laos, Cuba, and elsewhere were to be pursued in secret. Organized largely through the CIA, the American role in these conflicts was not supposed to come to public attention, and triumphs in them were to be celebrated in private by the few who knew. In June 1948, an innocuously titled Office of Policy Coordination (OPC) had been set up within the CIA, and given a mandate in NSC 10/2 to answer the "vicious covert activities of the USSR, its satellite countries and Communist groups." Through it, the CIA was to be freed to undertake "[a]ny covert activities related to propaganda, economic warfare; preventive direct action, including sabotage, antisabotage, demolition and . . . subversion against hostile states including assistance to underground resistance groups, and support of indigenous anti-Communist elements in threatened countries of the free world." Such actions were, however, to be "so planned and conducted that any U.S. government responsibility for them was not evident to unauthorized persons and that if uncovered, the U.S. Government can plausibly disclaim any responsibility for them."[15]

Between 1949 and 1952, the OPC experienced explosive growth: in personnel from 302 to over 6,000; in budget from $4.7 million to $82 million; in overseas stations from 7 to 47. In the decade 1953–1962, America's fighting would be done primarily by these CIA secret warriors, always employing a complex web of local peoples, mercenaries, and front organizations whose trail was never to lead back either to the CIA or the U.S. government. This kind of war seemed so unnatural to military men that most automatically shied away from it. In 1961, when the army was finally prodded by the Kennedy administration to upgrade its Special Forces, it tellingly opted to place the first Green Beret units sent to Indochina under CIA command.[16]

Because no boundaries were believed to constrain the enemy's efforts, no boundaries were to constrain America's secret warriors either. Ultimately, this meant that someday the "dirty" war would come home in the form of FBI Cointelpro operations against black groups, CIA operations against antiwar dissidents, and Nixon administration operations against the Democratic Party. Dirty tricks, black bag jobs, sabotage, all would become part of domestic politics as would the quasi-warriors themselves.

"War" had ceased to be a military operation. Left to the armed forces in those years was fantasy. The spacy war games that would be accessible to anyone with a personal computer in the post–Vietnam War era were then the property of the Pentagon. As guardians of the nation's nuclear strike force, with its apocalyptic scenarios, and of victory culture, with its nostalgic on-screen wars, they would prove war gamers par excellence. While the covert warriors fought by any means necessary on the "hidden" battlegrounds of the Third World, the armed forces were left wallowing in abundance, camping out on a global scale. When called upon once again to go to war, they entered Vietnam as an accumulation of abundance, of hardware and software to be delivered massively on an unseen enemy, and as an army of spectators whose leaders had matured writing war scenarios and whose troops had grown up watching them.

CHILD'S PLAY

For children in those years, there still existed an arena beyond the screen and largely outside either the pleasures of abundance or end-of-the-world terrors. They could disappear into a realm of war play where they would not act out a junior version of the new garrison state, pretend to be part of the SAC force, or shoot nuclear missiles at each other. Even though it was possible to buy "an exact automatic action replica of our Navy's newest atomic sub" or an H2O Missile, a water-powered "ICBM," there was something palpably unplayful in "nuclear toys." For obvious reasons, one could not lose oneself in them.

In a TV ad of that era for Lionel trains, a test pilot steps from his Grumman Tiger Jet to affirm that what's necessary for men and boys, when handling a dangerous machine, is "control." He hopes his son will learn such control on a new Lionel train with its railbound missile car. "You can learn to operate these Lionel missile launchers and fire these IRBM launchers by pressing a button . . . and remember, kids, you're in control."[17]

But children shrank from controlling the uncontrollable (as adults did from thinking the unthinkable), retreating instead into a sacramental version of American history in a "back yard" beyond the curiosity of the adult and still largely out of reach of corporate advertisers. For boys, in those years, the American way of war, whether on an American or an Asian frontier, was not a matter of death but an intense form of pleasure, an elemental happiness, and a rite (as well as right) of passage. That version of history in which the celebration lay in the slaughter remained central to the play and fantasy of the boys of the Vietnam generation. If anything, it gained in intensity and sunnyness in their world as it slowly drained from the grown-up one.

"It is hard to exaggerate the extent to which young boys . . . in the 1950s and early 1960s . . . grew up fighting an imaginary version of World War II," comments Christian G. Appy on the basis of interviews with and a careful reading of the writings of Vietnam veterans. "In patches of weed and clouds of imagination," veteran Tim O'Brien has written, "I learned to play army games. Friends introduced me to the Army Surplus Store off main street. We bought dented relics of our fathers' history, rusted canteens and olive-scented, scarred helmet liners. Then we were our fathers, taking on the Japs and Krauts along the shores of Lake Okabona."[18]

America's faith in its manifest destiny had unconsciously been relegated to the back yard, park, or floor. Sealed inside childhood, the war story seemed secure. Strikingly little was needed to act it out. With a Matty Mattel machine gun or a cap gun or a no-name toy rifle or a stick or a cocked thumb and pointing forefinger and the ability to negotiate or argue about who was dead and who alive, with woods or playground or yard or street (or, at home, generic fighting figures and a floor), you could engage in a sort of open-ended, instructionless war play.

Crucial as it was to boys' lives, war play was so little in the thoughts or concerns of adults that, except as it is hinted at in memoirs of childhood (especially those of Vietnam veterans), remarkably little has been written about it. There had been a burst of professional and parental concern about when "play goes warlike" during World War II. As the psychologist Arthur L. Rautman wrote in 1943, the shoot-the-Jap, bomb-those-Nazis play of children "excessively preoccupied with the war" might prove "a symptom of basic neuroticism and not . . . a desirable or wholesome . . . activity." But if worry about such war play briefly surfaced in professional journals and popular magazines, curiosity about it did not last out the war years.

Likely as war play might have seemed as a subject for Eisenhower-era child development experts, increasingly concerned with "juvenile delinquency" and "violence" in popular culture, it was largely untouched. Diane Levin, a researcher on childhood and war play who has conducted a search of the period's child development and play literature, could find little on the subject. As she remarked, "In each book, I could see exactly where an analysis of war play should have gone. It was as if there was a hole right after the obligatory discussions of boys' dramatic play and gender differences. Almost nothing was ever there." War play as a developmental activity with its "violent" acts made so little impression because it generally took place beyond the selling nexus and in a patriotic context so familiar as to be assumed harmless by adults.[19]

  If there is little information available on how children played at war and how they thought about what they did, there is some on what they played with. Though toylike soldiers have been found in ancient burial grounds, the earliest European toy soldiers whose use by children can be confirmed were a royal inheritance. Made from gold, silver, or lead, they were meant for those who would someday command real armies, the sons of kings or of the high nobility. Starting in the second half of the eighteenth century, however, the soldier as play toy spread quickly and in many forms: carved wooden soldiers for peasant children, cardboard cutout revolutionary war soldiers or soldiers of sawdust and glue in the United States, but especially highly detailed flat tin and solid lead soldiers, turned out in profusion by German and later French and English manufacturers.[20]

  In 1893, the English toy maker William Brittain, Jr., invented the lighter, cheaper, hollow-cast metal soldier; and the production of war toys achieved a commercial success and a "realism" that would soon turn a child's floor into something akin to a "battlefield" (as the invention of the cap pistol in the United States on the eve of the Civil War had given a new realism to the toy gun). The ability to create miniature soldiers inexpensively and in profusion opened up the possibility of enacting patriotic stories on one's own floor.

  The world wars spurred the development of toy soldier realism and speeded the production process. New weaponry scarcely made it onto the battlefield before replicas appeared in the playroom. The tank launched into battle in 1916 was in French children's hands by 1917. The armored vehicle, the mine, the motorcycle, and the antiaircraft battery all took a similar journey to the child's floor. In Germany, during World War II, writes historian George L. Mosse, soldiers gained even greater reality in pose, "at rest, playing cards, in action, saluting, goosestepping . . . [and] also . . . wounded, amputated, and dead."

  Antiwar sentiment emerging from World War I in both England and the United States led to the earliest recorded adult concern about the nature of children's war play. The call for "peace toys" was such that the American Soldier Company felt it necessary to produce a booklet for retail stores entitled "Good Reasons for NOT Buying Military Games," with all its pages blank.[21]

The toy soldiers that typified the immediate post–World War II years were the single color two-and-a-half- to three-inch hard plastic figures (soldiers, cowboys and Indians, knights) mass produced and sold, often by the bagful or in large boxed play sets. Small and crudely stamped out, they lacked expression, no less personality of any sort. Among the more expensive metal soldiers of the time, like the imported Brittains (which came in open-faced boxed sets), details of uniform and expression between officer and trooper might differ, offering slightly more individuality. Even hand-painted collector's figures were ordinarily done by unit or type rather than by individual personality, except in the case of major military figures like Napoleon.

Ally or enemy gained individuality not in production or instruction but in play. There was little need at the time to individualize—which would have meant, to explain—either the good or bad guys in the production process because neither the nature of the roles to be distributed, the rules of the game, nor the course of events was in doubt in the world of the child. There, American history was still in place.

I can vividly recall my own floor play strategies, developed so long ago. In that era of the large consumer item, the middle-class child's room was another kind of emptiness, for childhood was only then being discovered as a marketplace of significance. My room—one wall painted by my mother with marching soldiers—had a bed, a chair, a desk, a few games, numerous books, a six-gun and holster set, and an old wooden radio.

Then, of course, there were my soldiers and the stories about them circulating in my head. I had no blocks, though war play cried out for building materials, but books took their place. Piled up, they were mountains. Unevenly layered, they gained crevices and ledges. In two facing rows, they became cliffs on either side of a narrow defile. Indians, peering over *The Pony Express* or *Ben Franklin of Old Philadelphia*, commanded those heights. They "lay" on top of books or "crouched" behind them, fingering bows, tomahawks, or guns.

However, with their flat, protruding bases, those immobile figures, when laid down, looked dismayingly like they had fallen to the earth nose first. I sometimes dreamed of figures capable of changing their poses, or of being dead or wounded in realistic ways, or of weaponry that emitted actual battle sounds. But those fantasies (to become another era's reality) evaporated with the onset of the event itself: the hypnotic, oft-repeated moment of ambush when canyon walls echoed with the sounds of battle and bodies dropped like flies.

As the director of the primal scene in which the Indians lured the bluecoats into that Western groove, I could not help but notice something easy to avoid when you were a viewer—the essential dopiness of the cavalry. Why was it that the bluecoats always rode into that ambush? Their tactical stupidity only highlighted the cleverness of the Indians, making me more curious about them as a mass to be deployed.

Of course, I was the one who had to line up the bluecoats for their hapless procession into the Valley of Death. Because I was short a reasonable troop of cavalry or a full contingent of foot soldiers, I was forced to fill in with the odd redcoat and GIs of the green plastic variety. Choosing the order of the ride and who was to be handed over to destruction lent individual character and value to each treasured figure and emphasized the enormous pride I took in the best of my bluecoats. Yet, if the initial ambush was to be satisfying, death had to be faced.

Chosen first were the most lackluster figures, casualties of previous battles with chipped paint, broken limbs, or busted off rifles. These were to fall in the initial cascade of arrows, or by knife or tomahawk soon after. The crucial question was when to stop the killing of the bluecoats and begin the slaughter of the Indians. A satisfying cutoff point had to be found, especially given a countervailing temptation—to go all the way, to wipe out every last bluecoat. Sometimes it was powerful enough that I found myself almost siding with the Indians (which hinted at something novel hidden in this traditional sorting out process). Yet it was a temptation I never brought myself to test out.

For one thing, I possessed a bluecoat far too wonderful for death. This hand-painted, elegant cavalry officer sat easily astride a dappled gray horse, pistol dramatically drawn. From bridle to bedroll, bandana to boots, black mustache to white riding gloves, he was so lifelike his eyes seemed to sparkle. The exquisite, painful pleasure of the situation lay in calibrating how close I dared come to this soldier before the spectacle of slaughter began.

Amid the carnage, as arrows rained down, a few Indians would begin to fall. It didn't matter which ones, just that they dropped dramatically from the cliffs to the ground. There was no particular order, no special precedence in the roll call of Indian death. Their deaths simply had to satisfy certain standards of realism familiar to any moviegoer of the time. The chief was an exception. A red-jacketed Brittain, in his hand he held a silver-bladed tomahawk, clearly meant for scalping, and miraculously, his arm pivoted at the shoulder. As the only Indian with a distinguishing trait, he was invariably the last to die.

Nothing could have seemed more natural or more lasting than this kind of war play with its roots several hundred years old. Yet there were indications that, even in the unreachable world of children's play, the war story was undergoing change. The first subtle signs of this can be noted in the early 1950s, when "individualized" war toys—cowboys and frontiersmen linked to TV series like Hopalong Cassidy and Disney's Davy Crockett—swept into the child's world. The hard, plastic Hartland animal and horse figures produced in the 1940s now gained recognizable riders, ranging from the Lone Ranger and Roy Rogers to traditional western heroes.[22]

At the time, these passing fads of childhood, with their purchasable paraphernalia, seemed hardly different from others that had gone before. These toys with personas could still fit without confusion into the generic toy lineup on any floor, just as new, ever more realistic weaponry like Mattel's "fast-fanning" six-shooter could still shoot down quite traditional enemies. (The newer-style Cold War toys of the spy and intelligence agent didn't come into their own fully until the early 1960s.) When these TV-inspired crazes began to give "character" to the generic war toy, no one could have imagined that they were the beginning of a process that would someday leave war play and war toys nearly unrecognizable.

As folklorists Peter and Iona Opie have shown, children exhibit an amazing tenacity in holding onto what is culturally theirs. They repeat ancient rhymes, jokes, and ditties of all sorts (thinking them original or made up by friends and acquaintances) and regularly play games adapted to the moment but hundreds if not thousands of years old. That American children should have inherited the war story as their playful own, just as European children had once inherited the rituals of knightly battle discarded by adults, was not in itself extraordinary. Extraordinary was the fact that after its three hundred–year trip through a shared adult and child culture, it would take barely a generation to pass into the charge of children and then out of American society altogether.

ARCADIA AND APOCALYPSE

My father's gas station played its small part in fueling the world of militarized abundance, though my father was neither a militarist nor an army lover. His bitter comments about the "stupidity" of the regular army officers he dealt with were a commonplace of family life. Nor was my childhood militarized in any unusual way. The fantasy experience of war existed at the calm center of my largely eventless life. But wasn't this typical of the unique form of militarization the United States was experiencing then? The public, it seemed, was being mobilized and demobilized at the same time. Think of those popular TV comedies that recreated suburban life as a militarized activity. Didn't Sergeant Bilko of *The Phil Silvers Show* (1955–1959) and all the comic noncoms who followed offer up a gentler version of my father's critique of the army from bases, ships, even enemy prisons that seemed more like summer camps than the spartan encampments of warriors?

The United States was involved in a global "war," yet Americans were militarily unmenaced. The economy was churning out the most peaceable and the most warlike of big ticket items, and both were being sold to audiences migrating to the suburbs, intent on creating a carefree world of basement playrooms and backyard barbecues. The country was reimagining itself as a magic kingdom, a cornucopic mechanism for turning out the world's play toys and pleasure environments.

On the other hand, the country was being remodeled as an anxiety-ridden garrison state governed by a burgeoning national security bureaucracy and anchored by well-funded, overlapping intelligence, policing, and security agencies. Wholesale purges of leftists and dissidents were occurring at every level of society; attempts were being made to suppress any nationalist movement abroad that could be tarred with the brush of communism; and "defense intellectuals" were conjuring up games of chicken in which "the other side" would be pushed to the edge of the abyss by the first strike capabilities of the U.S. nuclear arsenal.

In 1950s America, the worlds of consumer arcadia and global fear, of twenty-four-hour-a-day television and twenty-four-hour-a-day airborne nuclear-armed bombers coexisted. In one of these worlds, Americans half-fancied that they had stepped beyond history into a postindustrial landscape of "affluence," where "leisure" might soon replace work almost entirely and the main problem was an inability to find problems. This vision of a suburbanized world without poverty engendered its own anxiety, for evidence was accumulating that abundance was nowhere near as satisfying as it was cracked up to be. In their new homes, women now found themselves trapped in a "female ghetto." "Life," as Sara Evans has written, "seemed to be passing them by: shopping trips became forays into the outside world, and husbands, who had less and less time to spend with their families, were now their major link to the public realm."[23]

From an only slightly different perspective, the leisure-filled existence in which everyone would have a similar wondrous house filled with the same wondrous goods looked like a "mass society" from which there might be no exit for the individual. Moreover, leisure was to be paid for by male breadwinners trapped inside large corporations that valued image over substance, outer acquiescence over inner strength, and group experience over individual initiative. Was this, then, just a looking-glass world? Someday, would the gray flannel–suited zombies of the corporate "rat race" meet the insects from the group-mind hive of communism halfway?

The feeling of entrapment in abundance also descended to the level of children, who were already spending startling numbers of hours in front of the television set learning that soon there would be endless buying possibilities for them, too. As for adults, so for children, from abundance arose suburban scenarios of quiet horror: often, no matter which way you looked other than at the screen, nothing seemed to be going on to the end of time. This sense of exitlessness was to haunt the activist children of the coming decade. As the organizers of the radical group Students for a Democratic Society wrote in their founding statement in 1962, "Beneath the reassuring tones of the politicians . . . beneath the stagnation of those who have closed their minds to the future, is the pervading feeling that there simply are no alternatives, that our times have witnessed the exhaustion not only of Utopias, but of any new departures as well."[24]

If in abundance lay a potentially debilitating sense of nowhere to go; something—whether the bomb or a Communist takeover—could still arrive from beyond that blank horizon before you even knew what hit you. What child of that era, jammed between the metal legs of a desk, hands protectively over head, could not testify that a fear of terrifying abstraction rested horrifyingly close to the society of affluence?†

Striking about this new state of being was its narrativeless quality. Abundance lacked plot, and when combined with the arbitrariness of either imagined end-of-story, that lack was itself terrifying. One might stumble unpredictably from the glut of affluence to the overabundance of military might, or from a dread of affluence to a dread of extermination, or even from "our" world into "theirs" without ever sensing that a border had been crossed. In this lay at least part of the fascination of Alfred Hitchcock's films of those years. His ordinary citizens crossed boundaries they hadn't imagined existed until they suddenly found themselves alone in the Bates Motel as the knife descended or on a deserted ribbon of highway in corn country as the crop duster made its first pass, machine guns blazing.[26]

Television, with its endless stories, seemed a bulwark against storylessness. Familiar forms of storytelling tumbled quickly into TV's safe

---

†As widespread as nuclear fears, fantasies, and dreams undoubtedly were among the young then, adults preferred to ignore them. The first attempt to study nuclear fears in children does not seem to have been undertaken until 1963, in the wake of the Cuban missile crisis, and another fifteen years passed before the subject was taken up seriously.[25]

haven. The guardians of television were few in number—mainly, four and then three networks—and they guarded the gate fiercely against apostasy of every sort. Anything appearing on screen was to be vetted for the aberrant, impure, or un-American. Inside that screen, fortress America fought back, defending itself against the ambushes of the forces of Evil.

Guns blazed in gangster shootouts, World War II battles, Cold War undercover operations, and western showdowns. Of 103 series listed for the 1958–1959 season, 69 fell into the "action-crime-mystery category"; and of them, none was more dominant from the mid-1950s through the early 1960s than the "adult" western, making up nearly one-quarter of all network nightly offerings by 1959. For adults and children alike, watching sheriffs, gunslingers, and cowboys walk an endless Main Street or patrol the savage frontiers of freedom on TV seemed a thrilling escape. Yet television proved a powerful motor for storylessness. The constant cycling of the dual worlds of blazing entertainment and enticing sales pitches had a corrosive edge all its own, and the war story's helpfulness in projecting a vision of the good life into the living room ultimately proved limited. While shimmering visions of ad-driven abundance cycled on, the consoling world embodied in that war story barely lasted out the decade on television. Hitchcock had it right. In the end, the most sensible stories to be made from such materials were tales of horror. From the intertwined worlds of dread 'n plenty, TV would offer no way out.[27]

As the new decade began, a young president would acknowledge a postwar loss of narrative. He would call upon other even younger Americans, promising "new frontiers" at the far reaches of the earth ("The great battleground for the defense and expansion of freedom today is the whole southern half of the globe . . . the lands of the rising peoples") and in previously "uncharted areas of science and space." By the mid-1960s, it seemed that only the young—or at least adolescents preparing to go off to war (or protest it)—could still take as an article of faith a story adults were suddenly finding themselves unable to replicate as entertainment. Just a few years later, not even the young could do so, and war as myth and play seemed to have been swept clean out of American culture.[28]

2

X Marks the Spot

PREVIOUSLY KNOWN AS Detroit Red and Big Red, Malcolm Little was called Satan by the other prisoners in his cellblock in Charlestown prison. In July 1947, only twenty-two years old and not quite a year and a half into an eight- to ten-year sentence for burglary, he had lost his name several times over. To the authorities—and sometimes even himself—he was now just a number. "You never heard your name, only your number," he would recall. "On all of your clothing, every item, was your number, stenciled. It grew stenciled on your brain."

"Satan" had already experienced most of the forms of containment America had to offer its subject populations. His mother had told him family tales of the fury of the Ku Klux Klan, and he suspected that his Garveyite father had been murdered by a white man in their hometown of Lansing, Michigan. As a boy, placed in a "detention home" run by a white woman, he had experienced the matter-of-fact containment offered a good Negro student. His English teacher in his all-white class had advised him to be "realistic about being a nigger" and consider becoming a carpenter, not the lawyer he dreamed of being.

As a young man, he had experienced the structural containment of the urban ghetto, whose hustling demimonde offered pathways mainly to jail, addiction, and death, and the cultural containment of a flight from blackness. Arrested for burglary before he was twenty-one, he underwent that most literal of containments—prison. His sentence, several years longer than the norm, was also a form of sexual containment. ("The judge told me to my face, 'This will teach you to stay away from white girls.'")

As he later saw it, he had been in a prison constructed by white people all his life. He would be twenty-three when he converted to a small Muslim religious sect, "the Lost-Found Nation of Islam here in this wilderness of North America." It was led by "a black man like us," Elijah (or Robert) Poole, the son of a Georgia sharecropper, who called himself the Honorable Elijah Muhammad. He had, he claimed, met "God, in person" in Detroit in 1930. God had taken the form of a man by the name of Wallace D. Fard. Through Fard, he believed, Allah had called on him to lead "the so-called Negro" out of a wilderness of whiteness and into a land of his own. Muhammad preached that "for centuries the 'blue-eyed devil white man' had brainwashed the 'so-called Negro' . . . [that] the black man was Original Man, who had been kidnapped from his homeland and stripped of his language, his culture, his family structure, his family name, until the black man in America did not even realize who he was."

Malcolm would feel that, in ceasing to eat pork, take drugs, or hustle, in following a man whose sympathies in World War II had lain with the Japanese, he had taken his first tentative steps out of containment years before his body was allowed beyond the prison walls. Through the Lost-Found Nation, he had begun to tunnel beneath a domestic Iron Curtain. In 1952, on parole, he would meet the Honorable Elijah Muhammad and later ceremonially divest himself of his "white slave-master name of 'Little' which some blue-eyed devil named Little had imposed upon my paternal forebears." In its place, he put an "X," symbolizing "the true African family name that he never could know." In 1953, while U.S. troops were still fighting along Korea's 38th parallel and negotiators at Panmunjom were arguing about where to establish another global boundary line of hostility, the "X" that Malcolm took on marked the spot where he had stepped beyond. Although the Nation of Islam was its own container, it gave him a language, a framework of analysis, that freed him to see America as an outsider, making him the second significant "X" of the postwar period.[1]

By July 1947, George Kennan had experienced most of the forms of possibility available to a promising white man. Born in 1904, in Madison, Wisconsin, he could trace his family back to a voluntary eighteenth-century immigration to America. His ancestors, he wrote in his memoirs, had been "a straight line of pioneer farmers, digressing occasionally into the other free professions. . . . Whoever emerged from such a family in the twentieth century emerged from it devoid of either pride or shame of station, without social grievance, oppressed neither by feelings of superiority nor of inferiority." His father, the first in his family to gain a college education, was the lawyer that Malcolm Little could not dream of becoming.

For reasons not to be found in his writings, from youth Kennan seems to have been a highly contained individual, with the detachment of an outsider, yet a drive to be inside. There was a Gatsbyesque quality to this relatively poor Midwestern boy who recreated himself as an aristocratic, European-oriented, conservative member of America's leadership class yet never lost a sense of not belonging. He attended a military school, then Princeton, and subsequently joined the Foreign Service. Trained as a Soviet specialist in Riga, Latvia, during its period of interwar independence ("almost the only place where one could still live in Tsarist Russia"), then in Berlin, Kennan was sent to the Soviet Union in 1933, as soon as the Communist regime was recognized by the Roosevelt administration.

Russia, though not communism itself ("a pseudoscience replete with artificial heroes and villains"), powerfully attracted him, perhaps because it promised an imperial world inconceivably distant from his own. On leave in 1936, he already found the United States an alien land. The embassy in Moscow, he felt, was "the only place in the world where, at that moment, [I] fully belonged." "Increasingly, now, I would not be a part of my country, although what it had once been would remain a part of me."

"Unlike many others who became professional observers of the development of Soviet power," he was later to comment, "I had never gone through a 'Marxist period.'" As someone who regretted the breakup of the Austro-Hungarian Empire, his political thinking ran toward nineteenth-century spheres of interest, and so in his analyses of the Soviet Union, he emphasized its specific territorial and state ambitions. During the Cold War, this stance would leave him immune to right-wing fantasies of Communist "grand designs" for global conquest. However, during this earlier period of liberal Democratic (and radical) hopes for a new cooperative relationship with the Soviet Union, his harsh policy advice would be ignored by his government. In two stints in Moscow (1933–1937, 1944–1946) he came to feel that dealing with Washington was like "talking to a stone . . . an unechoing silence." He saw himself as a man standing alone "on a chilly and inhospitable mountaintop where few have been before."

During diplomatic service in Nazi Germany and then in wartime Russia, Kennan experienced physical containment—quite literally during a five-and-a-half-month Nazi internment, only slightly less so when he found himself effectively isolated in the U.S. embassy in Moscow. During this second tour of the Soviet Union, he was especially horrified by the prison-land that Stalin had created for his own people (as well as for foreign diplomats).

As in the prewar years, Kennan warned of the Soviet Union's expansionist tendencies and of its responsiveness only to "manifestations of force." Discouraged that his cables to Washington "glided without perceptible effect off the slippery back of . . . official consciousness," he had begun to plan his early retirement when the State Department unexpectedly asked for his evaluation of Soviet policies. The result, in February 1946, was an 8,000-word broadside of anti-Sovietism, "all neatly divided, like an eighteenth-century Protestant sermon into five separate parts." Known as the Long Telegram, to Kennan's amazement, it created a sensation. "This telegraphic dissertation" passed through the highest reaches of government and was read by possibly thousands of high military officers and bureaucrats. With it, his "official loneliness came in fact to an end—at least for a period of two or three years."

In July 1947, *Foreign Affairs* magazine published an article by a Mr. "X" entitled "The Sources of Soviet Conduct." "It is clear," went its most famous passage, "that the main element of any United States policy toward the Soviet Union must be that of a long-term patient but firm and vigilant containment of Russian expansive tendencies . . . the adroit and vigilant application of counterforce at a series of constantly shifting geographical and political points, corresponding to the shifts and maneuvers of Soviet policy." X's anonymity was a thin fiction at best. No one who had seen the Long Telegram (which had been leaked to *Time* magazine a year earlier) could have doubted who the author was.

In this short, cogent essay, implicitly meant to rebut those in the Democratic Party who might still dream of some sort of accommodation with Stalin, Kennan used a term—containment—that stayed with policy makers through four decades of the Cold War. The United States, he claimed, had only to "hold the line," militarily as well as politically, until Europe was rebuilt and the world (which, for Kennan, largely meant "the West") would once again be a boundaried place. Patiently manning the globalized borderlands, American policy makers could either plan to undermine the Soviets or simply wait for their regimes to crumble, since their ideological appeal was only "the powerful afterglow of a constellation which is in actuality on the wane" (an image that perhaps owed something to atomic weapons in a document that otherwise ignored their impact). While Kennan undoubtedly yearned for a global politics in which threat would be containable within a modern, European-oriented *cordon sanitaire*, "containment" fit as well the familiar American image of the circling of the wagons (though his vision lacked the expansive optimism of the story that went with that circling).

Although in these documents more than in his other writings Kennan emphasized Marxism-Leninism as an unnerving force, he still could not

imagine it "spreading" like some mutant ooze or being injected like a
disease into the American or European social bloodstream (both popular
images of the time). He firmly believed that the enemy was out there,
potentially confinable within distinct territorial boundaries, and that to
"contain" them would also contain us. Fear would decrease with each
"firm" step American leaders took to stop the Russians "with unalter-
able counter-force at every point where they show signs of encroaching
upon the interests of a peaceful and stable world," wrote Kennan of still
devastated postwar lands.

Kennan was suddenly a star in the Cold War policy-making firmament
of the Truman administration. Brought back to Washington, he was
made a deputy commandant of the new National War College. There, he
held "a sort of academic seminar for the higher echelons of governmental
Washington." The next year, he was elevated to the head of newly
appointed Secretary of State George C. Marshall's Policy Planning Staff,
where he played a crucial role in shaping the Marshall Plan for the reconstruction of Europe. The outsider was now deep inside, and everyone
seemed to be listening. The shaper of "containment" policy found himself released from a lifetime of personal and policy containment.

Kennan was, however, too honest to long ignore the modern world.
Appalled by the crudities into which his containment idea was quickly
translated, he became uneasy with the enthusiasm of the new cold warriors for an arms race that left no room for the diplomat, and with the
military's World War II–style desire for total victory over the Soviet
Union. It soon became clear to him that what needed to be contained (in
part through a negotiated settlement in Europe) was the new weaponry of
global destruction that Washington and Moscow were both hell-bent on
creating.

After mid-1948, however, his recommendations were increasingly
ignored by colleagues who preferred a policy of military buildup, German
rearmament, and global military alliances. Within years, Kennan had
recanted his views on containment as a military policy. He would comment sardonically in his memoirs that much of his Long Telegram read
"exactly like one of those primers put out by alarmed congressional committees or by the Daughters of the American Revolution, designed to
arouse the citizenry to the dangers of the Communist conspiracy."

In the fall of 1950, he turned over his Policy Planning Staff duties to
Paul Nitze, one of the new breed of cold warriors, and took a "leave of
absence without pay" at Princeton's Institute for Advanced Study. After
a return to duty as ambassador to the Soviet Union in 1952, he went into
retirement. With his ideas increasingly anathema to officialdom, Mr. X

felt "a growing intellectual loneliness." He was once again a "stranger" in a strange land.[2]

In the meantime, America's leaders pursued their version of his policy with gusto, organizing a new world of acronymic alliances—NATO, CENTO, SEATO, ANZUS, OAS—around the mushy borders of "communism." The enemy was to be ringed from Eastern Europe to the Pacific Ocean, from his Southeast Asian extrusions to his outposts in the Americas with "lines" of military bases and a "wall" of weaponry. Plans were even drawn up for new armed outposts in that highest of all frontiers, the heavens. Thus was France's prewar Maginot Line experience recreated on a global scale.

The mental and political map of the globe was being redrawn in terms of new kinds of borders, divisions, and frontiers. There was now an Iron Curtain in the West, a Bamboo Curtain in the more pliable East, and crucial "parallels" in Korea and Vietnam. If Americans were organizing "front lines" in divided Europe and divided Asia, the enemy was doing so, too. Behind endless miles of barbed wire, they were locking their peoples in.

Nothing perhaps concretized this Maginot-style thinking more than the Berlin Wall. In the disaster of the actual wall as in the various metaphoric curtains, there lay bizarre reassurance that something like Kennan's original vision was indeed coming to pass. Each strand of their barbed wire, each new watch tower, offered proof that the globe was split into two clearly defined parts, "half slave and half free" as the phrase then went. The United States was now the leader of what was called—without either fine distinctions or the faintest hint of irony—the Free World, while its enemy ruled a vast slave-labor empire from Poland to the Korean peninsula.

Slavery would become the operative image of the Cold War years and so, for the first time, gain a centrality in the American story only because it could be shown to exist in the land of the enemy—in the "enslaved" nations of Eastern Europe, in the millions of "slave laborers" in the Soviet Union, and so on. No link, however, would be made between the uses America put Soviet slavery to and its own past or its segregated present (as later in Fannie Lou Hamer's famous retort, "No Vietnamese ever called me 'nigger'").

Yet there was also an undercurrent of doubt about what the various curtains, walls, and parallels were actually separating. For there was another acronymic world bound by none of them: CIA, KGB, SIS, FBI, MVD, NSA, GRU, DIA. It was a world in which the fiercest boundary builder for one side might be suspected of secretly building for the other;

in which you could lead more than one life, as did spies Kim Philby (for the Russians) and Oleg Penkovsky (for the British and Americans); in which each side had "intelligence" about the other that it would not have considered releasing to its own people. From this shared secret world, the enemy, contained by nothing, might suddenly emerge looking and acting just like "us."

VAMPIRES AND COMMUNISTS

Put yourself now on Main Street, U.S.A.; the sort of place any child of the 1950s remembers from civics class. Imagine two locales: a cornfield near a farming community and a town somewhere in mid-America. Whether in that cornfield where a mutilated body has been found or in the town's streets where citizens rush for shelter as night closes in, something is amiss.

In the cornfield, we meet fifteen-year-old Peter Gedra, his brother Edward, and his father Alec, refugees from Hungary, who arrived "soon after the end of the last war." They are examining the mutilated body. The father exclaims in shock, "I'd thought that we had left such horrors as werewolves behind us!" "Werewolves in America!" Peter mutters. A month later, after another victim is "torn to pieces and partially eaten" by the light of the full moon, a leering local sheriff accosts the father— "You come from Hungary don't you! Wolfsbane grows in Hungary! . . . We didn't have no killin's like this before *you* come here!"—and proceeds to execute him using a silver bullet. On the night of the next full moon, the embittered brothers split up to hunt the werewolf, whom Edward believes to be the sheriff. Armed with a slingshot and a silver coin filed to a point, Peter discovers the slavering beast in a field and slays it. In a fratricidal, Peter-and-the-Wolf-ish twist, however, the dying beast returns to human form not as the sheriff, but as brother Edward.

Meanwhile, in the all-American town, Harold, just off a train, listens to the last chime of a clock tower. Before setting off in search of his sister's house, he says of small-town America, like millions of city boys before him, "What a dead-looking place!" Later, his sister warns him not to venture onto the deserted streets, because vampires infest the town. ("Seventeen villagers murdered already! Blood drained!") Harold's no-nonsense disbelief in the superstitious townsfolk leads him to take a nighttime walk anyway. Finding a well-lit local restaurant, he orders dinner: "Juice, soup, roast with French fries, coffee, sherbet." Asked by the waiter whether he'd like his "roast clots" well done or medium, he chokes, revealing himself as a nonvampire. His own sister, in a blood-red dress, then elbows through a menacing crowd of vampire waiters and customers to inform him that "just like modern man, [vampires now] leave . . . the preparing to the professionals. This restaurant serves blood dishes . . . like a vegetarian restaurant serves vegetable dishes, blood-juice cocktail . . . hot blood-consomme . . . roast blood-clots . . . French-fried scabs . . . blood sherbet." At her command, the vampires grab him. ("Tie up his feet!" "String him up!" "A party!") In a parody of a lynching, they hang him upside down, insert a wine spigot in his neck, and proceed to make him an after-dinner aperitif. A hideous-looking hag named the Vault-keeper then offers up a mocking commentary: "Heh, heh! . . . That's what 'civilized' vampires do these days! They dine in Blooditarian Restaurants, open sundown to sunrise. Where is there one in your town, you ask? Well, some night if you feel up to it, look for it! You can tell it by the sign inside! It's in red. . . and it says, 'positively no nipping the waiters'!"

These two 1953 tales—"By the Fright of the Silvery Moon" and "Midnight Mess" from EC's line of horror comics, *Tales from the Crypt*—were among thousands of similar ones that comic book companies put out in the early 1950s. In such tales, the alien and unclean arose within marriage, family, and community, turning the normal, even sacred institutions of middle-class life into charnel houses of dismembered limbs and bloodless bodies. Carrying the punch of pint-sized pornography, they were invariably framed by the mocking laughter of a Crypt-keeper or a Vault-keeper.[3]

Only a few years earlier, comics—the reading matter of choice for the young men who went to war for America—had been all innocence, the home of "funny animals" and uncomplicated superheroes who single-handedly smashed "Japanazis." Within a decade of its birth, however, the comic book had become a site for the display of atrocities. Something had crept inside the most recent and childish of American story forms, making it almost unrecognizable. Opened to any page, the comic now displayed scenes that might have come from Hiroshima or Auschwitz.[4]

Comic books not only offered disturbing and titillating visions of mob violence, lynchings, and crime gone mad, but they snuck into the suburban home to mug the good life. (A henpecked husband murders his wife and stuffs her body bit by bit down the brand new garbage disposal he's bought her. The disposal has, unfortunately, been connected on the cheap so that when one of his friends turns on the kitchen faucet to get a drink, what comes out but . . .) Behind every innocent face, every upbeat but ordinary household object, a terrifying dreamscape of paranoid horror (and pleasure) lay revealed. "You pull down the oven door . . . just a crack! You step back horrified! The door falls open all the way! Inside is a brown-crusted, well-roasted corpse." Bon appetit, America![5]

Here, in the early postwar years, was an example of a new sort of ambush, a new kind of horror for which Americans were unprepared. There had long been a place in the American mind for the foreign operative or spy, for the lone traitor or even the band of alien conspirators ready to open the United States to foreign invasion or control, but not for an enemy who, when hounded into the light, looked like your neighbor—a Boston brahmin, a California longshoreman, a Minnesota farmer, a New York Jew—and insisted to the jailhouse doors, or even the electric chair, that he or she was your neighbor, and nothing more. As Richard Hofstadter has written, where "their predecessors discovered foreign conspiracies; the modern radical right [found] that conspiracy also embrace[d] betrayal at home."[6]

Nothing was more crippling to the story of America's march through history than the loss of an easily targeted foreign or racially alien enemy within, however much the identity of that enemy changed over time, as ward or protégé of the moment was sorted out from bestial foe. In the wake of Pearl Harbor, for example, *Life* magazine quickly published an article, "How to Tell Japs from the Chinese," to prevent enraged citizens from beating up Chinese-Americans. A photo of Ong Wen-hao, the handsome Chinese minister of economic affairs and ally, was paired with the scowling visage of Japanese General Hideki Tojo ("squat Mongoloid, with flat, blob nose . . . Japs, like General Tojo, show humorless intensity of ruthless mystics"). With guide arrows indicating key structural components of each face ("lighter facial bones" versus "massive cheek and jawbone"), *Life* offered a "rule-of-thumb from the anthropometric confirmations that distinguish friendly Chinese from enemy alien Japs." But these were the fine points of targeting the racial enemy. As had been true on the domestic frontier, in 1942 the enemy in Asia and his possible operatives in the United States still seemed easy enough to identify.[7]

Facing a white European enemy had always involved more complex problems of identification and targeting, such as in World War I, when a national hysteria arose over unseen German agents blamed for poisoning wells, spreading influenza germs, and even putting ground glass in Red Cross bandages. But those most suspected of holding pro-German attitudes could conceivably still be found in German-American communities with their own cultural institutions and customs, making containment of the enemy at home at least imaginable.[8]

Communism, on the other hand, proved bedeviling as an enemylike presence. It was never fully identified with or contained within any single ethnic or racial community. In the years after the Russian Revolution, communism would be denounced for its seemingly uncanny ability to insinuate itself into normal American society, and Russia would be vilified for its "Trojan horse" tactics in sneaking its operatives through the "gates" of America. With the rise of a militarily powerful Soviet Union, the difficulty involved in identifying Communist operatives and "true believers" in the United States made the post–World War II Communist enemy especially horrifying. There was no obvious rule-of-thumb for isolating Communists by dress, customs, language, or religion; nor, like Japanese-Americans during World War II, could they be rounded up and incarcerated by look.[9]

The Communist within was a frighteningly indistinct creature. Even propaganda images meant to alert the public to Communist characteristics lacked definition. Here is cultural critic Nora Sayre's description of the American Party member as seen in anti-Communist films of the early 1950s made by Hollywood's studios, usually based on scripts or popular books by government agents or informers:

> [M]ost are apt to be exceptionally haggard or disgracefully pudgy. Occasionally, they're effeminate: a man who wears gloves shouldn't be trusted. However, in films that feature dauntless FBI agents, it's very difficult to tell them apart from the enemy, since both often lurk on street corners in raincoats and identical snap-brims while pretending to read newspapers, and also because many B-actors lack distinguishing features: they simply look alike. Just when you assume that the miscreants are massing to plot, they turn out to be the heroes. But you can sometimes spot a Communist because his shadow looms larger and blacker than his adversary's . . . most are scruffy. . . . Communists "never keep their promises," and they're likely to go berserk when they're arrested.[10]

Communists were "termites boring within." They were "the Moscow masters of deceit," of "mirage" and "disguise." The less evidence there was of their presence, the more obvious it was that they or their sympathizers were secretly at work in society. Declining Party membership throughout the 1950s made them more, not less dangerous. "[N]umbers mean nothing, . . ." reported FBI director J. Edgar Hoover, "for there are those nations which have attempted to assess the threat of communism on the basis of numerical strength alone and they are eating the bitter fruit of Communist slavery for their shortsightedness."[11]

There were two approaches to the domestic containment of this elusive foe, neither necessarily exclusive of the other, but each based on an antithetical strategy, on a different assessment of the threat to "internal security." One was exclusion. Censorship, deportation, suppression, the purge, and the mobilization of surveillance resources were weapons in the exclusionist's battle to drive the "enemy within" from American shores. The other was inclusion. The politics of tolerance and of coalition, of the mobilization of all domestic groups, were weapons in the battle against communism abroad. Should America's national narrative be stretched to include peoples at home (and abroad) never before considered except as inferiors or enemies? Or should it be purged of "alien" elements; and if so, how was this to happen when the full resources of the state often had to be mobilized simply to identify a single Communist and separate him or her from the populace? This unresolvable tension between exclusion and inclusion, between the purge and paternalism, between vigilance and tolerance, was to mark the 1950s.

Exclusion was the response of the political right, much of the Republican Party, Southern Democrats, the military wing of the national security state, and domestic policing agencies. The purge was its chosen weapon, an attempt to enforce a national "conformity" that drew increasingly narrow boundaries around what was acceptable. In this urge toward "100 percent Americanness," the purgers paradoxically tended to cast their nets wider and wider in search of the enemy. "Rollback" at home proved a Sisyphean task.

Inclusion, the response of the "vital center," the liberal elite (now shorn of a more radical past and rearmed as anti-Communists), the globalizing corporation, and the CIA, was an attempt to expand the boundaries of the story to allow in a tamed version of the alien Other. The former racial enemy abroad and the problematic racial Other at home were both to be invited to join the struggle for global freedom.

Ironically, the right's approach was broader as its catchall categories of enemy-ness were no longer bounded by race, ethnicity, or religion. The right's tolerance for those (of whatever color, religion, or ethnicity) who would reveal the "many-headed monster" in its domestic lair was unbounded, while liberals, forced to confront the narrower category of race, found themselves coping with or warding off the demands of blacks at home and diverse nationalist and revolutionary movements abroad.

Neither approach, however, could long stanch the story's losses. While the right-wing response threatened to turn too many of "us" into the enemy, the vital center's raised the possibility that someday we might have to look at "our" story through other eyes. At home, containment proved a slapdash affair.

BUNKER CULTURE

The narrative forms that contained the war story had always had a childlike quality to them, a certain unchallenged, moving simplicity of language and vision, even when wedded to the most sophisticated technological processes—the movies and radio. In the 1950s, however, taking the inclusionary path meant letting in problem peoples who instantly lent the story more than a hint of atrocity. An inclusive western like *Broken Arrow* (1950) or a war film like *Home of the Brave* (1949) placed the viewer behind previously alien eyes through which—before a forced conclusion—whites suddenly looked like murderers, bigots, cheats, and liars.

Such films raised, even if in coded form, awkward questions about race relations at home and abroad. Starting with *Broken Arrow*, some westerns began to offer, as film critic Peter Biskind has noted, "a glimpse of a culture that embodie[d] utopian possibilities outside and against our own society." The film's initial Apache ambush and massacre of a party of white prospectors led not to a spectacle of slaughter but to a gush of explanation highlighting white acts of terror and greed for Apache land. "This was war," says scout and hero Tom Jeffords (Jimmy Stewart) "with cruelty on both sides."

Broken Arrow, according to its publicity materials, "shattered the barriers of color and hate"; and its casting of little-known white actors as Apaches (Jeff Chandler as Chief Cochise and sixteen-year-old Debra Paget as Jeffords' love interest) was meant to make the Indians "acceptable as human beings," in the words of producer Julian Blaustein. The film split the Other into Cochise, the noble "realist" with the human face, who could be assimilated to society, and Geronimo, the brutal and surly premature guerrilla fighter, who was to be ejected from it. Around the world, real countries would be called upon to make the Cochise choice—or face the consequences.[12]

The exclusionary path, on the other hand, plunged films into an anxiety-producing netherworld of horror. After all, the newest real-life exclusionary heroes, just then testifying before congressional committees, were a set of characters right out of the horror comics: individuals who had returned from the subterranean hells of communism to tell Americans bloodcurdling tales about their experiences with the undead. (Most anti-Communist films, made by studios protecting themselves from exclusionary purges, were however shunned by movie audiences.)

Any cultural product could contain both exclusionary and inclusionary impulses. In the science fiction films that prospered in the 1950s, exclusionary villains came from the other side of borders previously unimagined and unerringly headed for (or burst to life in) the United States with mayhem in mind. Boundaryless beings, they were scarier and easier to identify on screen than Communists: a "blob," a "thing," a "pod," radioactively reactivated monsters from the past or the mutating present (dinosaurs, ants, spiders, grasshoppers, even an octopus), or aliens from other planets or galaxies—all off any normal scale of observation and measurement. They were beasts or beings able to sop up all fears, capable of representing traditional nonwhite enemies and/or Communists and/or the nuclear threat at one and the same moment. Whether they were destroyed in the end by the sorts of scientific inventions and military interventions that often produced them in the first place or by the humblest of unscientific "weapons," like the germ or the garden hose, they invariably threatened an end to all that was good.

On the other hand, in the inclusionary mode, similar beasts or robots or space aliens turned out to be, if not lovable, then far wiser than Americans. Implicitly in a science fiction film like This Island Earth (1955), explicitly in one like The Day the Earth Stood Still (1951), the greatest enemy was no less terrifying a creature than ourselves. As in It Came from Outer Space (1953), "they" might look unsightly (particularly in 3-D), but it was Americans with their "mob" mentality who acted that way. The exclusionary films were apocalyptic and hysterical about them; the inclusionary ones about us. In either case, every stand in these films was potentially the last one. Whether the enemy came from the peripheries or the heartland, whether it was a monstrous Other or a monstrous vision of ourselves, the promise of extermination was not provisional and symbolic; and the attempt to wipe out the monsters, whether desperate and righteous or misguided and criminal, increasingly came to look less like an innocent spectacle of slaughter and more like a desperate act of horror.[13]

It wasn't just the on-screen spectacle that plunged into an underworld of horror. The actual weaponry of destruction would soon disappear into sunken "silos," storage facilities for one-way trips to Armageddon. If the world of abundance was a sunny-looking place, so much that mattered was now out of sight. It seemed only natural then for eyes, off screen as on, to turn to the skies, to the heavens, whether for a brief glimpse of onrushing destruction or for rescue.

Since at least the seventeenth century, there had been fantasies about life on other planets. The publication of H. G. Wells's War of the Worlds in 1898, however, placed an alien invasion from space on the human agenda. Even before World War I, prophetic eyes turned to the skies to imagine with fascination, horror, or (vis-à-vis racial inferiors) pleasure the growth of the ability to destroy from the air.

In 1912, Americans of all ages entered the space age with Edgar Rice Burroughs' hero John Carter. In a multitude of "red-blooded" pulp novels, Burroughs recreated the frontier on Mars, while sorting out the green, white, red, and yellow-skinned races found there. In the coming years, Buck Rogers would battle the "Red Mongols" of space in the "25th Century," and Flash Gordon would take on Ming the Merciless, "emperor of the universe," not just in pulp fiction but on the radio, on trading cards, and in comic strips. From the 1930s on, speculation about friendly and enemy "races" in space became a commonplace of pulp magazines, which offered up premonitory visions of future arsenals of annihilation that would rain down from the heavens. In World War II, the sorts of aerial incineration attacks that had previously been imagined in popular culture became reality, as did the first potential space weapons in Germany's V-2 rockets and, from Los Alamos, the nuclear weapons with which their successors would someday be armed.[14]

Only in the post–World War II years, however, did space aliens leave the environs of pop culture to visit Americans in person. "Flying saucers," or UFOs (unidentified flying objects) as they were called by acronym-conscious air force investigators, paid their first recorded visit to North America on June 24, 1947. Nine of them, "wav[ing] in and out of formation," were spotted by Kenneth Arnold, a forest service pilot and deputy sheriff, as they streaked at an estimated 1,200 miles per hour across the skies of Washington State, making a motion like "a saucer skipping over water." "Saucers" that looked like cigars, pie plates, fireballs, footballs, dumbbells, even ice cream cones visited the United States (and other parts of the world) erratically but in profusion in the 1950s, leaving behind a trail of blurry photos and adamant witnesses (sometimes upstanding citizens).

First "contact" was made by one George Adamski, a Southern California cultist who claimed that, on November 20, 1952, he met a blond Venusian with a prominent forehead near Desert Center, California. The Venusian, like many aliens to follow, seemed to have sprung from the inclusionary school of storytelling. He was here to warn humans against our "warlike ways" and to encourage us to halt nuclear testing as it was "upsetting the harmony of the universe." According to Keith Thompson, a New Age historian of the UFO experience, the spaceman—clearly a cognoscente of Cold War culture—informed Adamski that "many Venusians already lived in disguise among humans from various walks of life." In the years that followed, Americans encountered space aliens regularly, usually in deserted (often desert) locations, but once, so it was claimed, in the anonymity of a Greyhound bus station. (In the fiercest years of the Cold War in Catholic Europe, another type of space sighting became commonplace: public visions of saints and especially of the Virgin Mary.)[15]

In 1948, the air force instituted a long-lasting, semisecret investigation of reported UFO sightings. After all, if they were more than natural phenomena or products of mass hysteria, it was important to know whether the aliens were inclusionists ready to proffer the aid of an advanced civilization in the struggle against communism, or perhaps Russians conducting secret space experiments, which might pose distinct dangers to national security.

During World War II, citizens on the home front had mobilized to scan the skies for German or Japanese planes that would never arrive. The culture of the 1950s was beholden to that experience. Now, however, by the time you eyed the enemy it was too late. If danger seemed imminent, instead of heading up to the roof, you were to head down to the bomb shelter or basement. The skies were to be scanned not by the eye but by radar systems on the lookout for ghostly blips that might represent a flock of geese, UFOs, or a Russian attack. In pop culture, not only were the skies to be scanned, but so were the depths of the oceans, the Arctic ice pack, the past, the future, even (as in the film *Invasion of the Body Snatchers* [1956]) the basement where you were to hide: for no place was too distant or too close to home not to be threatened or threatening.

The UFO "controversy" was distinctly a creature of Cold War culture; and the various "contactees" who returned from the nether regions, expert in telling Venusians from the general populace and eager to testify, bore a resemblance to former Communists, informers, and defectors ready to help anti-Communist investigators tease Communists out of government or Hollywood. Yet, the "ufologists" were also almost the only group at the time to take on the national security state directly, assailing the secrecy that surrounded the government's UFO investigations and claiming a cover-up of information relating to the reality of space aliens. They demanded congressional hearings and wrote books excoriating the government for its hostile and deceitful behavior. In short, in the name of contact with friendly aliens, they declared the government to be an enemylike entity, guilty of the malign suppression of information crucial to the public. Because these cultists were considered beyond the pale, they may have been the only oppositional group in America in those years that no one bothered to accuse of communism.

Of course, the real alien threat from the skies that made everything else seem so uncontainable was the bomb, and the popular culture of that time was well dusted with atomic fallout. No one even thought it worth a comment that in Disney's cinematic retelling of *Twenty Thousand Leagues*

Under the Sea (1954), when Captain Nemo blows up his island to prevent his secret power source from falling into the wrong hands, a mushroom cloud rises over it, and even a slight Disney family comedy like *The Shaggy Dog* (1959) had its atomic secret–stealing villains.

No cultural product better caught the nuclear threat concealed in everyday life than the film *The Incredible Shrinking Man* (1957). After its opening credits scroll down a mushroom-cloud backdrop, Robert Scott Carey and his wife Louise are found on the deck of a small motorcraft in mid-Pacific. Soon the boat passes through an irradiated mist that envelops Carey while his wife is below deck. This reflected a real incident. On March 1, 1954, the Japanese fishing boat *Lucky Dragon V* with a crew of twenty-three passed through a cloud of radioactive ash from an American H-bomb test on Bikini Island. Most of the crew became ill soon after. On return to Tokyo, all were hospitalized and one subsequently died. (Americans living in states like Nevada, downwind from domestic bomb test sites, were then experiencing similar "mists.") The film, of course, mists over U.S. responsibility. The results of being irradiated are dealt with only as a medical problem. ("Carey was the victim of the most fantastic ailment in the annals of medicine!") Yet the bomb, held off as history, retained its power to dislocate.[16]

Returning to his home in suburban Los Angeles, Carey discovers he is undergoing "a deadly chemical reversal of the growth process." Unlike H. G. Wells' Invisible Man of an earlier era, who, though unseen, retained his normal relation to the world, Carey begins to shrink. He looks, at first, like a child in his father's too-large clothes. At three feet, he comments, "I felt puny and absurd, a ludicrous midget." Down to inches and living in a dollhouse, he mutters, "Every day it was worse, everyday a little smaller and everyday I became more tyrannical, more monstrous in my domination of Louise."

Daily life in the nuclear age only takes on its truly threatening quality, however, when Carey is hurled into a subterranean world. His loving kitty cat now reappears like some monstrous mutant feline, bloodies him, and knocks him down the laundry chute into the basement. There, he is stranded like Robinson Crusoe on Devil's Island or the Thief of Baghdad in hell, while his grief-stricken wife, believing the cat ate him, sells the house and departs.

"The cellar floor stretched before me like some vast primeval plain, empty of life, littered with the relics of a vanished race." A vast, empty box of safety matches makes a home; a pin, a sword; a leak, a flood; a crumb of stale cake, a feast. There, in his own home, he meets his night mare Friday, a gargantuan, hairy, black spider. ("I was no longer alone in my universe. I had an enemy, the most terrifying ever beheld by human eyes!") After destroying the spider, Carey "dwindles" completely off the scale of human measurement with the observation, "So close the infinitesimal and the infinite.... The unbelievably small and the unbelievably vast eventually meet like the closing of a gigantic circle."

The film caught and capitalized on a strange sense of disorientation linked to the bomb that led directly into the home. Containment was failing locally. However great U.S. power might grow, safety seemed beyond grasp; however narrowly an exclusionary line might be drawn around the suburban family, something threatening was already inside. As the 1940s ended, the government—and experts in fields from urban planning to medicine—began to emphasize the seriousness of organizing for survival in an atomic war.

While the government began to dig itself into mountainsides and organize post–atomic war lines of political succession, "real estate ads promised 'good bomb immunity.' *Newsweek* reported growing corporate interest in underground facilities. In upstate New York, an enterprising entrepreneur set up vaults for corporate records deep in an abandoned iron mine . . . [and] *Science News* warned of hucksters who were peddling backyard shelters, burn ointments, dog tags, flash bags, and 'decontaminating agents.'" Everywhere, a bunker mentality was being encouraged. The country was becoming "civil defense" minded, which meant that ordinary citizens were being urged to prepare today for tomorrow's hellish descent into the national basement.[17]

At least in its imagination, the United States was digging in. For the nuclear family, there was to be the privatized, well-stocked bomb shelter and the well-stocked, sheltered suburban home. In both, citizens were to find the ultimate in well-appointed bunker safety. The pleasures of the family bomb shelter were touted in government propaganda like the Federal Civil Defense Administration's pamphlet "Grandma's Pantry" ("Grandma's pantry was ready, is your 'pantry' ready in event of emergency?"), as well as in *Life* magazine's August 1959 celebration of one couple's honeymoon of "unbroken togetherness"—fourteen days in a twenty-two-ton steel and concrete private bomb shelter, twelve feet underground. "Contractors commercialized the idea," writes social historian Elaine Tyler May, "by creating a variety of styles and sizes to fit the tastes of consumers, from a '$13.50 foxhole shelter' to a '$5,000 deluxe "suite" with telephone, escape hatches, bunks, toilets, and geiger counter.'"

If the personalized shelter turned out to be more fantasy construct than construction boom, the same cannot be said for the ranch house. Through the Veterans Administration and the Federal Housing Authority, the government subsidized a new bunker culture in the suburbs centered on the single-family home. Federal dollars poured into highway and sewage systems that made a massive population shift to the suburbs possible based on the purchase of private homes. In the ranch house, the "mom" protected by her working husband was to raise a new generation of children, fortified by the products of abundance against all terrors. (Children per family soared from an average of 2.4 in the 1930s to 3.2 in the 1950s.)

Each family was to buy its own wagon train. This was bomb shelter abundance, the domestic equivalent of containment (as Elaine Tyler May has argued), a family version of national security. Sealed in the suburban home with its tamed "natural" surroundings—which, architecturally, had something of the look and feel of the bomb shelter—were "sex, consumer goods, children, and intimacy" as well as entertainment and whiteness.[18]

It turned out, however, that national security and insecurity were merging in the home, too. As in one of the period's many horror stories about unnatural possession, the children of the suburban dream were coming to seem both threatened and threatening. There was, in fact, something ominous in the multiplicity of everyday valences to which the idea of the enemy could now attach itself. Depending on your particular brand of obsessions and fears, the enemy could be lodged inside the government, the media and entertainment industries, the political parties, the labor unions, the intelligence agencies, or your own children.

Even as an obvious threat, the postwar enemy did not threaten in obvious ways. In 1957, to the astonishment of Americans, the backward empire of unfreedom launched the first satellite, *Sputnik*, into orbit. Yet the *Sputnik* "threat" turned out to be directed as much against the U.S. educational system as its military defenses. The grapefruit-sized satellite exposed America as technologically backward and aroused fears that its undisciplined next generation, evidently deficient in science, reading, and computational skills, would be no match for Russian youth. Who could have imagined that the response to the first Soviet "outpost" in space would take the form not just of funding missile-armed submarines but new physics and math programs?[19]

THE NEW WAR STORY

Nothing challenged the nature of American storytelling more in the 1950s than the freeing of blacks from aspects of their social, economic, and political confinement. By the end of the decade, the "Negro problem" was no longer largely a Southern one. A majority of blacks now lived in the North, overwhelmingly in urban areas, yet generally excluded from the good life increasingly available to white families. The retreat into bunker culture, an early version of white flight, was redrawing racial boundaries. As federal money poured into suburban areas, the segregated state of non-Southern society increased.

Whether in the suburbs or on TV, "America" remained reassuringly white. Even in the twilight world, whiteness was preserved. Although the CIA willingly employed faces of any color to man the foreign parapets of freedom, within its anonymous environs at home, it (like the FBI) was a blindingly white organization. Only in its executive dining room, where management could relax while being served by black waiters in "immaculate white coats," were black faces apparent. As late as 1967, less than 20 of its 12,000 nonclerical workers were black.[20]

While policy makers worried about countering an invisible enemy infiltrating nonwhite populations abroad, at home, a story of racial horror was slowly exfiltrating, and racial containment in the South was showing signs of faltering for the first time since Reconstruction. While some whites linked black demands to the Communist enemy, the civil rights movement rejected any exclusionary approach to "freedom." From Montgomery to Greensboro, from bus boycott to sit-in, its demand was "integration," and its language a soaring one, expressing a desire to merge into that sunny land of abundance and mobility. This was not the desire to "pass" for white but to "pass over" openly into a land officially declared available to all by piercing invisible yet fiercely policed boundaries not just around lunch counters, bus seats, and toilets, or even schools, housing, and workplaces, but inside heads.

To pass over meant, paradoxically, employing the means of the minstrel show, while bursting its boundaries. Civil rights leaders took up the exaggerated language of American perfection. Immaculate in suits and ties, polite and tolerant, blacks offered an audience of whites a minstrelsy of inclusiveness, a theatrical and incisive whiteface critique played out on black bodies. This disarming mirroring of the best the American tradition could promise threw into horrific contrast actual white acts. Long denied a role in the war story, blacks now put the only role ever offered them to critical use. In an aggressively "nonviolent" manner, they transformed the war story back into a tale of atrocities and turned whites—from Birmingham Police Chief Bull Connor to Alabama Governor George Wallace, from abusive students at the University of Mississippi to Klan bombers—into savages.

Each beautiful word, each perfect deed, was a mirror reflecting white acts. From beatings to hosings, from the firebombing of busses to the bombing of churches, from the mutilated bodies of murdered civil rights workers to those of abused schoolchildren, images of horror and horrific disproportion were displayed: one tired seamstress named Rosa Parks against a whole city of whites; a giant, armed white man loosing his dogs on unarmed black children; a mob of whites surrounding a few black adolescents. This fusing of America's most idealistic self-image with the horrors of its racial history was by the early 1960s being displayed before the eyes of millions of TV viewers and newspaper readers.

To accept the inspirational language of inclusion in this situation was to see the story in a new and shameful light. Within these novel narrative boundaries, sheriffs committed crimes against innocent citizens; the twelve angry men convicted; and when the savages took their captives off into the wilderness to torture them, the frontiersmen went back to bed. Who the settlers were and who the Indians were was unsettlingly clear in this un-war story.

In 1959, a white writer and "specialist in race issues" named John Howard Griffin, worrying that the racial situation in the South was a "blot on the whole country, and especially reflected against us overseas," donned a mask of blackness and "passed over." In 1960, he published a best-selling book, *Black Like Me*, a diary of his six weeks in blackface. In it, an inverted minstrelsy melded into sci-fi horror. The plot could be presented in this way: a human being decides to undertake a perilous voyage to a prison-planet inhabited by an alien and mistreated species. Through "a medication taken orally, followed by exposure to ultraviolet rays," he takes on the look of this alien race. ("[T]he face and shoulders of a stranger—a fierce, bald, very dark Negro—glared at me from the glass. He in no way resembled me. . . . I was imprisoned in the flesh of an utter stranger, an unsympathetic one with whom I felt no kinship. . . . The Griffin that was had become invisible.") This voyage is considered so dangerous that many, including not only lawmen from his own world but even some of the aliens, urge him to forgo his attempt.

Griffin, however, courageously decides to press ahead, become a Negro, and experience the degradations blacks regularly live with. After only six weeks in this alien prison of the flesh, he finds he can no longer take the humiliations his own kind dishes out and so "escapes" back to his planet.

The policeman nodded affably to me and I knew then that I had successfully passed back into white society, that I was once more a first-class citizen, that all doors into cafes, rest rooms, libraries, movies, concerts, schools and churches were suddenly open to me. After so long I could not adjust to it. A sense of exultant liberation flooded

through me. I crossed over to a restaurant and entered. I took a seat
beside white men at the counter and the waitress smiled at me. It was
a miracle. . . . I went to the rest room and was not molested. No one
paid me the slightest attention. No one said, "What're you doing in
here, nigger?"[21]†

Griffin's book, highly publicized at the time, was deeply influential.
Undoubtedly, either President Kennedy or one of his speech writers read
it before putting into a 1963 civil rights speech the striking line, "Who
among us would be content to have the color of his skin changed and
stand in [the Negro's] place?"[22]

There was irony in a white man in blackface bringing the message that
blacks were in a prison-land of degradation, abuse, and humiliation back
to the white world, for this was, naturally enough, no news to blacks. In
his autobiography, Malcolm X noted this. Whenever he heard what a
"frightening experience" Griffin's was, he replied, "Well, if it was a
frightening experience for him as nothing but a make-believe
Negro . . . then you think about what *real* Negroes in America have gone
through for four hundred years."

In 1959, when Griffin set off for that prison-planet, Malcolm already
was there, as he had always been. "[D]on't be shocked," he used to tell
black audiences, "when I say that I was in prison. You're still in prison.
That's what America means: prison." By now, however, Malcolm was
minister of the Nation of Islam's Mosque No. 7 in Harlem and had
almost single-handedly turned a tiny sect into a growing national black
separatist movement.

Though Malcolm often talked about whites collectively, he almost
never met them individually. Like many blacks, he was still "contained"
(a word he used) in a Northern urban ghetto. It was in 1959 that the
Nation of Islam was, for the first time, mapped into white consciousness
through a CBS TV documentary by Mike Wallace, "The Hate That Hate
Produced." Malcolm, fierce, angry, and remarkably self-contained, now
came to the attention of the media as the representative of black "hate
mongering." Scenes of the Nation's guards, the Fruit of Islam, proved
especially shocking to white audiences. Trained in self-defense tech-

---

†Griffin's may have been the first version of this scenario played out in real life,
but it was by no means the first acted out in postwar popular culture. In the film
Gentlemen's Agreement (1947), for instance, a WASP reporter (played by Gregory
Peck) took on the persona of a Jew to produce a series of articles on anti-Semitism
in America. "Listen," he exclaims, "I've even got the title, 'I Was Jewish for Six
Months.'" However, he, like Griffin, lasts only six weeks.

niques, these blacks, if not armed, at least had hands for weapons and looked like they might use them. Malcolm later compared the public reaction to "what happened back in the 1930s when Orson Welles frightened America with a radio program describing, as though it was actually happening, an invasion by 'men from Mars.'"

From Earth, the media phone calls began to pour in. In 1959, Malcolm, like Griffin, "passed over"—though in the opposite direction—bringing with him, uncontained and unrestrained, a language that should have seemed familiar to whites. He declared that blacks were in a "wilderness," endangered by inhuman beings capable of horrifying acts of torture, of captivities beyond measure; that blacks had to defend themselves and establish a land of their own. Without exception, he referred to whites as "devils," as "wolves," as "enemies"—all terms European settlers would once have recognized. He held up, in his own words, "a mirror to reflect, to show, the history of unspeakable crimes that [the white] race has committed against my race."

Unconstrained and unintimidated by white audiences, Malcolm X proceeded to turn three hundred years of an American narrative on its head. For whites, his was an unparalleled assessment of white society, of what it actually "contained," of what "inclusion" simply could not (or at least did not) include. ("Today, in many ways the black man sees the collective white man in America better than that white man can see himself.") While it was hardly the first assessment of the world of whiteness to be made by someone from that prison-planet, it was the first that whites seemed to hear. With the boundaries of an age-old containment crumbling, whites listened, initially with fear and anger, later with curiosity and even a certain respect, finally—among young, radical students first reading the autobiography that Malcolm left behind after his assassination—with fascination and admiration.

From living inside a "monster" to picking up "the gun," from sardonic mockery of American patriotism ("You have to be able to laugh to stand up and sing, 'My country 'tis of thee, sweet land of liberty.' That's a joke.... If you don't laugh at it, you'll crack up") to an emphasis on black power and an identification with Third World revolutionary movements, Malcolm presaged a decade to come, and he spoke in a dismantling voice strangely familiar to young whites. Possessed with a sense of the madness of those who controlled the planet, he knew just how uncontained white society really was. "The whole world knows that the white man cannot survive another war," he said. "If either of the two giant white nations pushes the button, white civilization will die!"[23]

It was the bomb, George Kennan realized relatively early in the 1950s (but too late to matter), that made containment inconceivable. He grew to view its use against Japan as "regrettable extremism." Even more so did he come to loathe the military mentality that believed "the normal objective of warfare was the total destruction of the enemy's ability and will to resist and his unconditional capitulation." Atomic weaponry made war of that sort either "suicidal or, if the adversary lacked such weapons, indiscriminately destructive to a degree impossible to contemplate." He found he did not even believe in the central tenet of Cold War thinking: "the reality of a Soviet military threat to Western Europe."

In his 1957 Reich lectures, his attack on nuclear strategy had the ring of dissident journalist I. F. Stone, not of a government insider. "If . . . indefinite competition in the cultivation of these weapons and their general proliferation was the best the future held for us, I would be tempted to say: 'Let us divest ourselves of this weapon altogether.'" Such weaponry, he proclaimed, was "sterile and hopeless."

The vision of his beloved Europe destroyed in the sort of nuclear war basic to military scenarios of the time sickened him.

> Let us by all means think for once not just in the mathematics of destruction—not just in these grisly equations of probable military casualties . . . let us ask ourselves in all seriousness how much worth saving is going to be saved if war now rages for the third time in a half-century over the face of Europe, and this time in a form vastly more destructive than anything ever known before.

Singularly, in those years, he accepted that atomic weaponry threatened "the very intactness of the natural environment in which, and in which alone, civilization would have a future. . . . We are not the owners of the planet we inhabit; we are only its custodians."

In "retirement" in Princeton, George Kennan found himself for the third time in his life contained, though now by his own former colleagues. Showered with praise but ignored, he became America's preeminent historian of containment—from Metternich to the post–World War I attempts to roll back the Russian Revolution. He, too, perhaps unbeknownst to himself, had stepped beyond. A figure to be nodded toward, but not listened to, his would be a strange and discordant voice of unintimidated, conservative sanity, a former X marking the spot where his own society threatened to leap off some cliff.[24]

3

The Enemy Disappears

OF THE GENERATION that grew up in the immediate postwar years, who doesn't remember the redness of maps? As projectors flickered in school cafeterias and auditoriums, the tentacles of red octopi slithered around globes and inky red blobs oozed across continents. In this visual horror story, the enemy—bloody and tyrannical—was known; his "plan" for world conquest indisputable. Yet the maneuvers of that enemy, spreading toward America, proved remarkably difficult to anticipate, for the ambush had globalized. While the Free World braced for communism to strike in Europe, it popped up in Indonesia, the Congo, any unlikely "hot spot" in a world otherwise frozen into armed stalemate.

The enemy about to light a flame to some obscure piece of global real estate was faceless in a new way. At any moment, he could be yellow, black, even white. He might be a "democrat" in a dictatorship, a "nationalist" under a colonial or neocolonial regime, a champion of religious rights in a nation run by pro-Western modernizers. He might speak any language and worship any pantheon of gods. Egypt. Laos. Cuba. Guatemala. Wherever Communists were, they looked, dressed, spoke, prayed like local people. In the United States, they claimed to be Jeffersonian democrats. "Communism," Party head Earl Browder had said, "is twentieth-century Americanism."

Only the indelible red stain of past conquests proved that a global "war" was in progress, its very name reflecting its puzzling nature. In 1947, thanks evidently to journalist Walter Lippmann, the phrase *Cold War* entered the vocabulary. A contradiction in terms, it stood in for the war whose name could hardly be spoken, the numerical successor to World War II that promised a future global meltdown.[1]

In this new "war," the enemy was shielded from view, his leaders in absentia. His capital was not a city like Berlin, Rome, or Tokyo, but a mysterious set of compounds; not Moscow but the Kremlin, whose ancient walls hid the modern synapses of power; not Beijing but Zhongnanhai, the walled leadership compound abutting the imperial precincts of the Forbidden City. Though the images of Russia's Stalin, China's Mao, Vietnam's Ho, Korea's Kim, Albania's Hoxha might blanket whole countries, they themselves often proved remarkably hard to locate. Despite significant outlays of money and energy, the American "intelligence" community generally could not uncover the simplest facts about their lives. Were they married? Did they have children? Mistresses? Favorites? Were they even alive? Mao Zedong, repeatedly rumored dead, disappeared from sight for months at a time. In the 1950s, when the Kremlin was still seen as the beating heart of a monolithic Communist movement, journalists or diplomats who regularly "penetrated" the Iron Curtain on official assignment, found Moscow an impenetrable series of curtains within curtains.

The task of revealing the hidden nature, capabilities, and intentions of this elusive enemy fell to a new cadre of experts. Their challenge was to ferret out and interpret the concealed statistics of enemy strength (the size of the military budget, the tonnage of the summer grain crop) from false enemy figures or possibly skewed assessments privately provided by U.S. intelligence agencies. The most respectable of these experts were a growing caste of academics—Kremlinologists—often trained at university-based but government-funded institutes for the study of communism. Part of their task was to tease enemy power relationships out of the most obscure clues and some of what they uncovered could not even be made public, for analyses based on classified information were by definition secret. So the attempt to reveal the enemy often had the unrevelatory effect of plunging scholars and their work into a hidden realm.

In a world in which information published by the enemy was untrustworthy, scholars, journalists, newspaper columnists, intelligence bureaucrats, and policy makers turned to the only person likely to have seen the real thing—the defector. The neutrality of the very word *defector* reflected the professionalization that the act of betraying one's country was undergoing. (Previously, the demeaning "turncoat" had generally been used.) Defectors came in many varieties. There were a few elite ones like Soviet Colonel Oleg Penkovsky who brought with them mental snapshots of the innards of the global enemy and scores of humbler figures like KGB assassin Captain Nikolai Khokhlov or cipher clerk Igor Gouzenko. "Debriefed" for months, even years, they were then offered new personas, sinecures, and lives. Some would become culture heroes, and their cautionary articles or books (ghostwritten by members of the intelligence community) best-selling horror stories. As instant experts on one world, they found themselves on Cold War career tracks in the other.[2]

There were more ordinary defectors as well, citizens who broke through one "curtain" or another, swimming to Hong Kong, crossing a barbed wire border somewhere in Eastern Europe, or after 1961, climbing over or tunneling under the Berlin Wall. These bottom-level informants were also debriefed, but for hours, not months, and no career track awaited them. Not for them the best-selling book or film, but the refugee study, the intelligence community's equivalent of the oral history.

The high-level defector was the rarest pearl in the secret world, his value beyond calculation. The CIA's China desk, as Phillip Knightley has noted, evidently "devoted nearly forty years to an effort to recruit its first Chinese official." Yet when the "walk in" defector appeared out of the blue at an agency doorstep anywhere in the world, the response was often not jubilation but dismay. CIA agents were taught to treat such defectors with extreme caution—they were sometimes simply turned away—for it was assumed that a defector not already targeted by our side was likely to be an enemy plant.[3]

Although intelligence bureaucrats developed elaborate methods for ascertaining the truthfulness of the defector's tale, those from "the other side" came without job references and were, by definition, beyond reliability. The only person who had seen the enemy firsthand might be anything from a self-aggrandizing self-promoter to a double agent. No matter what he brought with him to prove good faith, no information was too crucial not to be suspected by someone of being clever disinformation.

Not even Colonel Penkovsky, who passed some 5,000 Soviet documents into Western hands, was beyond suspicion. Given known Soviet successes in penetrating the British, German, and French secret services, this was only logical; but with the defection of KGB Major Anatoly Golitsyn in 1961, it led to a sort of madness. He came with purported information—that the Western European intelligence agencies had all been penetrated and that a Soviet "mole," identity unknown, was somewhere high in the CIA; as well as a theory that all schismatic lines in international communism including the Sino–Soviet rift were part of an elaborate disinformation plan intended to gull the West. In 1964, Yuri Nosenko, another KGB officer, defected, bringing with him information that contradicted some of Golitsyn's claims, particularly on the Soviet penetration of the CIA. James Angleton, head of CIA counterintelligence, believed Golitsyn to be genuine, and his search for the Soviet mole left the agency riven into camps of Golitsyn and Nosenko supporters —as well as a few who wondered whether Angleton himself might not be the mole, so destructive did his investigation seem. This was identification as nightmare: if the enemy was there, his invisibility was a mockery; if he wasn't, then who was?[4]

Increasingly, the world could be fathomed only by adepts. In the 1950s, congressmen, journalists, union leaders, academics, gossip columnists, publishers, television executives, foundation presidents, Hollywood studio chiefs—professionals in many walks of life—found themselves "within" the secret world, relying on experts who, in turn, relied on inherently untrustworthy individuals or on new forms of technowizardry. Electronic "eyes" and "ears" now began picking up traces of the enemy worldwide, but their products could be interpreted only by "cryptanalysts, traffic analysts, photographic interpreters, and telemetry, radar, and signal analysts, who convert[ed] the incomprehensible bleeps and squawks intercepted by their machines into forms usable by the substantive intelligence analysts," who produced material for, at best, a few thousand people with "high enough security clearances to see the finished intelligence product."[5]

Least equipped for the new struggle was the public, and so in congressional hearings, in the press and magazines, in books, in films, and on television, experts gave nonstop testimony on the enemy's identifying characteristics. Defectors, informers, double agents, ex-Communists, anti-Communists—improbable beings with terrifying tales—offered a confusing welter of clues to the enemy "in our midst" and so to an American identity increasingly in question.

Sometimes these clues had a World War II retread quality, as in FBI suggestions to "report all information relating to: Foreign submarine landings, poisoning of public water supplies . . . suspicious parachute landings, [and] possession of radio-active materials." On the other hand, the attempt to locate the Communist by more up-to-date criteria led only to muddle, as in "How to Spot a Communist," a *Look* magazine article by Leo Cherne. The Communist, Cherne claimed, was "not like other Americans. . . . Even his sex life [was] synchronized with the obligations of The Cause." Nevertheless, Cherne (in conjunction with *Look*'s editors) felt obliged to offer readers three elaborate checklists of Communist deviance: one to separate the "good cause" from the Communists "hiding" behind it ("Check all affiliations. . . . Does the group you support suddenly endorse other groups you know nothing about?"); one to separate Communist thought processes from American ones ("He considers a lie to be a legitimate political weapon"); and one to separate Communist traits from American ones ("Continually appearing as sponsor or co-worker of such known Communist-front groups as . . . the Civil

Rights Congress, the National Negro Congress"). There was, however, only one way to nail down one's suspicions. "[A]ctual membership in the Communist Party is 100 per cent proof but this kind of proof is difficult to obtain." By the FBI's World War II criteria, there were no saboteurs left to identify, and Cherne's lists offered such a murky set of traits that almost anyone might be fingered.[6]

The search for enemy identity had the paradoxical effect of solidifying the identity of the secret searchers, for in the postwar years, "intelligence" was coalescing into a way of life. In 1947, through the National Security Act, the secret world secured its own institutional identity with the establishment of the Central Intelligence Agency and of the National Security Council that would someday become a second cabinet, coordinating domestic, foreign, and military policies beyond the oversight of Congress or the public. Two years later, Congress exempted the CIA from making its "size, budget, methods, operations and sources" public, while the very existence of the National Security Agency (NSA), established by President Truman in 1952 to gather "communications intelligence," would be kept secret for five years.[7]

In those years, the intelligence "community" was gaining an identity by acting out a black-bag version of the aboveground life of abundance. In the Cold War underworld, the success ethic would be turned on its head. The higher one advanced, the more reticent one would become; the fuller one's upwardly mobile career, the blanker one's curriculum vitae. (CIA agents were, for a time, forbidden even to tell their wives who employed them or what they did.) Abundance itself would be publicly forgone. One's car would neither have too much chrome nor be too luxurious. Honors would not be publicly bestowed; professional papers would appear (if at all) in a classified CIA journal read only within the intelligence community. The small glories of the good life were to be hidden from sight. "Secret medals are awarded for outstanding performance," wrote former CIA employees Victor Marchetti and John Marks, "but they cannot be worn or shown outside the agency. Even athletic trophies—for intramural bowling, softball, and so on—cannot be displayed except within the guarded sanctuary of the headquarters building."[8]

Aboveground, they gave up everything, embracing the "mass," circulating unobtrusively by choice. In this, they bore a remarkable resemblance to popular images of the enemy they hunted. To act like "normal" Americans, they went under "cover," possessing other personas, other jobs, other pasts. As Philip Agee, a CIA employee who turned against the Agency, wrote of his secret life, "When you wake up in the morning, your mind goes click, okay, who am I today? All day long there is the same problem. Somebody asks you a simple question, 'What did you do over the weekend?' *Click.* Who does he think I am? What would the guy he *thinks* I am do over the weekend?"[9]

Because they were sacrificing everything then thought to make up the pursuit of happiness, the denizens of the secret world naturally viewed their anonymity in a heroic light. They took pride that their seamy acts in a twilit world left those aboveground safe and clean, democratic and strong. In their eyes, they were the gatekeepers, the true guardians of American freedom and identity. Unheralded and unappreciated, they alone protected the path into the underworld. With them on duty, no citizen ever had to look down.

But there was another side to this, for they presided not just over a haunted, but a haunting world. It was not for nothing that they came to be called spooks. As their community rituals implicitly mocked suburban bliss and the success ethic, so their unseen realm grew carnivorously beyond all bounds, dragging aspects of American identity underground.

In 1947, except for an FBI bailiwick in Latin America, the CIA with its 100 employees was alone in the field of foreign intelligence. Within two decades, it had 16,000 employees on its books (and untold thousands off); while the ten agencies concerned with foreign intelligence, ranging from the Defense Intelligence Agency to the Atomic Energy Commission's Division of Intelligence, had an on-the-books combined staff of 150,000. Abroad, covert operations had given way to wars. In Laos, 30,000 Meo tribesmen waged a CIA organized and funded war for years without Congress ostensibly being aware of it. U.S. intelligence operatives drew whole groups of people—Khambas in Tibet, Cuban exiles in Miami, Montagnards in Vietnam, Kurds in Iraq—into secret combat.[10]

A global geography of secrecy was developing. Spy aircraft patrolled the skies unseen, except by the enemy (and the public when a U-2 was downed by a Soviet missile); spy ships sailed the oceans unnoticed, except by the enemy; while stationary electronic listening posts encircled the Communist world, and satellite "eyes" would soon orbit in space "looking" over horizons and through clouds. The secret world was using secret technological advances to capture the identity of the Earth itself. Knowledge of its powers, peoples, and capacities was being transferred into a realm beyond oversight.

In a global war where the "front" was said to be "everywhere," the United States, too, became a secret battleground. While on television, in pop fiction, and in film, Americans experienced glorified versions of their new gatekeepers protecting them from fantastic versions of their enemies, the intelligence agencies and their aboveground allies began to gather information obsessively on their own suspect population of spywatchers.

Surveillance and investigation of Americans grew exponentially. By 1953, approximately one in five Americans in the work force—13.5 million people in all—had gone through some form of loyalty-security check for possible government or defense industry employment, and millions of secret dossiers for individuals had been created. The House Committee on Un-American Activities (HUAC) had a million such dossiers by 1949. The NSA intercepted up to 150,000 cables a month dispatched abroad and listened in on countless phone calls. Between 1952 and 1972, the CIA "reviewed" 28,519,414 letters sent overseas, sharing its discoveries with the FBI and other agencies. Offices were illegally entered and numerous burglaries committed. Between 1940 and 1978, the FBI alone employed at least 37,000 informers to report on Americans. Unknown to themselves, millions of citizens gained a dossier self, a shadow persona inside the secret world. This was identity politics, 1950s style.[11]

You could not stop "yourself" from entering that secret realm where, through "your" files, you could then be accused of acts of which you were ignorant. Even if the accusations were made public, you seldom had a way to confront the anonymous figures who had created your secret identity, or those who had made accusations against you. Often, you had no way of discovering who had accused you, or what it was you were being accused of, or even that you had been accused. Only the barest clues might exist to alert you to the events that had happened to your dossier self.

In the case of successful film and TV writer Millard Lampell:

quietly, mysteriously and almost overnight, the job offers stopped coming. . . . It was about three months before my [literary] agent called me in, locked her door, and announced in a tragic whisper, "You're on the [black]list.". . . She had not even been officially informed that I was a pariah. It was all hints, innuendoes and enigmatic murmurs. . . . Finally I ran into an old friend, a producer who had downed a few too many martinis, and he leveled with me. "Pal, you're dead. I submitted your name for a show and they told me I couldn't touch you with a barge pole.". . . and with a pat on my cheek: "Don't quote me, pal, because I'll deny I said it."

It took Lampell years to put together the obscure train of past associations that had made him into potential enemy material. In the meantime, he followed his dossier into the secret world. He was now, as he put it, one of the "twilight writers." Robbed of his ability to find work in his own name, he took on a cover:

In the end, I was writing under four different pseudonyms, including a Swedish name I used for sensitive art-house films. And there were two or three cleared writers willing to sign my work when the [TV] network or [ad] agency demanded a name with experience and a list of reputable credits. I had read Kafka, but nothing prepared me for the emotions of living in the strange world of the nameless. A script of mine won a major award, and I remember the queer feeling of being a nonperson when another writer went up to claim it.[12]

There was often no way to face what had happened to the "you" once lodged in the sunny world of the good life. Your acts, your past, your associations—in short, your biography—had been rewritten and possessed by someone else. As with radio commentator John Henry Faulk, who in 1962 won a libel suit against the private anti-Communist organizations that had blacklisted him, the struggle to return yourself to your own possession could involve endless years of litigation. For most, it ended in pain and failure—or worse.

The secret world was a growth industry. If maps of it had existed, they would have shown inky blots oozing from it to cover millions of individual lives and whole realms of government. Every government agency now had its own secret arm, and each of these grew and grew until there existed a vast secret bureaucracy whose elements alternately conspired with and competed against one another.

The government now had a public and a shadow face, and led a double life. In the 1950s, nothing symbolized this more than the Dulles brothers, John Foster and Allen, who controlled the public and secret aspects of foreign policy, respectively, one as secretary of state, the other as CIA director. One traveled half a million public miles, stepping off airplanes worldwide with a collapsible lectern to offer policy statements to the TV cameras. He publicly called on Americans to support a Republican program to "roll back" the Iron Curtain, free the "captive nations" of Eastern Europe, and threaten communism with "massive retaliation." The other brother traveled untold secret miles, addressing global audiences through a media all his own—CIA-funded operations like Radio Free Europe, Radio Free Asia, and Radio Liberation, which claimed to be "private, nongovernmental" services. Meanwhile, from Guatemala and Iran to Albania, he pursued "rollback" in private.[13]

That second netherworld absorbed more and more of the public realm. Even history became its property as hundreds of millions of pieces of paper, detailing every aspect of government planning and operation, fell from sight, stamped with newly minted categories of secrecy. Sealing off what it already possessed was not enough, however. The secret world also needed ready access aboveground. CIA agents, for instance, took "cover" inside the personas of government officials, journalists, business-men, scholars, and clergymen simply in order to travel the world openly and unrecognized. The twilight war demanded no less. To collect infor-mation on the enemy unnoticed, to transport arms and mercenaries worldwide unseen, to fight wars unwatched, the CIA had to set up its own cover institutions. To run money through the global veins and arter-ies of the secret realm, banks were needed that also operated as normal financial institutions. To get people and supplies to and from covert oper-ations, airlines were needed capable of carrying perfectly ordinary passen-gers. To get crucial information (or mis- or disinformation) to "surface" in the press, on radio, and on television, the necessary conduits had to be found (hundreds of journalists went on the CIA payroll over the years); publishers and magazines had to be funded and think tanks and founda-tions set up that would also think normal thoughts and fund normal proj-ects.

In this way, the disappearance of the enemy became the basis for a burgeoning new way of life with its own federal subsidy programs, its own definitions of abundance, and its own elaborate support systems. The proclaimed guardians of national security were deconstructing iden-tity aboveground and rebuilding it in the nether regions.

THE INFORMER AS STAR

In 1953, Lucille Ball, America's best-loved TV comedienne, was accused by gossip columnist Walter Winchell of being "red," because she had admitted to HUAC in 1952 that she had registered as a Communist in 1936 to "please" her grandfather. Though "cleared" by the committee the year before, she—and her top-rated TV show *I Love Lucy*—were endangered by Winchell's charges. This time she would be cleared by her husband, Cuban bandleader Desi Arnaz, who told the show's studio audi-ence, "Lucille Ball is no Communist. . . . I was kicked out of Cuba because of communism. [Actually, his parents arrived in Miami in 1933.] . . . Lucille is 100 percent American. She's as American as . . . Ike Eisenhower." As Cold War historian Stephen Whitfield recounts the moment, "The audience arose and cheered Arnaz, who called for his sob-bing spouse to come onstage: 'And now I want you to meet my favorite wife—my favorite redhead—in fact, that's the only thing red about her, and even that's not legitimate.'" Here was an oddity! A Cuban who based his claim to expertise on his (supposed) flight from communism could certify the "Americanness" of the country's premier comic.

As historian David Caute has noted, Senator Joseph McCarthy

> was the first right-wing demagogue in American history who denounced no specific racial, ethnic or religious group (unless it were Harvard professors and Ivy League diplomats!) . . . one of the appeals of McCarthyism was that it offered every American, however precarious his ancestry, the chance of being taken for a good American, simply by demonstrating a gut hatred for Commies.[14]

As a political phenomenon, McCarthyism aimed to mobilize anti-Communist fears to sweep Roosevelt Democrats, liberals in positions of power, as well as progressives and leftists of all sorts (including actual Communists) from government, the new defense industries, the media and entertainment industries, labor unions, and any other institutions of significance in American life. But in attempting to do so, it also helped transform America's enemies into beings who looked indistinguishable from "us."

As the power to define the enemy passed into a netherworld, where no simple, stigmatizing racial or ethnic shorthand existed, so, too, did the power to define the American. If the United States had been betrayed by a "Communist conspiracy" at, or close to the top echelons of government, as Senator McCarthy and others claimed, then those responsible, those in that "invisible government," from "the Red Dean," Secretary of State Dean Acheson, on down to various Far Eastern specialists in the State Department, were models of the WASP elite. Of this no one could have been more symbolic than Alger Hiss, the man Senator McCarthy and Congressman Richard Nixon accused of transmitting classified information to the enemy and, as an adviser to President Roosevelt at the Yalta conference, selling the United States out to Stalin.

Hiss, who had gone to Harvard University, clerked at the Supreme Court, risen in the State Department, and become president of the Carnegie Endowment for International Peace, in the words of historian John P. Roche, "wore no beard, spoke with no accent, [and] moved casually in the best circles. . . . Hiss looked like the man down the block in Scarsdale or Evanston, the man in the office across the hall on Wall Street or State Street. If this man could be a spy, anybody could." Worse yet, Hiss, the ultimate insider, adamantly refused to admit to anything but innocence.[15]

No wonder the public was in need of a new kind of expert in identity, one who, like an Orpheus returned from Hades, had either freely braved the horrors of the Communist underground or (like Whittaker Chambers in the Hiss case) awakened from the grasp of the group mind in time to wrest knowledge from the enemy. The loss of a clearly targetable enemy generated an unexpected, homegrown hero—the informer, domestic cousin of the defector, known to admirers as a patriot, informant, or friendly witness.

Previously, though an informer's testimony might have been used in court, the informer had been held in decidedly low esteem as the informal terms for him—snitch, squeeze, rat, stoolie—indicated. For an informer to certify one's patriotism would once have seemed a contradiction in terms. In the postwar years, however, the person most able to affirm the patriot's patriotism, the American's Americanness, became the informer; and he or she could affirm it solely by default. The informer could swear only that the patriot had not been seen skulking in the netherworld, had not appeared on the membership lists of the enemy's many front organizations, or, better yet, had been reviled or feared by the enemy. The enemy's invisibility placed the national character in the informer's hands.[16]

The informer alone could choose the role of hero, patriot, American, while others affirmed their patriotism by associating themselves with that choice. His path up from the underworld was an epic escape from captivity. He arrived—whether as a former Communist who had seen the light or an FBI agent planted among the enemy—seared by the flames of hell. The government investigator of subversive activities, the HUAC counsel who prepared witnesses to testify, the congressional representative whose investigative committee rooted out un-Americans all shared in the informer's glory. Like updated frontiersmen, their task was to rescue captives from Red savages in a dark and terrifying wilderness. Through them, the Mary Rowlandsons of a new age would offer terrifying testimony.

The former captives became not just "folk heroes," as Victor Navasky has called them, but "stars" in the Hollywood sense. For instance, Herbert A. Philbrick, who posed as a Communist for years at the behest of the FBI, testified in congressional hearings and at trials of Communist Party members, wrote a best-selling book, *I Led 3 Lives*, and became a columnist for the *New York Herald Tribune*, a professional lecturer, and a consultant to a hit TV series about his adventures with the same title as his book. ("Your best friend may be a traitor" was a typical script line.)[17]

Like movie stars, from an often obscure moment of discovery (later mythologized in the manner of any star's bio), many of them made their way to the big time of nationally televised testimony. Through hard work before state legislative committees and at local trials, the informing performer honed his or her skills. Take Harvey Matusow, former Party member, who worked as a professional informer for four years before, in a rare act, repudiating his own performances and explaining how they were created in his book *False Witness*. As Navasky describes it,

> Between 1951 and 1954, [Matusow] consulted with and testified for the Justice Department . . . , the Subversive Activities Control Board, the Permanent Investigations Subcommittee of the Senate Committee on Government Operations, the Internal Security Subcommittee of the Senate Judiciary Committee, the House Committee on Un-American Activities, the Ohio Committee on Un-American Activities, and the New York City Board of Education. By his own count he had testified in 25 trials and deportation proceedings and identified 180 persons as Communists as he worked his way up from the sticks to the informers' Palace—the McCarthy Committee. He also lectured for the American Legion, campaigned for candidates who could meet his fee . . . , wrote for the Hearst papers, and at one point had a radio program with fellow informer Howard Rushmore called *Out of the Red*.

Like Matusow, those who managed to emerge from the relative anonymity of local or regional informing found a life of fame available to them. A Philbrick Day was declared in Boston and a Matt Cvetic Day in Pittsburgh for the premier of *I Was a Communist for the FBI* (1951), a film based on his exploits. Honors and awards rained down.[18]

Although a labyrinthine network of congressional, loyalty board, and deportation hearings, security checks, and trials affected every part of society, no arena more fascinated the Communist hunter than Hollywood. There, perhaps 300 people had at one time been members of the "talent branches" of the Communist Party (including 50–60 actors, close to 150 screenwriters, and 15–20 producers, but not a single studio head); and a number of Communist screenwriters had written scripts almost devoid of anything that might pass for Party propaganda. Even films like *Mission to Moscow* (1943) and *North Star* (1943), based on a Lillian Hellman script, which in retrospect looked like egregious examples of Russian-inspired propaganda, were done at the behest not of the Party but of a wartime government intent on garnering public support for its alliance with the Soviet Union and were eagerly encouraged by the non-Communist liberals who staffed the Office of War Information.[19]

Congressional investigators were drawn to Hollywood for the obvious media attention movie stars and those associated with them garnered. However, another kind of affinity existed between that great story-making machine, the studio system, and the developing world of anti-Communist investigations. The various hearings not only drew on Hollywood's acting pool (voluntarily or not) in the fashion of a wartime mobilization of talent but organized themselves in a Hollywood-like fashion, for the anti-Communist investigatory "crusade" was a complex production process for the creation of a new-style war story in a boundaryless age. The FBI agents, informers, defectors, and ex-Communist testifiers were its stars, pampered, image-massaged, loaned from one "studio" to the next, and intimidated if, like a Matusow, they got out of line. Like Hollywood stars, they were surrounded by professional support teams to coach and direct their performances and publicists to project their images and protect them against detractors.

Along with stars like Philbrick in his red, white, and blue bow tie or Elizabeth Bentley, self-professed "Red Spy Queen," there were supporting casts of professional testifiers and a stream of bit players called forth to corroborate the tales from the netherworld the pros were offering up. The production's flaw lay not in its stars but in its villains. The "hostile" witnesses generally proved recalcitrant stand-ins for the enemy, refusing to testify to their own alien nature. With a few exceptions like the Rosenbergs, in trial after trial convictions were obtained, if at all, on procedural grounds, on relatively minor charges, or on charges jury-rigged for the occasion (many of which were soon overturned). Alger Hiss, after all, was finally convicted of perjury; Pete Seeger, leftist troubadour, of contempt of Congress; and Owen Lattimore, identified by Senator McCarthy as "Alger Hiss's boss in the espionage ring in the State Department" and Russia's top agent in the United States, of nothing at all. Ceremonies of guilt built around these disappointing facts lent an aura of enemy-ness to those who "hid" behind American rights. In the media, as in the various hearings, terms like "treason," "spying," and "subversion" were bandied about without the need for convictions in court. But an inability to produce the enemy looking and acting as an enemy should proved a fatal weakness.[20]

From such material, the anti-Communist production process molded an elaborate tale about shape-shifting monsters lurking, as in any child's nightmare, right under America's bed and intent on establishing a group-mind dictatorship by "treachery, deceit, infiltration . . . espionage, sabotage, terrorism and any other means deemed necessary" (in the words of the Internal Security Act of 1950). As the studio for this new adult horror story, the congressional hearing burgeoned in these years. While Congress authorized only 285 investigations between 1789 and 1925, 51 anti-Communist investigations were held during the 83rd Congress alone (1953–1954).[21]

As the Hollywood studios had churned out endless variations on a few film genres, so these hearings took their raw materials from confidential State Department personnel files, FBI files, the raw data of rumor and gossip from "red squads" and private right-wing groups, and the hearsay of spies, defectors, ex-Communists, and informers, and spun endless variations on a single fear-filled theme. The hearings themselves were a traveling road show. HUAC, for example, descended on scores of cities a year. In each, it produced a version of The HUAC Performance, in which the enemy was to be teased from a population of "red-blooded Americans" under the klieg lights of television, before the flashing bulbs of photojournalists, and in front of masses of reporters.

Despite their investigative form, these nearly continuous hearings of the early 1950s were highly stylized and largely ceremonial in nature. Roles were carefully predetermined, with testimony normally rehearsed in private before being put on public view. In its most ritualistic act, the "naming of names," witnesses identified those who had inhabited the Communist netherworld with them. The names were invariably already known to the committees, however, so the effect was incantatory rather than revelatory. In fact, puzzled "cooperative" witnesses sometimes reported being urged to offer fewer names at their public than their private sessions—for greater media impact. When Leo Townsend, screenwriter and former Party member, decided to testify, he called the FBI. "So two men came out to my home, and I told them all I knew. I discovered they knew more about it than I did; they knew every meeting I went to, they knew who was there.... I wasn't revealing anything.... [HUAC] had all those names."[22]

MAINTENANCE WORK

The war story's ability to make everything obvious with a minimum of explanation had given way to repetitious descriptions of a horrific enemy who could not be produced. A mobilizing fairy tale was being replaced by a chilling fantasy meant to engender panic and fear, one in which everything needed to be spelled out. Hostile witnesses had to be denied the possibility of facing their accusers, as if there was doubt that the hero could defend himself. Committee members and investigators had to employ bullying tactics and a pugnacious style of humiliation that gave this new story a distinctly defensive feel, even with abjectly repentant witnesses, as if no answer, however abject, could satisfy.

Constant maintenance work seemed necessary to prevent the story's collapse. A system reliant on the least trustworthy of witnesses had to put enormous energy into its own upkeep. Take the case of David Brown, a former Communist Party member approached by the FBI in 1950. "Faced with money difficulties and fearing for his job as a warehouseman if the FBI spoke to his employer, he decided to collaborate, receiving $5 for each report on a meeting advertised in the [Communist paper] *Daily People's World*, up to a maximum of $50 a month." As an FBI informer, he became executive secretary of the Rosenberg Defense Committee and, at the FBI's urging, tried to get himself readmitted to the Party. Failing in this, he sent the FBI reports about fictional Party meetings and later "pretended he had been kidnapped and murdered." On discovering his lies, the FBI "far from abandoning him as a neurotic perjurer, tried to persuade him to start again, but without success." Letting a David Brown drop from the system was potentially more dangerous than knowing that he would continue to produce wildly untruthful testimony.[23]

Understandably, hostile or uncooperative witnesses seldom grasped the nature of the hearings they were so forcibly attending. Those who resisted generally did so either on legalistic grounds (abridgment of rights) or by challenging the factuality of the various charges against them. The system, however, proved impermeable to attacks on the accuracy of its testimony. All such assaults simply signaled the need for further maintenance work.

The black singer, actor, and Communist Paul Robeson was an exception. In 1956, he responded to HUAC's attempts to cow him with unconcealed verbal contempt. When the committee director Richard Arens tried to badger him on the subject of his attitude toward Stalin, he responded, "I would not argue with a representative of the people who, in building America, wasted sixty to a hundred million lives of my people, black people drawn from Africa on the plantations. You are responsible, and your forebears." When Arens continued, "Tell us whether or not you have changed your opinion in the recent past about Stalin," Robeson shot back, "I have told you, mister, that I would not discuss anything with the people who have murdered sixty million of my people, and I will not discuss Stalin with you." As his hearing was ending, he added, "[Y]ou gentlemen . . . are the nonpatriots, and you are the un-Americans, and you ought to be ashamed of yourselves." In Robeson's public insistence that slavery was an American, not a Russian issue, that American history was murder, and that HUAC was an enemy institution lay a rare preview of the decade to come.[24]

Although the hearings system created a new story form for an era of triumphalist despair and indeterminate anxiety, it had a remarkably brief half-life. Its creators had not been wrong to feel on the defensive. The expenditure of energy involved in mobilizing the nation through constant infusions of fear and tales of horror led to exhaustion. By 1955, Senator McCarthy was gone, and mobilization through investigation attenuated in the years to follow.

By 1960, HUAC faced opponents who intuitively grasped its weaknesses. Student demonstrators, discovering that San Francisco's City Hall, the venue for local HUAC hearings, had been packed with right-wing supporters, began singing "The Star Spangled Banner" and chanting "Let us in!" (where, previously, opponents had pled to be let out). A small number of sympathizers already seated inside responded with cries of, "Let them in! Let them in!" HUAC's chairman, Representative Edwin Willis of Louisiana, called on the police to remove them. Witnesses subsequently did the unheard of, verbally attacking Willis and questioning his right to a congressional seat as he represented a district in which blacks could not vote. The next day the police turned fire hoses on student demonstrators, assaulted them with billy clubs, and flung some down the steps of City Hall. Each repressive act only increased their number.[25]

For the first time, an investigative committee had been theatrically and directly challenged and forced to take incommensurate steps against people who did not look like the enemy. This process would be repeated throughout the 1960s as young radicals attempted to seize control of the production's words and images. In 1966, for instance, members of the tiny Progressive Labor Party appeared before HUAC eager to "incriminate" themselves, as in this exchange between witness Richard Mark Rhoads and the committee:

MR. NITTLE: Were you a member of the Progressive Labor Movement between the period July 1964 and January 1965?

MR. RHOADS: I am very proud to state that, right now as I sit here before this Committee, I am a member of the Progressive Labor Party. . . .

MR. ASHBROOK: Mr. Chairman, in his own words he referred to "our Communist philosophy" or something of that sort. It was "our Communist." Is that what you meant to say, or are you denying it now?

MR. RHOADS: Are you trying to ask me whether I am a Communist or not?

MR. ASHBROOK: You are asking the question. Answer mine. . . .

MR. RHOADS: I certainly am. . . .

MR. POOL: Do you advocate the overthrow of the United States Government by force and violence?

MR. RHOADS: You gentlemen have some nerve to use "violence" when you are talking about what we advocate, because the United States Government is the prime user of violence against the people of the United States.

Blowing soap bubbles, Jerry Rubin, a Berkeley antiwar activist, appeared before the committee dressed as a Revolutionary War soldier; two years later, Abbie Hoffman appeared in an American flag shirt, which so enraged Capitol police that they tore it off his back, revealing a Cuban flag painted onto his skin. Finally, after two decades, representatives of "the enemy" were eager to show their faces—those of young, middle-class Americans. Not cowed, not trying to deny anything, they proudly entered their names and those of their "brothers" into the record. In the flamboyance of their "testimony," they parodied HUAC's reliance on ceremonial exaggeration. Capturing the instability at the heart of the HUAC production, they revealed the dreaded foe to be no less than a mocking, deconstructive voice long hidden in child culture.[26]

By the late 1960s, young radicals considered HUAC a toothless irrelevancy, while the various hostile witnesses, resistors, and blacklistees of the 1950s were beginning to be portrayed as heroic figures in a media that had previously stigmatized or shunned them. By the post-Vietnam era, the whole anti-Communist production seemed as strange and outdated as a Hollywood biblical spectacle, a form whose success and passing it largely paralleled. By the 1980s, even a president ready to recall with nostalgia much else about 1950s America carefully avoided their disinterment.

In retrospect, the anti-Communist purges were a way station on the road to an even more confusing version of enemy-ness, a production number in which the villain never quite made an appearance. True, the enemy had many stand-ins: ex-Communists and infiltrators of communism, spies, defectors, and informers; hostile and uncooperative witnesses; members of the American Communist Party put on trial and convicted under the Smith Act; various "aliens" deported; citizens whose passports were taken away; government officials and scientists who lost secrecy classifications (and so jobs) in loyalty hearings; performers and media personalities whose work lives disappeared into blacklists; and many ordinary citizens who lost livelihoods without ever walking on stage.

Even taken at face value, none of this quite added up to a vision of global evil. In addition, however tactically useful it was in the short term to have witnesses plead the amendment of their choice, lapse into silence, or be forced repeatedly to avoid committee questions (thus stigmatizing themselves as "Fifth Amendment Communists"), it lent the investigatory drama an aura of inaction. Despite the power of the state to level livelihoods, even jail opponents, here, too, was an unexpected stalemate; for here, too, victory was lacking.

Worst of all, the least cooperative witness was that enemy-within, the American Communist Party. Ready to act at the bidding of Stalin, its spies everywhere, its agents secreted in the uppermost reaches of government, its members strategically positioned in the mass media, its lawyers mocking revered constitutional rights and freedoms, its toughs ready to take over labor unions—this was the cumulative image of a party under the thumb of an alien power, preparing itself like so many maturing pods to possess the body politic. Wild scenarios of Party takeovers and Communist invasions were then commonplace. In film, there was *Invasion, U.S.A.* (1952), in which a Communist takeover turned out to be the shared hallucinatory fantasy of several bar patrons; in comics, "The Sneak Attack" from the first issue of *Atomic War* (1952); on television, *Red Nightmare* ("Presented by the Department of Defense," 1962); in magazines, the 1948 *Look* spread, "Could the Reds Seize Detroit?" with dramatically "enacted" photos. "Many factors," opined the *Look* piece, "make Detroit a focal point of Communist activity. Not the least of these is its geographical location. Only a narrow river separates the city from Canada, a foreign country. Ignoring the formalities of legal entrance, red agents can shuttle back and forth, as rumrunners did during Prohibition days."[27]

Whatever the hysterias of the moment, such fantasies forced a special burden on the anti-Communist production process, for the world's economic and military colossus was simply not going to be taken over by Communists. Even at the height of its strength just before World War II, the Party never had more than 75,000 members. By 1957, membership had plummeted to 5,000–10,000, an unknown but significant number of whom were FBI infiltrators and informants. Thanks to them, its membership roles and the minutes of its meetings had long been in FBI hands. From 1946 on, it had almost no influence on domestic politics or ability to promote a candidate or an issue, much less launch a countrywide takeover.[28]

Ironically, a process dedicated to the identification, uprooting, and destruction of the Party secretly found itself propping the Party up. Just as the credibility of the informer had to be burnished and protected, so, too,

the credibility of the Party had to be shored up in the face of painful realities. For behind the obsessive anti-Communist production process stood
not only a pitiful organization but a version of the same puzzling calculus
of power that could be seen in Korea. Looked at with a cold eye, a giant
was facing off against a midget, which was a new sort of horror story.

The purge that the anti Communist production number embodied
touched the livelihoods of, at a minimum, hundreds of thousands of
Americans, ranging from actual Party members to librarian Ruth Brown
of Bartlesville, Oklahoma, who lost her job for shelving magazines like
the *New Republic*, *Soviet Russia Today*, *Consumer's Research*, and
Negro Digest, as well as for taking part in "group discussions on race
relations." It was a purge that extended from the government—of the
State Department's twenty-two prewar China experts, only two remained in 1954—to the universities, where hundreds of professors and
graduate students were fired, expelled, or suspended, to labor, where
whole unions were, in effect, blacklisted. It brought what David Caute
has called the Great Fear to American society; yet rather than walling
Americans off from the enemy, it also brought a sense of enemy-ness
ever closer in ever stranger forms.[29]

There was already one great power whose fantastic and fantasy-based
purges of "enemies" had filled its society with fear and whose investigatory powers had focused on the theatrical revelation of an enemy-ness
that could be attached to anyone, no matter how powerful or insignificant. This was the Soviet Union, and the longer the American purge
went on, the more the similarities between the two fantasy systems of
story production grew (though the perils of the Soviet one bore no relation to those of the American one).

In 1961, Antonio Prohias, whose anti-Communist cartoons had made
him *persona non grata* in Castro's Cuba, began publishing a strip in an
American children's magazine. As characters, it had two pointy-nosed
spies, both wearing sunglasses, wide-brimmed hats, and monkish frocks,
each conducting a balletic secret war in an attempt to deceive and harm
the other. In their acts as in their looks, they were indistinguishable—
except for the fact that one was garbed in white, the other in black.
(Sometimes a gray spy showed up, and *she* always won.) Before novelist
John Le Carré's spies began to tell grown-ups in world-weary fashion,
"We're all the same, you know, that's the joke," children reading Prohi
as's "Spy vs. Spy" in *MAD* magazine's "Joke and Dagger Department"
experienced the Cold War as a series of ludicrous acts between two arbi-
trarily distinguishable quasi-warriors who had everything in common
with each other, and nothing with anyone else.[30]

While the Great Fear plunged adults into the horrorscapes of the secret world, a little fear came to haunt society as well. For locked inside the apparatus of abundance, those nearest to home seemed, on closer look, to be crossing over into a secret world of their own on a journey that left their parents mystified. One by one, America's children were being possessed, though what was possessing them (or what they were possessing) was a matter of debate.

4

The Haunting of Childhood

WORRY, BORDERING ON HYSTERIA, about the endangering behaviors of "youth" has had a long history in America, as has the desire of reformers and censors to save "innocent" children from the polluting effects of commercial culture. At the turn of the century, when middle-class white adolescents first began to take their place as leisure-time trendsetters, fears arose that the syncopated beat of popular "coon songs" and ragtime music would demonically possess young listeners, who might succumb to the "evils of the Negro soul." Similarly, on-screen images of crime, sensuality, and violence in the earliest movies, showing in "nickel houses" run by a "horde of foreigners," were decried by reformers. They were not just "unfit for children's eyes," but a "disease" especially virulent to young (and poor) Americans, who were assumed to lack all immunity to such spectacles.[1]

In the post–World War II years, adult unease about the young, while registering similar notes, gained in intensity from new realities, for adolescents (now labeled "teenagers") were organizing themselves in new and unsettling ways, distinct from and mocking of the frameworks and values of the adult world. They were creating (or responding to) new kinds of narratives. Many were ready to plunge into a culture of triumphalist despair with money in their pockets. They would be met by increasingly eager advertisers and businesses ready to retail their new narratives back to them in tamed form as part of a product-centered culture of adolescence.

In the 1950s, that era of big consumer objects, the car (owned by 75 percent of families by 1960), the TV (87 percent), and the washing machine (75 percent) entered the home (or the attached garage); so, too, did the first products of a new child- and adolescent-centered style and entertainment experience. From TV-inspired frontier paraphernalia to Barbie dolls, even the youngest children found themselves experiencing trickle-down economics, and, for the first time, they had an appreciable amount of money in their pockets with no need to contribute it to the family's welfare. Between 1944 and 1958, the teenager's average weekly income quadrupled from $2.50 to $10. By 1958, teen spending was an estimated $9.5 billion yearly, much of it in impulse purchases and almost all, for the first time, free from adult control. Teens now had the means to buy the small but thrilling fruits of abundance at will, just as the means of reaching them directly as a market—a movie screen shrunk down to living-room size—appeared in the home.[2]

To many adults, a teen culture beyond parental oversight had a remarkably alien look to it. In venues ranging from the press to Senate committees, from the American Psychiatric Association to American Legion meetings, sensational and cartoonlike horror stories about the young or the cultural products they were absorbing were told. Tabloid newspaper headlines reflected this: "Two Teen Thrill Killings Climax City Park Orgies. Teen Age Killers Pose a Mystery—Why Did They Do It? . . . 22 Juveniles Held in Gang War. Teen Age Mob Rips up BMT Train. Congressmen Stoned, Cops Hunt Teen Gang." After a visit to the movies in 1957 to watch two "teenpics," *Rock All Night* and *Dragstrip Girl*, Ruth Thomas of Newport, Rhode Island's Citizen's Committee on Literature expressed her shock in words at least as lurid as those of any tabloid: "Isn't it a form of brain-washing? Brain-washing the minds of the people and especially the youth of our nation in filth and sadistic violence. What enemy technique could better lower patriotism and national morale than the constant presentation of crime and horror both as news and recreation."[3]

You did not have to be a censor, a right-wing anti-Communist, or a member of the Catholic Church's Legion of Decency, however, to hold such views. Dr. Frederick Wertham, a liberal psychiatrist, who testified in the landmark *Brown* v. *Board of Education* desegregation case and set up one of the first psychiatric clinics in Harlem, publicized the idea that children viewing commercially produced acts of violence and depravity, particularly in comic books, could be transformed into little monsters. The lurid title of his best-selling book, *Seduction of the Innocent*, an assault on comic books as "primers for crime," told it all. In it, Dr. Wertham offered copious "horror stories" that read like material from *Tales from the Crypt*: "Three boys, six to eight years old, took a boy of seven, hanged him nude from a tree, his hands tied behind him, then burned him with matches. Probation officers investigating found that they were re-enacting a comic-book plot. . . . A boy of thirteen committed a lust murder of a girl of six. After his arrest, in jail, he asked for comic books."[4]

Not only was there a public hysteria over supposedly soaring rates of juvenile delinquency, but terrifying visions were conjured up of the young banding together in "gangs." Gang behavior seemed to offer frightening evidence that the delinquent children of the poor were entering the group-mind world of the enemy with switchblades and zip guns in their pockets. But the middle-class children of bunker culture were armed in their own way, for with soaring discretionary income they could now buy into a culture of their own, whatever their parents thought of it. Without necessarily leaving homes or neighborhoods, often while doing nothing more than dancing, listening, reading, or watching, they came to see themselves as separate and alienated from their parents, who in turn imagined them as "tainted," "contaminated," "poisoned," and "demoralized," not to say, "destroyed" as "future citizens." Teen acts of driving, dressing, embracing, speaking, moving, and fighting were portrayed as related atrocities. White children were shaking to what some adults began to call "leer-ics" or "nigger music."[5]

From the mid-1940s on, individually or en masse, the young were regularly portrayed as soft and vulnerable, hence ripe for enemy picking, or hardened and calloused, hence already aliens. In the public outrage over what was happening to the young, in a language so overheated as to seem, in retrospect, like parody, can be felt a seductive release of fears and tensions of the moment onto children.

BORDER CROSSINGS

Between the end of World War II and the Kennedy accession, childhood was the symbolic meeting point for two sets of fears, the place where two threatening kinds of un-American freedoms could be detected in a frozen world. The first was the fear that the domestic Other was escaping social and cultural containment. In the world of the child, the poor white—a missing figure in the pantheon of abundance—made a threatening reappearance as the juvenile delinquent; while the black outsider, still largely ignored in the adult world, materialized as the rock and roll singer.

The two—hood and performer, lower-class white and taboo black—merged in the "pelvis" of a Southern "greaser" who dressed like a delinquent, used "one of black America's favorite products, Royal Crown

Pomade hair grease" (meant to give hair a "whiter" look), and proceeded to move and sing "like a negro." Whether it was because they saw a white youth in blackface or a black youth in whiteface, much of the media grew apoplectic and many white parents alarmed. In the meantime, swiveling his hips and playing suggestively with the microphone, Elvis Presley broke into the lives of millions of teens in 1956, bringing with him an element of disorder and sexuality associated with darkness.[6]†

The second set of postwar fears involved the "freedom" of the commercial media—record and comic book companies, radio stations, the movies, and television—to concretize both the fantasies of the young and the nightmarish fears of grown-ups into potent products. For many adults, this was abundance as betrayal, the good life not as a vision of Eden but as an unexpected horror story.

Such fears mingled with larger fears of the Communist menace and nuclear annihilation. What made this strange brew so confusing—in addition to its surfeit of possible villains—was the fact that the young were not simply a symbolic territory on which adult fears could be played out. Some of them rushed to embrace the very nightmares their parents were conjuring up. In the rhythms of an unknown music, some were ready to discover a new kind of freedom story. In grown-up terrors, some found dark humor. Behind a frozen universe of abundance and destruction, some spotted pleasure, excitement, movement, energy.

Compared to the Great Fear, this little fear had an inchoate look, even though it involved some of the same "producers." FBI Director J. Edgar Hoover, for instance, was nearly as responsible for bringing the juvenile delinquent as the "masters of deceit" to public consciousness. Similarly, congressional hearings were held to tease the hidden manipulators of youthful minds as well as hidden Communists into the arena of public scrutiny. Of the two fears, the less familiar better illuminates the confusions of the time. Yet because the little fear centered on young people and because those who lost jobs produced comic books, not government

---

†At the time, confusing border crossings of all sorts were taking place in the music world. An early Presley hit, "Hound Dog," for example, was the work of songwriters Jerry Lieber and Mike Stoller, two Jewish adolescents. "We found ourselves writing for black artists, because those were the voices and rhythms we loved," recalled Lieber. Their song, written out of familiarity with black musical styles, was first recorded by black singer Big Mama Thornton, then picked up and popularized by Presley. Similarly, as increasing numbers of young whites were attracted to the rhythm and blues played on black radio stations, black DJs might be hired to train whites on white stations to sound black. "This was," comments music critic Nelson George, "blackface broadcasting in the extreme."[7]

policy, it is now largely dismissed as a laughable prelude to the coming of new life styles, and its main figures like Wertham are considered, if at all, as somewhat comic.[8]

What made this second Cold War production so fascinating was the inability of adults to give its elements a coherent narrative form. If the Great Fear's cast of characters had a uniformity imposed by the intersection of anticommunism and the secret world, the little fear had a bizarrely disparate cast, and not only was there no agreement on what was to be suppressed, but many of the phenomena chosen seemed, as part of a developing consumer culture for the young, irrepressible.

Take comic books. Even before the end of World War II, a new kind of content was creeping into them as they became the reading matter of choice for the soldier-adolescent. "By 1945," writes comics historian William W. Savage, Jr.:

> their artwork had developed a sexual orientation remarkable in a medium ostensibly still intended for juvenile audiences. A typical wartime cover might reveal in the foreground a scantily clad woman, tied with ropes or chains, at the mercy of some leering Axis villain, while in the background an American hero struggled forward, intent upon her rescue. The woman's clothing inevitably was torn to reveal ample cleavage and thigh, her muscular definition enhanced by forced contortion into some anatomically impossible position. Sometimes her clothing was completely ripped away, leaving her to face her tormentor clad only in her unmentionables.

Within a few years, "crime" comics like *Crime Does Not Pay* emerged from the shadows, displaying a wide variety of criminal acts for the delectation of young readers. These were followed by horror and science fiction comics, purchased in enormous numbers. By 1953, more than 150 horror comics were being produced monthly, featuring acts of torture often of an implicitly sexual nature, murders and decapitations of various bloody sorts, visions of rotting flesh, and so on.[9]

Miniature catalogs of atrocities, their feel was distinctly assaultive. In their particular version of the spectacle of slaughter, they targeted the American family, the good life, and revered institutions. Framed by sardonic detective narrators or mocking Grand Guignol gatekeepers, their impact was deconstructive. Driven by a commercial "hysteria" as they competed to attract buyers with increasingly atrocity-ridden covers and stories, they both partook of and mocked the hysteria about them.

Unlike radio or television producers, the small publishers of the comic book business were neither advertiser driven nor corporately controlled.

Unlike the movies, comics were subject to no code. Unlike the television networks, comics companies had no Standards and Practices departments. No censoring presence stood between them and whoever would hand over a dime at a local newsstand. Their penny-ante ads and pathetic pay scale ensured that writing and illustrating them would be a job for young men in their twenties (or even teens). Other than early rock and roll, comics were the only cultural form of the period largely created by the young for those only slightly younger. In them, uncensored, can be detected the dismantling voice of a generation that had seen in the world war horrors beyond measure.

The hysterical tone of the response to these comics was remarkable. Comics publishers were denounced for conspiring to create a delinquent nation. Across the country, there were publicized comic book burnings like one in Binghamton, New York, where 500 students were dismissed from school early in order to torch 2,000 comics and magazines. Municipalities passed ordinances prohibiting the sale of comics, and thirteen states passed legislation to control their publication, distribution, or sale. Newspapers and magazines attacked the comics industry. The *Hartford Courant* decried "the filthy stream that flows from the gold-plated sewers of New York." In April 1954, the Senate Subcommittee to Investigate Juvenile Delinquency convened in New York to look into links between comics and teen crime.[10]

Unlike the accused called before HUAC, William Gaines, the publisher of EC Comics, asked to appear before the hearings to defend horror and science fiction comics, a form he had almost single-handedly created. His testimony followed Dr. Wertham's. "It would be just as difficult to explain the harmless thrill of a horror story to a Dr. Wertham," he said, "as it would be to explain the sublimity of love to a frigid old maid. . . . The truth is that delinquency is the product of the real environment in which the child lives and not of the fiction he reads."

Perhaps the most famous moment in these hearings was this exchange between Senator Estes Kefauver and Gaines:

> KEFAUVER (holding up the cover of an issue of EC's *Crime SuspenStories*): This seems to be a man with a bloody ax holding a woman's head up which has been severed from her body. Do you think that is in good taste?
> GAINES: Yes sir, I do, for the cover of a horror comic. A cover in bad taste, for example, might be defined as holding the head a little higher so that the neck could be seen dripping blood from it and moving the body over a little further so that the neck of the body could be seen to be bloody.

Despite Gaines, the comics industry did not have the corporate clout to defend its products successfully. The business saw no choice but to promulgate a strict "comics code" ("All scenes of horror, excessive bloodshed, gory or gruesome crimes, depravity, lust, sadism, masochism shall not be permitted"); and crime and horror comics largely ceased to exist along with many of the companies that had produced them. With them went the original vitality of the comic book. Purged of alien intruders in the name of outraged parenthood, the comic remained for almost a decade a zombified form, losing fans by the millions.[11]

Within the year, Gaines had shut down EC's previously thriving business and was left with only one product, a ten-cent satiric comic he and Harvey Kurtzman had established in 1952. In 1955, he transformed it into a twenty-five-cent black-and-white magazine in part to avoid the code. Its name caught its sensibility—MAD (a name that would also be applied to a Kennedy-era nuclear strategy, Mutual Assured Destruction).

Of Gaines's now-defunct crime, horror, and "weird" sci-fi comics, all that remained was the mocking voice of the gatekeeper, but it proved more than enough when applied to the "weirdness" observable in society. MAD promptly turned it on the artifacts and cultural forms of the good life in the child's world and began to devour them with unparalleled comic relish. First, it cannibalized comic books themselves, dismembering anything that seemed "traditional" or "innocent" about them. In its hilarious pages, it turned Mickey Mouse back into vermin, a little rat-faced thug with a five-day stubble ("Mickey Rodent"); the innocent teenagers Archie and Jughead became chain-smoking juvenile delinquents ("Starchie"); the western hero, a fool ("The Lone Stranger"); and the triumphant superhero, an unbearable bungler ("Superduper Man!"). Soon MAD's creators turned their attention to television (the innocent puppet Howdy Doody became "Howdy Dooit!," a menacing pitchboy for products), to advertising, the movies, and finally politics.

The youngest audiences could now revel in the spectacle of America's mythmaking machinery being taken apart amid mocking, revelatory laughter. Though many parents could (and did) hate and denounce MAD, a "funny" magazine proved unsuppressible despite the "violence" of its deconstructive task.†

---

†It was a relatively short step from MAD to the stomping the American story took in the "underground comix" created over a decade later by a MAD generation. In Dan O'Neill's *Air Pirates Comics*, for instance, Disney characters were swept through the muck, fucking and cheating and swearing, while in "head comix," R. Crumb's Fritz the Cat, Mr. Natural, and other characters indulged in attitudes and acts that previously existed only in the nether regions of mainstream consciousness.

From the World War II years on, in fact, whatever young outsiders took as their own held an element of derision in it. Starting with the wartime "zoot suit," which mocked the proprieties of mainstream dress, young people "flaunted, celebrated, and exaggerated those things which prevailing social norms condemned." If they took the car for their own, they reshaped that symbol of mobility and family pleasure into the "hot rod," an exaggerated bundle of chrome and speed suitable for "joyriding," that is, sex and delinquency. When they took to the dance floor, as critic Barbara Ehrenreich has written, their music "bubbling up from America's invisible 'others' . . . mocked work ('Get a Job'), study ('Don't know much 'bout his-to-ry'), authority ('Charlie Brown, you're a clown'). It held out no professions, no career except that of the reckless 'Love Man,' not even a certainty of adulthood ('Teen Angel'). Its idea of time ('Rock Around the Clock') had nothing to do with a scheduled order of achievements."[12]

Against this youthful flaunting and haunting, adulthood proved unable to create a counterstory of its own. Witness page twelve of the February 23, 1957, *New York Times*, which carried a report that, at a meeting of the American Psychopathological Association, Dr. Joost Meerlo presented a new study suggesting a parallel between rock 'n' roll and St. Vitus Dance ("The Children's Crusades and the tale of the Pied Piper of Hamelin remind us," commented Dr. Meerlo, "of these seductive contagious dance furies. . . . A rhythmical call to the crowd easily foments mass ecstasy: 'Duce! Duce! Duce!' . . . as in drug addiction, a thousand years of civilization fall away in a moment. . . . We are preparing our own downfall in the midst of pandemic funeral dances").

There was also a brief report that "a more militant role by parent-teacher organizations in the fight against juvenile delinquency was recommended yesterday by a committee of junior high school principals," a briefer account of limits put on youthful bad habits ("Good Night to Kissing, Women's Hall at Michigan Puts Ban on Osculation"), a report on the sale of $20 million worth of Elvis Presley paraphernalia, and squeezed in at page bottom, an account of how "four teen-age winners of a 'Voice of Democracy' contest" had received from the Federal Communications Commission chairman $500 college scholarships "and gold recordings of their award-winning speeches."

Drawing these articles together was a continued-from-page-one piece—"Rock 'n' Roll Teen-Agers Tie up the Times Square Area, Line up at Theatre 18 1/2 Hours—175 Police Called"—with accompanying overhead photo of an antlike mass of teens barricaded in by a few policemen. The article reported not only the breaking of "previous records established for a week at the Paramount [theater] by Frank Sinatra, Nat King Cole, Dean Martin and Jerry Lewis," but "breakthroughs" of another kind. "They shouted, tried to crowd past policemen and burst screaming through wooden barriers set up to hold them in line. Policemen on horse-back were jeered as they galloped along ... trying to thwart break-throughs during the morning." The *New York Times* recorded various minor injuries, much messiness ("the street was littered with sand-wiches, apples and other lunch-box contents tossed at the police"), the shattering of a glass restaurant door and of the ticket seller's box, and—inside the theater—much screaming, "stamping" of feet in time to the music, and uncontrolled dancing "in the aisles, the foyer, and the lobby."[13]

The fascism of Mussolini, alien music, consumerism, medieval ill-ness, and juvenile crime were connected here only by the fact that teenagers had attended a "rock 'n' roll" show featuring popular black per-formers and emceed by a white radio deejay named Alan Freed. Events like this held a hint of horror because the more difficult a narrative was for adults to piece together, the more thrillingly coherent it seemed to teens. For the young, hysterical adult reactions confirmed the explana-tory powers of their new narratives.

In the 1950s, however, there were also adults who began to sense the drawing power of the stories emerging from teen culture and saw in them ways to take products directly into a new youth market. News of this market was brought to the corporate world almost single-handedly by someone just out of his teens. In 1945, as a nineteen-year-old college stu-dent, Eugene Gilbert set up Gil-Bert Teen Age Services in Chicago, employing teenagers to interview their own kind (who knew the species better?) and bringing news of their views, tastes, and purchasing power to businesses who had not had a clue. By the mid-1950s, Gilbert was run-ning four interlocking teen research organizations, had written a book, *Advertising and Marketing to Young People*, and was producing a weekly column ("What Young People Think") for newspapers nationwide. More important, he had convinced some of the nation's larger corporations that teens were the last marketing frontier, and that it was not teenagers but businesses who were aberrant if they did not take up the challenge.[14]

TEEN RIOTS AND MEDIA PANICS

On March 21, 1952, when Alan Freed, then a disc jockey for WJW in Cleveland, staged the nation's first live "rock 'n' roll" dance concert with an all-black cast of performers, what astonished him most were the more than 21,000 black and white teens drawn without significant advertising to an auditorium that had seating for only 10,000. The crowds so unnerved local authorities that they halted the concert halfway through, starting the first "teen riot" of the 1950s. In this way, a white DJ, a "nigger lover," launched "rock 'n' roll" as a dangerous national phenomenon.

By 1957, Freed had become the leading white promoter of rock and roll. His radio show could be heard on New York's WINS six nights a week, six-thirty to eleven, as well as on CBS radio stations nationally from nine to nine-thirty, and he had been successfully staging live concerts for five years. In his years of fame before he was felled by a rock riot in Boston and a "payola" indictment in New York, he often took credit for "inventing" rock and roll. Indeed, he was evidently the first to apply the term—a euphemism used by rhythm and blues singers for sexual intercourse—to the music, lending it an aura of newness rather than blackness that may have eased its way into the white world.[15]

But Freed was less inventor than invention. He had simply found himself at a tumultuous intersection where white adolescents were plunging into the cultural version of the secret world and black communities in search of promised freedoms were breaching the boundaries of containment. It was not Freed but white children in cities from New York to Los Angeles, Memphis to Atlanta, who first began to pick up unknown musical signals on the family radio.

Despite its centuries-long influence on American music, black music emerged from World War II in a particularly segregated and unequal state. The crooner-laden, family-oriented major record companies either did not produce black music at all or did so on small, separate "race" or "sepia" labels. Generally, such records could only be bought in stores in black communities and were not played on "white" radio or on most of the country's nearly half-million segregated juke boxes.

However, mainstream music had become bland and undanceable. Rosemary Clooney, Doris Day, and Perry Como were among established white singers of the day, and songs like "Oh, My Papa" and "Doggie in the Window," major hits. This was the horizonless music of suburban abundance, and it left an opening for independent record companies marketing black music to black audiences to reach into the white market. "Crying in the Chapel," Jubilee Records' 1953 hit by the black vocal group the Orioles, proved but an initial breakthrough in this regard.[16]

Meanwhile, as the 1950s began, radio stations were in chaos, their nonmusical content hemorrhaging into TV. With ratings plummeting, desperate stations opened themselves to almost any alien sound, particularly in the "empty" late-night hours, if an audience came with it. Whether Tex McCrary talked with Helen Gurley Brown about sex on campus, Jean Sheppard recalled his childhood, or Long John Nebel discussed UFOs, a new kind of uncensored talk beamed itself into the witching hours.

In addition, a mini-explosion of (mostly white-owned) black stations populated the far reaches of the radio dial as advertisers discovered the purchasing power of black audiences. On them, black DJs, playing R&B, blues, gospel, and jazz, began to offer up a galvanic, superheated style of broadcasting that drew on a heightened version of black speech. DJ Maurice Hulbert at Memphis's WDIA, for instance, was Maurice Hulbert, Jr., for the morning gospel show; Maurice the Mood Man for "Sweet Talkin' Time," a program "aimed at black housewives that emphasized mellow talk and sexy ballads"; and finally, jive-talking "Hot Rod," the "nighttime motor mouth" of the "Sepia Swing Club."[17]

In most cities, bored white teenagers could launch themselves on a voyage of discovery simply by fiddling with the radio dial. A random twist of the knob brought home a music guaranteed to shatter boredom. Rhythm and blues spoke openly of sexuality entangled with pain, and whatever tales it chose to tell, there was no way not to move your body. Though it spoke of a life experience alien to the white teenager, it spoke, too, of a situation in which thrills were to be torn from horror, which was comprehensible. In addition, the music that would become rock and roll was exciting because the singers were sometimes no older than the listeners.

If not for those unrecorded white hands fiddling the dial, Alan Freed would have continued playing classical music on "Record Rendezvous" at Cleveland's WJW. But Leo Mintz, whose record store sponsored the show, told Freed about white kids entering his shop in search of R&B and urged Freed to put the music on the air. So Freed tagged R&B onto the end of his classical program—until the requests started pouring in. Soon, he was calling himself "Moon Dog" and his program, "The Moon Dog Rock 'n' Roll House Party."

So black music and white teens took Freed over the top, and he never looked back or took anything but credit as the money began to roll in. But if Freed exploited his situation with gusto, he was no model of commerce. He dug the music too much, and throughout his career advanced black music and performers rather than the whitened versions of each being pushed by major record companies. In addition, as a grown-up, he was an unpalatable figure to institutionalize, representing an unsettling cross between a "white negro" and a sleazy salesman. At his stage shows, "he would appear in flashy clothes such as checkered sports coats and solid red jackets with silver buttons. He blew kisses to the audience and made his delivery with distorted vowels, in a raspy hoarse voice. He had a somewhat greasy look about him, with slight scarring on his face due to [an] auto accident."[18]

Freed's mix of pandering to, empathizing with, and exploiting young blacks and whites (and the music they were coming to share) would not be typical of the corporate producers of culture in the 1950s. Yet their response to the discovery that the young had spending money in their pockets and commercial minds of their own proved unnerving in its own right to adults, even as it reshaped youthful desires into acceptably tamer products. Unlike radio, the five major record companies, still geared to a "family" market, were initially unreceptive to the separate desires of a youth audience. So rock was largely left to small independent labels. In the mid-1950s, however, the majors began to move, ponderously at first, to appropriate this forbidden music and turn its "cannibal rhythms" into something more palatable.[19]

It was not just that they signed on some young, mainly white rock stars like Bill Haley and Elvis Presley (whose records sold 10 million copies, or 10 percent of the pop market in 1956), but that they turned their already extant stables of crooners into "rockers," providing toned down "white" versions of any black rock song that threatened to become popular. Even Pat Boone, with his suburban good looks and white buck shoes, found himself, somewhat to his dismay, riding simplified versions of Fats Domino's "Ain't That a Shame" and Little Richard's "Tutti Frutti" to gold record success. This custom (useful to radio stations that wanted to hold young white listeners without playing black music) was appropriately called "covering" a song. In the process, black singers were generally moved off the hit lists and back into the netherworld. In 1955, twenty of the top twenty-five records were by blacks; by 1958, only four of the top twenty-five represented black styles. Lyrics were cleaned up and new songs designed to reflect the least dangerous of teen desires. By decade's end, something still called "rock" was controlled by the major record companies, while the energy that had propelled audacious black musicians into the white teen world had been "covered."[20]

Like radio, the movie industry, too, was losing its dominant position as a family entertainment form, for television brought the screen conveniently to the viewer. Contributing to Hollywood's woes was a massive population shift from city to suburb, where only the drive-in theater, that breeding ground of hot-rod culture and teen sex, was available. In a decade and a half, audiences fell 50 percent from wartime highs and the studio system began to disintegrate. A sense of impending doom led the industry to gimmicks like 3-D, Cinerama, even AromaRama, to lure audiences back, and opened the movies up to dread and dissidence.[21]

No hearings, no outcry, no code of conduct could keep film producers from searching out the new teenage audience and putting images on screen that might thrill them. Although film production decreased by 25 percent in the early 1950s, the making of teenpics soared. Hollywood soon found itself supplying a teen market with prodigious numbers of cheap juvenile delinquency, rock and roll, dragstrip, sci-fi, and horror films starring teens. By the late 1950s, 52 percent of all moviegoers were under twenty.[22]

Though hemmed in by fears of congressional investigations and of adult outrage, Hollywood's moviemakers managed to produce in Marlon Brando's aimless biker in *The Wild One* (1954) and James Dean's middle-class *Rebel Without a Cause* (1955) appealing teen icons; while delinquents, as the historian James Gilbert has pointed out, were generally "pictured with enormous sympathy" and teens were invariably shown facing an adult society that did not understand their situation. Unlike early rock music or horror comics, teenpics—delinquency films, in particular—were, however, distinctly adult in their judgmental tone and in the punishments meted out for youthful misdeeds.[23]

TELEVISION DISCOVERS THE CHILD

Television, too, soon noticed its younger viewers, for by the end of the 1950s their existence on the marketing horizon was increasingly apparent. In 1958, for instance, a *Life* cover story bragged of "Rocketing Births: Business Bonanza." "In its kids," the article claimed, "U.S. has a recession remedy. . . . [T]he first of the postwar babies are beginning to constitute a huge market for teen-agers' goods and services."[24]

Although the TV set initially masqueraded as another piece of furniture, no household object had ever given off such an aura. It was as if some ghostly world were being called into existence right in the home. Like a cornucopia, it offered viewers miniaturized versions of all the forms of entertainment they had previously paid for—the dime novel, the pulp magazine, the comic, the minstrel show, vaudeville, the theater, the movies, the penny arcade, the parade, the political lecture, the newspaper, the newsreel, the police gazette, even the rodeo, the Wild West show, and the circus, and linked all of them to a purchasable vision of the good life.

In those years, the car and the TV became twin symbols of America's freedom to consume. With the car, one could consume space itself, go "freely" wherever the highway went in a state of comfort that increas ingly approximated home. No popular concept of freedom then existed without access to "wheels." Even the freedom of youthful rebellion was symbolized by the hot rod, the motorcycle, or minimally the thumb, which could propel you into the car and "on the road."

TV, however, offered an even more expansive kind of mobility, for one could miraculously go anywhere without leaving one's couch or bed. One could see the greatest show on earth for the one-time price of the screen-machine on which it was to be displayed. And what a vision was being given away! As television historian Erik Barnouw has written, "Every manufacturer was trying to 'upgrade' American consumers and their buying habits. People were being urged to 'move up to Chrysler.' Commercials showed cars and muffins and women to make the mouth water. A dazzling decor—in drama or commercial—could show what it meant to rise in the world."

By the mid-1950s, TV was taking its own message to heart. Sponsors were increasingly abandoning popular live drama series, which tended to focus on the grittier and more problematic aspects of everyday life for the "filmed episodic series of upbeat decor"; while ethnic urban comedies like *The Goldbergs* were being replaced by what critic David Marc has called "benevolent Aryan melodramas" like *Father Knows Best* and *The Adventures of Ozzie and Harriet*. Set in small towns or suburbs, these "transport[ed] the viewer to a kind of Eisenhower Walden." Show and ad now existed seamlessly in the same visual world. Never again would a working-class family like the Kramdens in *The Honeymooners* inhabit a living room furnished only with a single table, bureau, mini-icebox, and gas stove, or be so strapped for money that they couldn't afford a TV.[25]

An equivalent process took place in children's television. One way in which the new business first tried to get its $400–500 six-inch screen out of public spaces like bars and into family space was with the lure of wholesome children's programming, and soon enough the late afternoon hours came to seem like a vast puppet show inhabited by Howdy Doody, the Kuklapolitan Players, Rootie Kazootie, and other dolls, livelier in children's fantasies than any living character.

By decade's end, however, these dolls and puppets had all been swept aside with their grown-up hosts—the uncles, captains, and sheriffs from Buffalo Bob Smith to Soupy Sales. Early on, dressed up as cowboys, spacemen, or train engineers, but bearing some resemblance to sideshow barkers, they had served both as reassuring guides for the new child audience and pitchmen for sponsors' products. Though fascinating to children, they ill suited an environment meant to transmit the look of abundance that kiddie sponsors, too, wanted to sell with their products.

Although the first made-for-TV cartoon, the clever *Crusader Rabbit*, was not produced until 1950, children's television soon became a seamless landscape of fad-driven cartoons in which animated animals, spies, and assorted monsters chased each other into and out of increasingly stunning, animated ads. Here was a child's version of upbeat decor in which the selling of brand loyalty could proceed unimpaired.[26]

If TV offered the family a display window onto a glorious new world, its presence offered corporate advertisers a window into the home. A space previously impenetrable to the public gaze had been opened up to those with the necessary resources to "see" in. One of the first needs of television, then, was the means to see—that is, measure and gauge—the audience looking out. In 1950, the Neilsen Company, which already measured radio audiences, launched the Neilsen Television Index, issuing monthly show ratings based on a "mailable Audimeter" and an initial sample of three hundred households. By 1959, "Instantaneous Audimeter Service" was providing stations with overnight ratings. In this way, TV transformed the family into a commodity to be identified, measured, and sold to the sponsor via the "show."[27]

When television's sponsors looked into the family, one surprising discovery was the child as a separate consumer. From Shirley Temple dolls to Mickey Mouse paraphernalia, there had long been exploitable child-driven fads, but children had largely been approached as consumers through their parents' pocketbooks. If certain companies like cereal makers had advertised to "family" audiences on children's radio shows, direct advertising to children had been the most momentary, opportunistic, or marginal of activities for the most momentary, opportunistic, or marginal of products.

The comic book typified this. Its ads offered the young a two-bit con artist's version of the good life: get-rich-quick schemes ("Make Money! Get Prizes!"); instant methods for growing muscles, learning hypnotism, or developing breasts; collections of penny magic tricks, bags of nondescript toy soldiers, and worthless batches of foreign postage stamps. There was indeed something to upgrade here.

Advertisers moved slowly into children's TV. According to media historian J. Fred MacDonald, old B cowboy films and serials released into the late afternoon hours "played a key role in generating mass enthusiasm for the medium, especially among children," and first spurred the interest of bread, cereal, gum, and candy manufacturers. It was a cowboy, Hopalong Cassidy, with his "spine-tingling episodes never before shown on TV!" who first hinted at the market to come. In 1948, actor William Boyd gained TV rights to his old "Hoppy" movies and the right to make even more for television. He then parlayed his TV show into a host of celebrity endorsements and licensed products from jackknives (1 million

sold within ten days of their appearance) to black shirts for children—
"a singular marketing achievement since in American culture black
was associated with mourning or Italian Fascism." Other frontier figures
followed. Three hour-long *Disneyland* episodes on Davy Crockett in
1954–1955, for instance, produced a multimillion-dollar selling frenzy.[28]

However, the moment when those behind the screen first "saw" the
child as a separate market probably occurred in the fall of 1955. It was
then that Mattel, a small toy company, committed an unheard of half-
million dollars to reserve a weekly fifteen minutes of ad time on an hour-
long daily show Disney studios was developing for ABC. This commitment to the untested *Mickey Mouse Club* represented half the sum the
whole toy industry had previously put into all yearly advertising. The
new product Elliot and Ruth Handler, Mattel's owners, chose to push
was the Burp Gun, a cap gun "modeled after the machine guns used in
WWII jungle fighting." In early November 1955, their first ad showed the
son of the head of Mattel's ad agency stalking elephants in his living
room ("He never misses with that Burp Gun!"). Orders began flooding in
just after Thanksgiving. With the toy sold out in stores nationwide, President Eisenhower had to write Mattel directly requesting one for his
grandson. By Christmas, 1 million guns had been sold.

Two years later, the Handlers decided to test-market a fashion doll
with exaggerated breasts. Several hundred mothers and their children
were tested. The results, wrote former Mattel ad executive Cy Schneider,
"were astoundingly clear cut. Almost 100 percent of the mothers literally
hated the doll and felt it was too mature for their little girls. Most said
they would never buy it. Almost 100 percent of the girls, shown the doll
independent of their mothers, said they loved the doll and definitely
wanted to own it." Barbie was then launched via a TV ad campaign
aimed directly at the child, proving that the sponsor could now use the
television to bypass parents almost entirely and that toy lines might
thrive by having adult disapproval folded into them. Children might now
unnerve adults simply by buying a product.[29]

If sponsors and programmers recognized the child as an independent
taste center, the sight of children glued to the TV, reveling in their own
private communion with the promise of America, proved unsettling to
some adults. The struggle to control the set, the seemingly trancelike
quality of TV time, the soaring number of hours spent watching, could
leave a parent feeling challenged by some hard-to-define force released
into the home under the aegis of abundance, and the watching child
could gain the look of possession, emptiness, or zombification.

Fears of TV's deleterious effects on the child were soon widespread.
The medical community even discovered appropriate new childhood ill-

nesses. There was "TV squint" or eyestrain, "TV bottom," "bad feet" (from TV-induced inactivity), "frogitis" (from a viewing position that put too much strain on inner-leg ligaments), "TV tummy" (from TV-induced overexcitement), "TV jaw" or "television malocclusion" (from watching while resting on one's knuckles, said to force the eyeteeth inward), and "tired child syndrome" (chronic fatigue, loss of appetite, headaches, and vomiting induced by excessive viewing).

However, television's threat to the child was more commonly imagined to lie in the "violence" of its programming. Access to this "violence" and the sheer number of hours spent in front of the set made the idea that this new invention was acting *in loco parentis* seem chilling to some; and it was true that via westerns, crime shows, war and spy dramas, and Cold War–inspired cartoons TV was indiscriminately mixing a tamed version of the war story with invasive Cold War fears. Now, children could endlessly experience the thrill of being behind the barrel of a gun. Whether through the Atom Squad's three government agents, Captain Midnight and his Secret Squadron, various FBI men, cowboys, or detectives, they could also encounter "an array of H-bomb scares, mad Red scientists, [and] plots to rule the world," as well as an increasing level of murder and mayhem that extended from the six-gun frontier of the "adult" western to the blazing machine guns of the crime show.[30]

Critics, educators, and worried parents soon began compiling TV body counts as if the statistics of victory were being turned on young Americans. "Frank Orme, an independent TV watchdog, made a study of Los Angeles television in 1952 and noted, in one week, 167 murders, 112 justifiable homicides, and 356 attempted murders. Two-thirds of all the violence he found occurred in children's shows. In 1954, Orme said violence on kids' shows had increased 400 percent since he made his first report." PTAs organized against TV violence, and Senate hearings searched for links between TV programming and juvenile delinquency.

Such "violence," though, was popular. In addition, competition for audiences among the three networks had the effect of ratcheting up the pressures for violence, just as it had among the producers of horror comics. At *The Untouchables*, a 1960 hit series in which Treasury agent Eliot Ness took on Chicago's gangland (and weekly reached 5–8 million young viewers), ABC executives would push hard for more "action." Producer Quinn Martin would then demand the same of his subordinates, "or we are all going to get clobbered." In a memo to one of the show's writers, he asked: "I wish you would come up with a different device than running the man down with a car, as we have done this now in three different shows. I like the idea of sadism, but I hope we can come up with another approach to it."[31]

"A FLIMSY LITTLE TWO-LEGGED ANIMAL"

TV was a conundrum. Upsetting as its intrusion into the family could be, everything in the way it was organized was meant to mitigate against upset. First four, then three networks came to control the medium. Intent on offering sponsors the least jarring entertainment drawing the largest possible audiences, and policed by blacklisting publications and anti-Communist sponsors, network executives allowed few notes they recognized as discordant onto the air. TV's vision was largely exclusionary. In no other cultural medium were such efforts made to ignore any subject that might show the strain under which the American story was laboring. The question mark of the Korean War, which invaded the magazine, the novel, the war comic (where GIs began to die in prodigious numbers and sometimes unheroic ways), and the war film (where, as in *Retreat, Hell!* [1952], defeat came scarcely covered in the threadbare trappings of victory culture), made it into TV's ongoing fictions only with the appearance in 1972 of *M*A*S*H*.

Those figures of "Otherness" that rose to haunt society from within—the black, the beatnik, and the juvenile delinquent—were absent from TV's fictions. Even by 1950s' standards, television was white. As former CBS casting executive Ethel Winant recalled of its "Golden Years," "We never had any blacks on television. We never had a porter in a show. If a bag was carried, it was carried by a white conductor." Whites and blacks could be linked on screen only as master and servant, as a last name and a first name—Jack Benny and his manservant Rochester (*The Jack Benny Show*, 1950–1965) or the Hendersons and their maid Beulah (*Beulah*, 1950–1953)—and then rarely. In the movies, a black and a white, Sidney Poitier and Tony Curtis, could be yoked together as equals (*The Defiant Ones*, 1958), but not until Robert Culp and Bill Cosby hit the air as undercover agents in *I Spy* (1965) did television do anything similar. When NBC made crooner Nat "King" Cole the first black host of a weekly variety show in 1956, not one national sponsor could be found for him.[32]

In rare cases where racial issues arose, they could not be approached directly. Writer Reginald Rose, for example, proposed to CBS's *Studio One* a drama based on an incident in which white residents in a Cicero, Illinois, neighborhood had forced a newly arrived black family out. The outline was accepted with "one proviso. Network, agency, and sponsor were all firm about it. The black family would have to be changed to 'something else.' A Negro as beleaguered protagonist of a television drama was declared unthinkable." So the protagonist of "Thunder on Sycamore Street" became an exconvict.

The first interracial kiss did not arrive on television until November 22, 1968, and even then, at network insistence, *Star Trek*'s Captain Kirk had to turn his back to the camera to simulate placing it on Lieutenant Uhuru in outer space. Similarly, black music, by the mid 1950s a radio commonplace, made it onto network television from the waist up and by proxy only in the fall of 1956, when the upper half of Elvis Presley caused a national sensation on *The Ed Sullivan Show* (on which black musicians were not yet welcome), and in the following year as a vision of chaperoned whiteness when Dick Clark's *American Bandstand* went national. There, white teenagers, subjected to a dress and behavior code, danced in lackluster fashion to the latest hit records. The show was integrated—though barely—in 1957.[33]†

The beatnik never really made it onto TV at all, despite the fun poked at the lovable, dopey Maynard G. Krebs in *The Many Loves of Dobie Gillis* (1959–1963). Despite TV's multitude of comics, "sick" comedians like Lenny Bruce, Dick Gregory, and Mort Sahl, whose fast-talking "underground" nightclub acts were often an "angry response to mass society, the cold war, the indignities of Jim Crow, the denial of free speech, and a hypocritical web of traditions and taboos that gratuitously valorized religion and vilified sexuality," found no place on TV. The disintegrative force of Bruce's dirty acts and dirty words had no chance of making it past network Standards and Practices departments, while the hipster's cousin, the political radical, could be found on screen only as a dupe or enemy agent on shows like *I Led Three Lives*. As late as 1967, CBS censors cut singer Pete Seeger's performance of an anti–Vietnam War song, "Waist Deep in the Big Muddy," from *The Smothers Brothers Comedy Hour*, his first TV appearance in seventeen years.[35]

The juvenile delinquent appeared only in 1974 with the sweet, black-jacketed, but hardly rebellious "Fonzie" on *Happy Days*. The corrosive humor of *MAD* magazine (no less the stinging satire of singer Tom Lehrer or even the uncensored radio ramblings of a Jean Sheppard) had no place on the home screen until the arrival of the British-inspired satiric show, *That Was the Week That Was* in 1964, or even *Saturday Night*

---

†Alan Freed, too, tried his hand at a weekly TV show on CBS, but *Rock 'n' Roll Dance Party* was attacked for encouraging teen smoking (its sponsor was Camel cigarettes) and canceled when black singer Frankie Lymon of the Teenagers was shown dancing with a white girl. Presley's full body appeared on several shows including Milton Berle's, Steve Allen's, and Jackie Gleason's before Sullivan's. All received major ratings boosts as well as much invective. But it is the Sullivan camera angle that is remembered.[34]

Live in 1975. The horror comic and the science fiction movie, the 1950s genres that allowed the apocalyptic dreams of the age to be wrapped up in the Other from outer (or inner or under or in-between) space, did not reach TV until *The Twilight Zone* made its debut in 1959 (if one excepts *Alfred Hitchcock Presents* [1955–1965], an anthology show of terror and suspense in which evil often appeared victorious).

Well into the mid-1960s, TV was an ideological wagon train, circling constantly to ensure that it was the least haunted of entertainment forms. Yet its day-and-night commercial mission in family den or bedroom had an invasive feel to it. In any case, even out there in the safety of the "western" frontier, the story was being transformed almost imperceptibly into something less triumphantly American. The "adult western" burst onto the scene in 1955, sweeping aside its juvenile predecessors, as its car, cigarette, and beer sponsors swept aside the cereals, toys, and candy bars. In 1957, such shows took places 1, 2, 3, 4, 6, 7, and 10 in the cumulative yearly ratings, and they would dominate prime time into the next decade. Now, sheriffs like Marshall Matt Dillon in *Gunsmoke* entered saloons and downed drinks in the company of prostitutes, or like Gene Barry's *Bat Masterson* made the western hero into a "foppish dandy." Cowboys and gunslingers had assignations with women, married or not, and like James Garner's slick gambler *Maverick*, they could mock both themselves and a seedy, mean-spirited frontier world. They even began to take on some of the confusing trappings of the enemy. The hero could now dress in black and carry a card that said "Have gun, will travel" (as did Richard Boone's Palladin, that "knight without armor in a savage land"). With a sawed off carbine, like Steve McQueen's Josh Randall in *Wanted: Dead or Alive*, he could make a living as a bounty hunter, or even briefly in *Gunslinger* as an undercover agent—and be rewarded for it. Whether as a rootless wanderer or a soldier of fortune, TV's western hero, before the watching eyes of America, took his first cautious steps out of the "West" and into the shadows.[36]

At ten o'clock on Friday night, October 2, 1959, on CBS, a voice emerged from an image of spiraling galaxies to intone, "The place is here, the time is now, and the journey into the shadows that we're about to watch could be our journey." The show that followed about an amnesiac in an air force jumpsuit wandering through a deserted town was no better than workmanlike. (He proved to be a hallucinating astronaut-in-training in an isolation booth.) But at show's end, the same voice returned with riveting effect. "Up there, up there in the vastness of space, in the void that is sky, up there is an enemy known as isolation. It sits there in the stars, waiting, waiting with the patience of eons, forever waiting . . . in the Twilight Zone."

In a year when TV's top-rated shows were *Gunsmoke*, *Wagon Train*, and *Have Gun, Will Travel*, while *The Ed Sullivan Show* and *Father Knows Best* were still in the top twelve, TV made its initial foray into "the shadows." *The Twilight Zone* was the brainchild of Rod Serling, a writer who had made a reputation working for anthology series like *Playhouse 90* and had felt the narrow limits of the advertiser-driven medium. In one political drama for *Studio One*, Serling was to recall, "I was not permitted to have my Senators discuss any current or pressing problem. . . . In retrospect, I probably would have had a much more adult play had I made it science fiction, put it in the year 2057, and peopled the Senate with robots."

In 1958, Serling did just that, pitching a science fiction series to CBS whose premise would be "fear of the unknown working on you, which you cannot share with others." With CBS's agreement, television, for the first time, knowingly slipped into the territory of the science fiction film and horror comic. The inclusionist liberalism of the program fed on repeated visions of nuclear terror ("Underneath it all, behind the eyes of the men, hanging invisible over the summer night, is a horror without words. For this is the stillness before storm. This is the eve of the end"), on identity and boundary confusion (robots that couldn't be told from humans), on the alien within us ("[A] thoughtless, frightened search for a scapegoat has a fallout all its own—for the children, and the children yet unborn. And the pity of it is that these things cannot be confined to the Twilight Zone"), and on the cutting of Man down to just another creature caged in a local zoo on some distant planet ("You're looking at a species of flimsy little two-legged animal with extremely small heads whose name is Man"). All this was reinforced by a voice already familiar to childhood, a gatekeeper's voice whose dry, derisive tone hid a leveling laughter ("Practical joke wearing the trappings of nightmare, of terror, of desperation. Small human drama played out in a desert ninety-seven miles from Reno, Nevada, U.S.A., continent of North America, the Earth, and of course—the Twilight Zone").

While the show never broke into the top twenty-five, it built strong fan loyalty, drawing the liberal and the professional, but especially the young, to the underside, where they could thrill to the dismantling fear and confusion that lay in some secret world or at the end of time. "The appeal to children was a complete surprise to us," commented producer Buck Houghton. "We never thought of that. I don't think CBS did either; it was on at ten o'clock. We got a lot of nasty notes from parents saying, 'You're keeping the kids up.'" Not surprisingly, they also got lots of letters from teenagers, for in *The Twilight Zone*, the young recognized a voice of their own.[37]

In February 1962, speaking before the American Bar Foundation, the

Kennedy administration's Secretary of Defense Robert McNamara, like his president, summoned Americans into a darkling wilderness where the enemy lurked. Citing Soviet Premier Nikita Khrushchev's statement of support the previous year for "wars of liberation" in the Third World, he invited the country to support un-American acts in wars that were "often not wars at all." "In these conflicts," McNamara said, invoking a phrase Serling had already thrillingly appropriated, "the force of world Communism operates in a twilight zone between political subversion and quasi-military action. Their military tactics are those of the sniper, the ambush, and the raid. Their political tactics are terror, extortion, and assassination. We must help the people of the threatened nations to resist."[38]

Among those who would answer McNamara's call, even if in unexpected ways, were the teenage viewers of Serling's show. Soon, they would be playing out scenarios as ancient as the first hauntings of American history, as recent as Cold War terrors, as familiar as war games in back yards, as strange as those in any horror comic. As "Indian fighters" and "Indians," as interrogators and resistors, as warriors, defectors, and captives, as the brainwashed and as monsters, they would reveal shadow spaces only hinted at in the stories Americans had so recently told themselves and the world. As Rod Serling would have said, "Next stop, the Twilight Zone."

5

Entering the Twilight Zone

BY 1953, THE UNITED STATES had close to 1,000 A-bombs, H-bombs, and tactical nuclear weapons. In 1962, during the Cuban missile crisis, President John F. Kennedy commanded 112 sea-launched ballistic missiles, 284 land-based intercontinental ballistic missiles (ICBMs), 105 intermediate range ballistic missiles, and 659 nuclear-armed B-52s; while Soviet Premier Nikita Khrushchev, as historian Geoffrey Perret has noted, had only "150 long-range bombers of dubious worth and 35 ICBMs of proven unreliability." As it turned out, this was just the beginning. The Kennedy administration funded a 60 percent buildup of strategic nuclear forces as well as "battlefield" nuclear weapons, like a miniaturized atomic bomb two GIs could fire from a rocket launcher.

Certain military men had long considered a nuclear first strike against the Soviet Union. As early as 1950, the Strategic Air Command's Curtis E. LeMay urged the implementation of SAC Emergency War Plan 1-49, which involved delivering "the entire stockpile of atomic bombs . . . in a single massive attack," 133 A-bombs on 70 Soviet cities in 30 days. Such plans only grew more awesome. SAC's aim later that decade became the destruction of "more than 100 Soviet cities and towns, plus 645 military installations, in a single crushing strike . . . [in] less than a day."[1]

The Russians were as incapable of warding off such an attack as they were of delivering their minimalist arsenal to American shores. In fact, when *Life* magazine first tried to imagine such a scenario in 1949, the best it could come up with was the smuggling of a bomb into the country. Undramatic photos of a merchant ship and trucks on a highway were captioned, "Russian freighter unloads her cargo unmolested in U.S. port.

Atomic bombs could be exploded at dockside or transferred to trucks to be driven to target." In the mid-1950s, the Pentagon was still seriously considering defenses against similar scenarios.

Although the Soviet Union test-fired the world's first ICBM in August 1957 (two months before it sent aloft the first satellite), and John F. Kennedy slipped into the presidency in part by decrying a "missile gap," Soviet delivery systems were hardly in better shape in January 1961 than they had been twelve years earlier. Given the Soviet decision not to build a first generation of ICBMs, the ship-and-truck option was still probably their best bet—and President Kennedy soon knew it. Photographs from the new *Discoverer* satellite proved definitive. The Soviets had only 4 operational missiles, not the 50–500 of various intelligence estimates.[2]

As Robert McNamara was to learn just before becoming secretary of defense, the military's secret plan for blowing away the Communist world—2,500 targets in Eastern Europe, Russia, China, and North Korea—would have resulted in an estimated 360 million casualties without response, a one-way massacre so chilling that McNamara was stunned. While President Kennedy, in an interview in 1962, indicated that there were circumstances under which the United States might launch a first strike, these were idle words. No president proved willing to loose the massive one-way attack that seemed the logic of U.S. strategy, just as the many plans and threats, public and private, to use atomic weaponry in more "minor" ways in Iran, Korea, China, Indochina, and elsewhere "on the periphery" were never carried out.[3]

Constraints already existed to the implementation of this finale to the spectacle of slaughter. To deliver such a sneak attack would have made a mockery of victory culture. Although any plan—from a convulsive first strike to the use of nuclear weapons on Third World battlefields—always had its high-level proponents, and a number seemed to come within a hairsbreadth of happening, none ever did.

U.S. officials expressed this unexpected sense of constraint on their ability to make war to the fullest in two ways. First, they translated their hesitations into fears of how "our allies" or "the world" would react to the use of such weaponry. British Prime Minister Clement Atlee's cross-Atlantic rush to dissuade President Truman from using A-bombs in Korea attested to allied fears of U.S. nuclear intentions (and of the outbreak of World War III in Europe). However, as French requests for nuclear support in Indochina indicated, desires for the weaponry to be used also existed. Whatever other countries' fears and desires, a deeper restraining impulse was at work.[4]

The second way these constraints were expressed was as a form of hardheaded cost analysis and pragmatic puzzlement. This came into play whenever the possibility arose of bringing atomic weaponry to bear in the Third World. Once a first strike against the Soviet Union had been ruled out, upon what or whom could the bomb be dropped to offer a reasonable return on investment? Russian forces occupying northern Iran? A set of bridges over the Yalu River? The jungle around the besieged French outpost of Dienbienphu? ("You could take all day to drop a bomb. . . . No opposition. And clean those Commies out of there and the band could play the Marseillaise and the French would come marching out . . . in fine shape," recalled Air Force Chief Nathan Twining, who supported the use of three A-bombs there in 1954. "And those Commies would say, 'Well, those guys may do this again to us. We'd better be careful.'") But each place chosen that was not the Soviet Union seemed ludicrously disproportionate for weapons systems geared to wipe out large cities.[5]

That "deterrence" existed before any deterrent force came into being was the determining fact of the Cold War. Although critics of government policy making have been struck by revelations of how many times the United States considered using atomic weapons, the post-Nagasaki inability to use them, even when they resembled more ordinary weapons like artillery shells or land mines, was far more significant. The atomic stalemate preceded by well over a decade the Soviet nuclear strike force that was its explanation (and even briefly the development of "deterrence theory"), reflecting the limits of what the American story, American national identity, could withstand.

By the late 1950s, much of the public was aware that an atomic attack could not be restricted to its target. Strontium 90 and other radioactive elements released in aboveground bomb tests had traveled invisibly thousands of miles to land on the grass American cows ate and so entered the milk American children drank. Imagine, then, the effects on the United States of a massive first strike on enemy territory. In the long run, there was no way Americans could be protected from their country's greatest weapons except by an unpalatable program of disarmament (as a few peace organizations urged).

America's proudest technological achievement, its victory weapon, was driven into invisibility. Atomic secrecy was guaranteed through the Atomic Energy Act of 1946. Later, bomb tests went underground, as did nuclear missiles, while carefully crafted "friendly atom" propaganda covered over much evidence of the bomb's baleful effects on human health. Presidents spoke circumspectly, at best, of atomic policy, and the military's first-strike plans were so secret that even a secretary of defense might be kept partially in the dark about them.[6]

The weapons that should have been a boon to Americans and a terror to any enemy proved instead an embarrassment that had to be buried. To display them proudly in one's own country, no less brandish them abroad, was to shatter an image of "national security" crucial for domestic audiences. Yet if not openly tested for use and used, atomic arms radiated a sense of weakness, not strength.†

From the long rifle to the B-26, American arms had been a source of pride. The lopsided statistics of victory were always seen as due, in part, to the technological inventiveness of Americans. When fused with the character of the frontiersman or the jungle fighter, advanced weaponry made a one-against-many story possible, and there was nothing faintly shameful in that. Now, the uselessness of the nuclear arsenal became the unbearable and shameful torment around which global policy had to be built. Somehow, the enemy had to be convinced that tough-minded leaders would not hesitate to bring into play the very weapons they hesitated to use in conflicts from Berlin to Korea.

As the Eisenhower White House struggled in the post–Korean War years to keep military expenditures under control, policy makers fell back on the threat of the bomb. As Secretary of State John Foster Dulles spelled it out in 1954, the United States was not to respond to each thrust and jab of "the mighty landpower of the Communist world," but react "vigorously at places and with means of its own choosing"; with, in the euphemistic language of the time, "the further deterrent of massive retaliatory power." In other words, the United States was officially committing itself to turn conflicts with the enemy, large or small, anywhere in the world, into one-sided nuclear wars.[8]

---

†Paradoxically, in the wake of the Cuban missile crisis and the Atomic Test Ban Treaty of 1963, when a new generation of Soviet missiles first posed an actual threat to the United States, the nuclear issue disappeared from popular culture and political debate. The last end-of-the-world films appeared in 1964, fantasies of the nuclear destruction of America ceased in the media, and the bomb shelter program evaporated. By the mid-1960s, the nuclear issue proved of almost no interest to anyone. Even the National Committee for a SANE Nuclear Policy relegated nuclear matters to a back seat. "At a SANE executive board meeting in 1966, a catch-all entry called 'Disarmament—Nuclear Tests—Non-Proliferation' appeared far down on a long agenda otherwise given over to Vietnam and related issues." By 1969, SANE went so far as to eliminate "Nuclear" from its name. As soon as the extermination of Americans moved from futuristic fantasy to conceivable reality, it was repressed from national consciousness, not to resurface until the late 1970s.[7]

PAPER TIGERS AND GREEN BERETS

Such thinking appalled the Kennedy generation of war strategists, particularly future Secretary of State Henry Kissinger and future Kennedy military adviser General Maxwell Taylor. Taylor had been especially pained in the Eisenhower years to see money that might have gone into army coffers commandeered by the air force, simply because it then controlled the nuclear arsenal. To up-and-coming civilian strategists at universities and in government-supported think tanks, Dulles's "massive retaliation" seemed like a formula for paralysis. It offered policy makers no alternatives between the inconceivable—"a general atomic war in which there could be no real victory"—and the impossible—an acceptance of defeat locally around the globe.

According to General Taylor, the United States needed a more "flexible response" that could deal with Communist-inspired "brushfire wars" in the Third World without resort to nuclear weapons; one that, by recreating the preconditions for more "limited" styles of engagement, could "restore to warfare its historic justification as a means to create a better world upon the successful conclusion of hostilities." Here was an attempt at the level of military strategy to drive global slaughter underground, to relocate the first strike in the conceptual silo of last resort through an un-American act of self-conscious suppression.[9]

Previously, while warfare had been limited by the weaponry available and the state's ability to mobilize its resources, victory had been an endlessly expansive concept. With weapons of seemingly limitless destructive capacity, however, the idea of victory began to shrink. Soon, both superpowers would have to tacitly agree to restrict their struggles to areas where each could strive for a victory that would be largely symbolic of what could not now be done with abandon. Containment would become a policy directed at oneself—with the enemy's unspoken agreement.

As RAND's William Kaufmann, an early theorist of limited warfare, wrote in the mid-1950s, such wars would "perform a function midway between the abstractness of a show of force and the terrible concreteness of annihilative conflict. They [would] become partial or token tests of strength . . . indices of relative power." What they could not bring about was "a radical alteration in the distribution of power." No longer would a symbolic story be derived from warfare, for warfare itself had entered the realm of the symbolic. Previously, the ambush had been the small thing, merely representative of the vastness of the enemy's exterminatory desires. Now, victory would be the small thing, emblematic of a lost past of triumph.[10]

Limited war was a response to an odd fear: that America's vast power might make it a mockery in the world. As the enemy "nibbled away" at "the periphery of the Free World" through "indirect nonovert aggression" in lands convulsed by "revolution," they might be laughing as well as fighting. Indeed, there was evidence that such an attitude existed on "the other side." In a "talk" with journalist Anna Louise Strong in 1946, Mao Zedong had declared that "the atom bomb is a paper tiger with which the U.S. reactionaries try to terrify the people. It looks terrible, but in fact is not. Of course, the atom bomb is a weapon of mass destruction, but the outcome of a war is decided by the people, not by one or two new weapons."

In 1957, in Moscow to celebrate the fortieth anniversary of the Russian Revolution, Mao announced that "the international situation has now reached a new turning point. There are two winds in the world today: the East wind and the West wind. . . . I think the characteristic of the situation today is the East wind prevailing over the West wind." He then returned to his imagery of 1946, asking rhetorically, "Wasn't Hitler a paper tiger? Wasn't he overthrown? . . . U.S. imperialism has not yet been overthrown and it has the atom bomb, but I believe it too is a paper tiger and will be overthrown."[11]

The "limited war" theorists and Pentagon managers who moved into Washington in 1961 took the Chinese leadership's refusal to fear the bomb and its unabashed support for Third World "wars of liberation" quite seriously. Many of them read Mao for tips on guerrilla war, and he confirmed what was already in their hearts. For years, a number of them had, in effect, been saying that the United States was a paper tiger. Though they would hardly have put the matter in such terms, they saw their task as that of shoring up victory culture against a derisive voice still identified with the enemy, and so they chose an exaggerated, "hardheaded," tough-talking international style meant to counteract the slippage in U.S. prestige they felt they detected. To the new president and his associates, "weakness" was the only sin. Their love of "toughness" projected something like the bullying (and implicitly self-pitying) style of the HUAC investigator onto global politics. They were determined to make U.S. power "credible" again. But reestablishing "credibility"—a word that arrived with the new administration—proved problematic.

Behind a chorus of "determination" and "will" as well as a virtual cult of credibility lay a nagging sense of loss. This would become far clearer in the language of U.S. officials later in the decade as the war in Vietnam dragged on. "To prevent a situation from arising in which 'no nation can ever again have the same confidence in American promise or in American protection' is how President Johnson put it at a news conference in July of 1965," wrote Jonathan Schell. "To 'avoid humiliation' is how Assistant Secretary of Defense John McNaughton put it in a memo in January of 1966. To shore up 'the confidence factor' is how Assistant Secretary of State William Bundy put it in a speech in January of 1967. To prevent 'defeat and humiliation' is how President Nixon put it in a speech in November of 1969."[12]

Even in the Kennedy years, defending the credibility of U.S. power or its "reputation" proved a pale substitute for victory. Victory had been a self-evident state. If you looked at your humbled enemy, it was only for confirmation of what you already knew about yourself. Buried in credibility, however, was doubt. You now had to stare into enemy eyes to gauge your success, to see your national self. In other words, a certain power over the war story was being placed in enemy hands. It was no longer simply a matter of how Americans saw themselves or organized their own story but of the credibility others gave its account.

The Kennedy administration entered office with a sense that America, which should everywhere have been dominant, was everywhere in "crisis." The expansive, free, and mobile society identified with trail and highway, covered wagon and car, seemed paralyzed as the Eisenhower years ended. In his electoral campaign, Kennedy used his vigor and youth, his war record, his book *Profiles in Courage*, and Walt Rostow's telling phrase, "Let's get this country moving again," to establish *his* credibility as a man with a "can-do" look, a man with an eye to the future.

"What are we doing about guerrilla warfare?" was one of the new president's first questions. A devotee of limited war, he was aware that "a total solution is impossible in the nuclear age," and he understood that the United States faced a revolutionary new style of struggle. As he told Congress in May 1961, the enemy's "aggression is more often concealed than open. They have fired no missiles; and their troops are seldom seen. They send arms, agitators, aid, technicians, and propaganda to every troubled area. But where fighting is required, it is usually done by others, by guerrillas striking at night, by assassins striking alone . . . by subversives and saboteurs and insurrectionists, who in some cases control whole areas inside of independent nations."[13]

Kennedy proceeded to launch an unprecedented buildup of nuclear and conventional arms to give himself "flexibility" at every level. In addition, he raised the army's budget, insisting that it put aside scenarios of mega-war in Europe to lead the nation in the creation of new story material in the Third World. For fifteen years, U.S. leadership of the Free World had been uncontested, but the banner of freedom had been anchored in a war narrative increasingly ancient in feel. Now, succeeding a former general who valued CIA-style operations and took pride in keeping the country out of a traditional shooting war, Kennedy proclaimed the opening of a "new frontier." He would publicly take Americans, banners flying, into the "shadows," into the "gray areas" of the globe.

As the skills of the Indian had once provided a model for a Daniel Boone, so the revolutionary guerrilla would provide a model for the modern frontier fighter. Kennedy searched the writings of Mao Zedong and the Cuban revolutionary Che Guevara (as well as army guerrilla warfare manuals) for hints on how to construct his new frontiersman. He was determined to create a Natty Bumpo for the netherworld not from the quasi-warriors of the CIA (who had brought him the pain of defeat on Cuban beaches at the Bay of Pigs fiasco), but from the regular army. His new "counterinsurgency" warrior would be someone who could be mythologized and publicized rather than hidden in a cloak of secrecy and deniability that looked like shame.

Although the army had developed special forces for guerrilla forays behind enemy lines in World War II and had set up guerrilla units with an eye to future battles in Eastern Europe in the early 1950s, the Special Forces were anything but an elite unit in the Eisenhower years. No one who desired career advancement joined them at a time when the military wanted to have as little as possible to do with secret struggles in far-off lands.

To neutralize bureaucratic resistance to his counterinsurgency ideas, Kennedy formed a cabinet-level Special Group on Counter-Insurgency, which included his brother Attorney General Robert Kennedy and General Maxwell Taylor (whom the president brought out of retirement). Against the desires of the Joint Chiefs, he ensured that extra Pentagon funds would flow to the Special Forces, that their numbers would increase, and that they would have first access to the latest in weaponry.

Kennedy also proclaimed them his "favorite unit" and attended to their provisioning from head to foot. Over military opposition, he allowed them to wear flashy green berets and "personally supervised the selection of new equipment—the replacement of heavy, noisy combat boots with sneakers . . . and when the sneakers proved vulnerable to bamboo spikes, their reinforcement with flexible steel inner soles." At his orders, the "Green Berets" were the first military unit put into the field in Vietnam and soon became the media's military outfit of choice. There they did double duty, slipping invisibly through the jungles of

Vietnam, "preserving American liberty" in familiar frontier ways, while moving visibly through an imagistic world back home, mobilizing opinion in favor of limited war.[14]

As cultural historian John Hellmann has written, "By 1962 . . . [a]rticles depicted this hero striding forward from the walled city of containment and massive retaliation into the thrilling woods of America's mission." A *Saturday Evening Post* piece on these "Harvard Ph.D.'s of warfare," "Hot Weapon in the Cold War" by journalist Joseph Kraft, was typical. Its initial photo of Green Berets on a pontoon raft "paddling straight at the reader . . . like a canoe full of Rogers' Rangers emerging from the forest streams of the American past . . . was juxtaposed with the subheading 'At President Kennedy's urging, the Army is beefing up its Special Forces, the politico-military experts who are trained to combat Red guerrillas around the globe.'" These new rangers, Kraft emphasized, had "a detailed knowledge of weapons ranging from the bow and arrow to the howitzer." They would be capable of forest coups abroad and publicity coups at home.[15]

President Kennedy was determined to mobilize young Americans for a new type of warfare to be fought only to limited conclusions and largely beyond public view. As someone "born in this century, tempered by war, disciplined by a hard and bitter peace, [and] proud of our ancient heritage," he made an inaugural address that was a riveting example of triumphalist despair. He (or his speech writers) caught the upbeat sunniness of the inherited war story and mixed it with the downbeat, yet adrenalizing horrors of the postwar world to send a special message to "a new generation of Americans."

With almost his first words, Kennedy launched his presidency under the sign of the bomb, invoking its "power to abolish . . . all forms of human life." The bomb was the speech's presiding deity, its unlimited horror invoked six times in a few brief minutes: "before the dark powers of destruction unleashed by science engulf all humanity in planned or accidental self-destruction," "the spread of the deadly atom . . . that uncertain balance of terror that stays the hand of mankind's final war," and so on.

Such phrases had populated cautionary science fiction films for a decade. In Kennedy's eerie inaugural vision, all peoples, even those blessed with freedom and abundance, already inhabited a sci-fi world under the bomb. In this potential tomb-world, "in the hour of maximum danger," he called upon the representatives of freedom and unfreedom to "begin anew the quest for peace" among "people in the huts and villages of half the globe struggling to break the binds of mass misery." There, in a new-style global wilderness, Communist savages would be faced down in new forms of struggle. Though weaponry "sufficient beyond doubt" would still be needed, warfare might also occur on a battlefield labeled "peace," where "cooperation" would have its own "beachheads."

"Now," the new president called out stirringly, "the trumpet summons us again—not as a call to bear arms, though arms we need—not as a call to battle, though embattled we are—but a call to bear the burden of a long twilight struggle . . . a struggle against the common enemies of man: tyranny, poverty, disease and war itself." Although in this mobilizing speech, peace and peaceful struggle were emphasized, "peace" was now an aspect of a strange, new war story being assembled for an underground world.

From the beginning, the president called upon the young to enter the nether regions fearlessly to help him revivify that story. When he told a generation to "ask not what your country can do for you—ask what you can do for your country," he also reminded his listeners that "the graves of young Americans who answered the call to service surround the globe." But whatever the dangers, the mobilization he had in mind was a limited one, as befitted the sort of war he imagined needed to be fought.[16]

The young responded enthusiastically to his invitation to a "twilight struggle," and he quickly placed in the glare of public approval two twilit outfits for them to join—the Green Berets and the Peace Corps. As the counterinsurgent warrior was to meld in with the natives, bringing armed "civic action" and communal good works to the revolution-endangered, so the "idealistic, patriotic, freedom-loving, adventuresome youths" of the Peace Corps were to live alongside peoples threatened by the enemy's revolutionary false promises. Simply by virtue of growing up in the most advanced country on earth (and with the aid of an eight-week training course including congressionally mandated instruction in the "philosophy, strategy, tactics, and menace" of communism), these college graduates would perform "modern miracles." Through "community development" they would not only start those in "misery" on the upward path to abundance, but inoculate them against the virus of communism.

Like the Green Berets, the Peace Corps would be a new force for the limited battles to come on the peripheries. As Kennedy had said only a week before his election, "On the other side of the globe, teachers, doctors, technicians, and experts desperately needed in a dozen fields by underdeveloped nations are pouring forth from Moscow to advance the cause of world communism. . . . I am convinced that our young men and women, dedicated to freedom, are fully capable of overcoming the efforts of Mr. Khrushchev's missionaries who are dedicated to undermining that freedom." Even the name, the Peace Corps, resonated with the militarized confusions of this new struggle. In choosing it over the complaints of State Department bureaucrats, its director Sargent Shriver, the president's brother-in-law, "deprived the Communists of their virtual monopoly of the word 'peace.'"[17]

Although both outfits were important for the mobilization of public enthusiasm at home, the actual number of young frontiersmen would prove infinitesimally small. While the secret world of the spy, agent, intelligence analyst, and quasi-warrior continued to grow by leaps and bounds, the public face of limited war proved limited indeed. Despite the wash of admiration for both units and a surfeit of volunteers, the Green Berets grew by only a few thousand in the Kennedy years, while the Peace Corps reached its peak at 15,556 in 1966.[18]

Perhaps no generation in recent memory had been more deeply primed to be called to service than the maligned "soft" generation of the 1950s. When Kennedy reopened the Third World as a frontier area servicing the American dream, the response was instantaneous, and like the war that followed, it split along class lines. The Peace Corps would be the domain of young (mainly white) college graduates, the children of bunker culture, and would be viewed by the State Department as a suspect organization. Indeed, some of those who engaged in community organizing overseas on the government payroll would soon find themselves in a nearly oppositional relationship to officialdom. Similarly, the Green Berets would be frowned upon by the regular military and, like the Peace Corps, gain a rebellious aura. There, the previously troublesome juvenile delinquent, now a working-class idealist, could become a shadow ambassador/adviser to peoples under siege, combining the innocence of do-good civic action with the innocent blow-'em-away sensibility of American film. Like his president, he would be a caring warrior without an ounce of weakness.

In an era when "freedom" meant that, someday, consumer goods might rain down without surcease, the Peace Corps volunteer and the Green Beret alike were to enter an invisible struggle for the patience of the world's nonwhite populations. They were to offer American-style hope and practice American-style containment until, as former MIT professor and Kennedy adviser Walt W. Rostow was predicting, "developing" nations in the "first stage of economic growth" experienced American-style "takeoff." Counterinsurgency, whether imagined as limited war or limited peace, in the figure of the Green Beret or the Peace Corps volunteer, was to ameliorate and channel global desire. It was to stop "outside agitators" from " 'confiscat[ing] the revolution of rising expectations' by exploiting the growing pains of Third World nations."[19]

MOBILIZING YOUTH

What President Kennedy wanted was not a true generational mobilization, which might have threatened loss of control, but the look of mobilization to shore up the credibility of American power. Both the Green Berets and the Peace Corps were, in fact, marginalized once their presence had been widely publicized. If, however, the government was only willing to mobilize a few thousand young people, there were millions more with "rising expectations," ready to undertake some idealistic task, and a far more mobilizing call to national service had preceded Kennedy's into existence.

By the end of the 1950s, blacks were organizing not just to challenge white supremacy in the South but to demand that the United States live up to its "promises" nationally. The developing crisis over segregation and the growth of a civil rights movement ready to "fight" for freedom brought from the shadows the group that had always fit least comfortably the story's boundaries. This unexpected—and largely unwanted—mobilization of a previously invisible populace in the name of freedom and in a struggle against patience threatened to create a limitless space at the heart of the American experience.

What else was the Montgomery bus boycott of 1955, if not a local mobilization and a call to "arms." A home front population committed itself to undergo sacrifice and deprivation in order to provide front-line troops with transportation, funds, support systems, and food. This might have been a World War II scenario—or a guerrilla one, for the war front and the home front were located in the same place, and the fighters and their supporters were drawn from the same populace.

The rolling series of unofficial mobilizations that were the civil rights movement touched the same sense of idealism as Kennedy's twilight units, but the impulse came from elsewhere. If Kennedy's goal was to impose limits abroad, the civil rights movement's was to lift them at home. If Kennedy wanted to use public relations to jump-start the war narrative at the peripheries, the civil rights movement wanted to use bodies, white as well as black, to jump-start a new freedom narrative in the United States. Against such potentially destabilizing "nonviolence," the Kennedy administration found itself fighting a rear guard action.

In 1963, Martin Luther King, Jr., in an open letter from his jail cell in Birmingham, Alabama, addressed "moderate" white clergymen who had urged him to rein in "unwise and untimely" demonstrations. In response to their cautionary pieties, he cited the ways nonwhite peoples abroad were freeing themselves from colonial limits to advocate the immediate removal of limits at home.

> We have waited for more than 340 years for our constitutional and God-given rights. The nations of Asia and Africa are moving with jet-like speed toward gaining political independence, but we still creep at horse-and-buggy pace toward gaining a cup of coffee at a lunch counter. . . . We will win our freedom because the sacred heritage of our nation and the eternal will of God are embodied in our echoing demands. . . . One day the South will know that when these disinherited children of God sat down at lunch counters, they were in reality standing up for what is best in the American dream . . . thereby bringing our nation back to those great wells of democracy which were dug deep by the founding fathers in their formulation of the Constitution and the Declaration of Independence.[20]

A new, spontaneous, nonviolent mobilization of the young had indeed begun three years earlier, on February 1, 1960, when four black college students placed their bodies at a lunch counter in Greensboro, North Carolina. As sit-ins, kneel-ins, and wade-ins spread across the South, the leadership of the civil rights movement passed, in part, into the hands of idealistic black students, prefiguring other youthful mobilizations to come. The Student Nonviolent Coordinating Committee (SNCC), established in April of that year, declared in its brief founding statement, "By appealing to conscience and standing on the moral nature of human existence, nonviolence nurtures the atmosphere in which reconciliation and justice become actual possibilities."

In the youthful mobilizations of blacks (and some whites) that would fill buses, churches, jails, and streets, "the sacred heritage of America"— "justice" and "freedom"—was constantly held up to view. However, even in the seemingly simple slogan "Freedom Now" lay an unmeetable demand—that government and society support a new version of the American story, purged of the war story's exclusionary boundaries. Nothing made the youth mobilizations of the time more unsettling than this demand that the limits the war story imposed on freedom be rejected.

Though a language of battle would be used—"a new army of young people . . . would . . . invade the Deep South"—its reference point was not Indian fighting but that civil war at home whose "reconciliatory" celebrations had gone on too long. "We will march through the South, through the Heart of Dixie, the way Sherman did," wrote SNCC president John Lewis (in lines censored from his speech at the March on

Washington in 1963). "We shall pursue our own 'scorched earth' policy and burn Jim Crow to the ground—nonviolently. We shall crack the South into a thousand pieces and put them back together in the image of democracy."[21]†

"Put your body on the line" was a slogan of the Freedom Riders in 1962, and young bodies would be in motion everywhere, largely unbidden and unaided by adults. In the early 1960s, young whites, too, began to mobilize, not just in Africa or Latin America, but in sizable numbers in the South for Freedom Rides, Freedom Schools, and Freedom Summer, then nationwide. In 1963, inspired by SNCC, a small group of white radicals calling themselves Students for a Democratic Society (SDS) joined this larger movement, setting up an Economic Research and Action Project, whose goal was to build an interracial movement of the poor. Through scattered, underfunded pilot projects among poor or unemployed whites and blacks, these SDSers attempted to create a Peace Corps of their own meant to bring poverty and racial oppression out of an American twilight zone. Aware that they were a minuscule "minority" even on campus, they nonetheless dreamed of "stimulating" a "social movement . . . in campus and community across the country."

On June 12 of the previous year, fifty-nine of them—students, civil rights activists, children of the old left, and even a few union and leftist elders—had met for three days at an AFL-CIO workers' camp in Port Huron, Michigan, to develop a platform for "a new kind of politics." To

---

†It was hardly surprising that a group for whom the war narrative offered no place would attempt to purge it from American consciousness or that young white radicals, involved with and inspired by the civil rights movement, would do the same. However, for a tiny minority of white radicals another explanation may, in part, be in order. A few of the founders of Students for a Democratic Society and other early New Leftists had either been "red diaper babies" (that is, children of present or former members of the American Communist Party) or were raised in something close to a red-diaper culture. In the 1950s, that meant a culture under siege from the FBI, other government agencies, the courts, local red squads, and employers. Communist culture responded to such assaults by placing special emphasis on the Constitution, the Bill of Rights, and civil liberties. The Party had, in any case, long put the freedom story and blacks at the heart of its organizing efforts and so offered its young an oddly purified version of America's "heritage": the Brooklyn Dodgers and Jackie Robinson, not cowboys and Indians; Paul Robeson and Charlie Chaplin, not John Wayne; Tom Paine and Abraham Lincoln, not Davy Crockett and George Armstrong Custer. They demanded that America make good democracy, not good war. Perhaps only children brought up in the isolated Communist culture of the period could have received such a vision of America as a land of unarmed promise, or assumed that the armed Americans jailing, endangering, or driving their parents "underground" were un-Americans.

look at the founding manifesto that resulted, the Port Huron Statement, is to see in another form the triumphalist despair of the Kennedy inaugural. "We are people of this generation," it began,

> bred in at least modest comfort, housed now in universities, looking uncomfortably to the world we inherit. When we were kids the United States was the wealthiest and strongest country in the world, the only one with the atom bomb, the least scarred by modern war, an initiator of the United Nations. . . . Freedom and equality for each individual, government of, by, and for the people—these American values we found good, principles by which we could live as men.

Other than its lack of significant reference to Indochina among its lists of wars, crises, and revolutions, three aspects of this lengthy document are striking. First, here, too, the bomb reigned supreme. References to it riddled the text—"[T]he horrors of the twentieth century, symbolized in the gas ovens and concentration camps and atom bombs, have blasted hopefulness . . . a lifetime saturation with horror . . . the possibility of limited war becoming illimitable holocaust." The "presence" of "the Bomb" in the text was a reminder that every strategy for creating a better America might be pointless. "Our work is guided by the sense that we may be the last generation in the experiment with living."

Second, as confronting the invisible enemy overseas was central to Kennedy's vision, so bringing the invisible American to (white) consciousness was at the core of theirs: "[W]hite America is ignorant still of nonwhite America—and perhaps glad of it. . . . White, like might, makes right in America today. . . . The awe inspired by the pervasiveness of racism in American life is matched only by the marvel of its historical span in American traditions. The national heritage of racial discrimination via slavery has been a part of America since Christopher Columbus' advent on the new continent." In this statement, for the first time perhaps since the days of the abolitionists, a small group of whites accepted the black story as a (if not the) national one, transforming American history into a tale of horrors.

If the bomb presided over the war story and America's "sacred heritage" was "racial discrimination via slavery," the young manifesto writers could not quite decide on their own role in transforming the country. Were they in favor of a limited mobilization of resources for relatively modest reform—including a political realignment in which Southern "Dixiecrats" would be ejected from the Democratic Party—or of a new kind of mobilization centered on the formation of a "new left" on university campuses, but aimed at the future creation of a mass "participatory democracy"? Reflecting the faith and despair of the moment, they uneasily called for both.

Third, and least expected, was the half-hidden tone of nostalgia, even of sadness, that sometimes peeped through the text. Their childhood years, just past, were only half-ironically labeled an "American Golden Age." Children of the suburbs and abundance, distinctly middle class and desperate to believe in the unarmed promise of America, they were puzzled that they could feel so alone, that so few others seemed to notice anything was wrong.

The meeting at Port Huron provided them with the liberating thrills of comradeship and sex. They were transported by the participatory pleasures of a sleepless sorting out of their statement, which would mark the beginning of a national movement and a national moment. They connected and articulated the many aspects of triumphalist despair with a freshness that is still moving but also makes one shiver, for their analytic plunge into the invisible horrorscape of their childhood—racism, poverty, the "war economy," and the specter of world's end—had already made their growing-up experience of abundance seem distant and nostalgic.[22]

These, then, were the "children" of the era: in the 1950s, soft and scary, a haunting disappointment to their anxious elders; in the early 1960s, idealistic and impressive (or, if black, idealistic and threatening); by the late 1960s, more unnerving than ever. All the young people mobilized in that moment would hold something in common. Though from different class and racial vantage points, they would all experience a powerful sense of loss and betrayal by an older generation who delivered only one-half of the deepest promises of childhood, only the terrors—and the thrills—of the underground story.

In June 1961, while in Vienna to meet with Soviet Premier Nikita Khrushchev, President Kennedy held a private rendezvous with *New York Times* columnist James Reston. The president, felt Reston, had been "genuinely shaken" by Khrushchev's aggressive personal tactics, claiming that the experience was the "roughest thing in my life." "I think [Khrushchev] did it because of the Bay of Pigs," Kennedy confided. "I think he thought that anyone who was so young and inexperienced as to get into that mess could be taken, and anyone who got into it, and didn't see it through, had no guts." After assuring Reston that he would respond by increasing the military budget, he added, "Now we have a problem in trying to make our power credible, and Vietnam looks like the place."[23]

If limited war was the nuclear dilemma reduced to the peripheries and the need for credibility, the "domino theory" raised to the ethereal, then

Vietnam, almost by happenstance, was where the nuclear dilemma and domino theory, limited war and credibility, merged into a "test case" that could not be ignored. If you were born between 1943 and 1954, then you were nineteen sometime between 1962, when President Kennedy signed National Security Action Memorandum No. 124, calling for "proper recognition throughout the U.S. government that subversive insurgency ('wars of liberation') is a major form of politico-military conflict equal in importance to conventional warfare," and 1973, when the Paris Peace Accords were signed, officially ending the Vietnam War (almost) for Americans (though not for Vietnamese, Laotians, or Cambodians). It was possible, then, that you were among the 3 million Americans who went to Vietnam as soldiers (nineteen being the average age of the GI there), or among the several million antiwar protesters who were at one time or another active in some aspect of the Movement, as it was called—or, possibly, both.[24]

Each of these minority groups went into the war years carrying, close to their hearts, deep in their fantasies, from the culture of early childhood play and entertainment, a particularly pure and sunny form of the war story. Vietnam memoirs indicate that many of the young who joined the army to turn back the tide of communism went, initially, with a gung-ho attitude, even with a special sense of relief at being released from everyday life into a John Wayne version of American promise. A generation of young people, that is, took the same spirit of generosity and enthusiasm, the same call to sacrifice, into Vietnam and into opposition to it.

Vietnam, a "laboratory" (as General Maxwell Taylor called it) for limited war, was the place that led Americans back into the limitless, while the war story, already corroding in certain young heads as the new decade began, would within only a few years disassemble inside millions of others on college campuses, in ghetto communities, in the military in Vietnam, and not least in government offices in Washington. Sooner or later, everyone, young or old, willing or not, would enter the twilight zone and have an opportunity to discover the outer limits.

PART III

THE
ERA OF REVERSALS
(1962–1975)

I

THE FIRST COMING OF G.I. JOE

It was 1964, and in Vietnam thousands of American "advisers" were already offering up their know-how from helicopter seats or gun sights. The United States was just a year short of sending its first large contingent of ground troops there, adolescents who would enter the battle zone dreaming of John Wayne and thinking of enemy-controlled territory as "Indian country." Meanwhile, in that inaugural year of Lyndon Johnson's "Great Society," a new generation of children began to experience the war story via the most popular toy warrior ever created.

His name, G.I.—for "Government Issue"—Joe was redolent of America's last victorious war and utterly generic. There was no specific figure named Joe, nor did any of the "Joes" have names. "He" came in four types, one for each service, including the marines. Yet every Joe was, in essence, the same. Since he was a toy of the Great Society with its dreams of inclusion, it only took a year for his manufacturer, Hasbro, to produce a "Negro Joe," and two more to add a she-Joe (a nurse, naturally). Joe initially came with no story, no instructions, and no enemy, because it had not yet occurred to adults (or toy makers) not to trust the child to choose the right enemy to pit against Joe.†

In TV ads of the time, Joe was depicted as the most traditional of war toys. Little boys in World War II–style helmets were shown entering battle with a G.I. Joe tank, or fiercely displaying their Joe equipment while a

---

†Hasbro did later produce G.I. Joe Action Soldiers of the World, offering possible allies and enemies. As a 1967 comic book ad, "Adventures in the G.I. Joe Club with Andy & George," put it, "These new G.I. Joe action soldiers of the world are the greatest. . . . Y'know when you add these to [your] regular G.I. Joes . . . you have a battleground of the world." Though there was a Russian contingent, they were as clearly of World War II vintage as the Australian jungle fighters and the Japanese imperial soldiers. "And this area covered by soap flakes . . . is the snow-covered Russian Front. Here are the Russian infantrymen with their fur hats, DP light machine guns and order of Lenin medals. . . . Banzai!! Let's put the Japanese imperial soldiers on the Pacific Island! Hey. . . they have authentic field packs and Arisaka rifles." It seems, though, that most boys had only Joes.[1]

chorus of deep, male voices sang (to the tune of "The Halls of Montezuma"), "G.I. Joe, G.I. Joe, Fighting man from head to toe on the land,
on the sea, in the air." He was "authentic" with his "ten-inch bazooka
that really works," his "beachhead flame thrower," and his "authenti-
cally detailed replica" of a U.S. Army Jeep with its own "tripod mounted
recoilless rifle" and four "rocket projectiles." He could take any beach or
landing site in style, dressed in "the real thing," ranging from an "Ike"
jacket with red scarf to a "beachhead assault fatigue shirt," pants, and
field pack. He could chow down with his own mess kit, or bed down in
his own "bivouac-pup tent set." And he was a toy giant, too, nearly a foot
tall. From the telltale pink scar on his cheek to the testosterone rush of
fierce-faced ad boys shouting, "G.I. Joe, take the hill!" he seemed the picture of a manly fighting toy.

Yet Joe, like much else in his era, was hardly what he seemed.
Launched the year Lyndon Johnson ran for president as a peace candidate
against Barry Goldwater while his administration was secretly planning
the large-scale bombing of North Vietnam, Joe, too, was involved in a
cover-up. For if Joe was a behemoth of a toy soldier, he was also, though
the word was unmentionable, a *doll*. War play Joe-style was, in fact,
largely patterned on and due to a "girl"—Mattel's Barbie.

Barbie had arrived on the toy scene in 1958 with a hard expression on
her face and her nippleless breasts outthrust, a reminder that she, too,
had a secret past. She was a breakthrough, the first "teenage" doll with a
"teenage" figure. However, her creator, Ruth Handler, had modeled her
not on a teenager but on a German tabloid comic strip "playgirl" named
Lili, who, in doll form, was sold not to children but to men "in tobac-
conists and bars . . . as an adult male's pet." As Joe was later to hit the
beaches, so Barbie took the fashion salons, malt shops, boudoirs, and bed-
rooms, fully accessorized, and with the same undercurrent of exaggeration. (The bigger the breasts, after all, the better to hang that Barbie Wed-
ding Gown on.)[2]

Joe was the brainstorm of a toy developer named Stanley Weston, who
was convinced that boys secretly played with Barbie and deserved their
own doll. Having loved toy soldiers as a child, he chose a military theme
as the most acceptable for a boy's doll and took his idea to Hassenfeld
Brothers (later renamed Hasbro), a toy company then best known for producing Mr. Potato Head. In those days, everyone in the toy business
knew that toy soldiers were three-inch-high, immobile, plastic or lead
figures, and the initial response to Joe ranged from doubt to scorn to
laughter; but Merrill Hassenfeld, one of the two brothers running the
company, called on an old friend, Major General Leonard Holland, head

of the Rhode Island National Guard, who offered access to weaponry, uniforms, and gear in order to design a thoroughly accurate military figure. Joe was also given a special "grip," an opposable thumb and forefinger, all the better to grasp those realistic machine guns and bazookas, and he was built with twenty-one movable parts so that boys could finally put war into motion.

Hassenfeld Brothers confounded the givens of the toy business by selling $16.9 million worth of Joes and equipment in Joe's first year on the market, and after that things only got better. In this way was a warrior Adam created from Eve's plastic rib, a tough guy with his own outfits and accessories, whom you could dress, undress, and take to bed—or tent down with, anyway. But none of this could be said. It was taboo at Hasbro to call Joe a doll. Instead, the company dubbed him a "poseable action figure for boys," and the name "action figure" stuck to every war fighting toy to follow. So Barbie and Joe, hard breasts and soft bullets, the exaggerated bombshell and the touchy-feely scar-faced warrior, came to represent the shaky gender stories of America at decade's end, where a secret history of events was slowly sinking to the level of childhood.

For a while, all remained as it seemed. But Joe underwent a slow transformation that Barbie largely escaped (though in the early 1970s, facing the new feminism, her sales did decline). As the Vietnam years wore on, Joe became less and less a soldier. Protest was in the air. As early as 1966, a group of mothers dressed in Mary Poppins outfits picketed the toy industry's yearly trade convention in New York, their umbrellas displaying the slogan, "Toy Fair or Warfare?" Indeed, Sears dropped all military toys from its catalog. According to *Tomart's Guide to Action Figure Collectibles*, "In the late '60s . . . [f]earing a possible boycott of their 'war-oriented toy,' Hasbro changed Joe's facial appearance and wardrobe. Flocked hair and a beard were added to the figures. Hasbro liquidated strictly military-looking pieces in special sets, and by 1970 the G.I. Joe Adventure Team was created."[3]

Now, Joe was teamed with his first real enemies, but they weren't human. There was the tiger of the "White Tiger Hunt," the "hammer head stingray" of "Devil of the Deep," the mummy of "Secret of the Mummy's Tomb," and the "black shark" of "Revenge of the Spy Shark," as well as assorted polar bears, octopi, vultures, and a host of natural enemies in toy sets like "Sandstorm Survival." For the first time, in those years of adult confusion, some indication of plot, of what exactly a child should do with these toys, began to be incorporated into titles like "The Search for the Stolen Idol" or "The Capture of the Pygmy Gorilla." Not only was Joe now an adventurer, but his adventure was being crudely outlined on the packaging that accompanied him; and few of these new adventures bore any relationship to the war story into which he had been born.

This hipper, new Joe was, if not exactly gaining a personality, then undergoing a personalizing process. He no longer appeared so military with his new hairstyles and his "A" (for adventure) insignia, which, as Katharine Whittemore has pointed out, "looked just a bit like a peace sign." In fact, he was beginning to look suspiciously like the opposition, fading as a warrior just as he was becoming a less generic doll. By 1974, he had even gained a bit of an oriental touch with a new "kung-fu grip." In 1976, under the pressure of the increased cost of plastic, he shrunk almost four inches; and soon after, he vanished from the scene. He was, according to Hasbro, "furloughed," and as far as anyone then knew, consigned to toy oblivion.[4]

In this he was typical of the rest of the war story in child culture in those years. It was as if Vietnamese sappers had reached into the American homeland and blasted the war story free of its ritualistic content, as if the "Indians" of that moment had sent the cavalry into flight and unsettled the West. So many years of Vietnamese resistance had transformed the pleasures of war-play culture into atrocities, embarrassments to look at. By the 1970s, America's cultural products seemed intent either on critiquing their own mechanics and myths or on staking out ever newer frontiers of defensiveness.

Take Sgt. Rock, that heroic World War II noncom of DC Comics' *Our Army at War* series. Each issue of his adventures now sported a new seal that proclaimed, "make WAR no more," while his resolutely World War II–bound adventures were being undermined by a new enemylike consciousness. The cover of a June 1971 issue, for instance, showed the intrepid but shaken sergeant stuttering "B-but they were civilians!" and pointing at the bodies of five men, none in uniform, who seemed to have been lined up against a wall and executed. Next to him, a GI, his submachine gun still smoking, exclaims, "I stopped the enemy, Rock! None of 'em got away!" Inside, an episode, "Headcount," told the "underside" of the story of one Johnny Doe, a posthumously decorated private, who shoots first and asks later. "Hold it, Johnny!," yells Rock as Private Doe is about to do in a whole room of French hostages with their Nazi captors, claiming they're all phonies, "if you're wrong . . . we're no better'n the nazi butchers we're fightin' against!" Of Doe, killed by Rock before he can murder the hostages, the story asked a final question that in 1971 would have been familiar to Americans of any age: "Was Johnny Doe a murderer—or a hero? That's one question each of you will have to decide for yourselves!"

Two months later, in the August issue of *Our Army at War*, a reader could enter the mind of Tatsuno Sakigawa in "Kamikaze." Sakigawa, about to plunge his plane into the U.S.S. *Stevens*, recalls "when his mother held him close and warm! He remembered the fishing junk on which they lived . . . the pungent smell of sea and wind . . . he was at another place . . . in a happier time." As his plane is hit by antiaircraft fire and explodes, you see his agonized face. "FATHER . . . MOTHER . . . WHERE ARE YOU?" he screams. The scene cuts briefly to his parents on their burning junk ("H-help us . . . my son . . . help . . . "), and then to a final image of "the flames rising from Japan's burning cities! Houses of wood and paper . . . his own home." Tatsuno Sakigawa, the episode concludes, "died for the emperor . . . for country . . . for honor! But mostly . . . to avenge the death of his parents! The destruction of his home! The loss of his own life!" At page bottom, below DC's pacifist seal of approval, was a "historical note: 250,000 Japanese died in the fireraids . . . 80,000 died in the Hiroshima A-bombing."[5]

Even in that most guarded of sanctuaries, the school textbook, the American story began to disassemble. First in its interstices, and then in its place emerged a series of previously hidden stories. In the late 1960s, textbooks rediscovered "the poor," a group in absentia since the 1930s. By the early 1970s, the black story, the story of women, the chicano story, the Native American story—all those previously "invisible" narratives—were emerging from under the monolithic story of America that had previously been imposed on a nation of children. Similarly, at the college level, histories of the non-European world emerged from under the monolithic "world" story that had once taken the student from Egypt to twentieth-century America via Greece, Rome, medieval Europe, and the Renaissance.

These new "celebratory" tales of the travails and triumphs of various "minorities" arose mainly as implicit critiques of the One American Story that had preceded them or as self-encapsulated and largely self-referential ministories like that new TV form, the miniseries. In either case, they proved linkable to no larger narrative, though in the 1980s they would all be gathered up willy-nilly under the umbrella of "multiculturalism." Being celebratory, they needed no actual enemy, but implicitly the enemy was the very story that had until recently made them invisible. They were something like interest groups competing for a limited amount of just emptied space. The national story, which was supposed to be inclusive enough to gather in all those "huddled masses," which had only a few years earlier allowed textbook writers to craft sentences like, "We are too little astonished at the unprecedented virtuousness of U.S. foreign policy, and at its good sense," had now been cracked open.[6]

By the time Saigon fell in 1975, children like adults existed in a remarkably storyless realm. The very word *war* had been stripped out of children's culture and childhood transformed into something like an un-American event. The subterranean haunted and haunting quality of children in the 1950s had risen to the surface. The young were now openly threatening adults. Some were challenging American power with evidence of the destruction of minority children at home or out there ("Hey, hey, LBJ, how many kids did you kill today?"), while others, whether as political radicals, part of the counterculture, or GIs in Vietnam, seemed in the process of defecting to the Eastern enemy.

Yet, paradoxically, that victorious enemy was nowhere in sight—not in the movies, not on TV (despite the image of Vietnam as a television war), not even in the press. Where the Vietnamese should have been, there was instead an absence. Because it was impossible to "see" who had defeated the United States and hence why Americans had lost, it was impossible to grasp what had been lost. So American victimhood, American loss—including the loss of childhood's cultural forms—became a subject in itself, the only subject, you might say, while the invisibility of the foe who had taken the story away lent that loss a particular aura of unfairness.

So, in a final, strange reversal in that era of reversals, American postwar "reconstruction" would begin not in Vietnam, the land in ruins, which should have been but was not the defeated country, but at home in a land almost untouched by war, which should have been but was not the victor; and the rebuilding would focus not on some devastated physical environment but on the national psyche. In this postwar passage from John Wayne to Sylvester Stallone, from Pax Americana to Pecs Americana, this attempt to rebuild a furloughed American narrative of triumph, children were to play a special role.

2

THE INVISIBLE GOVERNMENT

There are two governments in the United States today. One is visible. The other is invisible. The first is the government that citizens read about in their newspapers and children study about in their civics books. The second is the interlocking, hidden machinery that carries out the policies of the United States in the Cold War.

The second, invisible government gathers intelligence, conducts espionage, and plans and executes secret operations all over the globe.

So journalists David Wise and Thomas B. Ross began their book, *The Invisible Government*. Published in 1964, it was the first serious attempt to describe and analyze the secret world of intelligence and national security.

This "invisible" or "shadow" government, Wise and Ross claimed, was "shaping the lives of 190,000,000 Americans." It was "a massive, hidden apparatus, secretly employing about 200,000 persons[,] . . . spending several billion dollars a year," and led by a "Special Group," a "small directorate, the name of which is only whispered." This group was practically beyond the political control of the president, and certainly beyond the oversight or control of Congress or the courts. The few high-powered men meant to control this growing government-within-a-government had "heavy responsibilities in other areas . . . [and] obviously [could] give no more than general approval and guidance to a course of action." The CIA and the other intelligence agencies, being practically free of oversight, were also free to chart and conduct something like their own secret foreign policy.[7]

Wise and Ross had given the concept of an "invisible government" a strange twist. In its 1950s origins as a McCarthyite term, the "invisible government" referred to a small group of highly placed traitors and dupes supposedly secreted within the government to assist a future Communist takeover. Wise and Ross's invisible government, however, was a creation of Americans, not the enemy (even if in response to the enemy's Cold War challenge), and it held out the frightening prospect of turning the government into something akin to an enemy entity.

In their book, Wise and Ross not only offered the first anatomy of U.S. intelligence and its varied secret operations worldwide but caught a

changing national mood vis-à-vis a government that only three years earlier had had its secret Bay of Pigs invasion of Cuba exposed as a disaster,
and only two years before had seemingly led the world to the edge of
annihilation during the Cuban missile crisis. Only the year before, its
young president had been murdered by a lone assassin, seemingly for no
discernible reason whatsoever. In its senselessness, that assassination
had cut short narrative possibilities. It was as if "The End" had quite
unexpectedly appeared on every screen in the country.

For the first time in history that November 1963, a nation had been
mobilized at couchside and plunged into electronic mourning. The television networks had stayed with post-assassination events from soon
after the shooting to funeral's end—four days, Friday to Monday, without
a single commercial, while at certain moments nine of ten Americans
tuned in. Viewers seemed to sense that they were at some unexpected
cutoff point, a possible unmarked exit into a storyless world.[8]

The national mood in the wake of John F. Kennedy's murder was so
unsettled and unsettling that the new president Lyndon Johnson urgently
convened a confidence-building commission of notables, including that
doyen of the national security state, former CIA chief Allen Dulles.
Headed by Earl Warren, the respected chief justice of the Supreme Court,
this group had the task of confronting quickly mounting "suspicions,"
"rumors," "theories," and "speculations" and reassuring the public that
no secret explanation of the assassination remained beyond public view.
Appointed on November 29, just seven days after the event it was to
investigate, the commission felt driven to complete its report before the
1964 presidential election.

The Warren Commission turned out to be something like a high-level
story conference. Its job, in essence, was to pound out an acceptable narrative of the assassination event that would account for its many oddi-
ties, ranging from the bizarre life story of the assumed assassin to his
murder by a petty criminal on national TV while in police custody. In its
final report released in September 1964, the commission acknowledged
the possibilities that existed for the construction of elaborate stories—
from enemy-led conspiracies to homebred plots—in its dismissive intro-
ductory comments:

> The Commission has found no evidence to show that Oswald was
> employed, persuaded, or encouraged by any foreign government . . . or
> that he was an agent of any foreign government . . . [or that the con-
> tacts which he initiated with] the Communist Party, U.S.A., the Fair
> Play for Cuba Committee, and the Socialist Workers Party . . . were
> related to Oswald's subsequent assassination of the President . . . [or]

that Oswald was an agent, employee, or informant of the FBI, the CIA, or any other governmental agency.

Elsewhere it denied that "any connections existed between Oswald and certain right-wing activity in Dallas which, shortly before the assassination, led to the publication of hostile criticism of President Kennedy." In place of such stories, the commission offered what, at the time, was thought to be the most consoling but proved the least satisfying of conclusions. The crime had been the handiwork of a disturbed lone gunman. It was an enemyless, plotless happening.

That initial "rush to judgment" (the title of an early attack on the commission's findings by lawyer Mark Lane) and the years of assassination controversy to follow revealed the degree to which not just the triumphal American story of August 1945, but the more confused and confusing Cold War version of that story had crumbled, although its forms were still everywhere in evidence. Secretary of State Dean Rusk had, for instance, appeared before the commission to defend the Russians. "I have not seen or heard of any scrap of evidence indicating that the Soviet Union had any desire to eliminate President Kennedy nor in any way participated in any such event. . . . I can't see how it could be to the interest of the Soviet Union to make any such effort."[9]

No wonder, in the confusion of the moment, the natural yearning for a story led many to wonder whether there wasn't more to the murder than a plotless, pointless mess. Perhaps the story was simply being withheld from the public. There was nothing illogical in this thought. After all, Americans were now living in a society in which it was almost a given that the more important the event, the less likely the public would have access to the necessary information on which to judge it.

The president, it was claimed, had been murdered by Lee Harvey Oswald, a former U.S. marine who had defected to and then returned from the Soviet Union with a Russian wife, who evidently had ties to right- and left-wing Cubans, to either the KGB or one or more U.S. intelligence agency. Here was the strangest part: the least satisfying explanation for the assassination in 1963 would surely have seemed the only obvious and convincing one to any commission of notables a decade earlier. A marine defector returns from Moscow and shoots the president— what other logical conclusion might there be than that he was a KGB-programmed assassin, rare proof of a Communist conspiracy to unman the United States and seize the world by disruption, terror, and subversion?

In fact, almost exactly that plot—a brainwashed POW returns a hero from the Korean War programmed by the Communists (with the agreement of his scheming, ambitious mother) to assassinate a popular liberal president—had played without great success in movie houses only the year before. The film, *The Manchurian Candidate*, employed the rejected version of the assassination-to-come not as tense, dark, anti-Communist melodrama, but as outright camp. No one today watching the fabulous vision of evil Communist brainwashers turning, in the mind of a benumbed POW, into a group of dowdy matrons at a tea party could doubt that the anti-Communist story was then in tatters, or that the very idea of "brainwashing," taken quite seriously in the wake of the Korean War, could no longer carry its cultural weight.

The major available storyline of the Cold War—in which the invisible Communist/Russian enemy infiltrated our world with mayhem in mind—proved implausible in the post-1963 period. Yet there was little question that the public was increasingly ready to entertain the thought that some kind of enemy-ness, some kind of organized evil, had managed to creep close to the president with deadly intent. As a result, the most unbelievable, un-American, and horrifying act since Pearl Harbor (the only one since then in which Americans individually would remember exactly where they were when the news reached them) was open to any interpretation except the most obvious anti-Communist one.

Kennedy's death, it seemed, might have been planned and committed by Castro's Cubans (who hated Kennedy for supporting the Bay of Pigs operation); or by Cubans who hated Castro (and hence Kennedy for not supporting a new Bay of Pigs operation); or by the Mafia, who loathed the Kennedy brothers even if mob women loved them; or by right-wing Sun Belt businessmen; or even (as conspiracy theorists began to mutter early on) by a cabal within the government, including members of the intelligence community and the military, angered over Kennedy's supposed desire to pull out of Vietnam; or in mix-and-match fashion by some combination of any of the above.

Most of these possibilities were picked up by New Orleans District Attorney Jim Garrison, who in 1967 charged a local businessman, Clay L. Shaw, with conspiring to assassinate President Kennedy. If the case proved nonexistent in court, that did not stop Garrison from pursuing endless paths of attack on the lone assassin theory. In 1970, in his book *A Heritage of Stone*, he outlined the vastness of the conspiracy that he believed lay behind Kennedy's death. In an echo of Wise and Ross, he wrote that its "operations all occurred in another dimension, a dimension which generally is not known to exist in our nation." As Edward J. Epstein has summarized Garrison's thoughts, in this other dimension was an "'invisible government [that] begins and ends with deception,' appropriates power to itself through assassinations, and conceals from the populace 'government force that is as criminal as the Germany of Hitler or the Russia of Stalin.' . . . To assure its invisibility, this elite employs technicians capable of inflicting on its enemies 'heart attacks, falls, shootings by "deranged" men and dozens of other kinds of misadventures.'" In this way, the assassination, meaningless on the surface, was pulled into a netherworld of secret operations in whose dimness it was impossible to tell "us" from "them."[10]

Had Oswald been a patsy for the real killers? Had there been two Oswalds (the real one and a look-alike)? As the years went by, the possibilities only seemed to multiply. All that was certain was the impossibility of creating a plausible assassination narrative in a world in which all crucial matters were meant to take place out of public sight; in which the government's natural response was to close to public scrutiny many of the relevant files compiled within that secret world, whose members might or might not have been complicit in the first place.

There was no contradiction between this sealing off of possibly crucial documents and, in the case of both the Warren Commission and the subsequent House Select Committee on Assassinations, the publication of voluminous reports and reams of accompanying documentation. The government was by now in the business of producing massive amounts of documentation and of classifying and filing huge amounts of it away under various categories of secrecy. As the forty-seven volumes of the Pentagon Papers were to prove, there was enough documentation to go around to obfuscate any situation or alternately to provide ammunition for almost any storyline, yet there was always more documentation that had not yet seen (and might never see) the light of day. Under the weight of such documentation (and its lack), to discern a plotline in a world run by "invisible" governments was a nearly hopeless undertaking. At one and the same moment, there was always too much to read and not enough to judge.

Daniel Ellsberg relates the following story:

During one period while I was a Special Assistant in the Pentagon, I directed the Message Center of ISA (International Security Affairs) to limit the [message] "traffic" sent to me daily to [only the highest classifications] of Top Secret, Nodis/Limdis [no distribution, limited distribution], and Eyes Only ["for the eyes only of the addressee"] messages on Southeast Asia; this cut my daily reading load to two piles of paper about two and a half feet high.[11]

In fact, one way Henry Kissinger garnered power from the national security bureaucracy on becoming President Richard Nixon's national security adviser in 1969 was to put it to work producing reams of paperwork in response to essentially bogus policy questions, while he and the president took control of actual policy matters.

Wise and Ross's book, then, was part of a process already well under way in the early 1960s by which one could imagine one's own government doing what previously only *they* did, and doing it for increasingly malevolent reasons. Certainly, it had become progressively easier to imagine the government as, in part, enemylike. This was reflected in several major films of the period: *Seven Days in May* (1964), in which a right-wing general linked to an incipient fascist movement attempts to carry out a *coup d'état* against a dovish president who has just signed a nuclear disarmament pact with the Soviet Union ("What I'm suggesting, Mr. President, is a military plot to take over the government!"); *Fail Safe* (1964), in which a computerized nuclear response system, too fast for human intervention, malfunctions and fails to stop an erroneous nuclear attack on Moscow, forcing an American president to save the world by nuking New York City; and *Dr. Strangelove* (1963), Stanley Kubrick's classic vision of the end of the world American-style, in which the atrocity is distinctly returned to American hands. ("I don't say we wouldn't get our hair mussed, but I do say no more than ten to twenty million people killed.")

In each of these films, the Russians were presented as an afterthought at best, rather than an enemy. In each, the enemy, ready to launch a first strike, whether against the White House or the Kremlin, whether with malice, by inadvertence, or in madness, was American. In each case, the most crucial and malign of events took place behind closed doors, and consequently the world either ended or threatened to end before ordinary people knew what hit them. This fictional vision of an invisible government of evil, power-hungry, or certifiably mad generals, as well as Nazi-style advisers and cold-blooded, end-of-the-world strategists, mixed easily enough with Wise's real-life exposé of Ivy League spymasters and Cuban foot soldiers in a secret war to make the world safe for America. As pseudonymous British author John Le Carré noted in his novels of the early 1960s, in the vast domains of the secret world where the Cold War was forever, "we" and "they" had more in common than either side did with its own people.

In *Fail Safe*, the following dialogue took place between the U.S. secretary of defense, various generals, and a think-the-unthinkable professor as American nuclear bombers headed for Moscow:

PROFESSOR: Every minute we wait works against us. Now, Mr. Secretary, now is when we must send in a first strike.

GENERAL: We don't go in for sneak attacks. We had that done to us at Pearl Harbor.

PROFESSOR: And the Japanese were right to do it. From their point of view we were their mortal enemy. . . . Their only mistake was they failed to finish us at the start and they paid for that mistake at Hiroshima.

GENERAL: You're talking about a different kind of war.

PROFESSOR: Exactly. This time we can finish what we start. If we act now, right now, our casualties will be minimal. . . .

GENERAL: You're justifying murder.

PROFESSOR: Yes. To keep from being murdered.

GENERAL: In the name of what? To preserve what? . . .

PROFESSOR: Those who can survive are the only ones worth surviving. . . . How long would the Nazis have kept it up, general, if every Jew they met had met them with a gun in his hand. But I learned from them, general. Oh, I learned.

GENERAL: You learned too well, professor. You learned so well that now there's no difference between you and what you want to kill.

In October 1962, during the Cuban missile crisis, as President Kennedy's advisers argued about whether to launch nonnuclear first strikes without warning on Cuban missile sites manned by Soviet advisers, Attorney General Robert Kennedy took a position similar to that of the fictional general in *Fail Safe.* "My brother," he said, "is not going to be the Tojo of the 1960's." This vision of the president as a possible sneak attacker and the United States as a potentially savage, first-strike nation—of an America, that is, as if seen through enemy eyes—had slipped behind the closed doors of government and lodged inside the heads of those who ran the state.[12]

3

PLAYING WITH FIRE

One day, in August 1965, Morley Safer, a thirty-five-year-old CBS reporter, Ha Thuc Can, his Vietnamese cameraman, and a sound man (actually a boy) named Thien accompanied marines in amphibious vehicles from the large American base at Danang to a cluster of hamlets called Cam Ne on a "search and destroy" mission. "Especially destroy," a marine lieutenant told Safer en route. "We've been taking fire from there every time we go by, and the gook head honcho in these parts told us to go teach them a lesson."

Safer, who for much of the previous decade had covered combat situations in the Middle East, Cyprus, and Algeria, was shocked by what he saw the marines do in Cam Ne. "Watching American boys, young and clean, *our boys*, carrying on like the other side's soldiers always did, and doing it so casually" was what unnerved him. Immediately after the mission, he filed a report for *Morning News Roundup*, a CBS radio show, on "the burning of Cam Ne." It caused consternation at CBS's New York headquarters. Fred Friendly, head of the news division, was awakened at home. On learning that there would be actual footage of American troops burning down a Vietnamese village, Friendly alerted CBS president Frank Stanton as well as Arthur Sylvester, assistant secretary of defense for public affairs at the Pentagon.[13]

CBS officials viewing Safer's film were also shocked. Not only were American boys not supposed to act this way, but television was not supposed to show them acting this way. But after nervously checking with Safer and evidently debating among themselves, they made his report the lead story twice on *The CBS Evening News with Walter Cronkite*: the first time, in that era before instant telecommunications, when Safer's telexed report was read over the air ("During the operation, the marines were telling the people in English to get out of their underground bunkers before they burned the houses. The people therefore stayed put, causing several close shaves, until pleas from this reporter that our Vietnamese cameraman should be allowed to speak to them in the Vietnamese language"); and again when the film was in hand.

Both reports were atypical at the time in their content, disturbing tone, and indication of a sizable gap between the official picture of the war and on-the-ground realities. "The day's operation burned down 150 houses, wounded three women, killed one baby, wounded one marine and netted these four prisoners. Four old men who could not answer questions put to them in English. Four old men who had no idea what an I.D. card was," one went in part. "Today's operation is the frustration of Vietnam in miniature. There is little doubt that American firepower can win a military victory here. But to a Vietnamese peasant whose home . . . means a lifetime of backbreaking labor, it will take more than presidential promises to convince him that we are on his side."[14]

The U.S. military's after-action report on Cam Ne came far closer to typical TV and press coverage of the time. The only structures burned at Cam Ne, the military claimed, were "fortified Vietcong bunkers from which the marines received fire. Others . . . were damaged by accident in the course of heated battle." To Safer, it was obvious that no battle had occurred. Of the three marine casualties, at least two had clearly been wounded due to "friendly fire," the only death was that of a ten-year-old village boy, and not a single weapon had been uncovered. In fact, Safer was to discover long after that Cam Ne had been destroyed only because a province chief, angered by the villagers' refusal to pay taxes, had wished to punish them.

The events at Cam Ne would seem less startling in the years to come when "Zippo jobs" and "Zippo squads" became commonplace terms; when American troops destroyed villages, salted fields, and dumped slaughtered livestock down village wells. But this was still August 1965, less than six months after the first marine battalion had landed at Danang. Americans had not long been in combat operations and TV was—as it would long be—more partial to reports on Americans rescuing Vietnamese orphans from the clutches of Communists, or, at worst, to what network reporters came to call "The Wily VC Got Away Again" stories.[15]

It was not, however, so much what Safer said that shocked as the particular set of images caught by his cameraman. They were perhaps the most disturbing of the war for those who saw them that August night. For they were the first (since the photos of Buddhist bonzes immolating themselves in the anti-Diem demonstrations of 1963) that broke through what TV critic Michael Arlen would later describe as the "routinizing film clips of combat on the evening news shows, those young TV correspondents standing beside some hillside outside Pleiku describing gunfire while we drank beer, played with our children, thought, felt God knows what."[16]

From the report's first words ("We're on the outskirts of the village of Cam Ne with elements of the First Battalion, 9th Marines"), the sight of Safer slightly bent above the tall grass, and the sound of shots ringing out, the camera carried the viewer into an already burning village. Through the Vietnamese cameraman's lens the viewer watched old and young rousted from their homes—thatched huts—by marines, bayonets at the ready. An old man with a goatee is obviously pleading for his home as Safer approaches mike in hand. ("This is what the war in Vietnam is all about. The old and the very young. The marines are burning this old couple's cottage because fire was coming from here.") Glimpses are caught of GIs moving impassively through this scene of terror. Before a viewer could question the voice-over's claim—that *Americans* were burning Cam Ne—the camera focused on a helmeted marine, his back to the viewer, arm outstretched toward the thatching on a roof, in his hand, a cigarette lighter; and indeed smoke, then flames begin to consume some peasant's home. There could be no question that a home was being burned, that others were being or would be incinerated in this village in which the "enemy" seemed no more than a collection of women, children, and old men.†

With this sequence of images, Morley Safer and Ha Thuc Can, a Canadian and a Vietnamese, returned fire, that atrocity against civilization and the act of settlement, to the war story as an unbidden horror committed by white intruders. It would no longer be the enemy who left the log cabin, the fort, the town in smoldering ruins. Fire was now in the wrong hands, a point only emphasized by the civilized innocence of the "weapon" the camera focused on that day. A minor convenience of the age of abundance, the cigarette lighter was meant to facilitate that moment of pleasure around the house, in the office, at a restaurant, but not, obviously, to torch house, office, or restaurant.

To accept such an unprecedented and un-American act on that most guarded of viewing screens meant accepting that one's government, one's countrymen could do—without visible emotion—what previously only they did. On the face of it, this had the look of alien propaganda. (After the report aired, Safer was threatened by a drunken officer shouting, "Communist Broadcasting System!" and shooting his pistol in the air.) Little wonder, then, that the CBS switchboard was deluged with outraged calls, many obscene, demanding an explanation and insisting that Safer's report should never have been aired.

It wasn't only ordinary viewers who were horrified and offended. The next morning, the nation's First Caller picked up his phone and dialed the nation's First Reporter, his old friend CBS President Frank Stanton. "Frank," demanded Lyndon Johnson, "are you trying to fuck me?" "Who is this?" asked a drowsy Stanton, for the First Caller had chosen a shockingly early hour to make his feelings known. "Frank, this is your President, and yesterday your boys shat on the American flag." Safer, Johnson insisted, must be a Communist.

When at Johnson's urging Safer was investigated by the FBI, the CIA, and finally the Royal Canadian Mounted Police, and the president was

---

†Given the uproar that followed, it is worth noting that the burning of Cam Ne was more organized and grisly than what was shown on TV. "As people stumble out of houses," Safer recalled in his memoirs, "marines, some with flamethrowers, others using matches, yet others with Zippo lighters, begin systematically to set fire to each hut." For an even grimmer account, see Private First Class Reginald "Malik" Edwards' story of the Cam Ne operation in Wallace Terry's fine oral history of black Vietnam veterans, *Bloods*: "When you say level a village, you don't use torches. It's not like in the 1800s. You use a Zippo. That's why people bought Zippos. Everybody had a Zippo. It was for burnin' shit down."[17]

informed that he was not a Communist, only a Canadian, he insisted, "Well, I knew he wasn't an American." Johnson remained convinced that Safer's report was an enemy plot, that he had somehow bribed a marine officer to get the shots he wanted. "They got to one of our boys," Johnson told his staff. The Vietnamese cameraman, like all Vietnamese in that war, was invisible and so beyond the bounds of the conspiratorial imagination of the First Caller (though not of some of his underlings). However, Johnson was not wrong to emphasize Safer's un-Americanness. Like British authors Graham Greene and John Le Carré, Safer's minimal outsiderdom undoubtedly helped explain his ability to "see" what U.S. reporters either saw but refused to acknowledge, or acknowledged but had not reported.

In his indignation and sense of betrayal, the First Caller was hardly alone at the top. From Marine Corps headquarters came the news that Safer's footage was a fake, that he had supplied the Zippo lighter and requested the performance. Secretary of State Dean Rusk came to believe the incident had been staged in an abandoned village used for marine training and maintained it was "common knowledge at the White House that the reporter was a questionable character with ties to the Soviet intelligence apparatus." Pentagon spokesman Arthur Sylvester, among others, worked to discredit Safer, telling CBS news executives that Safer was a "cheap Canadian. . . . Maybe a Canadian has no interest in our efforts in Vietnam and no realization that the Vietnam conflict is not World War II or Korea, but a new type of political, economic, military action."[18]

There was an odd calculus here. If fire had been the enemy's attribute in the war story, it had also been an important weapon in the U.S. arsenal. In World War II, the flamethrower and napalm had been crucial in the struggle to root Japanese soldiers out of fortified islands like Iwo Jima, while, in Europe and especially Japan, Americans had literally "fired the village." In a nighttime raid on Tokyo on March 9–10, 1945, the air force had cut a huge X of flames across the Japanese capital, constructed almost entirely of flammable materials. Then, for three hours, hundreds of B-29s had poured napalm-filled bombs, magnesium incendiary clusters, gasoline, and chemicals onto the inferno below. Uncounted tens of thousands of civilians were incinerated. Although publicized in the United States ("300 B-29's Fire 15 Square Miles of Tokyo," was the *New York Times* headline), the human carnage went largely unseen. Such fire raids were often described in the press as "'the bombing of factories and plants' undertaken against 'a fanatical foe prepared to fight to the death.'" Despite the fears of certain military men that the raids might make the United States seem "barbaric," the issue was never directly confronted, nor would it be in Korea, despite the massive use of napalm and the firebombing of the North Korean capital, Pyongyang.[19]

Fire was to be crucial in Vietnam, too, in the form of napalm and white phosphorus (which adhere to human skin while burning). But if this was a part of the war effort, seeing it on screen at home, except as a distant blooming of explosions, was not. Safer's report on American boys playing with fire jumped out of a relatively unthreatening landscape of war reportage. Far more typical at the time (and long after) were reassuring announcements of "dramatic American victories" accompanied by lopsided casualty figures; followed by combat reports showing American soldiers on patrol shooting into a distant line of trees or toward a group of huts where the enemy, viewers were told, was—or at least might be—located; followed perhaps by a shot of a body identified as a dead "VC" and sometimes scenes of wounded Americans. Alternately, the viewer might be shown helicopters landing and troops leaping out and rushing into the surrounding countryside in an unfinished vision of "progress." These represented the journalist's desire to pursue what Michael Arlen has called a "the next-day-the-First-Army-forged onward-toward-Aachen" approach to the war.[20]

Such more or less traditional war reports were supplemented by familiar noncombat sequences like ABC correspondent David Snell's report from "China Beach." Snell's voice-over went in part, "While pilots at nearby Danang air base prepare for flights north, the sun-soaked airman takes a fanciful flight of his own." Soldiers were shown frolicking in the waves and tossing a comrade in the air. In a brief beachside interview, a soldier complained to Snell, "Nine months away from America without round-eyes, without American girls, without one girl, my fiance," followed by shots of Vietnamese women in bikinis and Snell's comment, "The Vietnam war is, as they say, a different kind of war, but for the GI, there is still nothing like a dame."

The flood of coverage, at least until 1968, while hinting at problems in Vietnam, at ways in which it was a "different kind of war," was largely supportive of government policy. Where it diverged, particularly in the post-1968 period, it generally followed the widening fault lines of policy disagreement within the government. There was a way, however, in which the criticism that the media undermined the war effort, common among military men and government officials then and since, had a certain truth. A few images (as likely to have been still photos as TV footage) seemed to jump from the battlefield onto the home screen or into newspapers and magazines and were seared into public memory. Although sometimes initially seen by relatively small audiences, their shock value led them to be repeated many times over. These visual moments are still recalled today, often as if they were the sum total of, rather than exceptions to, everyday images from Vietnam. Yet they are remembered exactly because they stood out against a tide of increasingly unconvincing images of a war that would not go away.

Among them were the still photos and video of South Vietnamese police chief General Nguyen Ngoc Loan putting a pistol to the head of a shackled Vietcong suspect and shooting him in the streets of Saigon during the Tet Offensive in 1968; the shots of the U.S. embassy in Saigon partially taken over by NLF sappers in those same days; the still photos of prisoners in "tiger cages" on the South Vietnamese prison island of Con Son and of the My Lai massacre; and the 1972 photo and video of a young Vietnamese girl, napalmed by South Vietnamese planes, running naked down a road, her face contorted in horror and pain.

"The small village of Trang Bang found itself caught between the hammer and the nail of a murderous war," was how ABC correspondent George Watson began his report on the incident. "At 300 miles per hour it's easy to make a mistake. . . . Nobody is certain how many people were killed and injured, but these pictures tell the story of innocent human suffering far better than the weekly casualty reports and body counts." Here was no alien, no enemy, just a child at screen center mutilated by America's fire. It was as if that child had taken seven years to extricate herself from Cam Ne's burning homes and head toward American viewers crying in pain, a terrifying vision of what happens when the savages burn out the settlers.

The Vietnamese, a people subjected to a trial by fire, were visibly being transformed into victims and the Americans into savage aggressors. No wonder that, in 1965, the first of these broadcasts seemed to some Americans, including the president, like a message from the enemy. For the loss of the ability to use fire on the battlefield without committing an atrocity within the war story was a reversal of the first order.

4

INTO THE CHARNEL HOUSE OF LANGUAGE:
THE AMERICAN DREAM MEETS THE NIGHTMARE,
THE QUAGMIRE, AND THE BLOODBATH

How to explain the impression in the Vietnam years that the American colossus had stumbled off the beaten path of history into, as Richard Nixon put it, a "long, dark night of the American spirit"? Nothing was more puzzling to Americans than to find themselves suddenly trapped in a "nightmare" in which the most unnerving reversals of the known and expectable were taking place and from which waking did not seem an option. In this nightmare, every act, no matter how "well intentioned," managed to take on an aspect of the malign; every promise of "light at the end of the tunnel" seemed only to emphasize the increasing darkness inside. Even the language used to explain the war betrayed its users.

High officials, journalists, antiwar activists, GIs, Americans of all sorts regularly described the war or simply the times in terms of a bad dream and experienced a shared sense of disorientation. Vietnam was like an ambush that refused to end and for which no retribution proved satisfying. No images better captured that feeling of eternal ambush than those that flowed onto television sets in April 1975, in the last days of the war: South Vietnamese soldiers commandeering any sort of transport, shooting their way onto planes in wild panic; frightened refugees crowding all roads; desperate Vietnamese being beaten back by marine guards as the last U.S. helicopters lifted off from the American embassy rooftop in Saigon. Scenes of chaos, abject flight, wholesale loss—with never an enemy in camera range.

Jan Wollett, a flight attendant on the last "humanitarian" flight into Danang, caught the confusion of those final moments:

> When we landed it was very strange because we did not see a soul at first. . . . And then, as [our plane] started to taxi, a massive swarm of people came up and out of bunkers. Thousands—and I mean literally thousands—started racing toward us. . . . I was standing in the cockpit door looking out the front window. Then I realized that something really bizarre was going on. A group of people raced up next to the aircraft in a little truck. A man jumped off the truck and ran up in front of us . . . and he took out a pistol and started shooting at us. Suddenly, I had the fantastic feeling that I was in the middle of a John Wayne Western. And I thought, "Why are they shooting at us? We're the good guys."

Just as shocking were scenes of the abandonment of American goods. To the last second, Americans were psychologically unprepared for flight. Despite so many years of "withdrawal," left behind in the chaos of that rout was a catalog of the good life and a full range of the paraphernalia of nation building American-style; not just military equipment—planes, tanks, rifles, ammunition—beyond measure, but barrels of cash, reams of unburnt or unshredded files, vast air-conditioned base complexes built with American materials to American specifications, and on-line computer systems enumerating America's Vietnamese intelligence network.[21]

If the final images of flight, collapse, and abandonment were vivid, the enemy from whom Americans fled was as indistinct as the shadowy ogre in a nightmare where you run and run without daring to look back. Yet in that enemy's hands was left not just a cornucopia of destructive equip ment but the war story itself. This was indeed the terrifying culmination of what President Nixon had called a "nightmare [of] war without end," a time when "to millions of Americans it seemed we had lost our way."

To enter Vietnam in the first place had meant to find oneself in a world turned upside down, in which every natural American act gained an unnatural aspect as it was committed. For GI and counterculturalist alike, Vietnam was a "bad trip." As one Vietnam veteran testified, "When I got to Nam, it was like black had turned into white because I was totally unprepared. . . . You go over there with that limited amount of training and knowledge of the culture you're up against and you're scared. You're so scared, that you'll shoot at anything." Another described an incident in which his unit shot down women and children in a village:

> I was like in a state of shock and these guys did this so systematically like it was something done so many times before, it was easy. It didn't bother them, at least it didn't appear to bother any of them. You know the crime has been done and it is condoned, or it is covered up, and you get the impression that if this was not right, that someone would make an attempt to stop it, and since no one makes an attempt to stop it, this is the way it is supposed to be.

In Vietnam, as a GI who witnessed similar killings commented, "everything is backwards."[22]

Vietnam was literally an ambush waiting to happen. In approximately 90 percent of company-sized engagements the enemy initiated the action, and 80 percent of the time the element of surprise lay with that enemy. For the foot soldier, war largely meant walking, riding, or flying until the enemy decided to attack. Most of the time, the "grunt" was bait meant to draw the enemy into the "open," where American fire power could do the rest.[23]

For soldiers flown "in country" for a year's tour of duty, Vietnam often had the feeling of a dark, unbelievable dream. Many on arrival had next to no idea where they were, where or what Vietnam was, who exactly the enemy was (other than "communism"), and what the difference between "our" Vietnamese and "theirs" might be. From a "friendly" village might come deadly fire; from a "friendly" child, deadly misinformation. From "our" Vietnamese, cowardice and corruption; from "their" Vietnamese, awesome bravery and courage.

On arrival, you were no longer "in the world." Vietnam was the "boonies," or the "badlands," or "Indian country," a land to be "humped" while your days were counted until departure. There, you were released from civilized rules into horror and savagery in a place without inherent value, without a narrative of its own, evidently without history. When you died there, you were "wasted."

What was true for the foot soldier, experiencing war-as-bad-dream, victory-as-unending-ambush, was also true for the government officials and military men who made or carried out war policy. From the beginning, Indochina had been just another indistinguishable area in the "shadows" onto which the theorists of a new kind of war could project their ideas of struggle. Assignment to the country hardly changed this attitude. Even when American officials were physically in Vietnam, their attention was normally directed elsewhere. As General Maxwell Taylor, then U.S. ambassador to South Vietnam, commented at a staff meeting in 1964, "Failure in Southeast Asia would destroy U.S. influence throughout Asia and severely damage our standing elsewhere throughout the world. It would be the prelude to the loss or neutralization of all of Southeast Asia and the absorption of that area into the Chinese empire."[24]

No significant American official dealing with Indochina policy seems to have had either special knowledge about or interest in the Vietnamese, Laotians, Cambodians, or their past, or for that matter to have thought that lack of knowledge of the faintest importance in running a war there. To have worked with Filipinos in a counterinsurrectionary situation as had Edward G. Lansdale, or with Koreans in the last war, or with any other Asians at any time, or simply to have opinions on Asia was enough to fit an American to be an expert on Vietnam. In this sense, all Asians were to policy makers programmatically indistinguishable.

In the course of several decades of intense involvement with the area, the government called upon thousands of "experts" to deal with the war, yet few had any specific knowledge of the area. There was, in fact, almost no one to draw on. Even in the early 1970s, there were still only a handful of tenured professors in the United States with an expertise in Vietnam and a knowledge of Vietnamese. Former Undersecretary of State James Thomson, Jr., has written provocatively of the way in which the "shadow of the 'loss of China,'" and memories of the disastrous fates of a previous generation of State Department Asian experts led to the "banishment of real expertise" from the decision-making process. Yet the media, without a similarly fierce purge in its past or government control, replicated the phenomenon. With rare exceptions, journalists covering the war tended to cycle through Indochina on six-month tours of duty without knowledge of local languages, history, or culture.[25]

From General William Westmoreland ("The Oriental doesn't put the same high price on life as does the Westerner") to Henry Kissinger (overheard exclaiming of a resistant President Thieu of South Vietnam, "We'll kill the son-of-a-bitch if we have to"), Americans often found the Vietnamese hardly worthy of individual consideration. Lessons of the French war that preceded the American one were either ignored or forgotten. But then lessons of the American war were often ignored or forgotten as well by military and civilian officials who constantly shuttled through the area. Each arrived in the Indochinese blank, ready to make a name for himself by offering "new" solutions to "new" problems, and then move on. Typically, over half the generals who served in Vietnam, often in more than one post, did so for less than a year; and in one prestigious command area the average was only 7.6 months.[26]

What made Vietnam such a complicated experience for Americans was that, to the degree that they never arrived in the country, they also found it impossible to depart. The idea of "withdrawing" from Vietnam arose with the war itself. It was there from the beginning, though never as an actual plan. All real options for ending the war were invariably linked to "cutting and running," or "dishonor," or "surrender," or "humiliation," and so dismissed within the councils of government more or less before being raised. The attempt to prosecute the war and to withdraw from it were never separable, no less opposites. If anything, withdrawal became a way to maintain or intensify the war, while pacifying the American public.

"Withdrawal" involved not departure but all sorts of departure-like maneuvers—from bombing pauses that led to fiercer bombing campaigns to negotiation offers never meant to be taken up to a "Vietnamization" plan in which ground troops would be pulled out as the air war was intensified. Each gesture of withdrawal allowed the war planners to fight a little longer; but if withdrawal did not withdraw the country from the war, the war's prosecution never brought it close to a victorious conclusion. With every failed withdrawal gesture and every failed battle strategy, that sense of "nightmare" seemed to draw closer, and a feeling arose that the country had somehow been entrapped in Vietnam.

This may be the strangest aspect of any reading of the Pentagon Papers, that secret history of the war commissioned by Secretary of Defense Robert McNamara. No better documentation exists on the detailed nature of planning for upwardly ratcheted destruction in Indochina. Yet, among successive groups of planners one senses in the documents a growing feeling of inadvertence, helplessness, victimization, and self-pity. Not just GIs but the most powerful of the war managers came to feel that they had been drawn into a landscape of horror devoid of familiar landmarks.

So the war—with all its devastation—came to be, in part, about a very abstract subject: who had the power to define the "real" Vietnam. As the enemy fought its way into America's Vietnam, a confusing new set of war words gained currency, combining a desire to impose American reality on the Vietnamese, to defend it from the Vietnamese, and to hide it from the public. It was a withdrawal language that like various withdrawal strategies would get Americans only halfway home.

No word more encapsulated this confused process than the one that came to stand in for the whole experience. Vietnam, it was commonly said, was a "quagmire" that had sucked America in. This crucial withdrawal word seems to have entered the national vocabulary in 1964 with the publication of journalist David Halberstam's book *The Making of a Quagmire*. Like much of that vocabulary, it has refused to withdraw from political discourse ever since.†

"Quagmire" and its various cognates and relations—swamp, quicksand, bog, morass, sinkhole, bottomless pit—were quickly picked up across the spectrum of American politics. In 1965, Clark Clifford, then an unofficial adviser to the president, warned Johnson that Vietnam "could be a quagmire. It could turn into an open ended commitment on our part that would take more and more ground troops, without a realistic hope of ultimate victory." Writing in opposition to the war in 1968, Arthur Schlesinger, Jr., combined the images of quagmire and nightmare into a single image of horror. "And so the policy of 'one more step' lured

---

†In a singular discussion of the history of "quagmire" —in fact, a rare exploration of any of America's war words—Daniel Ellsberg, in *Papers on the War*, points out that the French had previously developed a version of the war-as-quagmire in Indochina, as in Lucien Bodard's book title *L'Enlisement* (literally, "The Bogging Down"; published in the United States as *The Quicksand War*). Ellsberg adds, "George Ball, one of the few U.S. officials who could imagine that American experience could be like French, was warned by De Gaulle that Vietnam was 'pays pourri,' a 'rotten country,' not suitable for tanks or Western politics, not, it was hinted delicately, white man's country." Within the American context, the fear of sinking into a land war in Asia was not new. Similar language had been used in reference to Korea. ("As you know, we are bogged down in Asia—trapped in Asia—a hundred thousand Americans killed or wounded," said anti-Communist radio commentator John T. Flynn in 1952.)[27]

the United States deeper and deeper into the morass. . . . Yet, in retrospect, each step led only to the next, until we find ourselves entrapped in
that nightmare of American strategists, a land war in Asia."

During the Tet Offensive of 1968, TV anchorman Walter Cronkite
ended a personal report on the war by concluding, "To say that we are
mired in stalemate seems the only realistic, yet unsatisfactory conclusion." Folk singer Pete Seeger sang his dismay over a war that left Americans "knee deep in the Big Muddy," and in 1974, an army commander
offered this assessment of the American dilemma: "The ultimate objective that emerged was the preservation of the U.S. leadership image and
the maintenance of U.S. integrity in having committed itself; it could not
then pull away from the quicksand in which it found itself."[28]

Embedded in war talk, the quagmire was never so much a description
of the war as a world view imposed on the war. A quagmire is "a bog having a surface that yields when stepped on." To the Vietnamese, their
country was not a quagmire. It was home and the American decision to
be there a form of hated or desired (or sometimes, in America's allies,
both hated and desired) intervention. For those who opposed the United
States, the war was a planned aggression of the most violent sort, the latest of many foreign invasions inseparable from Vietnamese history.

For Americans, the initial benefit of the word *quagmire* was that it
ruled out the possibility of planned aggression. The image turned Vietnam into the aggressor, not only transferring agency for all negative
action to the land, but also instantly devaluing it. It undoubtedly called
to mind as well movie scenes in which heroic white adventurers mis-
stepped in some misbegotten place and found themselves swallowed to
the waist, with every effort at extrication leading toward further disaster.

Here was no rich land to be settled. Its swampy nature made it value-
less as real estate and robbed the American presence of any suggestion of
self-interest. As a quagmire, the land became evidence of American
"good intentions." The United States was there only because the Vietnamese needed and wanted help. This geological Admiral Yamamoto had
"lured" Americans in and mired them there, ambushing an unsuspecting
country. Because the United States "stumbled" into this quagmire by
"mistake," the detailed nature of war planning was automatically denied.
In this way, "quagmire" offered an implicit explanation for involvement
in Vietnam (it sucked us in, once our good intentions had suckered us
there); and for why the United States remained so many years and battles
later (the harder it tried to leave, the more it was pulled down).

Its early adoption as a metaphor for the war indicates how quickly
Americans began to reimagine themselves as victims not victimizers. In

the "quagmire" can be seen the first glimmerings of a postwar sense that victimhood was the essence of national identity. In the idea of the land as aggressor lay the future obliteration of the memory of the Vietnamese victors; in an acceptance that all efforts at extrication only embedded Americans deeper in the muck of war lay proof that, had they been in control of events, all they would have wanted was to depart.

"Quagmire," of course, hardly captured the U.S. situation in Vietnam. There, detailed war planning, including the structured use of the spectacle of slaughter, came up against an organized, mobilized people, ready to resist foreign aggression under unimaginable levels of destruction for lengths of time inconceivable to American policy makers. What kept those policy makers in the war was not quicksand, but the thought that with the next ratchet up the scale of destruction and pain all this would somehow end *as it should* (and, to the last moment, disbelief that this was not so).

Seeing Vietnam as a quagmire, however, was one way in which Americans attempted to distance themselves from the war's reality. It was part of a language of self-deception and cover-up that painted an oddly flattering picture of a nation unfairly experiencing an "American tragedy." If such war talk proved a linguistic quagmire into which Americans quickly sank and from which they have never fully emerged, it was meant to de-Vietnamize the conflict, to withdraw the American gaze from any tragedy other than an American one, even while the United States continued to fight. It was meant to deflect attention from the centrality of the Vietnamese to the war and from the bloody nature of U.S. war plans. It was meant to take Americans part way home without an admission of defeat.

So the bloodbath that was Indochina was partly supplanted by a "bloodbath" the enemy was certain to commit the moment the United States withdrew. This future bloodbath of the imagination appeared in innumerable official speeches and accounts as an explanation of why the United States could not leave. In public discourse, this not-yet-atrocity sometimes became the only real bloodbath and an obsessive focus even of some of the war's opponents within mainstream politics. Activist Todd Gitlin recalled "the contempt with which [Tom] Hayden had told me of a meeting he and Staughton Lynd had with Bobby Kennedy, early in 1967. Kennedy, he said then, had been fixated on the dangers of a 'bloodbath' in South Vietnam if the Communists succeeded in taking over."

In his memoirs, Richard Nixon tells how Alexander Haig informed him of intelligence information indicating that the North Vietnamese and the NLF had "instructed their cadres the moment a cease-fire is announced to kill all of the opponents in the area that they control. This would be a murderous bloodbath." As the war's supporters could not seem to make the other side's actual atrocities carry the weight of American ones, this sea of blood to come weighed heavily in the United States' favor. Put another way, if the future was to be theirs, this was the one those Americans wished on them, for their bloodbath-to-come would effectively wash clean the bloodbath still in progress (as victory once might have, as the postwar bloodbath in Pol Pot's Cambodia indeed would). In the meantime, like "quagmire," "bloodbath" deflected attention from the nature of the struggle at hand, allowing American leaders to withdraw, but only so far, from the consequences of their war.[29]

The flaw in this war talk was the thought that what could not be faced would remain safely confined to faraway Vietnam. Yet, even as Americans "withdrew" from Vietnam, what could not be looked at there drew closer, until America was Vietnamized. Surprising numbers of young Americans began to proclaim the "illegitimacy" of authority and to create a new antiwar talk in which "withdrawal from Vietnam" had a very different meaning. For "quagmire," they offered "the system," "the Establishment," "corporate liberalism," and finally "imperialism"; for "mistakes," "war crimes"; for the worthlessness of the land, the worth of the Vietnamese people—and in some cases, a glorified Vietnamese Communist movement.

Here were the two nightmares of the 1950s, the two hauntings, the great and little fears, rising up as one to spook America. As in some 1950s science fiction fantasy, the enemy now looked exactly like your child! The wildest of these children were proud to proclaim their readiness to "smash Pig Amerikka" in the enemy's name and had no hesitation in claiming the language of both Cold War and Vietnamized America as theirs to do with what they would: "We're against everything that's 'good and decent' in honky America. We will burn and loot and destroy. We are the incubation of your mother's nightmare."[30]

"Nightmare," "quagmire," "bloodbath"—the war story had descended into the charnel house of history. There was a madness loose, not just in that distant land where American boys were committing un-American acts, but at home where the acts of other boys and girls had a distinctly un-American look.

5

THE PRESIDENT AS MAD MULLAH:
EMBRACING THE LOGIC OF MADNESS

If in the American Century the United States was to preside over global security and American dreams were to become global ones, then the president's job as commander-in-chief was to preside over victory culture. Yet nothing seemed less within presidential control in those years than the victory that was promised any wartime president. Lyndon Johnson told his most trusted advisers in 1967 that when it came to the war, he felt "like the steering wheel of a car out of control." Each presidential act only seemed to garner him more of the attributes of an enemy leader. "Hey, hey, LBJ, how many kids did you kill today?" chanted growing crowds of antiwar protesters. "That horrible song," Johnson called it. The president as baby killer, what story was he in? The world was "backwards" not just in Vietnam but in Washington.

"I will not be the first president of the United States to lose a war," Richard Nixon assured Republican congressional leaders in 1969. Nothing drove America's Vietnam presidents, Johnson and Nixon, more ruthlessly than the desire to avoid that most infamous of humiliations. For both, it was an inconceivable fate and yet, to the point of obsession, impossible to stop thinking about. Both, facing the specter of defeat, embraced a very unpresidential madness. Depending on which of his aide's memoirs one reads, under the strain of Vietnam and the collapse of his Great Society dreams, Johnson may have experienced something close to insanity. Nixon's madness being, in part, a consciously considered global strategy was, however, the more curious and revealing of presidential madnesses.[31]

Historically, Third World leaders who opposed imperial control were often not only demonized but imagined to be in some sense mad simply for taking on Western might. Throughout the latter part of the nineteenth century, for instance, the British faced down various "mad mullahs" in North Africa. Yet Ho Chi Minh, the North Vietnamese Communist leader, who would once have been portrayed as quite mad (or "fanatical," its ideological equivalent) for bringing such unbelievable punishment upon his people, remained a remarkably undemonized figure. He was pictured neither as a slathering ape like Tojo nor a frothing, dancing madman like Hitler. Despite his Oriental features, he was seldom drawn either as a Fu Manchu or a Ming the Merciless; or even as a miniature version of the monstrous, green-faced Mao Zedong of 1950s anti-Communist bubble gum cards, or of the thuggish Stalin of so many political cartoons. He remained a wispy old graybeard, a hard man to hate, more or less ignored for propaganda purposes by his opponents, while romanticized by some in the antiwar movement as "Uncle Ho," almost a member of the family. One of Lyndon Johnson's constant, private plaints took up this theme. As he told a group of senators after the Tet Offensive of 1968, "I wish [Senator] Mike [Mansfield] would make a speech on Ho Chi Minh. Nothing is as dirty as to violate a truce during the holidays. But nobody says anything bad about Ho. They call me a murderer. But Ho has a great image."

In the end, an American president, rather than Ho Chi Minh or General Vo Nguyen Giap, took on the mantle of madness. It was not just that Richard Nixon's domestic critics were ready to label him a madman but that, in his desire to end the war in a satisfying fashion, he was ready to label himself one. "I call it the madman theory, Bob," Nixon aide H. R. Haldeman reported the president saying:

> I want the North Vietnamese to believe I've reached the point where I might do *anything* to stop the war. We'll just slip the word to them that, "for God's sake, you know Nixon is obsessed about Communists. We can't restrain him when he's angry—and he has his hand on the nuclear button"—and Ho Chi Minh himself will be in Paris in two days begging for peace.[32]

Henry Kissinger, Nixon's national security adviser, was equally fascinated with the possible bargaining advantage of having the enemy imagine the president as an evil, potentially world-obliterating madman. "Henry talked about it so much," according to Lawrence Lynn, a Kissinger aide, "particularly at the time of [the invasion of] Cambodia—that the Russians and North Vietnamese wouldn't run risks because of Nixon's character."

According to investigative reporter Seymour Hersh, Nixon may have picked up the madman theory from Kissinger, who evidently first heard it from Daniel Ellsberg, the Pentagon staff aide and RAND researcher who, in 1971, leaked the Pentagon Papers to the *New York Times*. In 1959, Ellsberg had given two lectures on "the conscious political use of irrational military threats" at then-professor Kissinger's Harvard seminar.

Ellsberg called the theory "The Political Uses of Madness." In essence, he described a problem in bargaining theory: what to do when the available threat is so extreme or costly as to make it seem unlikely that a sane and reasonable person would carry it out. . . . Ellsberg postulated that one way of making the threat somewhat credible . . . would be for the person making the threat to appear not to be fully rational.

The main example Ellsberg had in mind was not a president but Adolph Hitler. "I didn't even imagine," Ellsberg told Hersh, "that an American president could consider such a strategy."

What made this fascination with the idea of a mad president more curious was that it fused with fears held by White House aides and advisers that Nixon might sometimes be impaired or nearing the edge of derangement. A number of his aides were aware of the fact that the president drank heavily at night and acted strangely. "My drunken friend," "that drunken lunatic," "the meatball mind," or "the basket case" Kissinger called him after receiving his share of slurred late night phone calls. "All of us were worried about this man's stability," Lynn commented. "We'd have glimpses of him and didn't know what to do with it." The United States, then, was prepared to confront its enemies with a carefully crafted vision of a mad president, while members of his own staff wondered if he wasn't, indeed, unhinged.[33]

This presentation of the presidential self represented loss of a very high order, something like, in fact, the defeat such a strategy was striving to avoid. If unlike any previous president, Nixon was willing for diplomatic purposes to let others imagine him mad, and if the evidence of that madness was to be his twitchy finger on the nuclear button, then the president was willing to present the spectacle of slaughter as an atrocity of inconceivable proportions. This was no longer a president as baby killer but as potential nation slaughterer, as world incinerator. The United States was now led by a man ready to portray himself as a mad emperor, a Ming the Merciless.

6

THE CROSSOVER POINT:
EMBRACING THE MADNESS OF LOGIC

To believe it possible to lose in Vietnam, when any measure of success—from dead enemy and captured weapons to cleared roads and pacified villages—pointed toward victory, seemed mad. Yet to accept the figures pouring in daily from soldiers, advisers, and bureaucrats was to defy the logic of one's senses. To make the endlessly unraveling situation madder yet, the impending defeat did not seem to be a military one; for those who directed the war regularly claimed that not a single significant battle had been lost to the Vietnamese enemy.

Take Khe Sanh, an isolated marine garrison near the Laotian border. In early 1968, it was besieged by North Vietnamese regular troops who, for months, held its outnumbered defenders in a state of bloody hostagedom. The battle made President Johnson so anxious that he had "a sand table map and photo murals of Khe Sanh [set up] in the basement of the White House so he could follow personally every detail of the siege." Fearing that he might preside over an "American Dien Bien Phu," he even forced the Joint Chiefs to put in writing their confidence that the outpost would not fall. Khe Sanh so obsessed him that the unfolding of the Tet Offensive did not fully divert his attention. Khe Sahn, however, proved no Dienbienphu. North Vietnamese troops suffered tremendous casualties there and the siege was finally lifted. Yet some months after this "victory," the outpost was abandoned and no presidential attention ever turned to it again.[34]

Similarly, the stunning South Vietnam–wide offensive launched during the 1968 Tet holiday truce was quickly declared an enemy "defeat." In a series of coordinated attacks, the North Vietnamese and National Liberation Front struck at five of the country's six largest cities, thirty-four provincial capitals, sixty-four district capitals, and numerous military bases—over one hundred major targets in all. NLF sappers even briefly captured part of the heavily fortified American embassy compound in the center of Saigon. General Westmoreland appeared at the embassy six and a half hours after the attack to denounce the Communists for "very deceitfully" using the truce period "to create maximum consternation." NLF soldiers held parts of Saigon for three weeks and parts of Hue, the old imperial capital, for almost a month until nearly every house in that city had been damaged or leveled in the fighting. South Vietnamese government troops were badly bloodied and American losses were high. To retake major urban areas, air power was called in. Saigon and other cities and towns were bombed. In perhaps the most infamous phrase of the war, an anonymous U.S. major said of the retaking of Ben Tre, "It became necessary to destroy the town to save it."[35]

All this broke over the American people in a wave of images of unexpected carnage, a home front televisual disaster whose effects were only heightened by the rosy administration prognostications that preceded it. Among the many officials enlisted to sell American prospects in Vietnam to the public, General Westmoreland had been summoned back to the United States the previous November to promote war "progress." In a National Press Club address, he had proclaimed, "The ranks of the Vietcong are thinning steadily. . . . We have reached an important point when the end begins to come into view."

Tet was visibly the wrong "end," a stunning setback, if not a breaking point in terms of public support for the war effort. Yet based on enemy dead—up to sixty thousand by some American estimates—Tet was declared, while in progress, a smashing defeat of the NLF. This "defeat" was announced by the president at his first post-Tet news conference, seconded by the military high command, and generally accepted by the media.[36]

Tet summed up the puzzle that was Vietnam. Victory somehow meant defeat, for to win you had to destroy what you "won," and to destroy what you won—the villages, towns, and cities of Vietnam, not to speak of its livestock, land, and people—was to ensure the enmity of those in whose name you fought. If it was true that there were no Alamos, no Little Big Horns there, all those years had an undeniable Alamo-like quality to them. Yet it seemed inconceivable that the North Vietnamese, no matter how fanatic their leaders or courageous their troops, could be *the* enemy. Whether North Vietnam was "a little fourth-rate power" (Henry Kissinger) or "a third-rate country with a population of less than two counties in one of the fifty states of the United States" (Joint Chiefs Chairman Admiral Thomas Moorer), how could it be responsible for the defeat-in-the-making of the world's preeminent power?[37]

This was the unspoken logic that drove those involved in the war's prosecution to conclude that, if victory was not in sight, there must be another explanation than military failure; that, in fact, only one people had the ability to defeat the United States, to sap its "will" to fight. In November 1969, on the eve of enormous antiwar demonstrations, President Nixon went on television to say as much: "And so tonight—to you, the great silent majority of my fellow Americans—I ask for support. . . . For the more divided we are at home, the less likely the enemy is to negotiate at Paris. Let us be united for peace. Let us also be united against defeat. Because let us understand: North Vietnam cannot defeat or humiliate the United States. Only Americans can do that."[38]

Candidates for this new enemy within were almost too easy to find. In the spectacle of the moment, various groups seemed to be auditioning for the part. Shots of young radicals marching under the colors of the NLF flag or chanting "Ho, Ho, Ho Chi Minh, NLF is gonna win" were common on television, as were images of black power advocates, black separatists, and black revolutionaries, speaking in a language that seemed to have nothing to do with the now comforting story of progress toward civil rights for all.

As in July 1967 in Detroit, Newark, Cleveland, and elsewhere, so in the wake of the assassination of Martin Luther King, Jr., in April 1968, America's "Vietnamese" launched their own "Tet" offensive of rioting, burning, and looting in 125 cities and towns. Fifty-five thousand troops had to be mobilized and rushed not into Hue or Saigon but into the inner cities to support overwhelmed police forces. Black rioters exhibited behavior and attitudes that seemed alien. A majority in Newark, for instance, in response to a question about whether they considered the country "worth fighting for in the event of a major war," replied in the negative.

There was sniping at police and troops, and it was rumored that disaffected black Vietnam veterans were using their skills in American cities—by implication, for the other side. Newspapers speculated about whether "guerrilla warfare," as the *New York Times* put it, "long a part of the rhetoric of Negro militants," might soon actually be put into practice in the streets ("Indeed, that phase may have already begun"). On TV, scenes from either "war" looked remarkably similar. "Television viewers . . . saw Washington itself defended by Federal combat troops, while columns of smoke from burning buildings towered above the Capitol." In his post-Tet press conference, the president linked the attacks that had "disrupted" life in Vietnam to the "disruptions" in Detroit. "A few bandits," he remarked, "can do that in any city."[39]

But these domestic "enemies" did not, in truth, fill the bill. Radical students restricted to college campuses (or to periodic demonstrations in Washington) and black rioters largely trapped in ghetto communities did not explain the failure to achieve victory thousands of miles away. Some in the military suspected that the real explanation lay with their own civilian leaders, who had not let them bomb the Vietnamese "back to the Stone Age." American power had never really been "unleashed," or had not been unleashed fast enough. The armed forces had been "handcuffed" by a president and his advisers too worried about Chinese entry into the war or about world opinion or about micromanaging military strategy. Despite the awesome levels of carnage inflicted on Indochina, they came to believe that the disproportionate numbers had not been disproportionate enough.

The internal enemy of record, however, proved to be the media. In the 1950s, the vision of a media infiltrated by the alien and un-American had been the thread that tied fear of communism to fear of the child. Now it was claimed that the media were offering the public something like an enemy's-eye view of the war, transforming military success into an impression of defeat. "NBC and the *New York Times*," commented President Johnson in a 1967 interview, "are committed to an editorial policy of making us surrender." Similarly, President Nixon sometimes spoke of the media as if it were a set of propaganda organs of Hanoi.

This view was fostered with a special intensity among those assumedly least likely to have viewed media coverage of the war—high-level military officers organizing and commanding the fighting in Vietnam. In a typical comment, a senior army general claimed in 1974 that the media had conducted "a psychological warfare campaign against the United States policies in Vietnam that could not have been better done by the enemy."[40]

Yet something rang hollow. None of these domestic enemies could believably be traced back to the enemy, and together they did not add up to defeat. Never had the treachery of the nonwhite adversary been more confounding. Every Vietnamese "victory" was accompanied by a one-sided slaughter; for unlike Pearl Harbor, their sneak attacks led to their deaths in vast numbers. Yet the United States, with its 553,000 troops and its air and sea armada was, in the end, forced to flee. It was as if defeat were some mysterious malady that appeared magically from the ether of victory.

In Vietnam, results did not faintly tally with calculations—and more than in any previous war, calculations were expectations; for Secretary of Defense Robert McNamara, former Harvard Business School professor and Ford Motor Company president, and his "whiz kids" or "computer jockeys," new-style defense planners from the world of corporate management and defense technocracy, were firmly convinced that the Pentagon could be managed in the same "scientific" and "efficient" manner as a business. They quickly put their numbers-crunching methods of cost-benefit analysis to work organizing a war in which anything that could be tabulated only seemed to confirm the ludicrous preponderance of American power.

In no war were the statistics of triumph so omnipresent and overwhelming. Sometimes it seemed that Americans in Vietnam did nothing but invent new ways of measuring success. There were, for instance, the eighteen indices of the Hamlet Evaluation System (HES), each meant to calibrate the "progress" of "pacification" in the South's 2,300 villages and almost 13,000 hamlets. Developed in 1966 at the behest of Secretary of Defense McNamara and CIA Director Helms, constantly refined and upgraded, nine of these indicators focused on rural "security" and nine on rural "development." Based on the information American advisers fed into HES, hamlets were rated from A ("A superhamlet. Just about everything going right in both security and development") to E ("Definitely under VC control. Local [government] officials and our advisers don't enter except on military operation").

There were also the many indices of the Measurement of Progress system. Its monthly reports, produced in slide form, included "strength trends of the opposing forces; efforts of friendly forces in sorties . . . enemy base areas neutralized . . . and the degree of government control of roads, population, etc." Then there were the figures on every form of destruction rained down on North Vietnam (sorties flown, tonnage dropped, "truck kills," and so on). In the South, special effort went into the creation of numerical equivalents for death. Visiting Washington officials received *son et lumière* briefings in which death was quantified in elaborate charts and diagrams. General Westmoreland had his "attrition charts," multicolored bar graphs illustrating various "trends" in death and destruction, while in the field, Lieutenant General Julian J. Ewell had his codified kill ratios of "allied to enemy dead," ranging from 1–50 ("Highly skilled U.S. unit") to 1–10 ("Historical U.S. average"). Collated, sorted out, broken down, interpreted, and illustrated, such statistics flowed tidally toward policy makers in Washington.[41]

This numerology of death was not just a set of passive measurements. The numbers were an active element in Vietnamese affairs. They initiated death as they recorded it, for it was on the basis of deaths recorded that future deaths were to be ordered up. The numbers would determine the next set of "quotas" to be met. Unless you entered the correct numbers into the ongoing flow, whether you were an officer or a bureaucrat, you stood little chance of advancement. Yet in a "backwards" world where few Americans could communicate with the Vietnamese, basic information might be unobtainable, numbers arriving from below had to be taken on faith, and pressure from above for victory statistics was constant, the production of numbers gained an irreality all its own.

On the ground, the MGR or "Mere Gook Rule"—"If it's dead and it's Vietnamese, it's VC"—meant you could produce your own bodies for the "body count," or even your own body count without the bodies to show for it. As First Lieutenant William Calley, Jr., on trial for his part in the My Lai massacre, testified, "You just make an estimate off the top of your head. There is no way to really figure out exact body count. At that time, everything went into a body count—VC, buffalo, pigs, cows. Something we did, you put it on your body count, sir. . . . As long as it was high, that was all they wanted." Often, the only limit on the body count was the need to produce (or explain the lack of) captured enemy weapons.[42]

In the same way, you could produce roads cleared, hamlets pacified, or trucks destroyed. This was something other than a matter of impreci-sion. This was war as fantasy. Yet the more fantastic (and unlikely) the figures became, the more horrifically destructive the war became; hence, the more likely that some horrific set of numbers was being produced.

In the field, the indices of success were often calibrated in the most detailed ways, as in the monthly Military Performance Indicator charts in which a complicated, weighted system of credits and debits gave each infantry division its "index of efficiency." ("Credits included enemy body counts, prisoners of war, and U.S. reenlistments. Debits included acci-dents, courts-martial, sicknesses, and all kinds of disciplinary problems," including drug taking.) If officers stood to gain career goals from the proper numbers, ordinary GIs might be offered bonuses in time off, medals, or money. Sometimes heightened production norms were emphasized through "contests." As *New York Times* reporter Gloria Emerson recorded:

> One contest in the 25th Division in 1969, called "Best of the Pack," was for the best rifle and the best weapons platoon in the 1st Battal-ion, 27th Infantry, which was known as the Wolfhounds. One award was a two-day pass for best weapons in Dau Tieng; the other, for best rifles a three-day pass in Cu Chi. . . . "Points will be awarded [the announcement said] for the following":
>
>   10- Each possible body count . . .
>   50- Each enemy individual weapon captured
>   100- Each enemy crew served weapon captured
>   100- Each enemy Body Count
>   200- Each tactical radio captured . . .
>   500- Perfect score on CMMI (inspection)
> 1,000- Each prisoner of war
>
> Points will be deducted for the following:
>
>   50- Each U.S. WIA (wounded)
>   500- Each U.S. KIA (killed)
>
> If a man was killed, his platoon was penalized and had less of a chance to win the pass.[43]

As in some perverse version of *The Price Is Right*, the products of abundance behind each curtain were bloody bodies. In this way did the army gain the look of the bounty hunter, ready to produce bodies on request. Completing a transformation of the cowboy hero begun on tele-vision in the previous decade, it now advertised itself with a card that said, "Have gun, will travel."

Of all the statistics, the "body count" caused the most controversy. In a war in which D-Day-like landings were uncontested publicity events and conquered territory might be abandoned within days, the body count was a way of quantifying what could not otherwise be envisioned. If killing the enemy was part of war, then a count of enemy dead seemed nothing to be ashamed of, and so, as an indicator of progress, it was incorporated into official military press briefings in Saigon. Once decoupled from victory, however, the body count gained a grim life of its own. Detached from reality yet producing reality, it became a death-dealing Catch-22.

Nowhere can the frustration over this decoupling of the statistics of slaughter from the war story's expected finale be felt more strongly than in the Pentagon Papers. Document after document reflects the chagrin, desperation, or despair that the war planners felt discussing (or straining to avoid discussing) some version of defeat ("retreat," "humiliation") in the context of the numerical signs of victory. Here, for instance, is a passage from an October 1966 memo Secretary of Defense Robert McNamara prepared for President Johnson:

The one thing demonstrably going for us in Vietnam over the past year has been the large number of enemy killed-in-action resulting from the big military operations. Allowing for possible exaggeration in reports, the enemy must be taking losses—deaths in and after battle—at the rate of more than 60,000 a year. The infiltration routes would seem to be one-way trails to death for the North Vietnamese. Yet there is no sign of an impending break in enemy morale and it appears that he can more than replace his losses by infiltration from North Vietnam and recruitment in South Vietnam. . . .

It is my judgment that, barring a dramatic change in the war, we should limit the increase in U.S. forces in SVN [South Vietnam] in 1967 to 70,000 men and we should level off at the total of 470,000 which such an increase would provide. It is my view that this is enough to punish the enemy at the large-unit operations level and to keep the enemy's main forces from interrupting pacification. I believe also that even many more than 470,000 would not kill the enemy off in such numbers as to break their morale so long as they think they can wait us out. It is possible that such a 40 percent increase over our present level of 325,000 will break the enemy's morale in the short term; but if it does not, we must, I believe, be prepared for and have underway a long-term program   [to] pursue the all-important pacification task with proper attention and resources and without the spectre of apparently endless escalation of U.S. deployments.[44]

The war effort was afloat in figures, utterly precise, yet fantastic. In 1968, for instance, the U.S. Military Assistance Command in Vietnam claimed an exact 15,776 VCI (Vietcong leaders or members of the Vietcong Infrastructure) "neutralized" at the village level (including 2,259 killed) by the Phoenix program, a CIA-organized attempt to contest NLF control of the countryside. This led to the setting of a quota of 21,000 "neutralizations" for the following year. Only 19,534 "neutralizations" (including 6,187 killed) were, however, recorded for 1969, because of what one government document called "an end of the year slump."[45]

Yet while the Phoenix program resulted in many deaths, its figures were unreliable. Scores that had little or nothing to do with the war were settled through the program. Bounties were paid to Vietnamese informants for evidence that "neutralization" had occurred ("on the presentation of a head or an ID card or an ear"), and extortion for protection from being denounced as VCI was commonplace. A significant percentage of actual VCI evidently bribed their way to freedom; whereas, lacking the money, innocent peasants rounded up to inflate the figures were tortured, jailed, or murdered. Program bureaucrats, under the same pressures for quota fulfillment as their military counterparts, produced doctored and inflated figures, suitable for promotion.[46]

Although the Phoenix program had a destructive effect on the NLF, there was no way to assess accurately the relationship the figures had to events on the ground. Assassinations and killings were seemingly underreported, and NLF "neutralizations" overreported in a war in which any dead Vietnamese could be called an NLF cadre without fear of contradiction. This was a dream world of destruction. The fantastic elaboration of the decoupled statistics of slaughter provided the war with its mad logic. Yet without an aura of triumph, the numbers proved a math from hell, and were so treated by the antiwar movement.

You did not have to oppose the war for the numbers to ring hollow, however; hence, the military high command's frustrated quest for the "crossover point," that moment when allied forces would kill more of "them" than they could replace through recruitment in South Vietnam or infiltration from the North. The promise of a crossover point held out hope that next month or next year Americans could regain a state of triumphalist innocence. Without that promise, the armed forces became a machine for the production of random death and destruction.

Here are Assistant Secretary of Defense John T. McNaughton's "notes" on an April 1967 conversation between President Johnson and Generals Wheeler and Westmoreland, then in charge of the war. Johnson's frustration and despair over lack of success in Vietnam had already

begun to overwhelm him. General Westmoreland started the discussion
by referring to a recent request for an additional two and a half divisions
of troops. Without them, the general added, "we will not be in danger of
being defeated, but it will be nip and tuck to oppose the reinforcements
the enemy is capable of providing." He then reminded the president that
"in the final analysis we are fighting a war of attrition in Southeast
Asia."

The president, hesitant over the political costs of dispatching more
soldiers to Vietnam, replied:

> "When we add divisions can't the enemy add divisions? If so where
> does it all end?" Westmoreland answered: "The VC and DRV strength
> in SVN now totals 285,000 men. It appears that last month we
> reached the crossover point in areas excluding the two northern
> provinces. Attritions will be greater than additions to the force. . . .
> The enemy has 8 divisions in South Vietnam. He has the capability of
> deploying 12 divisions although he would have difficulty supporting
> all of these. He would be hard pressed to support more than 12 divi-
> sions. If we add $2^1/_2$ divisions, it is likely the enemy will react by
> adding troops." The President then asked "At what point does the
> enemy ask for volunteers?" Westmoreland's only reply was, "That is
> a good question.". . . [Westmoreland then] explained his concept of a
> "meat grinder" where we would kill large numbers of the enemy but
> in the end do little better than hold our own. . . . Westmoreland con-
> cluded by estimating that with a force level of 565,000 men, the war
> could well go on for three years. With a second increment of $2^1/_3$ divi-
> sions leading to a total of 665,000 men, it could go on for two years.

Except as the raw statistics of slaughter, the enemy was invisible in
the government documents collected in the Pentagon Papers, and yet
confusingly powerful. As early as November 1964, in a Washington briefing for "senior officials," Maxwell Taylor, then ambassador to South
Vietnam, commented: "The ability of the Viet-Cong to rebuild their
units and to make good their losses is one of the mysteries of this guerrilla war. . . . Not only do the Viet-Cong units have the recuperative powers of the phoenix, but they have an amazing ability to maintain
morale."[47]

As for the policy makers, so for many Americans, the enemy, previously "faceless" yet substantial, was now dematerializing except in the
context of a slaughter that looked like nothing more than that—evidence
of a meatgrinder at work. To understand how victory culture was transformed into that meatgrinder, an obvious yet generally unacceptable fact

must be grasped. It was Vietnamese unwillingness to stop fighting, politically as much as militarily, that proved crucial to the war story's dissolution. The Vietnamese were, of course, intent on fighting a real enemy, not a societal state of mind. But it was a state of mind, a narrative, that Americans were intent on imposing on Vietnam, just as they were intent on building an American landscape of PXs and air-conditioned offices, of ice cream production plants and airfields on Vietnamese soil.

If the statistics of slaughter had been accepted by both sides as the ruling logic of the struggle, the United States should have won the war any day from the mid-1960s on. In the South, the degree of destruction was almost incomprehensible. In 1967, reporter Jonathan Schell flew in a series of small Forward Air Control planes over the "heavily populated coastal strip" of Quang Ngai Province. In the *New Yorker* magazine, he described what he saw:

> From the air, the roofs of houses that were still standing appeared as dark-brown squares; the ashes of houses that had been recently burned appeared as gray squares; and the rain-washed clay foundations of houses that had been destroyed more than a month or so earlier appeared as red or yellow squares. When houses had been burned by troops on the ground, their walls—of clay-and-bamboo or stone— were usually still standing, but the walls of houses that had been bombed or bulldozed were flattened, or strewn over the rice fields. The pattern of destruction was roughly the same throughout the densely populated area of fields and villages lying between the mountains and the sea. Villages remained standing in a long belt a few kilometres wide bordering Route 1. . . . The rest—with certain exceptions . . . —had been destroyed. . . . On the coastal side of Route 1 in Son Tinh [district]—again excepting the belt of a few kilometres along the road—from eighty to ninety percent of the houses had been destroyed all the way to the sea. . . . Like most of the province, the valley of the Song Tra Khuc was spotted with craters of all sizes. Craters from artillery fire, which were a yard or two wide, peppered the rice fields and the former villages, and craters from delayed-fuse bombs, which were as much as thirty feet across and seven feet deep, and many of which had filled with water, dotted the landscape with little ponds. Anti-personnel bombs, which explode on contact, had made shallow craters that spread out in rays across the fields, like giant yellow asterisks, and napalm strikes had blackened the fields in uneven splotches.[48]

It was a Vietnamese unwillingness to surrender in the face of a slaughter that only gained in statistical intensity that transformed the war story into a series of embarrassingly un-American-looking atrocities. From such slaughter came no payoff, no victory. The numbers endlessly confirmed American power; yet, by the sacrifice of untold lives, the enemy had somehow captured the only set of numbers worth having—the numbers of weeks, months, years that the fighting went on. In that war, longer than both world wars and Korea combined, the Vietnamese had wrested time from the American grasp. If there were two wars occurring at once, it was the Vietnamese who, at incalculable cost, made their "invisible" one predominant.

7

"SOMETHING RATHER DARK AND BLOODY": EMBRACING MADNESS

On the tenth of February 1675, came the Indians with great numbers upon Lancaster: Their first coming was about sun-rising; hearing the noise of some guns, we looked out; several houses were burning, and the smoke ascending to heaven. There were five persons taken in one house, the father, and the mother and a sucking child, they knocked on the head; the other two they took and carried away alive . . . another there was who running along was shot and wounded, and fell down; he begged of them his life, promising them money . . . but they would not hearken to him but knocked him in the head, and stripped him naked, and split open his bowels. . . . There were three others belonging to the same garrison who were killed; the Indians getting up upon the roof of the barn, had advantage to shoot down upon them over their fortification. Thus these murderous wretches went on, burning, and destroying before them. . . . One of my elder sister's children, named William, had then his leg broken, which the Indians perceiving, they knocked him on the head. Thus were we butchered by those merciless heathen, standing amazed, with the blood running down to our heels. . . . It is a solemn sight to see so many Christians lying in their blood, some here, and some there, like a company of sheep torn by wolves. All of them stripped naked by a company of hell-hounds, roaring, singing, ranting and insulting, as if they would have torn our very hearts out. . . .[49]

At 6:30 A.M. on March 16, 1968, all the enemy batteries installed around Son My started pounding the village for more than half an hour. The eleven choppers came in, strafing the locality and landing American troops whose sanguinary intention was visible on their faces. They shot at all that came in sight: men, women, children, elderly people, plants and animals, and destroyed everything: crops, fruit-trees, houses. . . . Vo Thi Phu, mother of a 12-month-old baby, was shot dead. . . . The baby, which tried to suck at its mother's breast, cried when it found only blood instead of milk. The Yankees got angry and shouted "Viet Cong, Viet Cong," and heaped straw on mother and baby and set fire to it. . . . After raping to death Mrs. Sam, a sexagenarian, the aggressors made a deep slash in her body with a bayonet. . . . Mui, 14, was raped and shut in her hut. The GIs set fire to it, guarded the door and pushed back the poor little girl who tried to run from the fire. . . . Worse still, the aggressors threw over one hundred women and children and many dozen old people into a canal dug in front of Mr. Nhieu's house and murdered them with machine-gun fire and hand grenades. The victims' corpses were disfigured beyond identification. . . . In one day only, 502 people including over 170 children were massacred, 300 houses destroyed and over 870 head of cattle killed. Our coastal village so green with coconut palms, bamboos and willows is now but heaps of ashes.[50]

With the publication of Mary Rowlandson's seventeenth-century captivity narrative, the European settlers of North America entered a cultural "Indian country." With the Vietnamese account of what became known as the My Lai massacre they left it. A subhamlet of Son My village known to the soldiers of the Americal Division as "Pinkville," My Lai 4 was located on the Battambang Peninsula in Quangngai province, South Vietnam. Like much of Massachusetts in Mary Rowlandson's time, the peninsula was thought of by the Americal's soldiers as "Indian country" and had been designated a "free-fire zone." Although Son My was the reputed headquarters of the 48th Vietcong Battalion, the Americal had twice swept through it, sustaining casualties without managing to confront the 48th. More than 90 percent of the division's casualties had, in fact, come not in battle but from land mines and booby traps.[51]

In the four months before First Lieutenant William Calley's platoon, one of three in Charlie Company, entered My Lai 4 as part of Task Force Barker, it had already been reduced by eighteen, without ever seeing the enemy. In briefings the previous day, however, they had been assured by company commander Ernest Medina, known to his men as Mad Dog, that this time they would meet the 48th head on, that this was their chance for revenge. Many of them were left with the impression that they were under orders to "level Pinkville." As Calley testified at his trial:

When my troops were getting massacred and mauled by an enemy I couldn't see, I couldn't feel, and I couldn't touch—that nobody in the military system ever described them as anything other than communism. They didn't give it a race, they didn't give it a sex, they didn't give it an age. . . . That was my enemy out there. And when it became between me and that enemy, I had to value the lives of my troops.[52]

Instead of the 48th Battalion, Calley's men found in the hamlet only women, children, infants, and old men, none armed, none resistant, many finishing breakfast. It was on these civilians—any one of whom might have been a Vietcong supporter—and the livestock, wells, crops, and houses of My Lai 4 that the Americans took out their pent up frustrations and their desire for vengeance against a deadly enemy they could not locate.

What made this massacre extraordinary—other than its size—among the many planned and unplanned horrors of that war was the nature of the journey it took to the homeland of "the enemy," to the United States. If the "other side" reported the massacre in Mary Rowlandson–like terms, those were largely the terms in which Americans, too, finally had to confront it. In the twenty months from that March morning in 1968 to December 5, 1969, when the My Lai photographs of military cameraman Ronald Haeberle appeared in *Life* magazine (with an African antelope and the promise of "Great Action Pictures" on its cover), the massacre seemed to rise inexorably through layers of official cover-up and denial, through what was left of victory culture, without losing the look of a horror as seen through the eyes of the massacred. Mary Rowlandson was now an Indian.[53]

The first stories about My Lai to appear in the United States—the morning after the massacre—were picked up from an army publicity release. No nonmilitary reporters had been near the scene. These reports proved fairly typical for the war. On its front page, for instance, the *New York Times* labeled the operation a significant success. "American troops caught a North Vietnamese force in a pincer movement on the central coastal plain yesterday, killing 128 enemy soldiers in day-long fighting." United Press International called it an "impressive victory," and added a bit of patriotic color: "The Vietcong broke and ran for their hide-out tunnels. Six-and-a-half hours later, 'Pink Village' had become 'Red, White and Blue Village.'" These dispatches from the "front" still had the ring of victory culture to them, yet they were a fairy tale My Lai, for none of the information in them was accurate.[54]

For over a year, no other version of the events was available to Americans, and so it might have remained if Ronald Ridenhour, a former GI who served with several witnesses to or participants in the massacre, had not been so deeply disturbed by their accounts. "My God, when I first came home," he later said, "I would tell my friends about this and cry—literally cry. As far as I was concerned, it was a reflection on me, on every American, on the ideals that we supposedly represent. It completely castrated the whole picture of America."

Ridenhour finally decided to compose a letter detailing what he knew:

> [I]n the following months I was to hear similar stories from such a wide variety of people that it became impossible for me to disbelieve that something rather dark and bloody did indeed occur sometime in March, 1968, in a village called "Pinkville" in the Republic of Viet-Nam. . . . Somehow I just couldn't believe that not only had so many young American men participated in such an act of barbarism, but that their officers had ordered it.

Mailed in April 1969 to the Department of the Army, the Defense Department, the Joint Chiefs of Staff, the State Department, the White House, various government officials, congressmen, and senators, it sparked an army investigation and in September the bringing of charges against First Lieutenant Calley.[55]

Though numerous officials and military men came to know at least some of the horrific details, months passed before news of My Lai made it into the media. On November 13, more than thirty newspapers picked up an article from Dispatch News Service, a little-known news agency, by Seymour Hersh, a former Associated Press reporter just then working on a book about the Pentagon. The story began, "Lieutenant William L. Calley, Jr., twenty-six, is a mild-mannered, boyish-looking Vietnam combat veteran with the nickname of 'Rusty.' The Army says he deliberately murdered at least 109 Vietnamese civilians during a search-and-destroy mission in March, 1968, in a Viet Cong stronghold known as 'Pinkville.'" Remarkable here was not the twenty months that had passed between the massacre and news about it, but that Hersh's piece had finally emerged not in "underground" papers like New York's *East Village Other* or Atlanta's *Great Speckled Bird*, but in the mainstream press, and that within weeks shocking photos of the massacre, taken while in progress, and network-televised confessions by some of those involved were unavoidable anywhere in the country.[56]

Cameraman Ronald Haeberle and army journalist Jay Roberts, from the 31st Public Information Detachment, had helicoptered into My Lai with Charlie Company. Only a week away from finishing his tour of service in Vietnam and carrying three cameras, Haeberle took many photos not just of bodies strewn everywhere but of those about to die. Of a photo of women and children huddled together, he later commented, "Guys were about to shoot these people. I yelled, 'Hold it,' and shot my picture. As I walked away, I heard M16s open up. From the corner of my eye I saw bodies falling, but I didn't turn to look." "This man," he wrote, of another, "was old and trembling so that he could hardly walk. He looked like he wanted to cry. When I left him I heard two rifle shots." "When these two boys were shot at, the older one fell on the little one, as if to protect him. Then the guys finished them off."[57]

Haeberle turned his black-and-white film of the massacre over to the army, but took the color shots back to Cleveland with him. There, he showed them to civic organizations as part of a Vietnam slide show. "They caused no commotion," he recalled. "Nobody believed it. They said Americans wouldn't do this." On November 20, some of his photos appeared in the *Cleveland Plain Dealer* and, soon after, in *Life, Time,* and *Newsweek.* That, combined with a November 21 *CBS Evening News* appearance by Paul Medlo, the first of numerous platoon members to offer confessional accounts on national television, induced a sort of national shock wave. Despite the tens of thousands of Asian bodies that had dropped on screen over the years, nothing like this had ever been seen. In *Life* magazine was a photo album from hell. No cover-up, not even a suppressive instinct at any level of society, prevented Lieutenant Calley, Sergeant Ernest Medina, Charlie Company, and implicitly the war effort from publicly taking on an aura of atrocity.[58]

Life published ten pages of "exclusive pictures, eyewitness accounts [of] the massacre at Mylai," labeled "a story of indisputable horror—the deliberate slaughter of old men, women, children and babies." Here they were, drenched in blood, surrounded by fire ("Huts were being torched with cigarette lighters"), in the embrace of almost any cruelty imaginable. ("One body, an old man, had a 'C' carved on his chest"; "A GI grabbed the girl and with the help of others started stripping her . . . 'VC boom-boom,' another said, telling the 13 year-old that she was a whore for the Vietcong"; "A GI was running down a trail, chasing a duck with a knife.") And these crimes were being committed by typical American "boys."

Remarkably, such accounts appeared in significant ways unchanged from NLF accounts of the massacre. The Vietnamese villagers were still the settlers; the Americans, the savage invaders, creating havoc in the world. In the United States, however, the nightmare of My Lai tended to be defined in different terms than in Vietnam. The horror—"an American tragedy," as *Time* magazine called it—lay largely in an inability to account for the Jekyll-and-Hyde reversals that My Lai seemed to have caused. What had led "almost depressingly normal . . . everymen . . . who at home in Ohio or Vermont would regard it as unthinkable to maliciously strike a child, much less kill one," officered by "just an average American boy," to commit such "patently demented" acts?[59]

If the central madness of the war was the need to fight an enemy who could not be seen, at least until death, then as in any horror story, it was in death that the most terrifying reversals occurred. In death, enemy bodies transmogrified into the mutilated corpses of so many innocents. In death, the terrorist became an infant; the VC messenger, a child; the VC whore, a girl; the VC suspect, an old man. The enemy, invisible yet deadly, once dead, became visible and harmless. Here, indeed, was an American nightmare, for here, too, the enemy had triumphantly disappeared.

Given the role reversals of My Lai, the spectacle of slaughter should now logically have passed into the hands of the Vietnamese "settlers." In fact, a tiny faction of American radicals, the Weathermen, instinctively grasped this. Identifying with peasant revolution in the Third World, they began in 1969 to call for the extermination of "Pig Amerikka," not just of the war-prosecuting government, but of ordinary white Americans ("honky bastards"). At a "National War Council" in Flint, Michigan, that December, Weatherleader Bernardine Dohrn hailed the Manson gang's murders of actress Sharon Tate and six other people in two Los Angeles houses. "Dig it, first they killed those pigs, then they ate dinner in the same room with them, then they even shoved a fork into a victim's stomach!" There was indeed an eerie parallel between the Manson gang, those perverse young longhairs eating dinner amid the murdered and mutilated bodies of the Tate household, and the "boys" of Charlie Company placidly lunching amid the bodies of their victims. This bringing of the atrocity into the dining room was an image any devotee of 1950s comic book culture would have recognized.[60]

If presidents were willing to embrace the logic of madness and generals the madness of logic, the foot soldier was left to embrace madness itself. Simply to survive to return to "the world" meant gaining expertise in the signs of enemy-ness. As with the Communist at home, the enemy in Vietnam had to be teased, HUAC-style, out of the undergrowth. But in a country where, to many soldiers, the inhabitants looked alike, spoke an incomprehensible language, and practiced alien customs, the task of even the expert was a daunting one. Under the circumstances, it was a small step from the knowledge that the enemy might be anywhere to the thought that the enemy was everywhere and that every Vietnamese was an enemy.

As one GI commented, in explaining a My Lai–linked massacre at a neighboring hamlet:

> The movements that were going on in the village, we just perceived that it was a VC village. There seemed to be different types of tracks. Like I said, when you're over there awhile you feel like you develop an ability to read a VC footprint or something like that. They always seemed to wear a type of tennis shoe or something. It just looked like a VC village to us.

It was enough to identify a village as "VC." To separate the villagers from the VC was beyond the skills not just of untrained GIs but of pacification bureaucrats and military strategists.

In contested areas, which meant much of the countryside, no VC expertise could definitively sort the enemy from the "friendlies." To disoriented GIs, like those in Charlie Company, the choices seemed visceral. As happened increasingly in the final years of the American ground war, the unit of "grunts" could turn a "search and destroy" mission into a "search and evade" one. They could, that is, simply leave a base perimeter and hunker down somewhere nearby while "on patrol." To do so was to declare the whole Vietnamese population off limits. Alternately, as with one soldier at My Lai who evidently purposely shot himself in the foot, an individual could disobey or ignore or avoid orders or even "frag" an officer who challenged his right not to fight. Another choice was to consider every "Oriental human being" (as the slaughtered were called in the initial military indictment of Lieutenant Calley) a "VC." Even a baby sucking at its mother's breast might, as a My Lai defendant claimed, be helping to conceal a hidden grenade.[61]

Frustration, anger, desire for revenge, rape, mutilation, torture, sadism, and the collection of body parts as souvenirs became something like norms in this backwards world in which the script American boys had followed since childhood no longer counted for a thing. The atrocity without the cleansing hope of victory became part of standard operating procedure; each act of horror, an unconscious mocking of American "ideals," an eating away at deeply held images. The generous GIs of victory culture entering a liberated town took on a new look in this new landscape. "First of all," testified Kenneth Ruth of the 1st Air Cavalry:

> we go into the village and ask people who they think are Viet Cong. So we were given two people that we were told were Viet Cong. What we do, is we took these two guys out in the field and we strung one of

'em up in a tree by his arms, tied his hands behind him, and then
hung him in the tree. Now what we did to this man when we strung
him up is that he was stripped of all his clothes, and then they tied a
string around his testicles and a man backed up about ten feet and
told him what would happen if he didn't answer any questions the
way they saw fit.

The enemy insignia, uniforms, and weapons brought home by the GIs
of victory culture became the collectible body parts of Vietnam. "[T]hese
white guys," recounted 1st Cavalry combat engineer Harold Bryant,
"would sometimes take the[ir] dog-tag chain and fill that up with
ears. . . . If we were movin' through the jungle, they'd just put the bloody
ear on the chain and stick the ear in their pocket and keep on going.
Wouldn't take time to dry it off. Then when we get back, they would nail
'em up on the walls of our hootch, you know, as a trophy."

The atrocity became mock-sport. "Kids would [line] up on the side of
the road," testified Sam Schorr of the 20th Brigade. "They'd be yelling
out, 'Chop, chop; chop, chop,' and they wanted food. . . . Well, just for a
joke, these guys would take a full can [of C-rations] if they were riding
shotgun and throw it as hard as they could at a kid's head. I saw several
kids' heads split wide open, knocked off the road, knocked into tires of
vehicles behind, and knocked under tank traps."[62]

On the other hand, in battlefield situations where the enemy acted in
a recognizably foelike manner, "their" Vietnamese ordinarily proved so
much more admirable than "ours." America's Vietnamese seemed like
the sorts of thugs white adventurers had once defeated single-handedly in
Hollywood films. They were corrupt, undemocratic, greedy, cruel, and
rapacious in relation to their own people and sometimes unwilling to
fight their own war. The enemy, on the other hand, often seemed like
"our kind of people." They were courageous, disciplined, willing to
endure terrible hardships, uncorrupt, and capable of mobilizing genuine
support among other Vietnamese. Major Charles Beckwith, the chief
American adviser to the special forces camp at Plei Me, reportedly commented after a siege of the camp was broken, "I'd give anything to have
two hundred VC under my command. They're the finest, most dedicated
soldiers I've ever seen. . . . I'd rather not comment on the performance of
my Vietnamese forces."[63]

Sometimes "they" looked so much like "us" that their enemy-ness
made no sense. In the spring of 1965, former military adviser John Paul
Vann returned to Vietnam as a civilian province pacification officer and,
shocked by the NLF's growth, wrote to a colleague:

There is a revolution going on in this country—and the principles, goals, and desires of the *other* side are much closer to what Americans believe in than those of GVN. I realize that ultimately, when the Chinese brand of Communism takes over, that these "revolutionaries" are going to be sadly disappointed—but then it will be too late—for them; and too late for us to win them. I am convinced that, even though the National Liberation Front is Communist-dominated, that the great majority of the people supporting it are doing so because it is their only hope to change and improve their living conditions and opportunities. If I were a lad of eighteen faced with the same choice—whether to support the GVN or the NLF—and a member of a rural community, I would surely choose the NLF.[64]

The flip side of this was a sense among some antiwar activists that the Vietnamese were saving the best of America from Americans intent on destroying it. In meetings with antiwar organizers, the Vietnamese were emphatic that their war was against an imperialistic government, not the American people, whose democratic principles were to be admired. As activist Tom Hayden explained of his return from antiwar burnout to launch the Indochina Peace Campaign, a congressional lobbying effort, "In a strange way, I had to learn it from Vietnamese propaganda, but the American people were fundamentally good. They had a good Declaration of Independence, a bill of rights, they weren't evil—and I was one of them."[65]

No matter what eyes you looked through, the United States seemed to be backing the wrong side. In this context, if the spectacle of slaughter was not ceded to the Vietnamese, it was, at least, lost to Americans as something that could fill a viewer with pride or pleasure. My Lai had taken Americans to the edge of what they could bear to see. Where the enemy had once been were now innocent victims. As triumphant fighters, the Vietnamese remained largely beyond view.

However, even the image of the enemy as victim proved so threatening that it called out for denial. Outside of the alternate world that housed the antiwar movement in college towns and communities, sympathy—no less empathy—for those murdered at My Lai seems to have been, at best, a minor aspect of the public's reaction. When Haeberle's photos first appeared in the *Cleveland Plain Dealer*, many readers phoned in to condemn the decision to publish them. Later, when shown to the Senate Armed Services Committee, only Senator Young of Ohio had a few compassionate words for the victims: "It's really terrifying and horrible, looking at a Vietnam woman—a young woman—standing up and begging, with young people all about her, and knowing that she would be killed an instant later by American bullets."[66]

More typical was the conclusion of a congressional subcommittee investigating the incident: "What obviously happened at My Lai was wrong. In fact it was so wrong and so *foreign* to the normal character and actions of our military forces as to immediately raise a question as to the legal sanity at the time of those men involved" [italics added]. Unsettling here was what seemed to be happening to Americans, not Vietnamese. Already, black urban uprisings, the assassinations of Robert Kennedy and Martin Luther King, Jr., and turmoil at the 1968 Democratic National Convention had brought home a sense of chaos and breakdown that Americans had been led to expect only in benighted lands like Vietnam.

To some, the United States was experiencing a "foreign" incursion, a new kind of sneak attack, and those dead bodies with their pretensions to innocence were part of the assault team. It was as if the babies, the cringing women, that pleading old man in Haeberle's photos had forced these horrific acts on otherwise ordinary GIs. The question they wanted answered was: Why hadn't the government done something to guard its boys? In a plea to the court on the day of his client's sentencing, George Latimer, Lieutenant Calley's main defense counsel, summed up this attitude: "When Lieutenant Calley went into the service of the United States Army, he was not an aggressive young man. Lieutenant Calley outside of an ordinary traffic violation was a good boy and he remained that way until he got into that Oriental area over there in Viet-Nam. Maybe, shall we say, he used bad judgment; maybe he became too aggressive. But who trained him to kill, kill, kill?"[67]

The members of Charlie Company, then, were the real victims of My Lai; "good boys" ordered into an impossible situation; scapegoats for misguided or evil government policies. The Invisible Government had struck again. On this point and around Calley as victim, the right and left, Governor George Wallace and Dr. Benjamin Spock, could meet and, in a limited way, agree. But many Americans seemed invested in a more blanket denial when it came to My Lai and Calley's conviction. In a *Time* magazine poll, 65 percent of Americans claimed not to be upset by the massacre. Telegrams, phone calls, and letters pouring into the White House, Congress, newspapers, and TV stations ran 100 to 1 against the Calley conviction and his sentence of life imprisonment. Veterans groups rallied to Calley, and draft boards in a number of states resigned in protest.[68]

Some professed to believe that no massacre had occurred, that an enemy fraud had been perpetrated on the public, that the photos were fakes. Blame was placed on the media for publicizing such photos and accounts in the first place. "Whose side are you on?" S. Lee of Beaver,

Pennsylvania, wrote *Life*. "I believe a new Communist tactic is recurring and they know they can rely on the liberals in the press as suckers," wrote a man from Baltimore. "I don't believe it actually happened," commented a Los Angeles salesman. "The story was planted by Viet Cong sympathizers and people inside this country who are trying to get us out of Vietnam sooner." Congressman John R. Rarick from Louisiana referred to My Lai as the "massacre hoax," while Senator Peter Dominick claimed that the My Lai reports, based on "unverified photographs," served "no public need to know."[69]

If in Vietnam the enemy could not be located, in the United States, the enemy, transformed into so many victims, had to be—with effort—not seen. Nonetheless, certain shocking thoughts about the enemylike nature of the government or simply of Americans proved irrepressible. In an official statement on My Lai, President Nixon was quick to call it an "isolated incident," particularly when compared to the "250,000 churches, pagodas, and temples" he claimed the marines alone had built "for the people of Vietnam" in the previous year. My Lai was, as Army Secretary Resor put it, "wholly unrepresentative of the manner in which our forces conduct military operations in Vietnam." Such sentiments were generally seconded by the media. Unlike the enemy's planned atrocity campaigns, My Lai was "an aberration." But in the defensiveness of such statements—and there were many at the time—one can almost hear what they were being defensive about. For they were all responses to a charge in the ether, even if largely unspoken: that the United States was embarked on a war that was criminal rather than misguided or mistaken.[70]

In 1945, the United States had stood in contrast to Nazi Germany, and the exterminatory impulse of the Holocaust had been walled off from the annihilatory impact of the atomic bomb. By the end of the 1960s, it had become almost impossible to think about the war without implicitly acknowledging, whether by preemptive refutation or avoidance, the suspicion that American acts had taken on a criminal cast. Nazism and the Nuremberg trials were on the brain. Chief counsel for the prosecution at Nuremberg, Telford Taylor, a supporter of sending combat troops to Vietnam in 1965, only five years later published *Nuremberg and Vietnam, an American Tragedy*. "But now," he wrote:

> the wheel had spun full circle, and the fingers of accusation are pointed not at others for whom we have felt scorn and contempt, but at ourselves. Worse yet, many of the pointing fingers are our own. . . . Accounts of the conduct of American troops, especially at Son My . . . have stung the national conscience as nothing else since the

days of slavery, and again Nuremberg is invoked as the symbol of con-
demnation.

Even those with no desire to take up such analogies found them
unavoidable. There were the soldiers of Charlie Company invoking the
Nazi defense to explain their actions. ("[I]f you're under orders, you're
going to be punished for not doing it and punished if you do. I didn't like
what happened, but I didn't decide.") There was *Time* magazine, in its
first account of My Lai, refuting the absurd charges of "critics abroad"—
those foreign elements again—who "glibly started making comparisons
with Nazi atrocities. Such comparisons are obviously spurious, if only
because Lidice and Babi Yar were caused by a deliberate national policy
of terror, not by the aberrations of soldiers under stress."[71]

Then there was the military command. In deciding how to deal with
possible My Lai trials, the military made every effort to avoid the spectacle of "two dozen or more American soldiers, including generals, lined up
in the dock like a little Nuremberg." In discussions with the Justice
Department, Pentagon officials emphasized that a "mass trial" was not
an option. Instead, the accused were assigned to bases across the country
where trial decisions would be made locally by each base commandant.
The effort to create the absence of Nuremberg confirmed, however, that
it had become a horrifying presence within the military imagination.[72]

Almost no book against the war was complete without comparisons of
American acts to German war crimes, of the American public to "good
Germans." In those years, no matter whose eyes you looked through, you
were likely to see Nazis. Tom Hayden, preparing for "an election year
offensive" with what he hoped would be massive antiwar demonstrations in Chicago during the 1968 Democratic National Convention, typically warned that there would be a showdown between "a police state
and a people's movement. . . . We will be saying NO from the streets . . .
many of us will not be good Germans under the new Nazis." Later, the
few thousand demonstrators who turned out under the threat of police
violence sensed themselves passing from analogy to reality. When they
looked at the Chicago police, who were mercilessly beating them, many
saw Nazis and chanted not only "the whole world's watching," but "*Sieg
Heil! Seig Heil!*" Others, however, saw only future comrades, oppressed
working-class whites, and in the confusion of the moment shouted out,
"Join us, join us." As the journalist Elinor Langer has written, "In the
middle of Chicago, at the nominating convention of one of America's
two major parties, half of us thought we were in Germany and half of us
thought we were in Russia." (The police charged the demonstrators,
screaming, "Kill the Commies!")[73]

From Robert McNamara to Henry Kissinger, those planning the war were being called fascists, Nazis, and war criminals by increasingly angry and confrontational demonstrators, while war crimes gained a history in America. The terms *genocide* and *holocaust* began to be linked to the experiences of the native peoples of the continent as well as those brought from Africa in chains. The criminals of the present day were made to stand in a line-up centuries old. Phenomena—the Klan, slavery, lynching—that had happened long ago in the South and had been considered aberrant to American history were now migrating northward and into the heart of the story as, on the left and in the counterculture, one, two, or three "k"s migrated into the country's name.

If the enemy was in the land and Nazi-like in conduct, who that enemy was depended on who was doing the looking, for in the eyes of right-wing academics and neoconservative intellectuals, young radicals sitting in on campus or demonstrating against the war were "brown shirts"; for Vice President Spiro Agnew, they were Nazi Storm Troopers or erstwhile KKK members; while Governor Rhodes of Ohio said of a group of "three or four" students he identified as responsible for "the most vicious form of campus-oriented violence" in his state, "They're worse than the Brown Shirts and the Communist element and also the night riders and vigilantes. They're the worst type of people that we harbor in America."[74]

It was not simply that Nazis, fascists, and Klansmen were everywhere in the American mental landscape, but that analogies were everywhere. America's singular journey, its unique mission in the world, was now discovered to be a journey of comparison—forget, for a moment, that the comparisons were to the most heinous regime ever to exist on the face of the earth.

8

THE WAR CRIMES OF DANIEL ELLSBERG

My Lai's epic journey to consciousness was paralleled by another twenty-month journey—of documentation from the netherworld of the national security state toward the light of day. These memos, analyses, intelligence reports, notes, and cables from the files of government agencies—all classified, all evidence of the bureaucratic planning and prosecution of a war—were first brought together due perhaps to the secret guilt or shame of Defense Secretary Robert McNamara. By 1967, he had lost confidence in his numbers-crunching methods of decision making, in the possibility of victory, and in his advice to two presidents. That summer, disillusioned with the war, he commissioned a study of the history of American involvement in Indochina that was to be "encyclopedic and objective" as well as top secret.

It took a task force of thirty-six scholars eighteen months to complete the project: seven thousand pages of documents and analysis housed in forty-seven volumes that were nonetheless incomplete. (McNamara, for instance, refused to allow the researchers to interview officials in key decision-making positions.) On its completion, every page of each volume was stamped "top secret—sensitive" and the copies locked away, largely unread even by those few officials and former officials who had access to them. The Pentagon Papers were to remain a clandestine archive, a collection assumedly (though no one knows McNamara's thinking on the subject) awaiting its future historians—or perhaps only a hidden counterbalance to the guilty conscience that the secretary of defense may have carried with him as he continued to advise the president on the war. If not for one man, the papers might have remained in that secret world forever.[75]

Daniel Ellsberg, Harvard graduate, marine lieutenant, crack pistol shot, joined the RAND Corporation, an air force–created civilian think tank, in 1959 and immediately found himself plunged into the heart of the secret world, that place where reasonable human beings considered strategies of global annihilation. There, he was put to work planning defenses against nuclear "surprise attack" and upgrading the fail-safe procedures that would prevent any unauthorized loosing of the nuclear attack force on the Communist world. To his surprise, on reading "the central nuclear war plan of the nation, the Joint Strategic Capabilities Plan," Ellsberg learned that the Soviet Union had no significant retaliatory capabilities. The Pentagon's "preventative" plan against nuclear war documented a one-way passage to annihilation for the enemy. Ellsberg recalled thinking that, with its estimated half-billion or more non-American fatalities, if put into action it would have made "Hitler's Holocaust look like a misdemeanor."[76]

Ellsberg was, however, a committed cold warrior, a true believer. In those years, he simply became a firmer advocate of civilian control over the military. He worked on crisis-management teams formed during the Cuban missile crisis and, in 1964, became special assistant to McNamara's Pentagon deputy, John McNaughton. There, he found his government colleagues "concerting, in secrecy, to plan and ultimately to wage aggressive war against North Vietnam." He accepted this "conspiratorial-style of policy-making," actively supporting policy planning on Vietnam.

In 1965, gung ho to hold the line against communism in Southeast Asia, he looked into rejoining the marines as a company commander. Instead, he went to Vietnam as part of a team put together by counterinsurgency strategist Edwin Lansdale and later became special assistant to Deputy Ambassador William Porter. In this period, he went on patrol and flew armed on at least one air reconnaissance mission. However, by 1967, when he returned to Washington with a case of hepatitis, he had grown disillusioned with the war. Soon after, he left the government "in large part," he wrote, "in order to oppose our policy—though still as an insider." He was, nonetheless, one of the first people invited onto the team that produced the Pentagon Papers and, as late as 1969, drafted a memorandum at the request of newly appointed National Security Adviser Henry Kissinger that laid out the "options" available to the Nixon administration in Indochina.[77]

Yet this trusted confidant to the powerful and writer of memos so secret few eyes would ever see them was slowly undergoing a change of heart that would lead him on a singular journey out of the secret government. Other officials, like McNamara, might leave quietly; a few like James Thomson, Jr., Roger Morris, or Anthony Lake would quit in protest, but with a certain decorum, and move on to other parts of the government, the think tank, or the university to await better times. For Ellsberg alone some eject button had been pushed that would send him through every position, every argument inside and then outside the government, for and against the war, and finally not only into a "new age" life style inhabited almost exclusively by the young, but beyond the specifics of My Lai and into the issue of war crimes and responsibility.

It was Ellsberg's hands-on experience in Vietnam that had first caused him privately to question the war. Like other disillusioned officials, journalists, and military men, including his friend John Paul Vann, he had initially criticized the inefficiency and stupidity of the war's prosecution. "I had thought," he commented, "that winning the war in Vietnam was a way of ending it." In the ensuing years, he passed through the whole range of war talk, through the misplaced good intentions and mistakes, the lack of sufficient force to win, the blunders, the quagmire, the tragedy of it all, first using that language, later dissecting it. He only gave up on victory culture in August 1969, "the last month that my writings expressed a concern with how we might have won in Vietnam."[78]

His study for the Pentagon Papers and then his study of them convinced him that Vietnam policy had been driven not by the idiosyncratic blunderings of five presidents, but by the "tacit, unquestioned belief" of

America's highest politicians and strategists "that we had had a right to 'win,' in ways defined by us." As Ellsberg saw it, the most powerful impulse driving the war machine was a presidential fear of losing Vietnam, of "what could happen to a liberal administration that chanced to be in office the day a red flag rose over Saigon." He began to see "stalement" there not as a "bankruptcy" of policy, but as policy itself, whose results in human carnage were obvious and predictable.

A powerful logic moved him from a consideration of the systematic planning necessary to keep such a war going to a belief that the officials responsible were guilty of war crimes. Even to raise the issue of war crimes and responsibility, however, an official previously involved in war planning would, in Ellsberg's words, have to "jump out of [his] skin," and out as well of what was left of the skin that held victory culture in place. As he first looked for potential allies, he was struck that, despite the disaffection of a number of ex-officials, most "seemed unwilling to take any more active part in antiwar efforts than they had while they were still serving the Government." It was in August 1969 that Ellsberg met "for the first time, face-to-face, Americans who were on their way to prison for refusing to collaborate in an unjust war." In September, upon hearing that the army was dropping charges against six Green Berets accused of assassinating an alleged Vietnamese double agent, he decided to xerox surreptitiously and release a copy of McNamara's secret study, stored and safeguarded at RAND. He did this to force the inner workings of the invisible government into a light not at the end of a tunnel. By this act, he saw himself taking responsibility for his own role in war planning. With a touching faith in the power of the revealed word to stir the soul, he hoped that publication of the secret record might encourage other officials or ex-officials to act; that a Congress, previously rendered impotent, might be moved to end the war; and that the public might be spurred to further acts of opposition.[79]

Characteristically, Ellsberg's first act of public revelation was undertaken in a secret and conspiratorial manner as a "leaker" of information. From the moment he slipped some of the documents past RAND's guards to their public appearance on the front page of the *New York Times* almost two years later, Ellsberg traveled the dovish wings of the Democratic and Republican parties trying to get some congressional figure to hold hearings on or make the papers public. In this, Ellsberg retained the instincts of an insider. Government still seemed to him the only proper venue for the release of secret information. Finally, in despair, he turned to the press, previously avoided for fear of opening himself up to prosecution, but also, perhaps, out of the insider's distaste for the journalist.

Ellsberg got in touch with Neil Sheehan, a *New York Times* reporter whom he had met in Vietnam years earlier. He took the step, in part, because he was impressed by "Should We Have War Crimes Trials?," a Sheehan roundup review of books on the war that appeared in the *New York Times* book review section. There, in words probably never before or after put in such uncompromising terms in the mainstream media, Sheehan wrote, "If you credit as factual only a fraction of the information assembled here about what happened in Vietnam, and if you apply the laws of war to American conduct there, then the leaders of the United States for the past six years at least, including the incumbent President, Richard Milhous Nixon, may well be guilty of war crimes."[80]

On June 13, 1971, the *New York Times* published its first article on the Pentagon Papers. Then followed the Nixon administration's unsuccessful attempt to enjoin publication in court (in part, on grounds of "aiding the enemy"), its unsuccessful prosecution of Ellsberg and several codefendants (in part, for violations of the Espionage Act), and its creation of a secret White House investigatory unit including a former CIA agent named E. Howard Hunt and a former FBI agent named G. Gordon Liddy. That unit—"the plumbers"—instructed to gather material that might discredit Ellsberg in case he became a "martyr" for the antiwar movement, would, among other acts, illegally break into the office of Ellsberg's psychiatrist.

Ellsberg, as the only insider now truly outside his "skin," was genuinely frightening to the administration. Henry Kissinger assured the president that he was "the most dangerous man in America today," a "fanatic" who "must be stopped at all costs." Who knew for whom Ellsberg, so familiar with the secrets of the national security state, might be a stalking horse. The Nixon administration, compiling its "enemies list," placed his name among the "most wanted." By "nailing" him, they hoped, in the words of Nixon crony Charles Colson, to strike at the "real enemy." However, whether that enemy was the Communists, antiwar radicals, congressional doves, the Democratic Party, the media, or a potentially traitorous bureaucracy was unclear. A secret black-bag crew, loyal only to Nixon, had to be organized because "enemies" were everywhere, and loyalty, even in the intelligence agencies, at a premium.[81]

Firsthand experience had convinced Nixon, his aides, and his close associates of something that was only a conviction from afar for young antiwar radicals. The president and his loyal few had no doubt that they were "in the belly of the beast," in a netherworld of jealous bureaucrats and spies, leakers and informers, potential turncoats and traitors. None could be trusted including FBI Director J. Edgar Hoover, who would not, they believed, fully investigate Ellsberg because his new wife Patricia

Marx was the daughter of a Hoover friend, the toy maker Louis Marx. If one wished to know one's enemies within the treacherous world of the national security state, then one had better wiretap, investigate, and do black-bag jobs on them oneself.[82]

In one of Ellsberg's last public appearances before the *Times* began to publish excerpts from the Pentagon Papers, he gave a speech entitled "The Responsibility of Officials in a Criminal War." In it, he recalled a conference he had attended the previous year. "I looked around a very large seminar table of participants—about forty distinguished people, among them Hannah Arendt and Telford Taylor—and it came to me that I was the only person present who was a potential defendant in a war crimes trial."

After relating his story and, through it, that of the national security state ("We have been in the process of fighting monsters without stop for a generation and a half, looking all that time into the nuclear abyss. And the abyss has looked back into us"), he wondered aloud about officials he had known who had opposed aspects of the war without making public their "special knowledge" of the nature of war planning. He questioned "the apparent lack of any strong sense of personal responsibility on the part of many of these individuals to take effective steps to help end the war." "Ought they—ought I—to feel such responsibility? . . . A starting point, it seems to me, lies in some profound comments on these questions by a man who had had twenty years in prison to reflect upon them in relation to his own life. A German, a Nazi—Albert Speer."

This was his message: American officials ought to look to a convicted Nazi war criminal for a sense of moral development. It is not hard to see why Ellsberg's might have been considered the ultimate bad trip. He was, in a sense, exactly what Kissinger called him, the most dangerous man in America, a nightmare come to life. For he was the first significant American defector. Like Philbrick, he had emerged from the Cold War netherworld, as if from the land of the undead, to tell his tale. Only this time, he was going to testify for them; and he brought back news of a new enemy in certain ways more frightening than the Nazi. "Albert Speer tells us he has no doubt that if Hitler had been given the atom bomb, he would have used it against England. But we have no doubt what we would have done with the atom bomb, since we did get it, and used it." The enemy had finally become "us."[83]†

---

†The Nazis remained the analogous war criminals of choice throughout the Vietnam years, although Japanese war crimes in Asia were a more logical point of comparison. Undoubtedly, the use of the atomic bomb against Japan (and the less than satisfying nature of the Tokyo War Crimes trials) helped de-emphasize memories of those crimes, but perhaps some unconscious sense of racial superiority

If Ellsberg alone emerged from officialdom to testify to the planning of war crimes, there were others who emerged en masse from the lands where the actual crimes were being committed—soldiers who had served in Vietnam and turned against the war. In April 1971, just two months before the Pentagon Papers came to light, hundreds of these Vietnam Veterans Against the War launched Dewey Canyon III (I and II had been invasions of Laos), a five-day "operation" of testimony in Washington, D.C. "A limited incursion into the country of Congress," they called it. According to reporter Gloria Emerson, "the veterans looked like men straggling back from a wilderness." Some on crutches or in wheelchairs, bearded, their hair long, wearing beat-up uniforms, carrying their discharge papers, they engaged in an extended antivictory parade to denounce the war they had fought in and threw back at the Capitol "medals for valor . . . stripes torn from sleeves. . . campaign ribbons and sometimes parts of dress uniforms." Fifty of them demanded to be arrested as war criminals, but they could, of course, find no one to arrest them.[85]

The VVAW had only months before convened the Winter Soldier Investigation in Detroit, the only war crimes "inquiry" the United States would hold. Ignored by the media, over 100 veterans (and 16 civilians) gave "firsthand testimony to war crimes which they either committed or witnessed." Beyond the unbearable nature of that testimony, the hearings were startling for the fact that here also were men who yearned to take some responsibility for what they had done, for nothing in victory culture was more taboo than to take responsibility for the atrocity-ridden nature of the spectacle of slaughter.[86]

With the Winter Soldiers as with Daniel Ellsberg, a limit had been reached. It was possible to accept the GI as a victim but not as a human being taking responsibility for a crime against humanity. There was no place for this in the American imagination. With "war crimes," as with Albert Speer as role model, the genuine frontier of what even a collapsing victory culture found acceptable had been discovered.

War crimes as charges are likely to be brought only in a court of law convened by a victorious power, and defeat, when it came, left none of its normal stigmata impressed on the "defeated" country. It was not simply that the Vietnamese victor could hardly impose its will, but that those forces in the United States that had opposed the war found themselves

---

was also involved in this choice of criminality. There were, nonetheless, rare moments when Japanese war crimes were cited, particularly the hanging of General Tomoyuki Yamashita, held responsible for 25,000 Filipino civilians killed by troops under his command.[84]

long before war's end in a state of collapse just as profound as that of the victory culture they opposed.

As a result, of all the charges of the antiwar movement, the ones that disappeared most quickly were those concerning war crimes—and the people who made them were as quickly forgotten. In the years to come, Vietnam veterans would be reimagined culturally, first as dangerous psychotics, then as the true victims of the war (in either case, certifiably beyond the bounds of responsibility). Similarly, Daniel Ellsberg, unlike other officials from the war-making regime, would neither be called upon for his thoughts nor held up as a symbol. He simply moved into a prolonged state of nonpersonhood. In this way, and without responsibility, were the limits of defeat reached in a country still more powerful and wealthy than any on earth.

9

AMBUSH AT KAMIKAZE PASS (II): THE INVISIBLE ENEMY TRIUMPHS

Hollywood produced countless war movies during World War II (all the fictional equivalents of Capra's *Why We Fight* propaganda series), and hundreds, if not thousands, of reworkings of that war between 1945 and 1965. In addition, throughout the 1950s, a subset of films, only partly in the World War II mold, were made about the Korean War, as were a handful set in Vietnam, including *A Yank in Indo-China* (1952) and *Five Gates to Hell* (1959). During the Vietnam War years, however, only one war movie, John Wayne's *The Green Berets* (1968), based on a best-selling novel by Robin Moore, was set in Vietnam. In the style of the "Children's Crusade Against Communism" bubble gum cards of the 1950s, it was largely an illustrated guide to the atrocities committed by the other side. "The last village I visited, [the Communists] didn't kill the chief," says Wayne's Green Beret colonel. "They tied him to a tree and brought his teenaged daughters out in front of him and disemboweled them. Then forty of them abused his wife and then they took a steel rod, broke every bone in her body. Somewhere during the process she died."

Superficially, *The Green Berets* resembled a John Wayne western down to the Indian-style attack on the Green Berets' outpost ("Fort Dodge"). Popular at the box office, the movie was picketed by war protesters and dismissed by critics as a failed throwback to another era. *Life*'s Richard Schickel "assured 'peaceniks' that as war propaganda the film was 'its own worst enemy.'" *Newsweek*'s reviewer began mockingly, "In the Alamo section of *The Green Berets*, when the yellowskins are about to overrun the fort and the air cavalry is nowhere in sight. . . ."[87]

What seems more curious today than that money-making film's "failure" was the fact that scores of similar prowar films were not made and that the one that was violated the conventions of the genre. The western and the war film, after all, had both been forms of historical explanation, "answers" to the question: How did this (the winning of the West, the taking of Iwo Jima) happen? In them, as with the most powerful myths and the best propaganda, uncomfortable questions were effectively addressed or repressed before the film began.

What is so odd about *The Green Berets*, then, is that (like the 1965 government propaganda effort, *Why Viet-Nam*) its makers felt obliged to begin with the Question. "Perhaps you could answer a question many of our subscribers ask," inquires a hostile journalist in its initial scene, a Green Beret press conference. "Why is the United States waging this ruthless war?"

The first of the many defensive answers that make up the bulk of the film is given by a Green Beret:

> Let me put it in terms we all can understand. If this same [war] happened here in the United States, every mayor in every city would be murdered. Every teacher that you'd ever known would be tortured and killed. Every professor you ever heard of, every governor, every senator, every member of the House of Representatives and their combined families all would be tortured and killed and a like number kidnapped. But in spite of this, there's always some little fellow out there willing to stand up and take the place of those who have been decimated. They need us . . . and they want us.

The film then follows the journalist into the war zone as the Answer is offered up again and again for his—and the viewer's—edification. But this only highlighted the question mark that hovered over all patriotic Vietnam-era products, and behind which, the film's makers assumed, lurked a hostile press and public, as well as the hostiles themselves. The Question revealed the mechanics of the western or war movie for all to see, and the inability to produce such films without defensiveness forced them out of the marketplace.

Although westerns had always functioned in part by analogy, framing and sorting out issues that were not faintly "western," Vietnam was a singular event in that it was fought culturally *only* by analogy. With the lone exception of *The Green Berets*, the war did not appear on screen directly in fictional form. Instead, it played itself out in a riot of analogous action in the war and western genres, even in road and gangster movies.

Hollywood experienced many unsettling reversals in those years, but none more symbolic than the arrival in 1964 of a new director—the Italian Sergio Leone—with his first "spaghetti western," *A Fistful of Dollars*. An avenging stranger rides into a Mexican border town on a mule and departs one hundred entertainment minutes later on a dray horse having cleansed the place of evil by cleansing it of humanity. Left behind are only riddled bodies. Here, before General Westmoreland even raised the possibility that the army might become a "meatgrinder," everyone in sight, including the stranger, was ground into visual meat.

In the hands of a sympathetic foreign director, the western hero was transformed into a mutant monster, and the sunny spectacle of slaughter into a nightmare. In Leone's film, everyone (except an innocent Mexican family) began to behave like the enemy. White or Mexican, lawman or criminal, everyone was an "Indian," and no act out of bounds. For this vision of a West transformed into a landscape of torture and atrocity, audiences offered up fistfuls of dollars.†

In the years that followed, like the western, the war movie crept closer to horror. In a film like *The Dirty Dozen* (1967), the Americans, not the Nazis, were the rapists, maniacs, and cold-blooded killers, men with names like A. J. Maggot who claimed they would rather "trust Hitler" than the U.S. Army. By the early 1970s, the "Good War," even in its down and dirty form, had lost its recyclable quality. The last significant group of World War II films, including *Patton* and *Tora! Tora! Tora!*, a joint American–Japanese Pearl Harbor extravaganza, appeared in 1970.[89]

On screen, whatever the genre, the state and the law now became monstrous entities, inflicting pain and death on rebellious white stand-ins for various oppressed and still largely unseen domestic minorities—and the Vietnamese. The countercultural druggies Captain America and

---

†In a notorious 1972 interview with Oriana Fallaci, Henry Kissinger explained his popularity by comparing himself to a cowboy: "I've always acted alone. Americans admire that enormously. Americans admire the cowboy leading the caravan alone astride his horse, the cowboy entering the village or city alone on his horse. Without even a pistol maybe, because he doesn't go in for shooting. He acts, that's all: aiming at the right spot at the right time. A Wild West tale, if you like." Though Kissinger was thinking of an earlier style of cowboy, with his Christmas bombings of Hanoi and his "mad" president he proved a figure from a spaghetti western.[88]

Billy (Peter Fonda and Dennis Hopper) were murdered in slow motion by Southern rednecks in *Easy Rider* (1969); Bonnie and Clyde (Warren Beatty and Faye Dunaway), uppity peasants out of a rural, Depression-era America, were riddled by the law's machine guns in a slow-motion ballet of death in Arthur Penn's 1967 film of the same name; while confused American soldier-bandits caught in a peasant revolutionary Mexico and a new era they failed to grasp were gunned down in a slow-motion last stand of horror in Sam Peckinpah's *The Wild Bunch* (1969). As the white hunter or scout had once embodied a war machine, single-handedly killing prodigious numbers of enemies with remarkable ease, inversely, just a few white rebels murdered incredibly slowly could turn the sunny spectacle of "them" dying into a nightmarish vision.[90]

In so many films of the period, aspects of Vietnam (as of the black, urban "Vietnam") were played out by implication. In the wake of My Lai, a group of anti-westerns was produced in which whites alone acted like "Indians" (that is, like whites). The Washita and Sand Creek massacres were used in *Little Big Man* (1970) and *Soldier Blue* (1970) to recreate My Lai (with clear reference to Haeberle's photos). In *Little Big Man*, Custer was reconceived as a vain buffoon, the spectacle of slaughter mocked ("Rifle against bow and arrow. I never could understand how the white world could be so proud of winnin' with those kinds of odds"), and whites portrayed as less than human.

Yet the western genre, however imaginatively inverted, was incapable of making sense of Vietnam. Even when whites became savage and rapacious "Indians," and Indians noble and innocent "settlers," the audience was left to identify with the losers, the defeated. When whites "lost" in last-stand films, there had never been a doubt of the final outcome beyond the screen. Now, when Indians won (audience sympathies, at least), there could be no doubt either. As with My Lai, in none of these films, in none of these analogies, could you see victors, only victims.

What did it mean to experience the enemy only by analogy? Already so elusive in Vietnam, that enemy proved even more so in the United States. No single image of Vietnamese evil, even of the most stereotypical kind, dominated the American imagination during those years—this, in a culture which had never previously lacked images of enemy-ness in which to ground its story. In fact, outside of a few humdrum comic books, you would have been hard pressed to find fictional representations of Vietnamese of any sort, no less of the enemy sort, in popular culture.

In Hollywood, it was common wisdom that Vietnam films—as yet unmade—would not be commercially or patriotically viable products, as in the publishing industry it was widely believed that Vietnam novels would go unread. The TV networks concurred, creating neither a series nor a single movie of the week on the subject. "Vietnam was like a plague," commented TV writer Howard Rodman. "If anyone touched it, your arm would rot away." In 1972, *M*A*S*H* finally breached television's bamboo curtain, though once again Vietnam existed only by analogy, with an older, unpopular war in Korea made to stand in for the one that couldn't be shown. In the same year, TV got its first "eastern," *Kung Fu*, in which a mystic fist-slinger, a half-Chinese rebel given to fortune cookie koans, searched the Old West for his long-lost brother. Still, there were no Vietnamese.[91]

Even in the press, where Vietnam was front-page news, the enemy was largely an absence. Until Harrison Salisbury arrived in Hanoi for the *New York Times* in December 1966, there were no firsthand reports from "the other side" either sought out by or largely available to the American media—and next to none thereafter. Of the Western press, only Agence France Presse had a reporter, Jean Raffaelli, stationed in Hanoi before 1966. Reports coming from enemy territory—whether Raffaelli's accounts of U.S. bombing in the North or the Australian Communist Wilfred Burchett's pieces on NLF guerrillas in the South—were generally "written off as either propaganda or the products of poor journalism by non-Americans." Commentary from the North Vietnamese or the NLF, while occasionally reprinted on the inside pages of a few newspapers like the *New York Times*, was taken even less seriously.

Salisbury's eye-witness accounts of "block after block of utter destruction" in North Vietnamese cities, citing damage statistics given him by his hosts, were immediately attacked. Pentagon spokesman Arthur Sylvester called Salisbury "Harrison Appallsbury" and his paper "The New Hanoi Times." The *Washington Post*'s Pentagon correspondent indicated that the reports were part of a new enemy tactic, "one as cleverly conceived as the poison-tipped bamboo spikes his men implanted underfoot for the unwary enemy," while the *New York Times'* Hanson Baldwin claimed in a front-page piece that Salisbury had swallowed "the Communist line almost hook, line and sinker."[92]

The enemy was similarly invisible on the TV news. In his study of the media and Vietnam, *The "Uncensored War,"* Daniel Hallin reported that he "never encountered a television story . . . that dealt primarily, or at any substantial length, with the political tactics, history, or program of the North Vietnamese or the NLF." What coverage there was of the enemy focused largely on the signs the enemy left behind—dead bodies, "VC suspects," blown bridges, punji stick traps, mines, atrocities—just as a crafty and elusive animal might leave droppings in its wake.

Of these signs, none were more significant than enemy atrocities. These were as purposeful and systematic as America's were isolated and aberrant. Atrocity reports, according to Hallin, used an "imagery of gratuitous savagery" and terrorism that

> drained [the enemy] of all recognizable emotions and motives and thus banished him not only from the political sphere, but from human society itself. The North Vietnamese and Vietcong were "fanatical," "suicidal," "savage," "half-crazed." They were lower than mere criminals . . . they were vermin. Television reports routinely referred to areas controlled by the NLF as "Communist infested" or "Vietcong infested."[93]

Facing a government incapable of giving evil a distinct and recognizable face yet doggedly pursuing its war of "attrition," some in the antiwar movement began searching out images of the missing enemy. They first took up ones of Vietnamese victimhood, of desolate Vietnamese children or innocent peasants ravaged in the southern part of the country, or of grief-stricken but determined bombing victims in the North, images that had once been "ours," even in Asia. In the 1930s, terrifying images of Japanese slaughter in China had helped mobilize public opinion in favor of more interventionist policies in the Pacific. The most famous, a photo of "an abandoned Chinese child, injured, bleeding, bawling on its haunches in the midst of the smoking destruction of Shanghai's railway station," appeared in a 1937 *Life* magazine and innumerable newsreels. Similar images were offered to children in the popular "horrors of war" bubble gum card series. ("War Against Women and Children. . . . Nanking, the most beautiful city in the world. . . . Japanese soldiers with fixed bayonets . . . both shooting and stabbing the fleeing and screaming Chinese. . . . Little children were killed by the hundreds. . . . Don't Let It Happen Over Here.")[94]

By the late 1960s, some in the antiwar movement, searching for more than an upside-down "horrors of war," had moved on to images of the Vietnamese as underdogs, not victims. They began to display pictures of the armed enemy—women as well as men—for which there was only one place to turn: the enemy. Though no National Liberation Front invitations were proffered to American reporters and the movements of Western journalists in North Vietnam, as in other Communist countries, were seriously circumscribed, Vietnamese images of themselves—or sympathetic images of them—were not hard to come by. They could be found in the NLF's English-language propaganda paper *Viet Nam Courier*, in North Vietnamese and NLF propaganda films like *Hanoi Tuesday the 13th* and *The Tet Offensive*, in Cuban posters and films like *79 Springtimes*, and in documentaries like *People's War* by the radical American film collective Newsreel, *Year of the Pig* by Emile de Antonio, and *Inside North Vietnam* by British journalist Felix Green.[95]

Images of the enemy as an armed and righteous force of underdogs became commonplace in the alternate world of the antiwar movement. On posters and flyers, in underground newspapers and on film, heroic and determined peasants in poses made popular by socialist realist art or small, lightly armed soldiers guarding giant American prisoners came to represent a new iconography of triumph. This was what victory culture looked like once it had been occupied by the enemy. Yet the significance of these images lay not in their capacity to enhance an understanding of the Vietnamese reality that produced them, but in their shocking ability to countermand the traditional war story. For the Vietnamese themselves, this amounted to another form of invisibility.

Whether your source was the alternate or the mainstream media, this combination of invisibility and invincibility lent Vietnam's revolutionaries a magical, suprahuman quality; yet, even in the wake of the Tet Offensive, the enemy did not quite make it onto the TV screen. In his book *Big Story*, former *Washington Post* Saigon bureau chief Peter Braestrup noted that the "Vietcong performance was not a major preoccupation of the television networks," even at that crucial moment in the war, "and direct reports on enemy thinking and behavior were few."[96]

Where the Vietnamese should have been, there was a missingness that lent the years from 1961 to 1975 an aura of mystery. An uncontainable, invisible enemy loose in the land had been feared and imagined in various forms since the 1940s. Now, *it* seemed to be at large; and no maneuvering on the battlefield could erect defensive barriers against what it was doing inside American heads. The worst horrors seemed to be occurring among the young inheritors of narrative and dream. No HUAC hearing, no science fiction film, no horror comic could have created a more unnerving scenario: children's brains and bodies, in Vietnam and at home, were being possessed. The two fears of the 1950s—the red scare and the child scare—had fused.

Meanwhile, the war story was in ruins. All those years in which the enemy could not appear on screen had taken a strange toll. As the enemy was forced in covert ways into the western and the war film, the genres themselves began to deconstruct before the eyes of the viewing public. Even the anti-western could not save the form. It proved impossible from within the dismantled forms of victory culture to imagine how to move forward. Having performed its critique, the anti-western had nowhere to go. One of the last—and canniest—of these films, Robert Altman's *Buf-*

falo Bill and the Indians or Sitting Bull's History Lesson (1976), took on the "invention" of the war story itself ("I'm going to Cody-fy the world!"), while offering sardonic analysis-by-analogy of various aspects of the war. ("You see, the difference between a president and a chief . . . [is that] the president always knows enough to retaliate before it's his turn.") However, it failed at the box office, while the war epics of the previous period dwindled down to box office disasters about military catastrophes. The frontier on screen seemed finally to close. The production of westerns dropped rapidly from an average of twenty-four a year in the early 1970s to four a year before decade's end. Ambush culture had been ambushed.[97]

10

BESIEGED

At home, the United States sometimes seemed to be not so much at war as on screen, for the singular focus of U.S. policy makers came to be the preservation of the look of victory culture. Vietnam was prime time for America's "reputation," disparate audiences were watching, and the ratings were all. In a memo to Robert McNamara in 1965, Assistant Secretary of Defense John McNaughton assessed why Americans were in South Vietnam:

> 70%—To avoid a humiliating U.S. defeat (to our reputation as a guarantor). 20%—To keep SVN (and the adjacent) territory from Chinese hands. 10%—To permit the people of SVN to enjoy a better, freer way of life. . . . We must have kept promises, been tough, taken risks, gotten bloodied. . . . We must avoid harmful appearances which will affect judgments by, and provide pretexts to, other nations regarding how the U.S. will behave in future cases of particular interest to those nations. . . . In this connection, the relevant audiences are the Communists (who must feel strong pressures), the South Vietnamese (whose morale must be buoyed), our allies (who must trust us as "underwriters") and the U.S. public (which must support our risk-taking with U.S. lives and prestige).[98]

As ratings sank, programming executives were fired or retired, and new ones came on-line proclaiming new programming concepts and new viewing schedules. But each time the result was the same—slaughter without victory, war without end. For all the Kennedyesque tough talk, McNaughton's sort of thinking turned out to be an unprecedented expression of weakness, for dominance was now hostage to what others thought of it. Since U.S. leaders were fighting not for victory as normally understood but to promote (as one might a dubious product) an image of victory, a traditional mobilization was not in order. "We have," bemoaned President Johnson, "no songs, no parades, no bond drives and we can't win the war otherwise." For this undeclared shadow war fought mainly by the children of the poor and working class, the public was to offer support solely by proxy and from afar. As a result, a great burden fell on the media, particularly television news. Only the media was to be mobilized, for who was more crucial in a battle of "looks" than the medium that brought little else but looks and styles into the home?[99]

No president had ever worked the media more assiduously or tried harder to control his image than Lyndon Johnson. He was excruciatingly aware of the power of the screen (as well as of the on-screen appeal of his predecessor, John F. Kennedy). Never had a president spent more time watching his own performance or watched it more critically, for he was endlessly frustrated that TV did not treat his basset-hound face, homey persona, and slow, twangy voice kindly. The television industry was Johnson's home front and he was constantly on the phone to network presidents, complaining, cajoling, stroking, threatening in order to assure that the images of "progress" in Indochina he thought the public ought to see actually appeared.

The president (or his underlings) worked hard among network anchormen and White House correspondents, doling out favors and twisting arms to muster the media troops daily in the good fight for evening news perfection. Johnson often geared his schedule and that of his government to TV time. He read his polls with care, gauging what a televised address or news conference might do for sagging ratings. (On one occasion, "support" for the war rose by 30 percent after a televised speech.) But this laying on of hands involved an implicit acceptance of loss as well, for Johnson was entrusting not just the national "reputation" but the "credibility" of the presidential self to his on-screen look. He was placing his image in the hands of poll takers and TV reporters.[100]

The barometer of Vietnam was to be presidential popularity, and by early 1966, "a steady erosion in public support [had] begun. . . . At least by the beginning of 1967, a plurality [of Americans] were saying they disapproved of Johnson's handling of the war," and this was without significant negative TV coverage. Johnson's increasingly desperate attempts to create quantified evidence of triumph at home collapsed when his numbers came up low both in the opinion polls and in the 1968 New Hampshire primary. It was then that he experienced the "humiliation," the loss of "reputation," that McNaughton and others had long feared.

His moment of defeat evidently occurred as he watched CBS anchorman Walter Cronkite, just back from a post-Tet visit to Vietnam, declare that the U.S. war was "mired in stalemate." At that moment, Johnson evidently turned to an aide and said, "It's all over." If he had lost Walter Cronkite, he told his press secretary, he had lost "Mr. Average Citizen." In the same way, David Halberstam writes, "his real farewell to politics was not the one most people remember, the surprise announcement on March 31, 1968, when he declared that he would not seek reelection, but a much more interesting and significant farewell given the next day in Chicago, where he had gone to face the National Association of Broadcasters and had in effect blamed them for his defeat and for defeat in Vietnam."

"As I sat in my office last evening, waiting to speak," Johnson told the broadcasters:

> I thought of the many times each week when television brings the war into the American home. No one can say exactly what effect those vivid scenes have on American opinion. Historians must only guess at the effect that television would have had during earlier conflicts on the future of this Nation: during the Korean war, for example, at that time when our forces were pushed back there to Pusan; or World War II, the Battle of the Bulge.

As ratings and images had once buoyed him, so now his troops, the image makers and poll takers, had failed him.[101]

Not surprisingly, Johnson and later Nixon, as well as much of the country's political and military elite, experienced the war primarily as a media betrayal. Vivid memories of the glories of actual triumph only made the helplessness that seemed to go with image politics and image war-making more profound. Presidents and generals came to feel like captives in an alien process. In this sense, America's First POW was never in the "Hanoi Hilton" but in the White House.

Ironically, those children of the suburbs who had once taken the war story to heart in movie theaters, on TV, in homes, and in back yards, felt even more deeply betrayed—by media image makers and image-manipulating presidents alike. For them, victory culture had been a matter of faith, and loss of faith in its images (and in those who made them) was a wrenching experience. As one SDS document fairly screamed out, "[T]he war against Vietnam is not 'the heroic war against the Nazis'; it's the big lie, with napalm burning through everything we had heard this country stood for."[102]

Many responded by fashioning their own images from what was left of the war story. In the domestic war of images that followed, they had two advantages over their adult leaders: they were the first generation to grow up in houses constantly filled with screen images; and they knew that to embrace imagery horrifying to adults was to achieve a certain pleasure. As a generation, they were tightly tied to images and yet felt free to manipulate them in ways alien to a Lyndon Johnson or a Richard Nixon. Without presidential access to TV, they sensed that television could be attracted to them. If "credibility" was at stake, then incredibility would be their response. They thought in a bold, imagistic style that should have had a familiar look to it. In those years when a president feared calling up the reserves or letting the term *mobilize* pass his lips, it was young radicals who joined an umbrella organization called the Mobe, created a home front, and called out the reserves.

The young began to dismantle the war story and redeploy its elements, as mechanics might strip an old car for its parts. Without ever straying far from the confines of that story, they transformed each symbol of triumph into a triumphantly possessed symbol of defeat. Take World War II's two-fingered V-for-victory (in which triumph and peace had been indissoluble). When a war protester now greeted a government official's arrival, it was with the sundered "V" of peace, a mocking "V" that proclaimed we-want-out.

Countless demonstrators sallied forth to a new sort of battle garbed in cast-off "good war" paraphernalia—secondhand army jackets, bombardier coats, bush hats. Initially without significant access to the media, the young reconceived the images of their childhood on themselves. They became distinctly modernist endeavors, living critiques or parodies of the familiar, their own *MAD* magazines. The particular images thus elevated were mainly of an enemy-ness recognizable from any of thousands of westerns: the Pancho Villa mustache, sombrero, and serape; the Native American headband and moccasins; the painted face or long hair of the "savage"; the valued "love beads" (those previously worthless baubles with which, everyone knew, Manhattan had so fraudulently been purchased); the peace (now, drug) pipe, and so on. In a continuous riff on an older imagery, the young donned "body paint," took on the aspect of the losers, and went on the peace path, wearing their incredibility.

This look of the tribal should not be mistaken, however, for an abandonment of techno-culture. Despite their denunciations of the media, a deep faith in the defining power of images on screen remained undiminished. Not only did they play theatrically to television using the upside-down imagery of the war story, but no one who demonstrated then could forget the experience of rushing home to see if the demonstration—perhaps your own image—had made it onto TV and so whether or not your event had really happened.

The counterpatriotic rituals of the "movement" had a familiar look. There were counterparades under the counterflags of the National Liberation Front; there were the Founding Father–like portraits of an avuncular Ho or a cheery-cheeked Chairman Mao, or Founding Mother–like ones of a sad-eyed Rosa Luxembourg that stared down from commune walls and workplaces. There were the buttons that proclaimed not "100% American," but "I'm an Americong."

The antiwar movement's "underground" press wrote of a war that had not yet made it to America, and its screenings were of grainy battle footage from "the other side." Some radicals wore rings made in North Vietnam from downed American airplanes. Others named their children after Mao or Che Guevara or the radiant Mme. Nguyen Thi Binh (as in "Dare to struggle, dare to win, live like her, Madame Binh"), whom the enemy, in a *coup de théâtre*, had sent to the Paris peace talks to negotiate with America's aging white men.

Countercultural youth pursued a similar path. If they discovered their version of un-victory culture in India or ancient China, and used the *I Ching, Tao Te Ching,* or *Rig-Veda,* rather than Mao Zedong's or Che Guevara's writings on guerrilla warfare as texts, it was still the mystery of the Vietnamese will to victory that gave conviction to the spiritual culture of the East. Domestically, young people invoked the war story's losers for spiritual or political strength, wisdom, and example: Carlos Castaneda's Yaqui Indian healer Don Juan or the visionary Black Elk for the counterculture; Sitting Bull or Geronimo for the politicos. If the counterculture thought tribally, so finally did student radicals, some of whom began to form small groups with names like the Quartermoon Tribe and the Proud Eagle Tribe.

As premature guerrilla fighters, low-tech conservators of the land, and spiritual guides to a world in which drug taking was not a recreational pursuit, Native Americans were elevated to the sacred status that the bluecoat, the cowboy, and the scout had once enjoyed. With a daguerreotype image of Geronimo holding a rifle, for instance, a leaflet, "Who Owns the Park?" opened up a defense of the "liberation" of an unused university-owned lot in Berkeley, California. Beginning with a history of how Spanish missionaries, the Mexican and U.S. governments, and finally the "rich men who run the University of California" had "ripped off" the land from the Costanoan Indians, it went on:

> We are building a park on the land. We will take care of it and guard it, in the spirit of the Costanoan Indians. When the University comes with its land title we will tell them: "Your land title is covered with blood. We won't touch it. . . . If you want it back now, you will have to fight for it again."

Only the phrase, "White man speaks with forked tongue" was missing.

The Weathermen, that final crazed offshoot of SDS, proclaimed a new "politics of confidence and . . . of victory." ("The Vietnamese people have won. . . . We have won, we won in Vietnam, that was a victory for us and for all people.") Using the slogan, "Bring the war home," they declared themselves "behind enemy lines," a "fifth column" for Third World revolutionaries living in the "heartland of a worldwide monster." "We are the sons and daughters of the enemy. . . . We are going to wipe out the imperialist state and every vestige of honkey consciousness in white people. . . . We have to force the disintegration of society, creating strategic armed chaos where there is now pig order." In a "declaration of a state of war" in which they announced their intention to go "underground," they declared, "we're not hiding out but we're invisible."[103]

There seemed to be no way, as horror comics had once been banned, to ban the young from glorying in the look, the stigmata of enemy-ness or embracing to the fullest triumphalist despair. This left America's leaders puzzled, frustrated, even enraged, but also fearful. They began to experience a strange loss of control at home paralleling the one in Indochina. Not just the symbols of victory culture, but its image-setting agenda was slipping from their grasp.

They instinctively felt that some invisible force, some adult and evil hand must lurk behind so much un-American activity. President Johnson set his people to work discovering the enemy that lay behind the protest movements of the time:

> Pressed by Johnson . . . to investigate the peace movement's international connections, the CIA reported back that "many [leaders] have close Communist associations but they do not appear to be under Communist direction," and that "connections between . . . U.S. activists and foreign governments are limited"—whereupon [Secretary of State Dean] Rusk said the CIA simply hadn't searched well enough, and Johnson was reportedly so unhappy he shook his finger in

the face of CIA director Richard Helms and said, "I simply don't understand why it is that you can't find out about that foreign money."[104]

In the Nixon White House, too, discovering the "foreign influences and financing of the New Left" had top priority. If Johnson brought the CIA into this process, the Nixon administration called on the CIA, FBI, NSA, and DIA as well as the White House's own hired operatives. The result was endless frustration, for the enemy, who could not be tracked to earth in Vietnam, could not be tracked down in the United States either.

Approaching domestic protest as if it were the enemy, the government infiltrated the antiwar movement as well as various black and white radical groups with startling numbers of agents, informers, and *agents provocateurs*. Phones were tapped, "movement" offices broken into, burglaries committed, dissension-causing disinformation sent out, and violent actions or internal conflicts provoked (in a few cases, among militant black organizations, with deadly results). In short, Cold War tactics, developed to counter the Communist enemy, were now turned on the putative inheritors of the story itself.[105]

Meanwhile, in Vietnam, an even more frightening transformation was under way. An army, made up increasingly of poor and working-class draftees, was threatening to come apart. Many of these troops had entered Vietnam, as some later put it, "like boys playing soldiers," only to find themselves in a war that bore no relation to screen expectations bred in their childhoods. ("In Flash Gordon," as one Vietnam veteran recalled, "no one ever bleeds.") If some arrived full of a John Wayne–like ardor ("Vietnam was my moment. . . . When I got there I kissed the earth because I considered it sacred ground"), most soon took up styles and attitudes that more closely matched their situation. As middle-class demonstrators mobilized in cast-off war dress, so GIs in the field visually demobilized, incorporating peace signs, graffiti ("eat the apple, fuck the Corps"), headbands, black power symbols, and drug paraphernalia into their uniforms. In a sardonic bow to the disgraced movie version of the war story, some called American headquarters in Saigon "Hollywood West," and with an angry nod to those beloved, controlled environments of their childhood, referred to Vietnam as "brown Disneyland," or "Six Flags over Nothing."

As the 1960s ended, statistics flowing back to Washington about the American war machine pointed toward an unimaginable nightmare. Drug taking was rampant (by 1971, up to 60 percent of returning soldiers admitted to some sort of use); desertions stood at seventy per thousand, a modern high; small-scale mutinies or "combat refusals" were at critical, if untabulated, levels; incidents of racial conflict had soared; and strife between officers ("lifers") and men was at unprecedented levels (reported "fraggings"—assassination attempts—against unpopular officers or NCOs rose from 126 in 1969 to 333 in 1971, despite declining troop strength in Vietnam).[106]

In 1971, Colonel Robert D. Heinl, Jr., author of the "definitive history of the Marine Corps," reviewed the evidence for *Armed Forces Journal*: "[T]he foregoing facts," he wrote, "point to widespread conditions among American forces in Vietnam that have only been exceeded in this century by the French Army's Nivelle mutinies of 1917 and the collapse of the Tsarist armies [of Russia] in 1916 and 1917." Like their stateside counterparts, soldiers were "turning on, tuning in, dropping out." In addition, despite sometimes deep, class-based feelings of resentment and envy toward middle-class demonstrators who managed to avoid military service, everywhere disaffected soldiers were in contact with the antiwar movement. According to Colonel Heinl's figures, as many as 144 underground newspapers were published by or aimed at soldiers ("In Vietnam," the *Ft. Lewis–McChord Free Press* typically wrote, "the Lifers, the Brass, are the true Enemy, not the enemy"); antiwar coffee shops for off-duty soldiers were being set up near bases; counseling and legal services were being organized for dissident GIs; deserters were being aided; and Jane Fonda's FTA (Fuck the Army) anti–Bob Hope revue had toured Asia to enthusiastic military audiences. More threatening yet, active duty soldiers in small numbers (as well as larger numbers of Vietnam veterans) were beginning to organize against the war.[107]

With a president desperate not to unsettle his domestic programs (or later increase middle-class protest against the war), and the need for troops for Vietnam on the rise, the military began to court increasing numbers of potential black recruits. In 1966, Secretary of Defense McNamara proposed "Project 100,000," a plan to lower military admissions standards to bring in large numbers of the "subterranean poor," curing them of "idleness, ignorance, and apathy" and rebuilding "the fabric of black society." In fact, in the years of most intense ground fighting, blacks, recruited or drafted, were disproportionately assigned to combat, took disproportionate casualties, and held disproportionately low ranks. (Blacks made up only 2 percent of the officer corps in Vietnam.)

Many black soldiers, especially those in the field, on confronting the more comfortable, whiter world of support units, had a distinct feeling that the war was elsewhere; that, as one put it, "I wasn't fighting the enemy. I was fighting the white man." It wasn't simply that familiar aspects of white racism from Confederate flags and cross burnings to racist graffiti were commonplace in Vietnam, but that blacks brought with them attitudes formed by the civil rights and black power movements, by black nationalist organizations and the Black Panther Party. In the same way, some soldiers joined those movements on return to the United States ("I joined the Black Panthers group basically because it was a warlike group. . . . I was thinkin' we needed a revolution. . . . And I was thinkin' about Vietnam. All the time").

Nothing had historically been more frightening to whites than the idea of blacks with guns. Now, as armed Black Panthers challenged the police in the ghetto streets of Oakland, California, and snipers fired on troops in urban riots, blacks seemed everywhere to be picking up the gun. In the popular imagination, a distraught army of deranged whites and white-hating, gun-toting blacks, hooked on drugs by malevolent Asians, were on their way home to kill—as the first films and TV shows that featured Vietnam vets suggested. They would be living time bombs, alien invaders in a new upside-down opium war. Even at home, it seemed possible that the army might not long remain under control and the United States itself might truly go up in flames.[108]

Fear of this, as much as of domestic protest, led in 1969 to the "Nixon Doctrine." According to Secretary of Defense Melvin Laird, the war would be "Vietnamized," using "indigenous manpower organized into properly equipped and well-trained armed forces with the help of materiel, training, technology and specialized military skills furnished by the United States." In other words, American troops would be withdrawn and U.S. air support increased. While in the post–World War II years, America's quasi-warriors had organized covert wars using foreign military personnel, here was the beginning of a new style of "limited war" that would carry into the post-Vietnam years. For the first time, Americans would openly fight wars by proxy, its battle tradition carried forward by U.S.-financed armies filled with foreigners.[109]

Little wonder that the leaders of the globe's most powerful government and military came to feel themselves not the besiegers of an enemy at the global peripheries but besieged by enemies in their own army and country. From 1966 on, it was increasingly difficult for those identified with the war's prosecution, from the president on down, to appear anywhere in America other than on military bases without facing a barrage of protest from young people, who treated government figures as if they were the emissaries of an enemy power or a hateful, alien civilization.

In November 1966, for instance, Secretary of Defense McNamara came to Harvard University to give a closed lecture to fifty students. The police car in which he attempted to depart afterwards was immediately surrounded by a dozen members of SDS, who promptly sat down. He was then trapped by hundreds of demonstrators and a shouted discussion began with a question about the war's origins:

> "It started in '54–'55 when a million North Vietnamese flooded into South Vietnam," McNamara said. "Goin' home!" someone shouted. . . . The next question asked for the number of civilian casualties in the South. "We don't know," Mac said. "Why not? Don't you care?" came the shouts. "The number of casualties . . . " Mac began, but was drowned out by cries of *"Civilian! Civilian!* Napalm victims!" A few [Progressive Labor Party] types in front were jumping up and down screaming "Murderer! Fascist!"[110]

There is hardly a more pathetic tale than the one President Nixon told of a predawn trip to the Lincoln Memorial in the company of his manservant Manolo Sanchez on May 9, 1970, as thousands of protesters gathered to demonstrate against the invasion of Cambodia and the National Guard killings of protesters at Kent State University and Jackson State College. There, as he recounted it, he tried to engage a group of bewildered, even uninterested demonstrators in conversation:

> I said, I know that probably most of you think I'm an S.O.B. but I want you to know that I understand just how you feel. I recall . . . when I was just a little older than you . . . how excited I was when Chamberlain came home from Munich and made his famous statement about peace in our time . . . and when I read Churchill's all-out criticism of Chamberlain I thought Churchill was a madman.

Offering sympathy for their goals, hoping that their opposition would not turn into "a blind hatred of the country," he suggested the broadening advantages of youthful travel, hymning the glories of Asia and the beauties of Prague, while they stared at him unresponsively or reacted with hostility. ("Then another spoke up and said, we are not interested in what Prague looks like. We are interested in what kind of life we build in the United States.") It was as if he, the president of the United States, were some hopeless freak. He could only watch himself helplessly, as if through alien eyes, as the first rays of the sun rose over the Washington Monument, for he had lost control over his own image.[111]

A feeling of victimization gained hold among the highest officials in the land as they peeped out from Washington windows at unarmed young Americans (and some of their elders) marching upon them. As early as October 21, 1967, approximately 100,000 mostly youthful demonstrators paraded through lines of soldiers, bayonets at the ready, and onto the grounds of the Pentagon. There, in a derisive gesture to victory culture, they raised an NLF flag on a "liberated" flagpole. With Secretary of Defense McNamara and high-ranking military officers watching, a group of hippies began to "exorcise" and "levitate" the Pentagon, while other demonstrators relieved themselves against it, camped out on its lawn, smoked dope, and in one case, made love in front of a line of "bewildered" soldiers.[112]

Sometimes U.S. leaders ostentatiously pretended *not* to notice. Johnson announced a trip to his Texas ranch to avoid one demonstration, while Nixon proclaimed himself absorbed in a televised football game during another. Whether officially looking or not, they saw the demonstrators as the demonstrators saw them. In his memoirs, Clark Clifford, adviser to President Johnson and McNamara's successor as secretary of defense, recalled his furtive sense of looking at the almost-enemy in Washington:

> As I was driven through the streets . . . to my office, I would sometimes see antiwar demonstrators through the thick bulletproof windows of the automobile. Even though I opposed the war, I could not relate to these people. . . . While I understood their desire to end the war, I was appalled that many of the demonstrators, in their anger at the government, seemed to side actively with the communists. Such acts as flying the Vietcong flag or burning the American flag were deeply offensive to me. The war was a tragic mistake, but it was wrong to glorify the enemy, who were at that moment killing Americans the same age as many of those demonstrating in the streets. The fact that we would not be able to achieve our original objectives was cause not for celebrating but for mourning.[113]

For Nixon and his circle of aides, advisers, and officials, a sense of besiegement was reality itself; for enemy-ness was everywhere: among recalcitrant Vietnamese allies; the antiwar opposition ("The terrorists of the far left would like nothing better than to make the President of the United States a prisoner in the White House"); the press ("The press is the enemy." "Their whole objective in life is to bring us down"); various Hollywood actors and actresses like Paul Newman involved in "Radic-Lib causes"; Democrats who opposed the president ("consciously aiding and abetting the enemy of the U.S.") or who like Clifford had once been involved in Vietnam policy making ("turncoats"); the Democratic Party itself and its chairman Lawrence O'Brien as well as its 1972 presidential candidate George McGovern ("bemused with surrender" and ready to perform "an act of betrayal" over Vietnam); CBS correspondent Daniel Schorr ("a real media enemy"); Edward Kennedy and the rest of his clan; and every variety of "fashionable" or "with-it" "elitists."[114]

All those enemies wanted, it seemed, was to "get" Richard Nixon, and so no Cold War method of covert assault was now inapplicable at home. As White House counsel John Dean described such Nixonian thinking in practice, "[G. Gordon] Liddy laid out a million dollar plan that was the most incredible thing I have ever laid my eyes on: all in codes, and involved black bag operations, kidnapping, providing prostitutes to weaken the opposition, bugging, mugging teams." The Democratic Party was to be "infiltrated," as were the presidential campaigns of Senators Muskie and McGovern. And all this was to be performed by former or present employees of the CIA and the FBI as well as quasi-warriors previously trained by the invisible government to bring down Castro's Cuba.

This secret war against the "enemy" was hardly restricted to the larger society. It permeated the White House, for the president and his closest advisers believed that enemy-ness existed within the highest reaches of government. When National Security Council aides William Watts, Anthony Lake, and Roger Morris resigned to protest the invasion of Cambodia, Kissinger's NSC deputy Alexander Haig called them "traitors," referring as well to aide Morton Halperin, suspected of leaking policy information to the press, as a "Communist." Every office, every cabinet position, every bureaucratic outpost had, potentially, been penetrated. "Nobody," as Nixon commented, "is a friend of ours."[115]

The war had finally come home. Constant vigilance against betrayal was necessary. With Nixon's encouragement, Kissinger ordered wiretaps of various of his aides, including his closest friend on the NSC, Helmet Sonnenfelt, as well as figures in the Defense Department. The president, in turn, ordered his key aides to spy on Kissinger, something former Kissinger aide and later presidential confidant Alexander Haig did in any case. Kissinger and Nixon conspired to make sure that Secretary of State William Rogers and Secretary of Defense Melvin Laird were both kept "out of the loop" and created their own "back channel" to the Joint Chiefs; while Laird developed his back channels, particularly to Admiral Noel Gayler of the National Security Agency, in order to learn about the latest in Kissingerian diplomacy. In the meantime, Joint Chiefs Chairman Admiral Thomas Moorer organized an operation to spy on Kissinger, including the infiltration of and black-bag operations against the NSC; and the president wired just about every room in the White House without the knowledge of anyone except aide H. R. Haldeman.[116]

In the Nixonian scheme of things, only two potential allies of consequence remained—the Russians with whom, unlike the Democrats, one might achieve "détente," and Communist China. A new relationship with the former "expansionist" enemy in Asia was seen as a means to disrupt the Vietnamese war effort and possibly achieve a pro-American peace, which would disarm Nixon's opponents at home. Though often hailed as the greatest of his (and Kissinger's) foreign policy triumphs, the "opening" to China had the hallmarks of desperation from the first signals sent to the Chinese leadership through Yahya Kahn, the Pakistani dictator, to Nixon's arrival in Beijing for a "summit" without an assurance that Mao Zedong would meet with him.

The mad mullah's image was now at the enemy's mercy. As Kissinger put it in his memoirs, "We had made the two great Communist powers collaborators in holding our home front together." Nixon's global triumphs were all that stood between him and the final assault on the White House by his encircling enemies—the liberal media, the antiwar opposition, congressional foes, the Democratic Party, and the Watergate committee. Could there have been a greater reversal? The only true friends he had left resided within the cloistered walls of the Zhongnanhai leadership compound in Beijing.[117]

The Nixon White House was an unintended end point for the kind of "limited war" imagined by Kennedy-era strategists. While the war expanded into an Indochina-wide inferno, with American planes bombing from the outskirts of Phnom Penh to Haiphong harbor, the "war" at home seemed to narrow to the environs of the White House. By March 21, 1973, containment policy had gained a more limited meaning in the Oval Office. As counsel John Dean explained to the president, describing his attempts to keep the Watergate affair from unraveling before various investigative bodies, "I worked on a theory of containment. . . . To try to hold it right where it was." All that was left of the "domino theory," the fear that losing a single country like Vietnam to communism would cause other non-Communist nations to collapse in rapid succession, was Dean telling the president, "What really troubles me is . . . will this thing not break some day and the whole thing—domino situation—everything starts crumbling, fingers will be pointing. . . . And the person who will be hurt by it most will be you and the Presidency."[118]

Indeed, within months the last boundaries had fallen, the last domino had collapsed. Just about every close associate of the president was under indictment except Henry Kissinger, and the heavy-drinking mad mullah had been tracked to his hideout. After three hundred years, here was defeat. But unlike in Vietnam, where a tank would drive through the gates of the Presidential Palace in Saigon to accept the surrender of interim president Duong Van Minh; in Washington, no tank was about to arrive. Instead, Nixon boarded a helicopter with all due ceremony and began the first leg of his flight into California exile, while Gerald Ford, his vice president, took over the government. In the United States, unlike Vietnam, the opposition was part of the collapse. In each country, "reconstruction" was about to begin.

II
RECONSTRUCTION

The war mysteriously robbed Americans of their inheritance. On screen and off, they were transformed from victors into, at best, victims; from heroes into, at worst, killers; their leader, a self-proclaimed madman; their soldiers, torturers; their democratic public, a mob of rioters and burners; their army, in a state of near collapse; their legislative bodies, impotent. They had become the world's most extraordinary (because least expected) losers.

The only official heroes left were the prisoners of war held by Hanoi until 1973. Though some of them, like their Korean War predecessors, returned burdened by "confessions" broadcast over enemy radio as well as accusations of collaboration and collapse, they were seen by the Nixon administration as a blessing and made the centerpiece of a rare government-sponsored celebration, Operation Homecoming. For this publicity event, meant to mark the end of the American role in the war, they were wined and dined at the White House, greeted by the president, and entertained by Bob Hope.

What made them heroic, however, was a set of traits—victimization and degradation by a savage and inhuman foe, years of helplessness, enforced passivity—previously associated with the white female captive. Incarcerated under harsh conditions, sometimes tortured, absent in certain cases for a decade or more, they had also missed the period in which the war story was impaled. Now, returning by air from the nowhere of captivity, relics of a past seemingly beyond recapture, they were emblematic figures of loss. They could step off the plane bringing them home, saying, "God bless America," and whatever the government stage-managing involved, their comments had credibility. Like astronauts returning from a space voyage, their credentials as Americans were in order exactly because they had been gone all those years. Through their long-suffering absence, they alone could testify to the world that had been lost.

As the last helicopter lifted off from the roof of the U.S. embassy in Saigon in April 1975, a new era began that was not to end until the first helicopter landed triumphantly on the roof of the American embassy in Kuwait in March 1991. That era—of reconstruction—stretching across sixteen years from one embassy rooftop to another was strange indeed. The victorious country from which the first helicopter fled had suffered as many as 3 million dead (not counting Laotian and Cambodian casualties). In the South, 9,000 of 15,000 hamlets were in ruins, 19 million tons of herbicide had been sprayed on the land, and unexploded ordnance was everywhere. There were an estimated 1 million widows, 879,000 orphans, 181,000 disabled people, and 200,000 prostitutes. All six of the North's industrial cities had been severely damaged (three razed to the ground), as were 28 of 30 provincial towns and 96 of 116 district towns. Vietnamese farmers had lost 1.5 million farm animals, and the now unified nation had not even a minimal industrial plant left.[119]

The defeated country toward which that helicopter headed—for the aircraft carrier on which it landed off the Vietnamese coast was a seaborne slice of America—had suffered its own violence, property damage, and death. Numerous Reserve Officers' Training Corps buildings on college campuses across the country had been set on fire or bombed by antiwar protesters, as had draft boards, induction centers, federal buildings, and an army mathematics research building at the University of Wisconsin, where a graduate student had died. Significant bomb damage had been done to a Pentagon bathroom, the Capitol atrium, various corporate headquarters or showrooms, and a Bank of America branch office burned down by rioters in Santa Barbara, California. This war-related damage involved many millions of dollars in losses, not including the costs of National Guard and state troops, of police units, of federal, state, and local agents, and of the informers put to work infiltrating and disrupting the antiwar movement as well as encouraging some of the property damage it caused.

As for human damage, 58,000 Americans died and another 300,000 were wounded in Indochina. (Another 60,000 or more veterans are believed to have committed suicide in the postwar years.) Domestically, there were perhaps twenty Vietnam-related deaths (including the shootings of students at Kent State and Jackson State and of James Rector during Berkeley's People's Park demonstrations), several cases of paralysis due to police beatings, thousands of injuries of greater or lesser severity, and tens of thousands of arrests. Military forces on the home front, mainly policemen, suffered fewer but still numerous injuries.

To this must be added the violent upheavals in the country's black ghettos. In Detroit alone, forty-three people ranging from looters to a national guardsman died in 1967 and property damage was estimated at $40 million. The devastation and subsequent triaging of inner-city areas proved a signal that a new era was on the way, for in the postwar period, such areas would be treated like extensions of Vietnam and informally embargoed. For them there would be neither reconstructive fervor nor reconstructive funds. There, as in devastated Vietnam, the promise of an American-organized future of abundance would be decisively abandoned.[120]

In 1975, the defeated country nonetheless remained the world's preeminent power. If a postwar era of reconstruction was to take place, the question of what was to be reconstructed, where, and for whom seemed murky. In a final reversal in that era of reversals, the idea of reconstructive aid was up for grabs. The province of the victor, such aid had been to international relations what charity was to class relations. As with Germany and Japan after World War II, defeated countries were to be reconstructed along lines useful to the winners, and the process was to confirm the generosity of vision that lay behind the crushing, triumphant pursuit of the enemy to the point of abject surrender. Reconstruction was to call forth rituals of gratitude in the reconstructed that would emphasize a deeply held American sense of benevolence.

During the Vietnam War, there were two spasms of reconstructive planning. The first crystallized in a speech President Johnson gave at Johns Hopkins University on April 7, 1965, just two months after ordering ongoing air strikes against North Vietnam and only days after quietly changing the marine role in South Vietnam from base defense to active combat patrol. According to the A.C. Neilsen Company, 60 million Americans watched the president on all three networks (while others listened on the radio). Johnson invoked "a world where each people may choose its own path to change," the "principle" for which American "ancestors fought in the valleys of Pennsylvania . . . [and] for which our sons fight tonight . . . in the jungles of Vietnam." He tried to answer the "why" question, cited the dangers of "the deepening shadow of Communist China" in Southeast Asia, assured the world that "we will not grow tired," and stated a desire to hold "unconditional discussions" on ending the war with North Vietnam (though not with the National Liberation Front, dismissed as "agents" of the North).

Packaged with this was an emotional vision of a peaceful Southeast Asia, premised on a multinational, reconstructive scheme to develop the Mekong River in which the North Vietnamese would be offered a place "just as soon as peaceful cooperation is possible." That river, the president claimed, could "provide food and water and power on a scale to dwarf even our own TVA." In discussing this carrot-and-stick package of air power and water power, "rockets" and "schools," Johnson cited the "generosity" of the American people "in times past in these works" and indicated that the United States would make "an investment" of $1 billion.[121]

This reconstructive offer was part of what one Johnson aide called "a policy of minimum candor," for the speech was crafted as a cover for further escalation and an attempt to pacify a restive U.S. and international public. Yet Johnson undoubtedly took seriously his proposal that, in the acceptance of defeat (even if negotiated rather than imposed), the enemy would find the solace of the good life. He even invoked a redemptive vision of technological reconstruction from his own childhood: "In the countryside where I was born, and where I live, I have seen the night illuminated and the kitchens warmed and the homes heated where once the cheerless night and the ceaseless cold held sway." After the speech, he assured his press secretary Bill Moyers that "old Ho can't turn me down."[122]

Certainly, Johnson had a fervent belief in his country's reconstructive abilities, for what was his Great Society program if not an attempt to launch a second era of reconstruction at home? His proposal, then, was still a recognizable American vision being offered, even if in bad faith, to the enemy. Yet buried in it was the seedling of something new. In the weeks preceding the speech, pressure to move from bombing to the bargaining table had been growing. In the New York Times, Max Frankel (backgrounded by administration officials) wrote a front-page commentary the next morning indicating that the intent of the speech was "to erase the impression that the President and his country were heartless, stubborn and unreasonable where peace was at stake," as well as to "regain for President Johnson some of the stature, sympathy and respect that President Kennedy enjoyed around the world." The speech, the New York Times noted in the penultimate paragraph of its lead article, "was picketed by pacifist groups urging an American withdrawal from Vietnam and carrying such signs as 'End the war—Not the world.'"[123]

Its reconstructive impulse was novel because it was directed more toward repairing damage to public consciousness and to the image of the Johnson presidency than toward the damaged lands of Indochina, and because it arose not from an expectation of victory but from incredulity that the future in Vietnam might not be American. It was less an offer of aid than a bizarre cry for help.

Within years, to propose even so shaky a reconstructive program had become politically impossible. So when, on January 27, 1973, Henry Kissinger and North Vietnam's Le Duc Tho initialed the Paris Peace Accords, the public document said only, "In pursuance of its traditional policy, the United States will contribute to healing the wounds of war and to postwar reconstruction of the Democratic Republic of Viet-Nam and throughout Indochina." More details for the funding of the "postwar reconstruction of North Vietnam" had been agreed upon, but their existence was noted only in a secret protocol to the accords, a letter signed by President Nixon and addressed to Prime Minister Pham Van Dong, offering between $4.25 billion and $4.75 billion in postwar aid "without any political conditions."

The existence of this protocol was emphatically denied by the Nixon administration. "We have not made any commitment for any reconstruction or rehabilitation effort," testified Secretary of State Rogers before a House committee on February 8, 1973. Small wonder, for the $4 billion-plus was offered not as the generous fruits of triumph but as reparations, the sums normally paid by a defeated nation to its conquerors, and the Vietnamese saw it as such. It was a bribe to procure Vietnamese assistance in putting a good face on defeat.[124]

This protocol was never honored. The U.S. government later claimed that the North Vietnamese had reneged on the Paris agreements, the completeness of their victory in 1975 being the ultimate evidence of their deceit. With that defeat, President Ford extended a wartime embargo of North Vietnam to all Indochina, froze Vietnamese assets, vetoed its membership in the United Nations, and declared the "book closed" on the war. His successor Jimmy Carter added only that the destruction in the war had been "mutual." Briefly, the Carter administration showed a willingness to open relations of some sort, if only the Vietnamese would give up the insulting idea of reparative aid. They indignantly refused. In response, an angry Congress forbade the State Department to negotiate "reparations, aid, or any other form of payment" to Vietnam.[125]

Even had relations opened then, they would have been no more than a passing event. Deeper confusions made them impossible. No one in the governing elite, Republican or Democrat, pro or antiwar, was about to forgive (no less ask forgiveness of) Vietnamese Communists for not succumbing to the spectacle of slaughter. No less was any administration going to claim responsibility for the devastation that was now Indochina. To ask the most minimal "forgiveness"—though it might have begun a true healing—was beyond possibility, while the normal pathways to the reconstruction of a defeated enemy had long since been destroyed.

The only path left, the one long chosen, was to look upon the war as an experience in American victimization and to see the United States as the nation in need of reparations. If even in flight from Vietnam, the United States hardly fit the image of a defeated nation, the postwar project of its leaders nonetheless became a new kind of domestic reconstruction.

In the late 1970s, ex-President Nixon could write, "We had won the war militarily and politically in Vietnam. But defeat was snatched from the jaws of victory because we lost the war politically in the United States." He was hardly alone in his thoughts. Soon, in revisionist scholarship as in popular culture, the war would be recast as one in which the United States more or less fought itself—and lost. If, then, "we" had won *and* "we" had lost, it was up to us to rebuild and to do so in the image of what had been lost. This reconstructive path, because in the deepest bad faith, created its own desperate confusions. The inability to find a fully satisfying explanation for victimization turned the era of reconstruction into an era of overexplanation. As a people, it was said, Americans had been "traumatized" and were suffering from a "Vietnam syndrome." They had experienced a profound loss that could no longer be captured in the idea of "losing" a country. Instead, they had evidently lost something of value in Vietnam. Certainly, they had lost a generation identified with a decade—the 1960s—to the enemy.[126]

So, in one of the many strange reversals of the period, postwar reconstruction began not in Vietnam, the land in ruins, which should have been but was not the defeated country, but in the United States, a land physically almost untouched by war, which should have been but was not the victor; and the rebuilding would focus not on some devastated environment but on the American psyche. In this postwar passage, this attempt to rebuild a narrative of triumph, children were to play a special role. For that footage of a helicopter lifting off from an embassy in abject defeat to be rolled back, so that it might land in glorious triumph, childhood had to be rescued from its foreign captivity and returned to American possession.

PART IV

AFTERLIFE
(1975–1994)

EMPTY SPACE

On the evening of May 25, 1977, a dazed thirty-two-year-old movie director, with one success to his name, was finishing a Herculean two weeks "mixing" his latest film for European audiences. Breaking for dinner, he and his wife headed for Hamburger Hamlet, a restaurant across the street from Mann's Chinese Theater in Hollywood, only to run into heavy traffic and sizable crowds. Coming around a corner, he spied the title of his new film in giant letters on the theater marquee. It was opening day. "I said, 'I don't believe this,'" he recalled. "So we sat in Hamburger Hamlet and watched the giant crowd out there, and then I went back and mixed all night. . . . I felt it was some kind of aberration."

Director George Lucas had already celebrated his teenage years in *American Graffiti* ("Where were you in '62?"), the surprise hit of 1973, which sparked a wave of nostalgia for the years before Vietnam and inspired the TV series *Happy Days* (1974). As a moviemaker, however, he had had a desire to reach even deeper into his California boyhood, to return to those moments when he had acted out World War II scenarios with toy soldiers, or watched old Flash Gordon serials, cowboy and war films on television. Like movie audiences (as box office receipts of the time indicated), he wanted to reverse the cinematic cannibalism of the 1960s. In this, he stood apart from directors as disparate as Robert Altman, Stanley Kubrick, Arthur Penn, Mel Brooks, and his own mentor Francis Ford Coppola, who for years had been dismantling space and horse operas, war and detective films; in fact, all familiar on-screen space.

"There's a whole generation," he would later say, "growing up without any kind of fairy tales." Although he undoubtedly identified with the countercultural politics of the time, his was a conservative vision. Instinctively, he wanted to still the mocking voices and return the movie audience not just to his own childhood but to a childlike viewing state. Throughout the early 1970s, he struggled to construct a script that would rebuild the missing war story in outer space. The heavens had been empty since, at the end of the 1960s, Stanley Kubrick blasted an American astronaut into a fetal state in *2001: A Space Odyssey; Planet of the Apes* took its astronauts on a mocking journey to a postnuclear Earth where humans were not the dominant species; and the U.S.S. *Enterprise* of TV's *Star Trek* left the "final frontier" to be mothballed.

In 1975, Lucas signed on with Twentieth Century Fox to produce a space film that (he reassured his wife) "ten-year-old boys would love." To make it, he had his costume designer study books on World War II uniforms and Japanese armor, while he turned to films ranging from Frank Capra's *Battle of Britain* (1943) to *The Bridges at Toko-Ri* (1954) to construct dogfights in space. In casting, he avoided white ethnics like Dustin Hoffman and Al Pacino, who had played on-screen rebels for years, in favor of unknown WASP-y actors who might bring to mind the one-dimensional whiteness of his movie past.

Summoning up enemies from his screen childhood, he patterned his evil emperor on Ming, ruler of Mongo in *Flash Gordon* (as well as on Richard Nixon), and cloaked his dark Jedi, Darth Vader, in gleaming black visor and body suit. Although there would be no blacks on screen, he hired the black actor James Earl Jones to play Vader's hissing techno-voice. In Chewbacca, the "Wookie" with the Mexican cartridge belts strung across his hairy chest, the Others of the previous decade from ascendant ape to Native American would be returned to their rightful place. This nonwhite would not even be capable of Hollywood-style broken English; only of King Kong-ish howls of frustration or rage (made by mixing bear, walrus, seal, and badger calls).

In early 1977, the almost finished film seemed an unlikely candidate for success. Fox's research showed that the word *war* in a title would turn off women, that robots would turn off everyone, and that science fiction was a dead category. Fox's board of directors had only reluctantly financed the film; and at a special screening, those directors who did not go to sleep were outraged. As movie theater owners showed little enthusiasm, the film opened in only thirty-two theaters nationwide.

Not in his wildest flights of fancy did Lucas imagine that his cinematic vision would sweep all before it, that his reconquest of a child audience and of "the kids in all of us" would be crucial to the reconstruction of a narrative of triumph, that he would help give a new look of entertainment to the design of war and reintroduce the spectacle of slaughter to the many screens of America.[1]

About two years before *Star Wars* opened, a twenty-year-old MIT student, Peter Hagelstein, applied for a fellowship to the Hertz Foundation. Among its board members was Edward Teller, "father" of the H-bomb and a founder of Lawrence Livermore National Laboratory, a government nuclear weapons research facility in Northern California. Although John

D. Hertz (of rental car fame) had set up the fellowships to "foster the technological strength of America" vis-à-vis the Soviet Union and some recipients were recruited into Livermore's weapons research by those interviewing them, the foundation advertised only that "[t]he proposed field of graduate study must be concerned with applications of the physical sciences to human problems, broadly construed."

Hagelstein was offered a fellowship and a summer job at Livermore by Lowell Wood, his interviewer and head of Livermore's O Group. Its young scientists were working on designing a "third generation" of nuclear weapons (the first two being the A and H bombs). According to Hagelstein, Wood told him only that they were working on "lasers and laser fusion, which I had never heard of before, and he said there were computer codes out there that were like playing a Wurlitzer organ. It all sounded kind of dreamy. . . . The lab made quite an impression, especially the guards and barbed wire. When I got to the personnel department it dawned on me that they worked on weapons here, and that's about the first I knew about it."

In the summer of 1976, he went there full time, while continuing Ph.D. work at MIT. He was a young man who "hated bombs" and "didn't want to be associated with anything nuclear." He was even romantically involved with an antinuclear activist who picketed the lab. But he was held by a dream of creating a laboratory x-ray laser that would allow scientists to "see" various biological processes, and by the appealing young men of O Group, with their jeans and long hair, all-night work habits, countercultural élan, and perverse humor. (Once, they even "took up a collection" to buy Lowell Wood a Darth Vader costume.)

The year that *Star Wars* soared into box office heaven, a senior O Group scientist came up with a new concept for using a nuclear explosion to "pump" enough focused energy into a laser to turn it into a weapon. In the summer of 1979, Hagelstein appeared at a meeting where the use of an underground nuclear explosion to test out the idea was being discussed. Dazed from twenty straight hours of work, he made a suggestion—"The mouth just said it"—that was to lead to a laser device dubbed Excalibur and successfully tested in November 1980. While Hagelstein's dream of a laboratory x-ray laser faded, "his" weapon became the centerpiece of a different sort of fantasy.

In February 1981, the trade journal *Aviation Week and Space Technology* reported the x-ray laser's heavily classified existence, saying that, "mounted in a laser battle station" in space, it had "the potential to blunt a Soviet nuclear weapons attack." The magazine's account was accompanied by a hyper-realistic, futuristic "artist's drawing" showing a snazzy battle station that "bristled with long laser rods," an image the mainstream media picked up, thus marrying the look of war to the look of *Star Wars*.

By 1982, Teller had taken news of Peter Hagelstein's laser directly to Ronald Reagan. Space lasers and other third-generation weapons, he assured the president, "by converting hydrogen bombs into hitherto unprecedented forms and by directing these in highly effective fashions against enemy targets would end the MAD [Mutual Assured Destruction] era and commence a period of assured survival on terms favorable to the Western alliance." Even a young weapons researcher whose doctoral thesis ("Physics of Short Wavelength Laser Design") mentioned three science fiction novels featuring beam weapons could hardly have imagined that one spaced-out suggestion would become a crucial part of a multibillion-dollar national fantasy to create a "protective shield" over the reconstruction of war on Earth.[2]

TEENAGERS IN SPACE

Now that Darth Vader's breathy techno-voice is a staple of our culture, it's hard to remember how empty was the particular sector of space *Star Wars* blasted into. The very day the Paris Peace Accords were signed in 1973, Richard Nixon also signed a decree ending the draft. It was an admission of the obvious: war, American-style, had lost its hold on young minds. As an activity, it was now to be officially turned over to the poor and nonwhite.

Those in a position to produce movies, TV shows, comics, novels, or memoirs about Vietnam were convinced that Americans felt badly enough without such reminders. It was simpler to consider the war film and war toy casualties of Vietnam than to create cultural products with the wrong heroes, victims, and villains. In *Star Wars*, Lucas successfully challenged this view, decontaminating war of its recent history through a series of inspired cinematic decisions that rescued crucial material from the wreckage of Vietnam. To start with, he embraced the storylessness of the period, creating his own self-enclosed universe in deepest space and in an amorphous movie past, "a long time ago in a galaxy far, far away." Beginning with "Episode IV" of a projected nonology, he offered only the flimsiest of historical frameworks—an era of civil war, an evil empire, rebels, an ultimate weapon, a struggle for freedom.

Mobilizing a new world of special effects and computer graphics, he then made the high-tech weaponry of the recent war exotic, bloodless, and sleekly unrecognizable. At the same time, he uncoupled the audience from a legacy of massacre and atrocity. The blond, young Luke Skywalker is barely introduced before his adoptive family—high tech peasants on an obscure planet—suffers its own My Lai. Imperial storm troopers led by Darth Vader descend upon their homestead and turn it into a smoking ruin (thus returning fire to its rightful owners). Luke—and the audience—can now set off on an anti-imperial venture as the victimized, not as victimizers. Others in space will torture, maim, and destroy. Others will put "us" in high-tech tiger cages; and our revenge, whatever it may be, will be justified.

In this way, *Star Wars* denied the enemy a role "they" had monopolized for a decade—that of brave rebel. It was the first cultural product to ask of recent history, "Hey! How come *they* got all the fun?" And to respond, "Let's give them the burden of empire! Let's bog them down and be the plucky underdogs ourselves!"

Like Green Berets or Peace Corps members, Lucas's white teenage rebels would glide effortlessly among the natives. They would learn from value-superior Third World mystics like the Ho-Chi-Minh-ish Yoda in *The Empire Strikes Back* and be protected by ecological fuzzballs like the Ewoks in *Return of the Jedi*. In deepest space, anything was possible, including returning history to its previous owners. Once again, we could have it all: freedom *and* victory, captivity *and* rescue, underdog status *and* the spectacle of slaughter. As with the Indian fighter of old, advanced weaponry *and* the spiritual powers of the guerrilla might be ours.

Left to the enemy would be a Nazi-like capacity for destroying life, a desire to perform search-and-destroy missions on the universe, and the breathy machine voice of Darth Vader (as if evil were a dirty phone call from the Darkside). The Tao of the Chinese, the "life force" of Yaqui mystic Don Juan, even the political will of the Vietnamese would rally to "our" side as the Force and be applied to a crucial technical problem; for having the Force "with you" meant learning to merge with your high-tech weaponry in such a way as to assure the enemy's destruction. Looked at today, the last part of *Star Wars* concentrates on a problem that might have been invented after, not fourteen years before, the 1991 Persian Gulf War: how to fly a computerized, one-man jet fighter down a narrow corridor under heavy antiaircraft fire and drop a missile into an impossibly small air shaft, the sole vulnerable spot in the Emperor's Death Star.

Here, Lucas even appropriated the kamikaze-like fusion of human and machine. In Vietnam, there had been two such man–machine meldings. The first, the bombing campaign, had the machinelike impersonality of the production line. Lifting off from distant spots of relative comfort like

Guam, B-52 crews delivered their bombs to coordinates stripped of place or people and left the war zone for another day. The crew member symbolically regained humanity only when the enemy's technology stripped him of his machinery—and, alone, he fluttered to earth and captivity. At the same time, from Secretary of Defense McNamara's "electronic battlefield" to the first "smart bombs," Vietnam proved an experimental testing ground for machine-guided war. Unlike the B-52 or napalm, the smart bomb, the computer, the electronic sensor, and the video camera were not discredited by the war; and it was these machines of wonder that Lucas rescued through the innocence of special effects.

In James Bond films, high-tech had been a display category like fine wines, and techno-weaponry just another consumer item for 007. For Lucas, however, technology in the right hands actually solved problems, offering—whether as laser sword or X-wing fighter—not status but potential spiritualization. This elevation of technology made possible the return of slaughter to the screen as a triumphal and cleansing pleasure (especially since dying "imperial storm troopers," encased in full body carapaces, looked like so many bugs).†

Not only would George Lucas put "war" back into a movie title, he would almost single-handedly reconstitute war play as a feel-good activity for children. With G.I. Joe's demise, the world of child-sized war play stood empty. The toy soldier had long ago moved into history, an object for adult collectors. However, some months before *Star Wars* opened, Fox reached an agreement with Kenner Products, a toy company, to create action figures and fantasy vehicles geared to the movie. Kenner president Bernard Loomis decided that these would be inexpensive, new-style figures, only 3³/₄-inch high. Each design was to be approved by Lucas himself.

Since Kenner could not produce the figures quickly enough for the 1977 Christmas season, Loomis offered an "Early Bird Certificate Package"—essentially an empty box—that promised the child the first four

---

†As Lucas rescued the machinery of war from debacle in Vietnam; so, too, he rescued special-effects technology from the deconstructive efforts of the previous era. He hired veterans of Kubrick's *2001* to help him, for Kubrick's numbed-out astronaut had ridden down the same cramped corridors that in *Star Wars* would be filled with futuristic ack-ack fire. In that initial special-effects extravaganza of our age, a deadened astronaut was in need of a circuit transplant from a rebellious and menacing adolescent computer. Lucas lifted Kubrick's technology and Hal, his machine-with-a-personality, out of *2001* and robbed them both of threat. It was in this way that the stick hurled by Kubrick's prehuman landed nine years later.³

figures when produced. The result was toy history. In 1978, Kenner sold over 26 million figures; by 1985, 250 million. All 111 figures and other *Star Wars* paraphernalia, ranging from lunch boxes and watches to video games, would ring up $2.5 billion in sales.[4]

By the early 1980s, children's TV had become a *Star Wars*–like battle zone. Outnumbered rebels daily transformed themselves from teenagers into mighty robots "loved by good, feared by evil" (*Voltron*) or "heroic teams of armed machines" (*M.A.S.K.*) in order to fight Lotar and his evil, blue-faced father from Planet Doom (*Voltron*), General Spidrax, master of the Dark Domain's mighty armies (*Sectaurs*), or the evil red-eyed Darkseid of the Planet Apokolips (*Superfriends*).

Future war would be a machine-versus-machine affair, a bloodless matter of special effects, in the revamped war story designed for childhood consumption. In popular cartoons like *Transformers*, where good "Autobots" fought evil "Decepticons," Japanese-animated machines transformed themselves from mundane vehicles into futuristic weapons systems. At the same time, proliferating teams of action figures, *Star Wars*–size and linked to such shows, were transported into millions of homes where new-style war scenarios could be played out.[5]

In those years, *Star Wars*–like themes also began to penetrate the world of adult entertainment. Starting in 1983 with the surprise movie hit *Uncommon Valor*, right-wing revenge fantasies like *Missing-in-Action* (1984) returned American guerrillas to "Vietnam" to rescue captive pilots from jungle prisons and bog Communists down here on earth. In a subset of these—*Red Dawn* (1984) and the TV miniseries *Amerika* (1987) are prime examples—the action took place in a future, conquered United States where home-grown guerrillas fought to liberate the country from Soviet imperial occupation. Meanwhile, melds of technology and humanity ranging from Robocop to Arnold Schwarzenegger began to proliferate on adult screens. In 1985–86, two major hits featured man-as-machine fusions. As Rambo, Sylvester Stallone was a "pure fighting machine," with muscles and weaponry to prove it; while in *Top Gun*, Tom Cruise played a "maverick" on a motorcycle who was transformed from hot dog to top dog by fusing with his navy jet as he soared to victory over the evil empire's aggressor machines, Libyan MIGs.

It took some time for political leaders to catch up with George Lucas's battle scenarios. In the years when he was producing *Star Wars*, America's post-Vietnam presidents were having a woeful time organizing any narrative at all. In the real world, there seemed to be no Lucas-like outer space into which to escape the deconstruction job Vietnam had done to the war story. The military was in shambles; the public, according to pollsters, had become resistant to American troops being sent into battle anywhere; and past enemies were now negotiating partners in a new "détente."

Gerald Ford, inheriting a collapsed presidency from Richard Nixon, attempted only once to display American military resolve. In May 1975, a month after Saigon fell, Cambodian Khmer Rouge rebels captured an American merchant ship, the *Mayaguez*. Ford ordered the bombing of the Cambodian port city of Kampong Son and sent in the marines. They promptly stormed an island on which the *Mayaguez* crew was not being held, hours after ship and crew had been released, and fought a pointless, bitter battle, suffering forty-one dead. The event seemed to mock American prowess, confirming that rescue, like victory, had slipped from its grasp.

Jimmy Carter, elected president in 1976, had an even more woeful time of it. Facing what he termed a Vietnam-induced "national malaise," he proposed briefly that Americans engage in "the moral equivalent of war" by mobilizing and sacrificing on the home front to achieve energy independence from the OPEC oil cartel. The public, deep in a peacetime recession, responded without enthusiasm. In 1979, in a defining moment of his presidency, Carter watched helplessly as young Islamic followers of the Iranian Ayatollah Khomeini took fifty-two Americans captive in the U.S. embassy in Teheran and held them for 444 days. In April 1980, "Desert One," a military raid the president ordered to rescue the captives, failed dismally in the Iranian desert, and the president was forced to live out his term against a televised backdrop of unending captivity and humiliation that seemed to highlight American impotence.

Only with the presidency of Ronald Reagan did a Lucas-like reconstitution of the war story truly begin at the governmental level. The new president defined the Soviet Union in Star Wars–like terms as an "evil empire," while the army began advertising for recruits on TV by displaying spacy weaponry and extolling the pleasures of being "out there" in search of "the bad guys." In Nicaragua, Angola, Afghanistan, and elsewhere, the Reagan administration managed to portray the forces it supported as outnumbered "freedom fighters" struggling to roll back an overwhelming tide of imperial evil. This time, we would do the hitting and running, and yet we—or our surrogates—would retain the high-tech weaponry: mines for their harbors and Stinger missiles for their helicopters. Meanwhile, planners discovered in an intervention in Grenada that, with the right media controls in place and speed, you could produce the equivalent of an outer space war fantasy here on earth. No wonder that a group of junior officers at the Army Command and General Staff

College at Fort Leavenworth responsible for aspects of the ground campaign used against Iraq in 1991 would be nicknamed the Jedi Knights.[6]

THE GRAPHIC DESIGN OF WAR

President Ronald Reagan, elected in 1980 on the promise of a "new beginning" for America, still faced a troubled national landscape in his third year in office. A massive rearmament program, begun during the Carter administration, was going well amid a revival of Cold War tensions, and he himself was receiving adulatory media attention as the "Great Communicator." Yet, despite his insistence that the Vietnam War had been a "noble cause," the public, according to pollsters, remained deeply reluctant to see troops committed to battle abroad. Worse yet, an oppositional mood seemed on the rise, though its focus was no longer an ongoing war on Earth but a future one in space.

If Vietnam was still largely blanketed in silence, nuclear war and human extinction were the subjects of the moment. From Jonathan Schell's best-selling 1982 book *The Fate of the Earth* (with its "Republic of Insects and Grass") to the hit 1983 film *War Games* about a teenage hacker who uses a government computer system to accidentally launch World War III (Computer: "Shall we play a game"; Teenager: "Let's play Thermonuclear War"), the country once again filled with nuclear fears. In films, novels, TV shows, the statements of religious organizations, and the writings of scientists, a new antinuclear mood was apparent. In 1983, several scientists including Carl Sagan introduced the idea that a relatively small nuclear exchange might cause a "nuclear winter," while 100 million Americans watched the missiles leave their silos in *The Day After*, a highly publicized TV movie-of-the-week.[7]

In the late 1970s, a grass-roots movement first began to form around the dangers of nuclear power as an energy source. In 1979, a near catastrophe at the Three Mile Island nuclear power plant in Pennsylvania, and the release of Jane Fonda's film *The China Syndrome* about just such an incident, helped mobilize support. By the beginning of the new decade, a nationwide Nuclear Freeze movement was attacking the MAD policies of both superpowers, while a torrent of antinuclear protest culminated in a 750,000-person demonstration in New York City in June 1982.

On March 23, 1983, President Reagan tacked several paragraphs onto a speech calling for greater defense spending against a renewed Soviet threat, challenging the nation and the "scientific community" ("those who gave us nuclear weapons") to undertake a vast research and development effort to create an "impermeable" antimissile shield in space that would render nuclear weapons "impotent and obsolete." This shield would offer "new hope for our children in the twenty-first century" by protecting Americans from nuclear attack just as, he later explained, "a roof protects a family from rain." Labeled the Strategic Defense Initiative (SDI), it was to be based on the "third-generation" nuclear work being done at Livermore Lab and other government-funded research centers— not just x-ray lasers, but chemical lasers, exotic particle beams, and other fantastic concepts in weaponry.[8]

Now, like his antinuclear opponents, the president had attacked the very idea of Mutual Assured Destruction, offering instead technological optimism and an innocent "defensive" weapons system. This would be "mutual assured survival." He even ventured at one of his later press conferences that the United States might someday be willing to share this defensive technology with the Russians. The president's critics quickly pointed out SDI's operational improbabilities and mocked this "movie president" for proposing a Hollywood-style defense fantasy. On the Senate floor the day after the speech, Ted Kennedy attempted to infantilize the project by dubbing it Star Wars. Politicians, editorial writers, cartoonists, religious figures, military strategists, and scientists jumped into the fray, and the name stuck.

But Reagan's critics had badly misjudged him. "In the first place," Gary Wills has written, "*no one* understood all [SDI's] multiple if sketchy projections. There were more dreams—and the key parts of those, classified—than tested components to it. It was more an expensive and glamorous wish than a single project." Ronald Reagan's reluctant acceptance of "Star Wars" as a label for SDI ("If you will pardon my stealing a film line—the Force is with us," he commented genially) proved intuitively on the mark. Unlike his critics, he grasped the Star Wars–like promise of sleek, futuristic, good machines that would destroy bad enemy machines far off in space.[9]

In addition, he grasped the promise of such a "good" weapons system for clearing the American mind, the way you might clear a computer screen, of visions of the previous war. His critics, wedded to a no-fun adult world, did not understand the magical power of war as a childhood game to make adults feel as good as children again. The most sober scientific research, the most bizarre sci-fi fantasy, and the most toylike high-tech weaponry could now mingle in a childlike American defensive system.†

---

†For the president, SDI may have rung a special bell, for in 1940 he had starred in a film, *Murder in the Air*, in which he had to stop a spy from stealing an advanced

The synergy proved fantastic. Designers moving from the military-industrial to the computer to the high-tech toy worlds could develop the wildest products imaginable—talking cockpits and talking dolls, laser weaponry and laser tag, video tracking systems and video game systems. The high-tech design of *Star Wars* moved on to TV cartoons, to video games, to Star Wars, the embryonic weapons system, to Star Wars, the newscast (with animated space weapons surrounded by the talking heads of High Fronticrsmen, government officials, sci-fi writers, and scientific experts), and to Star Wars, the proto-war.

In April 1982, Margaret Thatcher's British government, with one eye on the by now accepted version of the media's role in Vietnam, went to war with Argentina over the distant Falkland Islands. No foreign correspondents were allowed, and visuals of British disasters took up to twenty-three days by sea to reach TV screens, thanks to the Royal Navy. Lacking visuals, the nightly news reconceived the conflict in Star Wars–style graphic design; and so a grim little episode that was more slaughter than battle became, through cartoonlike animation, the first visually fun war of the post-Vietnam era—and U.S. government officials were watching the show. Military journals would, for instance, subsequently offer copious advice to the Pentagon on how to adapt British news management techniques, including the exclusion of unsympathetic correspondents from the battle zone, to ensure "favorable objectivity."[11]

Someday, the Empire would strike back. War culture, uncoupled from its recent past, had reentered American life, initially as childish fantasy, then as a "childlike" multibillion-dollar research and publicity endeavor. Innocence was rearming itself to embrace slaughter. Military men were

---

electrical beam weapon capable of knocking an enemy plane from the sky. ("Yes, Doctor, and wait 'till you see it in action. It not only makes the United States invincible in war, but in so doing promises to become the greatest force for world peace ever discovered.")

His supporters were also aware of the importance of children to SDI. One pro-SDI group released a TV ad that showed a child's crayon drawing of "a family standing outside a little house." A young girl then extolled the virtues of SDI: "I asked my daddy what this 'Star Wars' stuff is all about. He said . . . [i]t'd stop missiles in outer space . . . so they couldn't hit our house. Then nobody could win a war, and if nobody could win a war, there's no reason to start one. My daddy's smart." As she spoke, "a protective dome magically appeared over the family and their house, enemy missiles bounced harmlessly off the dome, the sun smiled, and the American flag flew overhead."

Such ads so upset George Lucas that he sued two pro-SDI groups for using his movie title. His lawyer claimed that children would be "turned off by [the ado] . . . and would shy away from the movie and its spinoff products, such as dolls, toys, comic books, cookies, paper cups, watches, candles and bubble bath." But he lost.[10]

going back to school in places like the National War College and the Defense Information School to sort out how to give better war at home the next time around; while the historical reversals introduced in *Star Wars* lodged in the culture and began to replicate.

THE DOMINANT WHINE

The United States emerged from Vietnam with only two aspects of its war story still intact: victimhood/underdog-ness and captivity. Stripped of the rest of the story, each had taken on a strange new look. Being outnumbered by a savage enemy and subject to treacherous ambush had always been the war story's starting point. As captivity necessitated rescue, so ambush necessitated the defensive acts of conquest and slaughter. Although the captivity account could descend into self-pity (as in nineteenth-century "frail flower" narratives, in which white women suffered endless humiliations at the hands of Indian captors), it remained largely a justification for triumphant white acts to follow.

That Vietnam offered a new sense of victimhood was clear long before the war ended, as in President Nixon's 1970 suggestion that the United States might soon be reduced to the status of "a pitiful, helpless giant." The image of America as a diminished and unfairly constrained giant would carry through the postwar years. The sense of aggrievement and self-pity that lay behind it was summed up in the insistence that the country would never again fight a war under constraints. As President Bush put it on the eve of the war with Iraq, "No hands are going to be tied behind backs. This is not a Vietnam."

The image was not a new one. The idea of a military "shackled" by politicians fearing nuclear conflict had arisen during the Korean War and again in Vietnam. However, its repetitive post-Vietnam use reflected a particular sense of aggrievement. After all, in everyday speech, the challenge, "I could beat you with one hand tied behind my back," is a bravado offer of voluntary restraint and an implicit admission that fighting any other way would make one seem a bully. Hidden in the image, then, was a most un-American acceptance of the United States as a bully nation, whose "unleashing" was to be a policy goal.[12]

As a sense of victimhood and aggrievement spread into domestic society, some whites came to see themselves as just another unfairly oppressed minority. With George Wallace's 1972 third party presidential campaign and the Supreme Court's 1978 decision in *Bakke v. University of California*, whites began to reposition themselves not as a dominant majority but as dominant victims. The underside of dominance turned out to be the right to the dominant whine.

So the lost war story would be reconstructed around the only materials available: a sense of national aggrievement and a series of captivities without rescue. The ur-captivity narrative of the period was that of the American prisoners of war whom, it was claimed, the Vietnamese, Cambodians, and Laotians had not returned in 1973. POWs had first become a war issue in 1969, when, according to the historian H. Bruce Franklin, the Nixon administration demanded a Vietnamese accounting of Americans missing in action and the early release of POWs. Soon, officials began denouncing the unwillingness of the other side to do so as "unprecedented" and "barbaric" (though it was the normal way of war). That same year, the administration helped organize the National League of Families of American Prisoners and Missing in Southeast Asia, and by 1970 had created a new issue: "concealed prisoners."

POWs and MIAs soon became an explanation for the country's continued presence in the war. "[A]s long as there are American POW's in North Vietnam," declared President Nixon in 1971, "we will have to maintain a residual force in South Vietnam." As its failed 1970 commando raid on North Vietnam's Son Tay prison camp indicated, the rescue of captives no longer seemed within America's capability; and so captivity became a focus not for triumphant action, but for self-pity.[13]

If the POW/MIA issue was initially an artificial creation, however, the war's end changed that. "Live sightings" of MIAs poured in, and their existence gained a reality that no analysis of the forces promoting the search for them could account for. Ghostly photographs of the missing multiplied; and the more these were declared forgeries, the more real the MIAs became, until a vast percentage of Americans believed in them. They continued to roam the sealed off former battle zones; no matter how many times they were "rescued" in movies, books, or on TV, or the Vietnamese denied their existence, they could not be dismissed. They were like UFOs rising from the rubble of the war story. They were the afterlife.

AMBUSH AT KAMIKAZE PASS (III):
VIETNAM MOVIES

A defining feature of the war story had been its essential simplicity, its childlike unself-consciousness, its lack of explanation. At war's end, however, there were scenes within consciousness impossible to absorb without explanation. A new "simplification" would soon follow. Public dissatisfaction with the war would be reduced to the "Vietnam syndrome," transforming complex opposition into simple illness. An array of American acts that seemed like crimes would be replaced by the "barbaric" Vietnamese treatment of POWs. A remarkable range of domestic protest would be reduced to the single (possibly mythical) act of "spitting" on returning troops. The complexities of the antiwar and antidraft movements would be replaced by the lone desecrations of the "flag burner"; the chaotic story of loyalties in the military and connections between soldiers and antiwar civilians would be transposed into that figure of pathos, the mistreated Vietnam veteran; and madness would be returned to Qaddafi of Libya, Khomeini of Iran, and other "mad mullahs."

In turn, a few symbols would expand to fill a space emptied of complexity. The flag, for instance, would grow to gargantuan proportions or be displayed in prodigious numbers at any celebratory event; its in-your-face presence, an insistence on the return of pride in country. The larger it became, the more aggressive the whine of aggrievement behind it; the more the flag burner became the focus of "debate," the more burning would be returned to the true savages of the Vietnam years.

This process took place not just in the political arena but on movie screens, where "Vietnam" would soon be refought in largely emptied jungles. However, the process of creating a simplified war took time. The first significant Vietnam films—*The Deer Hunter* (1978), *Coming Home* (1978), and *Apocalypse Now* (1979)—were box office successes, yet raised a confusion of political issues and angers. From the entertainment industry's point of view, all three were quagmire films—as excessive and indigestible as the war.

Director Michael Cimino's *The Deer Hunter*, a sprawling, male-bonding film, broke new ground in its portrayal of Americans as captives and victims but created a media uproar by reversing certain defining images of the war. Here, Americans in watery tiger cages were forced by their captors to play Russian roulette (reversing the infamous image of General Loan executing a Vietcong suspect during Tet). What made the film especially uncomfortable, though, was its vision of Americans in endless flight or in states of unbearable degradation and humiliation in Vietnam. To its final moments, a desolate singing of "God Bless America," it was about unparalleled loss.

Jane Fonda's *Coming Home* took a different point of departure, for it skipped the war (and the Vietnamese) entirely, focusing only on its cost to Americans—literally so in the case of Luke (Jon Voight), a paraplegic vet. In doing so, it began the transformation of the vet's image from psychotic killer to sensitive victim. However, its antiwar politics, its display of protesters, its references to American atrocities (army wife: "I got [a letter] from Dink this morning. All he said was, I got you another ear. Poetic, huh?") as well as the presence of its star, brought disturbance to the screen. "Hanoi Jane," as Fonda was labeled by war supporters after being photographed seated on a North Vietnamese antiaircraft gun, had long been a symbol of antiwar activism and betrayal; for it had been a shock when Barbarella, the sex goddess, landed on Earth, only to reject the American dreamscape.[14]

The jungle travails and cost overruns of Francis Ford Coppola's *Apocalypse Now* led it to be promoted as a quagmire film. It broke ground in portraying the war largely as an insular struggle for the American soul. However, it also offered audiences their only chance to experience from a peasant's viewpoint the annihilating terror of attacking U.S. helicopters. With its sardonic view of the war effort and its crazed length, it seemed an object lesson in why the war should not be refought by Hollywood.

A half-decade of on-screen silence followed before *Rambo: First Blood Part II* (1985) brought *Star Wars* down to earth in Vietnam with a box office bang. A superhuman guerrilla hunk, a one-man X-wing fighter, trained in the jungle skills of Ewok and Vietcong alike, Rambo was "the chosen one." Of "Indian-German descent," he appropriated all roles: machine and human; male and female; Green Beret, captive, and rescuer alike. Distancing himself from "our" high-tech weaponry ("I always believed that the mind was the best weapon") and destroying theirs, he nonetheless retained a New Age, high-tech weapon for himself—a black crossbow with missile-tipped arrows.

He was on a postwar mission to rescue the tiger-caged POWs of *The Deer Hunter*. His domestic enemies of choice were weak Washington bureaucrats ("What if some burnout POW shows up on the six o'clock news? . . . Y'want to bomb Hanoi?"); a pusillanimous Congress ("Do you think somebody's going to get up on the floor of the United States Senate and ask for billions of dollars for a couple of forgotten ghosts!"); an oppositional media; and unseen antiwar spitters who fought "a quieter war, a war against all the soldiers returning." The imprisoned Rambo at film's beginning is visibly a shackled giant. Subsequently lied to by his government, tortured on an electric rack by a Russian officer, and beaten by the Vietnamese, who lower him enchained into a literal quagmire of shit, he would be in every way degraded and humiliated—thus, preparing *them* for the slaughter.

The reversals of *Star Wars* were here unclouded by Lucas's confused political agenda. Rambo was Victim, Rebel, and Savior; the Vietnamese (and their Russian overlords) were the ones who were bogged down. If they now possessed the only air force in Vietnam, they had lost the Force; so, alone, Rambo proves capable of knifing, garroting, electrocuting, blowing up, and smothering in mud prodigious numbers of them, all without losing his sense of self-pity. When asked at carnage's end, "What is it you want," eyes brimming with tears, he replies pleadingly, "I want what [the MIAs] want, and every other guy who came over here and spilt his guts and gave everything he had, once. For our country to love us as much as we love it."

It turned out that the "good wars" of screen history could not be brought back without a form of overexplanation that verged on the grotesque. Traditionally, brute physique had been the least of the qualities the western hero needed to enter "Indian country." His strengths were, if anything, visually understated, not a spectacle in their own right. Even John Wayne was no giant. Rambo's gargantuan musculature, however, was a form of explanation. He bulged with visible strength, while the camera repeatedly took roller coaster rides over his mountainous muscles, reiterating that he was such a hero.

What had once seemed natural now needed not just fulsome illustration, but the sort of cartoonish exaggeration that would previously have passed for mockery. Everything had to be similarly overdetermined because it had to be relearned. To feel good now involved damnable effort and strain. If Rambo was not violated and victimized again and again, then the slaughter to follow somehow could not take place. No more, as in *The Searchers* (1956), would only John Wayne see what the savages did to his family. Now, viewers would have to see it for themselves, many times over. No longer were you at home wherever the wagons circled and defending yourself no matter what you did. Only an endless victimization gained you the right to an on-screen spectacle that once was as American as Kansas in August.

In 1986, Oliver Stone's *Platoon* picked up where *Coming Home* and *Apocalypse Now* had left off. Now, there would be a second cinematic path out of Vietnam. In *Platoon* and the many "noble grunt" films to follow, all that was left of the war was the white foot soldier, a beleaguered underdog on whom fell its full tragedy. (Blacks were, at best, background figures.) All but the years of the American ground war were gone; the air war ceased to exist; the war's origins were missing in action; the war's planners and military strategists, beyond sight and memory (though, as in *Good Morning, Vietnam* [1987], low-level bureaucrats could be reviled); and the youthful antiwar movement, except in its spitting mode, invisible.

The Vietnamese, almost totally excised from these films, were either

shadowy fighting figures, babbling, terrified victims, or as in Stanley
Kubrick's fierce *Full Metal Jacket* (1987), plot devices. Only in a single,
easily missed moment in *Good Morning, Vietnam* was it even suggested
that the United States might have been "the enemy." The civil war in
Vietnam had, according to critic Pat Aufderheide, moved "inside the platoon," a struggle between two sergeants, the good and bad halves of the
American soul. As Director Stone's stand-in Chris comments, "We didn't
fight the enemy, we fought ourselves, and the enemy was in us."[15]

In such films, slaughter was still embargoed as a spectacle of pleasure.
It remained a criminal act that mainly triggered conflict among grunts
over American values. Only in 1991, while Iraq's dazed armies were
being dismembered in the Persian Gulf, were Americans again able to
cheer slaughter in an earthbound film that was not a right-wing fantasy
of vengeance. In Kevin Costner's hit *Dances with Wolves*, a rebellious
ex–Civil War soldier and sensitive white man voluntarily goes MIA on
the beautiful western plains. There, he establishes contact with the
Sioux, the Ewoks of that time. The Costner character is a Luke Skywalker come to earth—white, young, alone, in search of wisdom from
the Other, and possessing high-tech weaponry, a cache of army repeating
rifles. The rebel figure is now firmly us. If every other white is cartoon-
ishly evil or crazed, they are the history we have shed. They are Vietnam,
we are not; and the proof is that we are willing to turn our technology
over to the Ewoks of Earth so that they can defend themselves from their
enemies—the Pawnees.

Implacable, murderous, and cruel, the Pawnees emerge from the horizon bent on destroying "our" home (the Sioux village). With punkish
haircuts and fierce facial paint jobs, they are not Native Americans but
the treacherous Indians of movie history rising up to be slaughtered.
What had changed here—and it indicated the limits the Vietnam era still
imposed—was that whites, now freed to slaughter Asians and Arabs in
right-wing films, had not gained that right vis-à-vis the people central to
the spectacle. In *Dances*, something far more tortured had to happen to
recreate a facsimile of that spectacle. The Costner character had to hand
over the rifles to his embattled friends so that they could conduct a
splendid slaughter of the primitively armed Pawnee aggressors. To the
audience's cheers, the admirable Other did the job.

In the 1980s, a Rambo-dreaming president, National Security Council,
CIA, and military establishment began to plan an agenda of intervention
abroad based on a desire to wipe the memory of defeat and domestic
opposition from the face of the earth. Developments on screen, in Vietnam comics like *Nam* and *Vietnam Journal*, in the "grunt" novels and
memoirs that flooded from publishing houses, in Vietnam snuff novels

like the *M.I.A. Hunter* series, in revisionist works of history, and on TV in *China Beach* and *Tour of Duty* paralleled such off-screen governmental desires. The narrowness of the script that passed for the war, whether in its liberal or its right-wing versions, was striking enough to seem agreed upon. If this wasn't a culture of propaganda, that was only because no one seemed fully aware of what they were doing.

THE URGE TO EXPLAIN

What was most striking about President Reagan's much praised and criticized actorly "ease"—even his ease of error—was the level of effort, planning, and outright strain that surrounded it. Layers of publicists, handlers, pollsters, and managers worked to script his every step and word. He seemed never to move from his bedroom (where he relaxed watching old movies) without the media frame that public relations could construct around him. As the memoirs of those who surrounded him attest, he was not just a passive but a largely absent personality. It was not hard for him to believe anything about himself; that, for instance, he had been away at war during World War II (when he had never strayed far from Hollywood) or that he had photographed the liberation of a Nazi death camp. As a man who had trouble keeping track of his own story, his context had to be constantly manufactured for him.[16]

It became a cliché of the Reagan–Bush years to note that never had so many political handlers and "spin doctors" been so concerned to control the image of the moment as presented in the media. The media itself began to offer regular glimpses of the framework of control for the stories they were reporting—the marks, for instance, carefully chalked out by aides to indicate where the president should stand for the perfect photo opportunity. Similarly, in election coverage, "spin doctors" appeared on TV to analyze the spin they had just put on an event, while reporters discussed the process of being spun. Though this often passed for exposé, how the public was being controlled was less emphasized than how their leaders and attendant publicists were *in control*, how firm was their grasp on the technology of presentation.

This reconstructive image of images—of how "they" had prepared the frame for "our" viewing—was itself a reduced and controlled image that served as an antidote to feelings of discontrol engendered by Vietnam. The desire not just to control images but to be seen as in control of them was but another form of overexplanation meant to call up memories of the power presidents had once exercised without such display. The Reagan administration even altered what was overt and what covert in the exercise of state power to satisfy this urge. Although secret operations grew ever more elaborate (as the Iran-Contra affair indicated), a parallel need also grew—to display to the public the sorts of foreign policy manipulations that once would have been secret. So the "covertness" of the administration's war against Nicaragua's Sandinista government was publicly promoted as a signal that future Vietnams would remain under control.

This half-to-be-seen edifice of manipulation declared—and secretly pleaded—that the president was again in control, partially by offering glimpses of the ways in which he was controlled. Yet the more a vast market research and publicity apparatus had to be mobilized to organize and sanitize what was on screen, the more what remained visible had to be subjected to elaborate special effects simply to give it the look of narrative. At the heart of the many celebratory evocations of patriotism in those years, there often seemed to be no story at all. Typical were the XXIII Olympic Games in Los Angeles, taken up by the Reagan administration in 1984 as a celebration of its "America is back" reelection campaign theme. Indeed, after years of losses to Communist bloc athletes, the prodigious number of medals won were hailed as proof of a return to glory days. Yet the Soviets did not attend. A full-scale Cold War Olympics had been triumphantly promoted that lacked the other side.

Every exaggerated, overreferential event could in some fashion be traced back to Vietnam. Take the names of two military interventions of the period: Operation Urgent Fury (Grenada, 1983) and Operation Just Cause (Panama, 1989). There was nothing about Grenada that called for urgency or fury. The "hostaged" American students at a medical school on the island were in no visible danger, no less actual or implied captivity; and the new regime, whose supporters had just murdered Prime Minister Maurice Bishop and overthrown his revolutionary government, was anxiously trying to reassure the students and the Reagan administration of that.

The real fury of military and civilian planners came from a "memory" of betrayal in Vietnam ("the first war in our history during which our media were more friendly to our enemies than to our allies," as President Nixon put it) and was aimed neither at the Grenadan regime nor at the Cubans on the island, but at the media and potential antiwar forces at home. The "urgent" referred to a desire to carry out a war that, unlike Vietnam, would happen so swiftly the media could not cover it nor the public mobilize against it. The Pentagon press pool was left behind during the invasion and then banned from the island for their own "safety" while the fighting progressed. Instead, the administration offered its own "news" videos to the TV networks; mostly rescued-hostage shots of, as the *Washington Post*'s Tom Shales put it, "American students smiling, blowing kisses and flashing the 'V' sign as they were escorted off the island under military protection." The war ended with the president declaring victory over Vietnam's imagined legacy. "Our days of weakness are over. Our military forces are back on their feet and standing tall."[17]

Operation Just Cause, the invasion of Panama, was similarly referential, a Ramboesque whine in response to the charge that Vietnam had been an unjust war. In campaign names, Rambo's muscles, giant flags, and too-large "victory" parades lay the obsession with Vietnam transposed. The reversals of the Vietnam years were being displaced by a cartoonlike re-creation of victory culture. Yet politicians could not but open their mouths to exult that Americans had "kicked the Vietnam habit" before Vietnam stumbled out. The more the world was reorganized into "not-Vietnam" events and the war said to be "behind us," the more like some uneasy spirit it refused to depart.

THE SECOND COMING OF G.I. JOE

The reversals of history first introduced in *Star Wars* were picked up by a fast-developing toy business in the 1980s. Every "action figure" set would now be a *Star Wars* knock-off, and each toy company faced Lucas's problem. In post-Vietnam war-space, how would a child left alone in a room with generic figures know what to play? *Star Wars* had offered a movie universe for its toys to share, but a toy on its own needed another kind of help.

About the time Ronald Reagan came into office, Hasbro began to consider resuscitating G.I. Joe, for the world of war play was still distinctly underpopulated on earth, if not in space. As the toy company's executives were aware, Joe retained remarkable name recognition, not only among young boys (who had inherited hand-me-downs from older siblings) but among their parents. The question was, what would Joe be? At first, Hasbro had only considered marketing "a force of good guys," but according to H. Kirk Bozigian, Hasbro's vice-president of boys toys, "the [toy] trade said, who do they fight?" Hasbro's research with children confirmed that this was a crucial question.

In fact, blasting an action figure team into a world in which, as Bozigian put it, "there was a fine line between the good guys and the bad guys," called for considerable grown-up thought. Although Joe was to gain the tag line, "a real American hero," the G.I. Joe R&D and marketing group ("all closet quasi-military historians") early on reached "a conscious decision that the Soviets would never be the enemy, because we felt there would never be a conflict between us." Instead they chose a vaguer enemy—"terrorism"—and created COBRA, an organization of super-bad guys who lived not in Moscow but in Springfield, U.S.A. (Hasbro researchers had discovered that a Springfield existed in every state—except Rhode Island, where the company was located.)[18]†

But teams of good and bad guys weren't enough. Children needed context. A "history" had to be written for these preplanned figures, what the toy industry would come to call a "backstory." Then a way had to be found for each figure to bring his own backstory, his play instructions, into the home. First, "Joe" was shrunk to $3^3/_4$-inch size, so that his warrior team could fit into the *Star Wars* universe. Next, he was reconceived as a set of earthbound fantasy figures (rather than "real" soldiers) and armed with *Star Wars*–style weaponry. A Marvel comic book series lent the toys an ongoing story form, while Hasbro pioneered using the space on the back of each figure's package for a collector card/profile of the enclosed toy. Larry Hama, creator of the comics and of the earliest profiles, calls them "intelligence dossiers." Each Joe or COBRA was now to come with his own spacy code name (from Air Tight to Zartan) and his own "biography." Each "individualized" team member would carry his story into the home on his back.

Take "enemy leader, COBRA Commander." Poisonous snakes are bad news, but his no-goodness was almost laughably overdetermined. Faceless in the style of Darth Vader, his head was covered by a hood with eye slits, reminiscent of the KKK, his body encased in a torturer's blue jumpsuit, leather gloves, and boots. Here is his "dossier":

> Primary Military Specialty: Intelligence.
> Secondary Military Specialty: Ordinance (experimental weaponry).
> Birthplace: Classified.
> Absolute power! Total control of the world . . . its people, wealth, and resources—that's the objective of COBRA Commander. This fanatical leader rules with an iron fist. He demands total loyalty and allegiance. His main battle plan, for world control, relies on revolution and chaos. He personally led uprisings in the Middle East, Southeast Asia and other trouble spots. Responsible for kidnapping scien-

---

†The Russians did not totally disappear. In Marvel's *G.I. Joe* comic books they would still be an enemy, but a secondary one. By issue seven (January 1983), the Joes and the Reds had already sealed their first temporary alliance. "A moment ago they were enemies . . . now they fight together against the greatest evil in the world!" COBRA, of course.

tists, businessmen, and military leaders then forcing them to reveal
their top level secrets. COBRA commander is hatred and evil personi-
fied. Corrupt. A man without scruples. Probably the most dangerous
man alive!

Other than the telltale reference to Southeast Asia, he was an enemy
uncoupled from the war story. Only the profile that came with him separated him from Snake-Eyes, a good guy with Ninja training who also
came encased in a blue jumpsuit with slits for eyeholes.[19]

Launched in 1982, the new G.I. Joe was to prove the most successful
boy's toy of the period. By the mid-1980s, Joe had an every afternoon animated TV show that put special effects battles with COBRA constantly
within the child's field of vision. After Joe, war play on "Earth" would be
in the reconstructionist mode. Carefully identified teams of good and bad
figures, backed by collector's cards, TV cartoons, movies, video games,
books, and comics, as well as a host of licensed products stamped with
their images, would offer an overelaborate frame of instruction in new-
style war play. All a child had to do was read the toy box, turn on the TV,
go to the video store, put on the audio tape that accompanied the "book,"
or pick up the character's "magazine" to be surrounded by a backstory of
war play. Yet the void where the national war story had been remained.

By 1993, Hasbro had produced over 300 G.I. Joe figures with "close to
260 different personalities" and sold hundreds of millions of them. No
longer a masked man and his lone sidekick, but color, price, and weapons
coordinated masked teams, these "characters" on screen and on the
child's floor were by-products of an extraordinary explosion of entrepre-
neurial life force, for the business impulse behind war play was childhood's real story in the 1980s. The intrusive, unsettling world of commercial possibility that had first looked through the screen at the child
three decades earlier represented the real victory culture of the postwar
child's world.[20]

The new war story it produced had only a mocking relationship to a
national story, for all "war" now inhabited the same unearthly, ahistori-
cal commercial space. Even Rambo, transformed into an action-figure
team for children, found himself locked in televised cartoon combat with
General Terror and his S.A.V.A.G.E. terrorist group. While various Ninjas
and Native Americans brought their spiritual skills to the good side,
everywhere the "enemy" remained a vague and fragile construct, a
metallic voice stripped of ethnic or racial character; and everywhere the
boundary lines between us and the enemy, the good team and the bad
team, threatened to collapse into a desperate sameness.

In its characters, names, and plots, the new war story relied on constant self-mockery. The enemy, once the most serious of subjects, was now a running joke. The evil COBRA organization, as described by Hasbro's Bozigian, was made up of "accountants, tax attorneys, and all other kinds of low lifes that are out to conquer the world." The mocking voice of deconstruction was alive and selling product in children's culture—as with that mega-hit of the late 1980s, the Teenage Mutant Ninja Turtles.[21]

In the new war play universe, you did need a scorecard to tell the players apart. In the comic book world, for example, the story had become so self-enclosed that it was nearly impossible to pick up an *X-Men* comic and have any sense of where you were if you hadn't read the previous twenty issues. Here is part of the dossier of a 1991 Marvel comics supervillain from one of 160-odd similar bubble gum cards. His code name is Apocalypse.

> Battles Fought: 6344
> Wins: 3993 Losses: 2135 Ties: 216
> Win Percentage: 63%
> Arch-enemies: X-Factor
> First Appearance: *X-Factor* #5, June 1986
> Apocalypse believes that only the strong survive, and that the weak must be destroyed. In his quest to weed out those he deems unfit to live, he manipulates various factions of mutants to battle each other to the death. . .
> Did You Know: Apocalypse's former headquarters, a massive sentient starship, now serves as the headquarters for his arch-enemies, the super hero group known as X-Factor.

Though a sort of story was recaptured and with the help of television made to surround the child constantly, behind the special effects was an eerie inaction—of which, at an adult level, the war in the Persian Gulf would be symbolic.

OPERATION NOT-JUNGLE NOT-QUAGMIRE: RECONSTITUTING WAR

On August 1, 1990, Iraqi leader Saddam Hussein, a former ally, ordered the invasion of the small oil emirate of Kuwait and became America's global enemy number one. His decision offered American officials an opportunity to eradicate the Vietnam experience by untying the giant's hand outside the western hemisphere, largely because, at the end of the 1980s, the evil empire had bogged down in its own land and begun to disaggregate. Such an unexpected ending to the Cold War was like an invitation to an open script conference.

For George Bush's administration, Iraq offered endless possibilities for appealing scenarios. An evil north, a police state run by a cruel dictator, had invaded a good south across an international border, the very scenario less than successfully promoted in Vietnam. Like North Vietnam (and unlike Grenada or Panama), Iraq seemed a formidable enemy: the world's "fourth largest army," battle-hardened in an eight-year war with neighboring Iran, equipped with high-tech Soviet weaponry, outlawed chemical weapons, and soon, possibly, nuclear or biological arms. But what Iraq most offered the reconstructionists was *emptiness*. To the extent that Iraq was imagined at all, it was as a desert, a sandy blank on the map on which, as with some Hollywood back lot, any facade might be erected. The single image chosen was Saddam Hussein's face, large as a flag, mountainous as Rambo's musculature; a dreamscape of evil.

For a decade, the demonized face of a single leader, from the cunning Qaddafi's of Libya to the pock-marked Noriega's of Panama, had stood in for the enemy of the moment. Yet the jerry-built nature of the "enemy" in the Persian Gulf War would be particularly striking. Abuse of the enemy from "kick his ass, take his gas" t-shirts to President Bush's drawled "Sadaaaam"s would largely be restricted to the person of the dictator. (Hussein's pervasive personality cult—his face seemed to be plastered on every wall space, every watch face in Iraq—would only make this easier.) In the media, even acts of pillaging and raping by Iraqi troops occupying Kuwait would be more or less attributed to him.

The faceless horror of a savage racial enemy would now be reduced to a single, individualized face complete with "intelligence dossier." Saddam, like the COBRA commander, would enter the home via the TV screen with instructions in place, while the Iraqis would become a nation of no-traits in the blankness of their country. Visceral hatred toward Iraqis would be lacking. With the exception of a few references by American pilots to Iraqi soldiers scattering like "cockroaches," even the relatively rare dehumanizing images—sheep in a fold, a "turkey shoot"— would be mild by any historical standard. Not generally in evidence would be bugs, vermin, indistinguishable hordes, or terms like "gook" with which American English has proved so richly inventive. No phrase more summed up the general lack of race hatred toward the Iraqi populace than the oft-repeated American desire to "get the job done" in the Gulf.

As a Vietnam stand-in, nothing in Iraq's situation was comparable to Vietnam's. The United States was to take revenge for a jungle war on a land without cover, for a war of popular mobilization on a war-exhausted country of demoralized conscripts; for fears of becoming embroiled in a conflict with China and the Soviet Union on a country without significant allies; for an inability to throttle the Vietnamese in their "sanctuaries" on a country without a safe haven.

Yet through this new close encounter of the third (world) kind, that old "nightmare" was to be reversed, point by point. In this war, there would be no "body counts." The only statistics of death would be "weapons counts" (how many Scud missiles, tanks, or gunboats had been put out of action); the only destruction would be of the inanimate (hence, the repeated video footage of bridges and buildings blowing up); and there would be no "body bags," for there would be no bodies. Instead of Saigon's "five o'clock follies," there would be preplanned global news conferences; instead of the peace sign, the yellow ribbon; instead of posttraumatic stress disorder, pre-traumatic stress counseling; instead of "spit upon" vets, gargantuan "welcome home" parades; instead of a humiliating final helicopter flight from the embassy roof in Saigon, a liberatory helicopter landing on the embassy roof in Kuwait City; and around it all would be those familiar glimpses of the framework of control, those constant reminders of who was firmly in charge.[22]

This would once again be a screenable war, calibrated for anxious thrills like an Indiana Jones film or a theme park ride. But to return its audience to the childlike days of triumph of another era, the government would have to invest the resources once reserved for war in the managed creation of a war story.

CHILDHOOD ENGULFED

From the beginning, the Bush administration dealt with its Persian Gulf troops as if they were potential MIAs. Their situation was framed in a language previously reserved for hostagedom: an army of "kids" (as the president called them) awaited rescue and a quick return to American shores. This was reflected in the war's omnipresent patriotic symbol, the yellow ribbon, which, throughout the 1980s, had been a symbol of American captives in Lebanon and elsewhere in the Mideast. Applied to the Gulf crisis, the yellow ribbon emphasized the role of U.S. troops as victims.†

Meanwhile, as the war unfolded, young children at home experienced feelings that, as portrayed in the media, bore a resemblance to the "Vietnam syndrome" their parents were supposedly casting off. On a Saturday morning news special for children, ABC anchorman Peter Jennings fretted ("All over America this morning American children are worried about war"); newspapers and magazines ran anxious articles ("Imaginations Run Wild About War," "When Little Children Have Big Worries"); respected or beloved figures from Jonas Salk to Mr. Rogers soothed ("There isn't anything that casual observers can do to help make a difference in the Persian Gulf, but there's a lot we can do right in our own homes"); popular counselors like Dr. Joyce Brothers offered advice ("Dear J.T.: Talk with your children about whatever they fear, and remember that in violent times, as when a nation is at war, it's important to reassure children by addressing unasked questions"); instant books offered children help ("Sometimes it's worse just imagining about things" than being in "a real war"); and on radio, in classrooms, children's museums, and day care centers, concern about children's anxieties and fears became a significant war theme.[23]

This wartime outpouring of solicitousness for children not in a war zone was unprecedented. Certainly, Americans had never previously imagined their children as possible "casualties" of or in any way hostage to the enemy. Now, children who had for years wielded laser swords and shaken sound bracelets that recreated the whoosh of missiles being launched or grenades landing were suddenly imagined as being in need of psychic rescue. Yet the most threatening wartime act most of them would experience was the commandeering of the TV set by their parents when they might have been watching the Ninja Turtles fight off the evil Shredder.

In the days after the bombing of Iraq began, a plethora of experts were

---

†Because the troops were already imagined as hostages, there was confusion about how to handle the small number of military personnel captured by the Iraqis during hostilities (a few of whom were shown, looking battered, on Iraqi TV). Were they heroes simply for being there or cowards for saying a few words? Either way, once released, the POWs seemed like awkward presences. In the end, they rode in a few parades and then were largely ignored. Their memoirs were not requested. Miniseries were not produced. It was as if, on returning, they went MIA in America.

mobilized to advise parents and caregivers in a new style of adult activism; and they offered help in close to a single voice. "How to Talk to Your Child About the War" from Work/Family Directions, a Boston-based group that helped organize corporate child care, was typical. With its toll-free number "for more information or to talk to a knowledgeable child care specialist," it struck the basic note immediately: "This pamphlet has been developed to help adults understand how children may view the war. It also provides useful recommendations to ease the stress and fears your child or a child you care for may be experiencing because of the war." It took for granted that something must be done and that adult activism inside home or school was to be highly recommended. For the child with "excessive concerns" about the war, "professional help" might even be in order.

"What children don't have is the ability to understand the war like an adult. Instead, they see the war through their own world, sometimes causing them to be afraid of things that could, in fact, never happen." Young children cannot grasp "the complexity of war" because they have not yet fully developed the capacity to reason. "Their images may be oversimplified stereotypes, like 'good guys always win.'" In such descriptions, the undeveloped nature of the child was used to elevate the understanding of the adult helper being mobilized. This was the same adult perched in front of the TV set watching an on-screen war production that had taken more than a little from child culture.

Children were incapable of understanding on their own "how far away the war [was]. . . . Even ninth-graders have fears that a bomb could drop in their own backyard." In their minds, they were as much "in" the Gulf as the troops and so became a second set of potential MIAs in a reconstituted American war drama. Naturally, the parents' first task was to rescue the child and bring him or her "home," reestablishing familiar "family routines." For the war's duration, that home was to be a caring support center, staffed by sensitive parent-therapists observing the symptoms of disturbance. ("Their feelings may show up in other ways, such as being cranky or having nightmares, or may be subtly . . . expressed in their play.") The parent-therapist had to be ready to spot war disturbance even in children who seemed to "show no interest in the war."

Everywhere adults were urged to "help" children achieve war closure by taking on an "active role." "While children need to know it is not their job to end the war, they may feel better knowing they can at least play an active part in the war effort." They could explain their feelings in letters to the president and their congressional representatives, or "if your family knows someone in the Gulf or wants to 'adopt' a soldier your child can send drawings, stories, photographs, and audio tapes." Another typical handout from Philadelphia's Please Touch Museum, "Suggestions for Helping Young Children Respond to WAR," pointed out that "[c]hildren's imaginations, especially when fed by outside sources of words and images, can often create far worse scenarios than reality," and suggested that "children, like adults, feel better about overwhelming events when they feel that they can do something to help. You can find out the names of servicemen and women from your community and write them letters or send them care packages."

"Adoption" was not, however, presented as an act of home front support for the war effort like radio character Jack Armstrong's World War II "Write-a-Fighter Corps," in which "more than a million children . . . pledg[ed] to write once a month to a service person as well as collect scrap and tend their victory gardens." Instead, it was to be part of a therapeutic healing process. In this common suggestion of that moment (and its Pentagon-inspired converse, that soldiers "adopt" classes of children back home), the two groups of American "kids" were linked together as mutual war victims.[24]

Replacing the [American] parent and the [American] child in such documents with the [Iraqi] parent and the [Iraqi] child, however, revealed their strange, narcissistic nature. For behind this outpouring of worry about and advice on caring for the war-endangered American child lay the obsession with Vietnam, the impulse to obliterate from memory a time when images of Vietnamese children in distress due to American acts seemed to dominate American consciousness. Now, in the exaggerated fashion of the day, on every screen, in every medium, the images would be of our children returned to our care. As in *Star Wars*, so in the real world, we would once again have all the roles. The heroes, the victims, even the activists would be overbooked for, not against, the United States, and the basic scenario of the endangerment of the child would be back in American hands.

PRODUCING WAR

In the new version of victory culture, the military spent no less time planning to control the screen than the battlefield, and the neutralization of a potentially oppositional media became a war goal. In a daily round of televised press conferences and briefings, military and civilian spokesmen purposely addressed television viewers over the shoulders of reporters unceremoniously scrambling to ask questions. These televised events made explicit and visual the sidelining of the reporter in bringing war news to the public. According to a *Washington Post* reporter, the journalists unlike their military briefers looked like "fools, nit-pickers and egomaniacs . . . a whining, self-righteous, upper-middle class mob jostling for whatever tiny flakes of fame [might] settle on their shoulders." The briefings, commented spokesman Lieutenant General Thomas Kelly, were "the most significant part of the whole operation [because] for the first time ever . . . the American people were getting their information from the government—not from the press."[25]

The military assessment of the Gulf War as a media event was summed up by Barry Zorthian, chief Pentagon public affairs spokesman in the Vietnam era. "The press lost," he told the National Press Club as the war was ending. With this assessment, most journalists, editors, and media executives as well as critics of the war and the media were in agreement. Government planning to control the media, many years in the making, had been impressive. On the ground in Saudi Arabia, layers of military control had been inserted between the journalist and the "action," as well as between journalist and newspaper or newscast. As *New York Times* reporter Malcolm W. Browne put it, the "pool" system, developed by the military, essentially turned the journalist into "an unpaid employee of the Department of Defense, on whose behalf he or she prepare[d] the news of the war for the outer world."[26]

Reporters generally blamed journalistic defeat on censorship and began dreaming of techno-fixes that would make matters better in the future. News organizations, commented Philip Shennon of the *New York Times*,

> are surreptitiously planning the technology that will make all sorts of things possible. . . . We're told that in the next two years, we'll be able to have a satellite phone that will fit into a very small suitcase. If you can get into a car and head out to where the battlefield is, you'll be able to file your story almost instantaneously. . . . I think we'll have a better war next go around.[27]

Yet those who claimed that the media lost the Gulf War—that censorship, press pools, and military handlers galore represented an epic government triumph over reportorial independence—had not seen the screen for the pixels. If the military was intent on reconstituting a national war story, in part by sidelining the media, there was another powerful force at work with another kind of story in mind, and it, too, was the media. What Americans saw with the televised bombing of Baghdad on January 16, 1991, was the birth of a new coproduction process that might be called "total television." The war in the Gulf was the ur-production of the new media conglomerate, for which the war proved promising exactly because the boundaries between military action and media event broke down in such a way that military planning could become media reality.

Total television had its antecedents neither in traditional war reportage nor in national war mythology. It was not even the child of the Vietnam War, which in its inability to adhere to precise scheduling or achieve the closure television craves, was hardly America's first television war. Instead, total TV was born in certain mesmeric moments when the whole nation seemed to be mobilized at couchside to stare at the same images across many channels. Starting with the Iran hostage crisis in 1979, these generally had the theme of America or Americans held hostage—most humiliatingly in Iran; most tragically in various terrorist plane-nappings and murders; most pathetically in NASA's *Challenger* space shuttle disaster, in which a schoolteacher's life was hostaged to the failure of U.S. technology; most absurdly in the drama of a little girl hostaged to the elements by a fall down a Texas well shaft; most triumphantly in images of American students kissing American soil after their "rescue" from the island of Grenada.

From the media's point of view, most of these events were, fortunately, quite limited: one kidnapped plane on an airport runway; one embassy surrounded by a crowd; a few film clips of an explosion replayed a hundred times—all surrounded by talking heads—or one small war in a distant place with minimal government-supplied visuals. To create more expansive scenarios would have been ruinously expensive without outside help. Even Ted Turner's Cable News Network (CNN), set up for twenty-four-hour-a-day media events, would have felt the financial strain if left purely to its own devices. It was not enough to mobilize an audience; new forms of sponsorship were needed.

Here, the corporate context for Gulf War–style total television needs to be recalled. During the 1980s, media giants like Time-Warner and Rupert Murdoch's News Corporation were being stapled together, and under their roofs distinct media forms were blurring into vast TV/movie/newspaper/magazine/book/music/theme park entities. However, to put such entities together was to incur billions of dollars of debt. The burden of this debt—and a crumbling advertising market by decade's end—gave rise to pressures to "downsize" these unwieldy new entities. Fewer personnel and cheaper production methods were needed to make them financially palatable to nervous owners (or anxious potential buyers). General Electric, Capital Cities, and the Tisch Family operation, which had come to control, respectively, NBC, ABC, and CBS, also faced an assault on their audiences and their advertisers from cable television and Murdoch's new Fox network. In turn, the swift erosion of network dominance in the late 1980s led money managers to hack away at prestigious but often unprofitable news departments.

If the Persian Gulf War revealed the media's ability to mount technical operations on an unprecedented scale, it also exposed the need of these financially pressed media giants (and their upstart competitors) for sponsorship on a scale hitherto unimaginable. This was what the Bush administration seemed to offer—an outside production company able to organize a well-produced, subsidized event that could be channeled to the American (and increasingly, the global) public at, relatively speaking, bargain basement prices.

With its million or more uniformed extras, its vast sets, and its six-month preproduction schedule filled with logistical miracles (and a few fiascos), the production, the Gulf War, involved intense military–media cooperation on a global scale. All through the winter of 1990, the production had its built-in "coming attractions"—the many variations on "showdown in the Gulf," which teased the viewer with a possible January opening on screens in domestic multiplexes nationwide. It had its dazzling *Star Wars*–style graphics, its own theme music and logos, and its stunningly prime-timed first moments (Disneyesque fireworks over Baghdad). As a show, it was calibrated for controlled thrills, anxiety, and relief from its opening laser-guided, *son et lumière* spectacular to its final triumphant helicopter descent on the U.S. embassy in Kuwait.

To succeed as a coproduction, however, the Pentagon had to offer the networks five things, the first of them being funding based on a relatively limited financial contribution from the networks themselves. This was accomplished by a State Department–Pentagon financing team that sought out foreign investment much as any Hollywood production team might have—from the Japanese, the Germans, the Saudis, and so on; $50 billion for "foreign rights," money that ensured a break-even point on the government side of the enterprise almost before the first missile left the ground. The second was the ability to organize round-the-clock, on-location support systems across a vast theater of operations; third, a pre-edited flow of visuals available to all channels; fourth, control over access to the production's set, thus limiting inter-network competition and consequently network costs (these last two usually fall under the rubric of "censorship"); and finally, the sort of precise scheduling and closure that television needs.

At the Pentagon, much thought had gone into matters of scheduling and closure, partially from a post-Vietnam desire to create a Third World battlefield where maximal weaponry and minimal U.S. casualties would make public support axiomatic. In the 1980s, a new wave of "smart" (and not-so-smart but highly destructive) weaponry was brought on line or upgraded to complement an impressive Vietnam War–era arsenal. As a result, in the Persian Gulf, the superiority of U.S. weaponry made slaughter on a vast scale and with an eye to television's tight time requirements possible.

What President Bush could, then, promise the nation—and the media corporation—was a war that could be scheduled, and this promise was structured not only into war planning but into the minds of the war makers. As Bob Woodward reported in *The Commanders*, "In the White House, Bush, Quayle, Scowcroft and Sununu gathered in the small private study adjacent to the Oval Office to watch television. When the sounds of bombing could be heard behind the voices of the reporters still in their Baghdad hotel rooms, Bush, visibly relieved, said, 'Just the way it was scheduled.'"[28]

The largest threat to the Gulf production was this pressure for closure, built into the logo-ized form, "The War in the Gulf, Day X" (itself a creation of the Iran hostage crisis). Offered up twenty-four hours a day, a "war" only days old might quickly seem weeks or months old, as viewers abandoned the routines of daily life (and the daily TV schedule) for vast doses of a single on-screen production. As a result, the Gulf production held the possibility (much feared at the time) of recreating "Vietnam" without the endless years of fighting. It was this anxiety about closure, or lack of it, that gave the production much of its tension and drawing power.

From all involved—network executives, advertisers, programmers, government officials, reporters, soldiers, and viewers—came a longing for the reassurance of a quick return to normalcy, which was forthcoming from the war's first moments. A striking feature of the war was how often the viewers were told that it was unfolding "on schedule." Nearly every military news conference included such a reminder, and the schedule being referred to was clearly television's.

In the past, the reporting of war had often been successfully controlled by governments, while generals had polished their images with the press or—like Omar Bradley and Douglas MacArthur—had employed public relations staffs to do it for them. But never had generals and war planners gone before the public as actors, supported by all the means a "studio" could muster on their behalf and determined to produce a "program" that would fill the day across the dial for the full time of a war. Behind the multiple daily press conferences of the various actors—each in his distinctive fashion-camouflage outfit, each wielding his sitcom quips and put-downs, each giving his impression of the Victorious General or the In

Control Press Spokesman—lay a globe-spanning network of scriptwriters, makeup artists, fashion consultants, graphic designers, production managers, film editors (otherwise known as "censors" or "escorts"), even a military version of a network Standards and Practices department with its guidelines for on-air acceptability. Military handlers made decisions—like refusing to clear for publication the fact that Stealth pilots viewed X-rated movies before missions—reminiscent of network show-vetting practices.[29]

Unsurprisingly, the approximately 1,600 reporters, mostly camped out in high-tech hotel lounges and makeshift press centers in Dhahran and Riyadh, Saudi Arabia, watching the war on TV just like viewers at home, saw the military's media role mainly as a censorious one. But only military pre-editing of virtually all aspects of the war made total television a six-week-long ratings hit. Hence, despite the uneasiness of some journalists on the scene, the TV networks understandably offered no significant protest over the censoring and controlling mechanisms of the Bush administration, which were largely in their interest. In fact, no well-known media company joined publications like the *Nation* or New York's *Village Voice* and individual journalists like *Newsday*'s Sydney Schanberg in a wartime legal challenge to Pentagon censorship policies.[30]

The Gulf production launched a major new form of the program-length commercial similar to those pioneered by toy companies in the previous decade that turned cartoon shows into animated toy catalogs. It was as if the whole post-Vietnam era had built toward this forty-three-day-long ad, intent on selling domestic and foreign markets on the renewal of American qualities as well as on the specific weapons systems that were renewing those qualities. In this sense, the Gulf War was a response to the Japanese and European economic challenges in that it emphasized the leading-edge aspects of the country's two foremost exports: arms and entertainment.

What made this program-length ad unique, though, was its length and the fact that its newness and defining style unexpectedly threw into question the nature of normal TV advertising. If *this* was the Ad, then what were those? Although CNN, ready-made for total TV, experienced rising ad rates and revenues during the war, for the networks it was another story. Non-CNN advertisers were unsure how their ads would coexist with "war" in this puzzling new version of entertainment time. Of course, what they, like so many media experts and military consultants, feared was a visually bloody war of body bags and body counts, the very war that the military had spent seventeen years organizing out of existence.

The failure of advertisers to grasp the nature of this new media experience and join the production team helped make it into a financial fiasco for the big three networks. They found themselves showing a vast commercial while losing revenue from advertisers who felt more comfortable inside sitcoms like *Cheers* than inside the cheering framework of a war to destroy Iraq. NBC, which like CBS ran behind ABC in the ratings, claimed losses of $55 million on its war coverage, including $20 million in withdrawn ad revenue.[31]

This confusion over sponsorship reflected total television's primitive state, as well as certain flaws in the military production team. With a generally adversarial attitude toward the media and a strong belief in its responsibility for defeat in Vietnam, the military consciously inhibited the flow of fresh images that would have fed television's voracious appetite. In a study done before the Vietnam War ended, former army general Douglas Kinnard sent a questionnaire to 173 army generals who had commanded there. Among the 67 percent who replied, most felt, as one senior general put it, that the media had conducted "a psychological warfare campaign against the United States policies in Vietnam that could not have been better done by the enemy." Eighty-nine percent declared themselves negative toward the press, 91 percent toward television. It was one of only two subjects on which they achieved near unanimity.[32]

Little surprise, then, that for former junior officers like H. Norman Schwarzkopf, who had served under such generals in Vietnam and were now in charge of planning the media event in the Gulf, this was a grudge match. In military eyes, the media more than the absent Iraqis had the look of enemy-ness. From lowly "handlers" to generals, many were driven by a powerful desire to "defeat" the media this time around. In their desire to shut the media down, they significantly retarded the Gulf production as a visual spectacular, even though there was little evidence that reporters freed from military restraints would have produced anything but more enthusiastic visuals and copy, suitable to the production's needs.[33]

In addition, an inability to control all participants in the war proved an obstacle to the successful closure the war planners had taken for granted. The ground war, for instance, was carefully rounded off at "100 hours." The figure was justified, in Vietnam War terms, by a lack of desire to "bog down" in a future Iraqi "quagmire." This cutoff point, as General Schwarzkopf has written, was chosen by administration officials who "really knew how to package an historic event." However, the official closure of the war-as-media-production did not close down Saddam Hussein, or Shia rebels in southern Iraq, or Kurdish rebels in the north.

Within weeks, piteous images of Kurdish refugees flooded the media, forcing the administration to half-reopen the war.[34]

Similarly, from the Iraqi side, unexpected video of wounded, dead, and grieving civilians at Baghdad's Public Shelter 25, where a U.S. missile incinerated over 300 people, intruded into a production planned for its vision of machine death, not human gore. In reactions to those images and to Peter Arnett's CNN reports from the Iraqi capital, it was briefly possible to feel the panic the uncontrolled image elicited in the military. Nonetheless, the attempt to choke off any visual messiness undercut the Gulf production's staying power as a war narrative.

The military production team had taken on the task of defining and delivering the range of shots that would constitute the war's on-screen reality, but what they provided, sometimes grudgingly, was largely grainy videos of missiles and bombs obliterating (nonhuman) targets, upbeat sequences about high-tech warriors doing their jobs, shots of planes taking off and landing or of magnificent penile machines firing projectiles into magnificent desert skies, and access to the Patriots-greet-incoming-Scuds fireworks extravaganza. Though a far cry from the Grenada and Panama news blackouts, this was still visually thin stuff. There was no way to combine such isolated sequences into even a passing narrative of war.

Limited visuals forced the networks to fall back on replays or talking heads. Undoubtedly, military experts like ABC's Anthony Cordesman or CBS's forcibly retired air force general Michael Dugan were meant to be Monday Night War's color commentators, but if so, they seemed eternally trapped at half-time with no game to call. Although each day's show was packaged with ever more dazzling logo material and theme music, and viewers were invited to breach computer-recreated versions of the (largely imaginary) "Saddam Wall," in the end, there was no war out there to be seen. Except for oft-repeated footage from the "battle" of Khafji, hardly a bit of evidence could be mustered for the war-ness of this war story.†

No greater problem faced the military–media production team than its

---

† The closest the production came to presenting scenes of slaughter as on-screen entertainment was at the deserted Saudi Arabian border town of Khafji. In this sole Iraqi ground attack of the war, there was an eerie parallel to *Dances with Wolves*. Qatari and Saudi troops, America's "Sioux," armed with the latest U.S. weaponry, were pushed forward with heavy U.S. air support to retake Khafji. TV cameras advanced with them and recorded shots of dead and wounded Iraqis. As in *Dances*, it was only when the Other took up our weaponry that such scenes could be put on screen without the taint of atrocity.

inability to establish a suitably epic flow of visuals, no less an epic story at the heart of its production. From the initial "battle in the Gulf," the 1981 dogfights with Libyan MIGs over the Gulf of Sidra, through the invasions of Grenada and Panama, the Reagan and Bush administrations had engaged in a decade-long experiment in the controlled presentation of battle triumph. In the Persian Gulf, however, any sense of what form a lasting, empathetic war narrative could take without a military struggle in which to ground itself was missing in action.

Off screen, events were closer to a mass execution than a war. No Iraqi aggressors fell from their charging camels in the sort of on-screen battle for which film tradition called. No armies could be discovered clashing in their multi-thousands, nor could tank battles—billed, before the war, as potentially the largest since World War II—be shown ranging across vast desert vistas. The crucial production number, D-day (renamed "G [for ground war]-day") turned out to be no day at all. The penultimate event of the post-Vietnam era in which the not-Vietnamese were to be crushed in battle had to be elided because at the heart of this technically awesome spectacle was an embarrassingly unwatchable slaughter. The best that could be offered were shots of bedraggled Iraqis emerging from their dugouts to surrender or of Iraqi-commandeered cars, trucks, and buses turned to charred rubble by U.S. planes on the road out of Kuwait City.

Only when some journalists—"unilaterals" who had evaded military controls and others loosed by the military—dashed into Kuwait City was there a hint of an on-screen story. If the liberation-of-Paris-style crowds were sparse in population-decimated Kuwait, at least the visuals flowed and Charles Jaco, Dan Rather, and the others could simulate war reporters of the past down to the last safari jacket.

If the Persian Gulf War's lack of a story accounts, in part, for its remarkable disappearance from U.S. politics and culture, it was not for want of the footage of death. This was a screen war at the "front" as well as in the White House, the Pentagon, and at home. Cameras shooting through the night-vision gun sights of Apache AH-64 attack helicopters, for instance, caught graphic scenes of confused and helpless Iraqi soldiers being "blown to bits" by unseen attackers. "The Iraqi soldiers looked like ghostly sheep flushed from a pen—bewildered and terrified, jarred from sleep and fleeing their bunkers under a hellish fire," wrote the *Los Angeles Times*' John Balzar, who viewed the film with officers of the 18th Airborne Corps at a briefing tent on the Saudi border. "Even hardened [U.S.] soldiers hold their breath as Iraqi soldiers, as big as football players on the television screen, run with nowhere to hide. These are not bridges or airplane hangars. These are men." But such outtakes were never released by the military, for they would have been appropriate only for a horror story, not a war story.[35]

The war to reestablish war, American-style, vaporized as a triumphant event while the yellow ribbons were still fluttering. Although intervention abroad remained an ever present option, the process that had begun in 1945 now stood complete. As a three-hundred-year-old construct, the enemy had evaporated. A typical end-of-war photo in *Newsday*, labeled "Heroes at Work," showed an armed American soldier standing guard over the desert. Below him, the sands dropped away, perhaps into a bunker where some Iraqi conscript lay buried. It was impossible to know, for though the GI was "doing his job," no enemy was in sight to certify his "heroism."[36]

With cameras switched on in nose cones, a high-tech machinery of war had been launched into the emptiness of the sky, heading toward a land without people, in search of a cartoon version of evil. In the meantime, in the missing space that was not "desert," but village, or bunker, or mosque, or street, a slaughter had occurred without anger, race hatred, or a desire for revenge. There were no last stands to repay, no Pearl Harbors to remember. All the confetti in the world snowing down on "victory" parades could not obscure what was gone.

The war had barely ended in visually bloodless, *Stars Wars*–style, machine-versus-machine destruction, when a familiar nightmare rose to the president's lips. Having exulted, "By God, we've kicked the Vietnam Syndrome once and for all" just after the cease-fire in March, by May George Bush found himself talking with his advisers about a possible "quagmire" in northern Iraq. "Last week important policy makers began to apply what they called 'the Q word' . . . to the problem developing in the area along Iraq's border with Turkey." But neither truncated words, nor a truncated "war" could purge Vietnam from the mind.[37]

The pseudo-pageants essential to the narcissistic—and fragile—war story of the era of reconstruction lacked staying power. Like so many childhood fads, they had brief half-lives. Little wonder that no major toy company took a chance on creating a Desert Storm set of action figures, or a major movie company a Desert Storm film. In fact, the packs of Desert Storm bubble gum cards, the Schwarzkopf dolls, and the t-shirts showing Saddam Hussein's forehead pierced by a Patriot missile were quickly packed away, and two years later, when the departing president again launched air strikes against Iraq, there was no story to bring back. Like a bad sequel, Gulf War II flickered quickly on and off screen in January 1993; its most dramatic videos, of missiles that missed their targets. In Iraq, more people died, but in the United States, all that remained of the twenty-four-hour-a-day, blood-pumping, all-channel, media–military spectacular was the promise of a new form of television and the possible new global stories of commerce it represented.

Total television points toward a world in which more fully meshed media systems will need to discover new, more powerful sponsoring relationships that can raise to a higher power the single-sponsor show (*The Alcoa Hour, General Electric Theater*) of a simpler corporate age. Whether the nation, even the superpower, at war will sponsor some of the next century's global "shows" is, however, open to question. If in the Persian Gulf War, the global media conglomerate was still willing to produce an American war story for a global audience, the "national" interests of future, even more global media entities are unknown, and what form their shows will take—whether at screen center will be slaughter or some friendlier sport—we can hardly guess.†

THE *N*TH COMING OF G.I. JOE

The commercial world has clearly indicated that it can thrive and prosper without a successful national narrative. It has other tales to tell. Like the movie and music industries, the toy industry, though still corporately located in American space, is increasingly intent on creating product that will sell beyond all boundaries. "American" battle tales of the future, like the "American" media companies promoting them, are likely to freely appropriate elements from other cultures in a new transnational selling space, just as in the 1980s they began to borrow themes, graphic design, and animation styles from Japan.

Of course, commercial culture is not likely to reject any narrative that mobilizes people to watch and buy, whether national or not. However, the question of whether a revivified war story could reanchor victory cul-

---

†In the United States, sports may already have come closer than war to meeting the story needs of total TV. In the 1980s, leagues, seasons, games, and TV outlets for sports of every sort expanded so dramatically that a single overlapping web of sports viewing possibilities came into existence. As an ongoing generic narrative, sports may be the perfect analog for storylessness. On the one hand, there is always a story—the race for the pennant, the cup, the championship. On the other hand, it is in the nature of sports that the story be constantly forgotten and seasonally reconstituted. Certainly, sports proved more effective in mobilizing audiences at couchside long term than did the one-sided wars from Grenada to the Gulf.

ture in American consciousness (no less sell significant product) seems settled, not because its elements, which run deep in our history, have ceased to exist, but because it has proved impossible to force out of consciousness the quarter-century of that story's dissolution. Its boundaried and triumphant "innocence" cannot be "recalled" in the same way that the knowledge of the making of atomic weapons cannot be forgotten.[38]

Do Americans, then, have the capacity, the resources, or the need to create a new national narrative of any sort, and, if so, how would such a narrative be linked to a war story? Certainly, the rise of (as well as opposition to) "multiculturalism" in its race-, gender-, and sex-based storytelling forms reflects such a need. The attempt to uncover, express, and in some sense celebrate experiences and points of view previously ignored within the boundaries of the story seemed initially to promise a future revised and far more "diverse" yet inclusive national tale.

However, the new plural (rather than pluralistic) tales have not proven assimilable into a single alternative national one; for each—the story of African-Americans, women, gays, the poor, the Chinese-, Japanese-, Korean-, Hispanic-, or Native American—had something of the self-enclosed, self-referential feel of all the other productions of the era of reconstruction. The various separate, if not separatist, stories that have been gathered together under the vague and unevocative umbrella of multiculturalism seem to bear the same relationship to the American story as the anti-westerns of the 1970s did to the film story, or the anti-war movement to American politics. Implicitly or explicitly, they remain part of the breaking down of one story, not the building up of another. Without the larger story—or at least a memory of it to play off of—they may have no national existence.

Whether a national story will even be sustainable for a superpower in a world of transnational media entities intent on their own styles of global storytelling is questionable. The peculiar limits of any such national rebuilding efforts seem clear when the world where childhood and commerce mix is explored, for in the business of childhood can be felt an energy that drives all narrative possibilities before it, herding them (and their consumers) toward a stripped down, storyless global environment. Like the souped up dinosaurs of *Jurassic Park*, that business feeds well on the reduced narrative carcasses of more than one culture, creating special effects screen rides (not unlike, but better than those of the Persian Gulf War) that in allied theme parks owned by the same companies can be turned into . . . actual special effects rides. In child culture, storylessness has been a success. There, the collapse of the war story resulted, from a business point of view, in the story of the century.

. . .

In February 1992, I found myself with H. Kirk Bozigian, Hasbro's vice-president of boys toys, in the labyrinthine Hasbro toy display at the American International Toy Fair in New York City, where toy lines for the coming season were being shown to "the trade." We passed through pastel rooms where blond women in white dresses demonstrated baby dolls and fluffy white kittens in sweet whispers and then, in the gender-segregated world of toys, stepped into the dark, cavernous world of the boy. There, we came upon the war toy that seemed to have outlasted the war story itself. Hundreds of millions of action figures after his rebirth, G.I. Joe was still a top ten toy.

Joe, it was clear, had been running hard to survive in a confused world. In the previous two years, he had incorporated "Red Star" and "Big Bear," two members of the "Soviet October Guard," into his team of Good Guys, passed through an "eco-warrior" phase, and prevented COBRA's "most sinister attack to date, destruction of the Earth's . . . fragile ecological system." Bozigian was now preparing to send a new force onto television, into comics, and into the toy stores against yet another enemy. His Drug Elimination Force was even planning a brief alliance with evil itself—COBRA—so that both could turn their expert attentions to the deadly drug lord Headman and his Headhunters in a battle for "Main Street U.S.A."

Bozigian was describing Joe's new "toyetic features," mini-special effects, while behind us a demonstrator in an all-black Ninja outfit complete with plastic knives and swords showed off one of those features to dark-suited adult toy store buyers—"a special battle flash action weapon that fires a burst of light when the weapon is launched." In a nearby alcove, a demonstrator dressed as a Joe boomed out a pitch for "the awesome G.I. Joe Headquarters" with its "positionable spring activated missile launchers! . . . It's got a working searchlight! Five battle sounds, and a series of explosions triggered when you knock down the tower!" At the sound of an explosion, he shouted, "We've been blown! Send the medics!"

Among the hordes of Joe "recruits" ("Wet-Suit," "Heavy Duty," "Gung Ho") and COBRA "villains" ("Firefly," "Destro") carefully displayed in these rooms, my eye was caught by the "Ninja Force," six "masters of hand-to-hand combat," three good and three evil, all with "spring-action martial arts features." However, their names, dayglo colors, weaponry, and faceless design offered an uninstructed outsider no clues to separate the Joes from the COBRAs, the good guys from the enemy, "us" from the inhuman Other.

Joe, already a survivor of his own demise, has been both an actor in the collapse of the war story and a witness to the ways in which special effects succeeded for a time in masking the loss of a victor's culture. He remains a "real American hero" to a generation of children for whom the enemy, horrific yet ill defined, lives in our shadow, threatening always to become us. In a world without and beyond the war story, there are undoubtedly ever more chilling secret realms, hopeless yet thrilling, terrifying yet magnetic into which to plunge, for we all now live in the afterlife, and what the path out of the ruins may be neither Joe nor we understand.

NOTES

TRIUMPHALIST DESPAIR

1. Franklin D. Roosevelt, "War Message to Congress," in *Great Issues in American History: From Reconstruction to the Present Day, 1864–1981*, rev. ed., edited by Richard Hofstadter and Beatrice K. Hofstadter (New York: Vintage Books, 1982), pp. 401–3; "War," *Life* (December 15, 1941): 27; "America Goes to War," *Life* (December 22, 1941): 13.
2. John W. Dower, *War Without Mercy: Race and Power in the Pacific War* (New York: Pantheon Books, 1986), p. 152; John Morton Blum, *V Was for Victory: Politics and American Culture During World War II* (New York: Harvest/HBJ, 1976), pp. 95–105.
3. See Richard Slotkin, *The Fatal Environment: The Myth of the Frontier in the Age of Industrialization, 1800–1890* (Middletown, Conn.: Wesleyan University Press, 1986), for a brilliant exploration of how the frontier myth absorbed or offset these boundaryless internal phenomena. Slotkin's frontier myth trilogy, *Regeneration Through Violence: The Mythology of the American Frontier, 1600–1860* (Middletown, Conn.: Wesleyan University Press, 1973), *Fatal Environment*, and *Gunfighter Nation: The Myth of the Frontier in Twentieth-Century America* (New York: Atheneum, 1992), is an indispensable, pioneering guide to our culture's "Indian country."
4. "NSC 68, A Report to the National Security Council," *Naval War College Review*, May–June 1975, pp. 67, 80–81; "NSC 141, Reexamination of United States Programs for National Security," in *Documents of the National Security Council, 1947–1977*, edited by Paul Kesaris (Washington, D.C.: Microfilm Publications Project of the University Publications of America, 1980), p. 84.
5. Kenneth Keniston, *Young Radicals: Notes on Committed Youth* (New York: Harvest/HBJ, 1968), p. 48.

6. I. James Quillen and Edward Krug, *Living in Our America: History for Young Citizens* (Chicago: Scott, Foresman, 1956), p. 32.

7. Kirkpatrick Sale, *SDS* (New York: Vintage Books, 1974), p. 219.

8. Dower, *War Without Mercy*, pp. 15–23.

9. William J. Blakefield, "A War Within," *Sight and Sound* 52 (Spring 1983): 133.

10. James C. Thomson, Jr., "How Could Vietnam Happen? An Autopsy," *Atlantic Monthly* (April 1968): 50.

11. Henry Steele Commager, "On the Way to 1984," *Saturday Review* (April 15, 1967): 68; Peter Gessner, "A Guide to Anti-War Flicks," in *The Movement, a New America: The Beginnings of a Long Revolution*, edited by Mitchell Goodman (Philadelphia/New York: Pilgrim Press/Knopf, 1970), p. 407.

STORY TIME

1. Richard Drinnon, *Facing West: The Metaphysics of Indian-Hating and Empire-Building*, rev. ed. (New York: Schocken Books, 1990), pp. 42–43.

2. From the 1906 silent movie, *Attack on Fort Boonesboro* through hundreds of films ranging from *Drums of the Desert* (1927) to *Fort Yuma* (1955), the attack on the whites' fort (often with "flaming arrows") was a convention of the screen western as it had been of the dime novel, even though such attacks were historically rare. See Ralph E. Friar and Natasha A. Friar, *The Only Good Indian . . . The Hollywood Gospel* (New York: Drama Book Specialists, 1972), p. 188, esp. pp. 294–95, for a list of films in which such attacks occur.

3. Michael H. Hunt, *Ideology and U.S. Foreign Policy* (New Haven: Yale University Press, 1987), p. 46; Ruth Miller Elson, *Guardians of Tradition: American Schoolbooks of the Nineteenth Century* (Lincoln: University of Nebraska Press, 1964), pp. 73–74.

4. Drinnon, *Facing West*, pp. 44–45.

5. Michael Paul Rogin, *Ronald Reagan, The Movie and Other Episodes in Political Demonology* (Berkeley: University of California Press, 1987), pp. 145–46; Richard Slotkin, *Regeneration Through Violence: The Mythology of the American Frontier, 1600–1860* (Middletown, Conn.: Wesleyan University Press, 1973), pp. 73, 88; Drinnon, *Facing West*, p. 53.

6. Rogin, *Ronald Reagan*, p. 46.

7. Henry Nash Smith, *Virgin Land: The American West as Symbol and Myth*, rev. ed. (Cambridge: Harvard University Press, 1970), p. 4.

8. James W. Loewen, "History Textbooks and the First Thanksgiving," *Radical Historian's Newsletter* 65 (November 1991): 13.

9. Peter Wood, *Black Majority: Negroes in Colonial South Carolina from 1670 Through the Stono Rebellion* (New York: Knopf, 1975), pp. 42 ff., 219–20. See also Elson, *Guardians of Tradition*, p. 332, on the Americanness of being outnumbered in battle.

10. Drinnon, *Facing West*, p. 17; Slotkin, *Regeneration Through Violence*, p. 38.

11. Slotkin, *Regeneration Through Violence*, pp. 39, 42; Smith, *Virgin Land*, pp. 175–77.

12. Peter Dimock, "The American Revolution as Legitimating Social Narrative: George Bancroft's History and American Collective Memory," Paper presented at the Organization of American Historians, Chicago, 1992, pp. 6–7.

13. James D. Hart, *The Popular Book: A History of America's Literary Taste* (New York: Oxford University Press, 1950), pp. 40–41; see also Richard Slotkin and James K. Folsom, eds., *So Dreadful a Judgment: Puritan Responses to King Philip's War, 1676–1677* (Middletown, Conn.: Wesleyan University Press, 1978).

14. June Namias, *White Captives: Gender and Ethnicity on the American Frontier* (Chapel Hill: University of North Carolina Press, 1993), pp. 29–34.

15. Ibid., pp. 29–34; Smith, *Virgin Land*, pp. 112–20; Elson, *Guardians of Tradition*, pp. 310–12.

16. Bernard Bailyn, *The Peopling of British North America: An Introduction* (New York: Knopf, 1986), pp. 112, 115–16, 119.

17. George M. Frederickson, *White Supremacy: A Comparative Study in American and South African History* (Oxford: Oxford University Press, 1981), pp. 24–25; Slotkin and Folsom, eds., *So Dreadful a Judgment*, p. 33.

18. William H. Goetzmann, *Exploration and Empire: The Explorer and the Scientist in the Winning of the American West* (New York: Vintage Books, 1972), pp. 4–6, 303 ff.; see also Joseph Kastner, *A Species of Eternity* (New York: Knopf, 1977).

19. Elson, *Guardians of Tradition*, p. 80.

20. Hunt, *Ideology and U.S. Foreign Policy*, pp. 40–41, esp. pp. 19–45 for a stimulating discussion of "greatness" and "liberty"; Smith, *Virgin Land*, pp. 55–56.

21. Eric Foner, *Reconstruction: America's Unfinished Revolution, 1863–1877* (New York: Perennial Library/Harper & Row, 1989), p. 72.

22. James M. McPherson, *Battle Cry of Freedom: The Civil War Era* (New York: Oxford University Press, 1988), pp. 854, 859; Elson (*Guardians of Tradition*, p. 5) points out that American history "was not generally a required [school] subject until after the Civil War."

23. McPherson, *Battle Cry*, pp. 274, 797, 808.

24. Ibid., p. 850; Nathan Irvin Huggins, *Black Odyssey: The African-American Ordeal in Slavery*, rev. ed. (New York: Vintage Books, 1990), pp. 237–39.

25. Edward Tabor Linenthal, *Sacred Ground: Americans and Their Battlefields* (Urbana: University of Illinois Press, 1991), pp. 90–96, 105–8, 119.

26. See Nell Irvin Painter, *Exodusters* (New York: Knopf, 1976).

27. Nathan Irvin Huggins, *Harlem Renaissance* (New York: Oxford University Press, 1973), pp. 244–301; Toni Morrison, *Playing in the Dark: Whiteness and the Literary Imagination* (New York: Vintage Books,

1993), pp. 9, 35; see also David Nasaw, *Going Out: The Rise and Fall of Public Amusements* (New York: Basic Books, 1993), for the ways nineteenth- and twentieth-century public entertainments and spectacles of all sorts parodied blacks while excluding them from the crowd or audience.

28. Trudier Harris, *Exorcising Blackness: Historical and Literary Lynching and Burning Rituals* (Bloomington: Indiana University Press, 1984), p. 2; Frederickson, *White Supremacy*, p. 251.

29. Harris, *Exorcising Blackness*, p. xi.

30. Huggins, *Black Odyssey*, pp. xi–xviii. This extraordinary introduction to the 1990 edition of this book should be read in its entirety.

31. J. Hoberman, "How the Western Was Lost," *Village Voice* (April 27, 1991): 50; Richard Slotkin, *Gunfighter Nation: The Myth of the Frontier in Twentieth-Century America* (New York: Atheneum, 1992), p. 231.

32. Robert Sklar, *Movie-Made America: A Social History of American Movies* (New York: Random House, 1975), pp. 18 ff.; Nasaw, *Going Out*, pp. 160–62; Friar and Friar, *Only Good Indian*, p. 78.

33. Kevin Brownlow, *The War, the West, and the Wilderness* (New York: Knopf, 1979), pp. 224–35; Slotkin, *Gunfighter Nation*, p. 707.

AMBUSH AT KAMIKAZE PASS

1. James Bromley Eames, *The English in China* (London: Curzon Press/Harper and Row, 1909), p. 506; John Ellis, *The Social History of the Machine Gun* (Baltimore: Johns Hopkins University Press, 1986), pp. 86–87.

2. V. G. Kiernan, *From Conquest to Collapse: European Empires from 1815–1960* (New York: Pantheon Books, 1982), pp. 66–72, 86; Ellis, *Machine Gun*, pp. 89–90.

3. Evan S. Connell, *Son of the Morning Star: Custer and the Little Big Horn* (New York: Harper & Row, 1984), pp. 223–27; John W. Dower, *War Without Mercy: Race and Power in the Pacific War* (New York: Pantheon Books, 1986), p. 105.

4. Frances Fitzgerald, *America Revised: History Schoolbooks in the Twentieth Century* (Boston: Atlantic-Little Brown, 1979), p. 90.

5. Ralph E. Friar and Natasha A. Friar, *The Only Good Indian . . . The Hollywood Gospel* (New York: Drama Book Specialists, 1972), pp. 31 ff.

6. Michael Wood, *America in the Movies or "Santa Maria, It Had Slipped My Mind"* (New York: Delta, 1976), pp. 131–35; Friar and Friar, *Only Good Indian*, pp. 281–83; see also John E. O'Connor, *The Hollywood Indian: Stereotypes of Native Americans in Films* (Trenton: New Jersey State Museum, 1980).

7. Henry Nash Smith, *Virgin Land: The American West as Symbol and Myth*, rev. ed. (Cambridge: Harvard University Press, 1970), p. 103.

8. Richard Slotkin, *Gunfighter Nation: The Myth of the Frontier in Twentieth-Century America* (New York: Atheneum, 1992), pp. 278-92.

9. Jeanine Basinger, *The World War II Combat Film: Anatomy of a Genre* (New York: Columbia University Press, 1986), pp. 87-107, an invaluable book on war films; Ruth Miller Elson, *Guardians of Tradition: American Schoolbooks of the Nineteenth Century* (Lincoln: University of Nebraska Press, 1964), pp. 333-34; Paul Fussell, *Wartime: Understanding and Behavior in the Second World War* (New York: Oxford University Press, 1989), p. 120.

10. Fussell, *Wartime*, p. 138.

11. On the failure of OWI to rein in Hollywood's impulse to demonize the Japanese, see Clayton R. Koppes and Gregory D. Black, *Hollywood Goes to War: How Politics, Profits and Propaganda Shaped World War II Movies* (New York: Free Press, 1987), pp. 248-77; Ronald Spector, *Eagle Against the Sun: The American War with Japan* (New York: Free Press, 1985), pp. 409-10.

12. Julian Smith, *Looking Away: Hollywood and Vietnam* (New York: Scribner's, 1975), pp. 182-86. Generally, the films of full-scale battle against the Nazis that often come to mind when World War II movies are mentioned were postwar creations.

13. Edward F. Murphy, *Heroes of WWII* (New York: Ballantine Books, 1990), pp. 54-56; John Toland, *The Rising Sun: The Decline and Fall of the Japanese Empire, 1936-1945* (New York: Random House, 1970), pp. 245-46. For the kamikaze as the Japanese experienced it, see Haruko Taya Cook and Theodore F. Cook, *Japan at War: An Oral History* (New York: New Press, 1992), pp. 305-36.

14. Basinger, *World War II Combat Film*, p. 234.

15. John F. Kennedy, "Radio-TV Address of the President to the Nation from the White House," in *The Cuban Missile Crisis, 1962: A National Security Archive Documents Reader*, edited by Lawrence Chang and Peter Kornbluh (New York: New Press, 1992), pp. 150-54.

PREMONITIONS: THE ASIAN DEATH OF VICTORY CULTURE

1. Though there is a vast country-by-country (and even regional) library of books on post–World War II Asia, Asia as an area has played a distinctly subsidiary role in Cold War historiography. Akira Iriye's *The Cold War in Asia: A Historical Introduction* (New York: Prentice-Hall, 1974), almost the only volume to announce itself on the subject, in fact, stops chronologically short of the actual Cold War in Asia; while Robert M. Blum's *Drawing the Line: The Origin of the American Containment Policy in East Asia* (New York: Norton, 1982) makes it only to 1950. Otherwise, Thomas J. McCormick, in his *America's Half Century: United States Foreign Policy in the Cold War* (Baltimore: Johns Hop-

kins University Press, 1989), with his idea of a Rimlands War, "a twenty-year contest for the rimlands of Northeast Asia, Southeast Asia, and Taiwan," is particularly provocative and useful; as on the early years is Bruce Cumings in *The Origins of the Korean War: The Roaring of the Cataract 1947–1950*, vol. 2 (Princeton, N.J.: Princeton University Press, 1990), pp. 35–157. Still, it is remarkable that there is no single history of the Cold War in Asia.

2. Michael S. Sherry, *The Rise of American Air Power: The Creation of Armageddon* (New Haven: Yale University Press, 1989), p. 351; Paul Boyer, *By the Bomb's Early Light: American Thought and Culture at the Dawn of the Atomic Age* (New York: Pantheon Books, 1985), pp. 291–318.

3. Boyer, *Bomb's Early Light*, pp. 4–5; Sherry, *American Air Power*, p. 202; Richard Rhodes, *The Making of the Atomic Bomb* (New York: Simon and Schuster, 1986), pp. 664–65.

4. Boyer, *Bomb's Early Light*, pp. xix, 3, 14, 67; "The 36-Hour War," *Life* (November 19, 1945): 27–35.

5. "Preview of the War We Do Not Want," *Colliers* (October 27, 1951): 14, 19, 20; J. Fred MacDonald, *Television and the Red Menace: The Video Road to Vietnam* (New York: Praeger, 1985), p. 45.

6. Boyer, *Bomb's Early Light*, pp. 336–37.

7. Harold R. Isaacs, *Images of Asia: American Views of China and India* (New York: Harper Torchbooks, 1972), pp. xvii–xxiii, 216 ff.

8. Ibid., pp. 68, 226–27; John W. Dower, *War Without Mercy: Race and Power in the Pacific War* (New York: Pantheon Books, 1986), p. 166.

9. Stephen J. Whitfield, *The Culture of the Cold War* (Baltimore: Johns Hopkins University Press, 1991), p. 43; Clayton R. Koppes and Gregory D. Black, *Hollywood Goes to War: How Politics, Profits and Propaganda Shaped World War II Movies* (New York: Free Press, 1987), pp. 223–36.

10. Ross Y. Koen, *The China Lobby in American Politics* (New York: Harper & Row, 1974), p. 87; Ronald Steel, *Walter Lippmann and the American Century* (Boston: Atlantic–Little, Brown, 1980), p. 466.

11. Koen, *China Lobby*, pp. 13, 15, 206; David Caute, *The Great Fear: The Anti-Communist Purge Under Truman and Eisenhower* (New York: Simon and Schuster, 1978), p. 46.

12. Caute, *Great Fear*, pp. 55–56, 305, 315–17; Koen, *China Lobby*, p. 207; Jon Halliday and Bruce Cumings, *Korea: The Unknown War* (New York: Pantheon Books, 1988), pp. 159–60, 194.

13. Halliday and Cumings, *Korea*, pp. 155–57.

14. Ibid., pp. 154–55, 165; Melvin P. Leffler, *A Preponderance of Power: National Security, the Truman Administration and the Cold War* (Stanford: Stanford University Press, 1992), pp. 398, 406; Geoffrey Perret, *A Country Made by War: From the Revolution to Vietnam—the Story of America's Rise to Power* (New York: Vintage Books, 1990), p. 468.

15. Leffler, *Preponderance of Power*, p. 325; "NSC 68, A Report to the National Security Council," *Naval War College Review*, May–June

1975, p. 97; Ernest R. May, "Cold War and Defense," in *The Cold War and Defense*, edited by Keith Nelson and Ronald G. Haycock (New York: Praeger, 1990), p. 45.

16. Halliday and Cumings, *Korea*, p. 126.

17. Perret, *Country Made by War*, p. 451.

18. Halliday and Cumings, *Korea*, p. 128; Boyer, *Bomb's Early Light*, pp. 340–41; MacDonald, *Television and the Red Menace*, p. 31.

19. U.S. Department of State, *The Hate America Campaign in Communist China* (Washington, D.C.: U.S. Department of State, 1953), p. 99.

20. Callum A. MacDonald, *Korea: The War Before Vietnam* (New York: Free Press, 1986), pp. 253–56; Halliday and Cumings, *Korea*, pp. 207–8.

21. The only use of "Korean syndrome" I have discovered occurs in the *Pentagon Papers*. In a 1965 memo that Assistant Secretary of Defense John McNaughton wrote to Secretary of Defense Robert McNamara, he mentions the possibility of "large U.S. troop deployments [being] blocked by 'French defeat' and 'Korea' syndromes." New York Times, *The Pentagon Papers* (New York: Bantam Books, 1971), p. 433.

WAR GAMES

1. See, for instance, Jean Bethke Elshtain, *Women and War* (New York: Basic Books, 1987), pp. 15 ff.; Nancy Carlsson-Paige and Diane E. Levin, *Who's Calling the Shots: How to Respond Effectively to Children's Fascination with War Play and War Toys* (Philadelphia: New Society, 1990), p. 6; also author interview with Carlsson-Paige and Levin.

2. On Pentagon assistance to and oversight of commercial films about World War II, see Julian Smith, *Looking Away: Hollywood and Vietnam* (New York: Charles Scribner's Sons, 1975).

3. Paul Fussell, *Wartime: Understanding and Behavior in the Second World War* (New York: Oxford University Press, 1990), p. 53.

4. Paul Kennedy, *The Rise and Fall of the Great Powers: Economic Change and Military Conflict from 1500 to 2000* (New York: Random House, 1987), p. 384.

5. Peter C. Rollins, "Victory at Sea: Cold War Epic," *Journal of Popular Culture* 6, no. 3 (1973): 467–68.

6. For the above, I've relied on and taken all quotes from J. Fred MacDonald's invaluable *Television and the Red Menace: The Video Road to Vietnam* (New York: Praeger, 1985), pp. 111–21.

7. Ariel Dorfman, "Evil Otto and Other Nuclear Disasters," *Village Voice* (June 15, 1982): 43.

8. For those working-class and poor boys who did dream of becoming soldiers, see Christian G. Appy, *Working-Class War: American Combat Soldiers and Vietnam* (Chapel Hill: University of North Carolina Press, 1993), pp. 44–85.

9. Michael S. Sherry, *The Rise of American Air Power: The Creation of Armageddon* (New Haven: Yale University Press, 1987), pp. 187–93;

John Morton Blum, *V Was for Victory: Politics and American Culture During World War II* (New York: Harcourt Brace Jovanovich, 1976), p. 100.

10. *Life* (February 7, 1944): 9; (September 18, 1944): 15, 21; (November 19, 1945): 17.

11. Stephen J. Whitfield, *The Culture of the Cold War* (Baltimore: Johns Hopkins University Press, 1991), p. 74; Sidney Lens, *Permanent War: The Militarization of America* (New York: Schocken Books, 1987), p. 15.

12. Ernest R. May, "The U.S. Government: A Legacy of the Cold War," in *The End of the Cold War: Its Meaning and Implications*, edited by Michael J. Hogan (New York: Cambridge University Press, 1992), pp. 218, 226–28.

13. Seymour Melman, *The Permanent War Economy: American Capitalism in Decline* (New York: Simon and Schuster, 1974), p. 20; Whitfield, *Culture of the Cold War*, p. 31; Geoffrey Perret, *A Country Made by War: From the Revolution to Vietnam—the Story of America's Rise to Power* (New York: Vintage Books, 1990), pp. 471–75; Maxwell D. Taylor, *The Uncertain Trumpet* (New York: Harper, 1960), p. 173.

14. Michael McClintock, *Instruments of Statecraft: U.S. Guerrilla Warfare, Counter-insurgency, and Counter-terrorism; 1940–1990* (New York: Pantheon Books, 1992), pp. xvi, 28; H. W. Brands, *The Devil We Knew: Americans and the Cold War* (New York: Oxford University Press, 1993), p. 61.

15. McClintock, *Instruments of Statecraft*, pp. 29–30.

16. Melvyn P. Leffler, *A Preponderance of Power: National Security, the Truman Administration, and the Cold War* (Stanford: Stanford University Press, 1992), p. 490; McClintock, *Instruments of Statecraft*, p. 181.

17. Sydney Ladensohn and Ted Schoenhaus, *Toyland: The High-Stakes Game of the Toy Industry* (Chicago: Contemporary Books, 1990), p. 60; Ira H. Gallen, *Television Toys: A Video Series*, vol. 1 (New York: Video Resources NY, 1990).

18. Appy, *Working-Class War*, pp. 60–62; see Ron Kovic, *Born on the Fourth of July* (New York: Pocket Books, 1977), pp. 54–56, for another veteran's vivid account of such childhood war play; and Robert Jay Lifton, *Home from the War, Vietnam Veterans: Neither Victims Nor Executioners* (New York: Basic Books, 1985), esp. pp. 239–42, for more on the childhoods of antiwar Vietnam vets.

19. William M. Tuttle, Jr., *"Daddy's Gone to War": The Second World War in the Lives of America's Children* (New York: Oxford University Press, 1993), pp. 134–38; Arthur L. Rautman, "Children's Play in War Time," *Mental Hygiene* 27, no. 4 (October 1943): 550–52; author interview with Nancy Carlsson-Paige and Diane E. Levin.

20. Antonia Fraser, *A History of Toys* (London: Weidenfeld and Nicolson, 1966), pp. 51, 61, 86, 102, 149–52; Leslie Daikin, *Children's Toys Throughout the Ages* (London: Batsford, 1953), pp. 137–51. I was also helped by visits to the displays of toy soldiers at the Forbes Magazine

Galleries in New York City and at Leksaksmuseet (the Toy Museum) in Stockholm, Sweden.

21. George L. Mosse, *Fallen Soldiers: Reshaping the Memory of the World Wars* (New York: Oxford University Press, 1990), pp. 139–44; Fraser, *History of Toys*, p. 184. See also H. G. Wells' account of his own adult war-gaming with toy soldiers, *Little Wars* (London: Arms and Armour Press, 1970).

22. Carol Markowski and Bill Sikora, *Tomart's Price Guide to Action Figure Collectibles* (Dayton, Ohio: Tomart, 1991), p. 8.

23. Barbara Ehrenreich, *Fear of Falling: The Inner Life of the Middle Class* (New York: Pantheon Books, 1989), pp. 19–22; Sara Evans, *Personal Politics: The Roots of Women's Liberation in the Civil Rights Movement and the New Left* (New York: Vintage Books, 1980), p. 8.

24. James Miller, *"Democracy Is in the Streets": From Port Huron to the Siege of Chicago* (New York: Torchstone/Simon and Schuster, 1987), p. 330.

25. Very little has been written on nuclear fears in children during the Cold War era. See Robert Coles, *The Moral Life of Children* (Boston: Atlantic Monthly Press, 1986), pp. 243 ff.; Paul Boyer, *By the Bomb's Early Light: American Thought and Culture at the Dawn of the Atomic Age* (New York: Pantheon, 1985), pp. 355, 419 n. 11.

26. Special thanks to Jonathan Cobb for this thought about Hitchcock. *Psycho* (1960) and *North by Northwest* (1959) are the films referred to.

27. Erik Barnouw, *Tube of Plenty: The Evolution of American Television* (New York: Oxford University Press, 1975), p. 231; J. Fred Macdonald, *Who Shot the Sheriff? The Rise and Fall of the Television Western* (New York: Praeger, 1987), p. 55.

28. John F. Kennedy, "The New Frontier in Space," in *A History of Our Time: Readings in Postwar America*, 2nd ed., edited by William H. Chafe and Harvard Sitkoff (New York: Oxford University Press, 1987), pp. 126–29.

X MARKS THE SPOT

1. For Malcolm X, and for specific quotes, I have relied on: Malcolm X (as told to Alex Haley), *The Autobiography of Malcolm X* (New York: Grove Press, 1966), pp. 36, 152, 197, 199; Peter Goldman, *The Death and Life of Malcolm X*, 2nd ed. (Urbana: University of Illinois Press, 1979), pp. 32, 35–40.

2. For George Kennan, and for specific quotes, I have relied on: George F. Kennan, *Memoirs 1925–1950*, rev. ed. (New York: Pantheon Books, 1984), pp. 5–6, 30, 68–69, 77–79, 230, 293–95, 306; *Memoirs 1950–1963*, pp. 88–89; "The Sources of Soviet Conduct," *Foreign Affairs* (July 1947): 566–82; *The Nuclear Delusion: Soviet-American Relations in the Atomic Age* (New York: Pantheon Books, 1982), p. xii; Fred Inglis, *The*

Cruel Peace: Everyday Life and the Cold War (New York: Basic Books, 1991), pp. 87–95; Richard J. Barnet, "A Balance Sheet: Lippmann, Kennan, and the Cold War," in *The End of the Cold War: Its Meaning and Implications,* edited by Michael J. Hogan (New York: Cambridge University Press, 1992), p. 117.

3. "By the Fright of the Silvery Moon," *Tales from the Crypt* (EC Comics) 1, no. 35 (April–May 1953), in *Tales from the Crypt,* vol. 4 (West Plains, Mo.: Russ Cochran, 1979); "Midnight Mess," *Tales from the Crypt,* no. 35 (April–May 1953), in *Horror Comics of the 1950s* (New York: Nostalgia Press, 1971).

4. Thanks to Art Spiegelman for this thought from a lecture at the School of Visual Arts, New York City; also Abe Peck, *Uncovering the Sixties: The Life and Times of the Underground Press* (New York: Citadel Press, 1991), p. 11.

5. "Indisposed," *The Haunt of Fear* 1, no. 25 (May–June 1954), in *The Haunt of Fear,* vol. 5 (West Plains, Mo.: Russ Cochran, 1985); "Death of Some Salesmen!," *The Haunt of Fear* 1, no. 15 (September–October 1952), in *The Haunt of Fear,* vol. 3 (West Plains, Mo.: Russ Cochran, 1985).

6. Richard Hofstadter, *The Paranoid Style in American Politics and Other Essays* (Chicago: University of Chicago Press/Phoenix, 1979), p. 24.

7. "How to Tell Japs from the Chinese," *Life* (December 22, 1941): 81.

8. John Higham, *Strangers in the Land: Patterns of American Nativism 1860–1925,* 2nd ed. (New York: Atheneum, 1975), pp. 207–8; see pp. 194–212 for a fascinating exploration of this hysteria about German-Americans.

9. Richard M. Fried, *Nightmare in Red: The McCarthy Era in Perspective* (New York: Oxford University Press, 1990), pp. 49–50.

10. Nora Sayre, *Running Time: Films of the Cold War* (New York: Dial Press, 1982), pp. 80–81.

11. Frank J. Donner, *The Age of Surveillance: The Aims and the Methods of America's Political Intelligence System* (New York: Knopf, 1980), pp. 105–6; David Caute, *The Great Fear: The Anti-Communist Purge Under Truman and Eisenhower* (New York: Simon and Schuster, 1978), p. 114.

12. Peter Biskind, *Seeing Is Believing: How Hollywood Taught Us to Stop Worrying and Love the Fifties* (New York: Pantheon Books, 1983), p. 231; see pp. 230–40 for a striking discussion of the "cult of the Indian" film, as well as Richard Slotkin, *Gunfighter Nation: The Myth of the Frontier in Twentieth Century America* (New York: Atheneum, 1992), pp. 366–78; John E. O'Connor, *The Hollywood Indian: Stereotypes of Native Americans in Films* (Trenton: New Jersey State Museum, 1980), pp. 49–54.

13. Again, I have relied on Biskind's provocative *Seeing Is Believing,* pp. 102–59 (as well as my own viewing of these films).

14. Michael S. Sherry, *The Rise of American Air Power: The Creation of Armageddon* (New Haven: Yale University Press, 1987), pp. 1–21; Slotkin, *Gunfighter Nation,* pp. 195–211.

15. For all details of the American encounter with UFOs, I have relied on Keith Thompson, *Angels and Aliens, UFOs and the Mythic Imagination* (New York: Addison-Wesley, 1991); William Christian, Jr., "Religious Apparitions and the Cold War in Southern Europe," in *Religion, Power and Protest in Local Communities: The Northern Shore of the Mediterranean*, edited by Eric R. Wolf (Berlin: Mouton, 1984), pp. 240–41. Thanks to Marilyn Young for directing me to Christian's piece.

16. Richard B. Finn, "Lucky Dragon Incident," *Kodansha Encyclopedia of Japan*, vol. 1 (Tokyo: Kodansha, 1983), pp. 75–76.

17. Paul Boyer, *By the Bomb's Early Light: American Thought and Culture at the Dawn of the Atomic Age* (New York: Pantheon Books, 1985), pp. 325–26.

18. I have relied here on the pioneering work of Elaine Tyler May, *Homeward Bound: American Families in the Cold War Era* (New York: Basic Books, 1988), esp. pp. 3, 106–7, 136–37, 170, 207.

19. Geoffrey Perret, *A Country Made by War: From the Revolution to Vietnam—the Story of America's Rise to Power* (New York: Vintage Books, 1990), p. 476.

20. Stephanie Coontz, *The Way We Never Were: American Families and the Nostalgia Trap* (New York: Basic Books, 1992), p. 30; Victor Marchetti and John D. Marks, *The CIA and the Cult of Intelligence* (New York: Knopf, 1974), pp. 277–79.

21. John Howard Griffin, *Black Like Me* (New York: Signet Books, 1960), pp. 8–16, 119.

22. William H. Chafe, *The Unfinished Journey: America Since World War II* (New York: Oxford University Press, 1986), p. 214.

23. X, *Autobiography of Malcolm X*, pp. 238, 268, 285, 347, 381; George Breitman, ed., *Malcolm X Speaks: Selected Speeches and Statements* (New York: Grove Press, 1965), p. 8; Goldman, *Malcolm X*, pp. 25, 158.

24. Kennan, *Memoirs 1925–1950*, pp. 309–10, 464; *Memoirs, 1950–1963*, pp. 246–47; *Nuclear Delusion*, pp. 6–10.

THE ENEMY DISAPPEARS

1. Todd Gitlin, *The Sixties: Years of Hope, Days of Rage* (New York: Bantam Books, 1987), p. 68; Ronald Steel, *Walter Lippmann and the American Century* (Boston: Atlantic–Little, Brown, 1980), p. 445.

2. Gordon Brook-Shepherd, *The Storm Birds: Soviet Postwar Defectors* (New York: Weidenfeld & Nicolson, 1989), p. 15.

3. Philip Knightley, *The Second Oldest Profession: Spies and Spying in the Twentieth Century* (New York: Norton, 1986), p. 298.

4. Ibid., pp. 300–13.

5. Victor Marchetti and John D. Marks, *The CIA and the Cult of Intelligence* (New York: Knopf, 1974), p. 93.

6. Nora Sayre, *Running Time: Films of the Cold War* (New York: Dial

Press, 1982), pp. 92–93; Leo Cherne, "How to Spot a Communist," *Look* (March 4, 1947): 21–25.

7. Knightley, *Second Oldest Profession*, p. 248. On the NSA, see James Bamford, *The Puzzle Palace: A Report on America's Most Secret Agency* (New York: Penguin Books, 1983).

8. Marchetti and Marks, *CIA and the Cult of Intelligence*, pp. 273, 287–88; Thomas Powers, *The Man Who Kept the Secrets: Richard Helms and the CIA* (New York: Pocket Books, 1981), pp. 21–22.

9. Knightley, *Second Oldest Profession*, pp. 341–42.

10. Marchetti and Marks, *CIA and the Cult of Intelligence*, pp. 79, 118; Powers, *Man Who Kept the Secrets*, p. 44.

11. Sidney Lens, *Permanent War: The Militarization of America* (New York: Schocken Books, 1987), pp. 47, 53; Frank J. Donner, *The Age of Surveillance: The Aims and Methods of America's Political Intelligence System* (New York: Knopf, 1980), pp. 11–12, 27, 137, 275.

12. Millard Lampell, "I Think I Ought to Mention I Was Blacklisted," *New York Times*, August 21, 1966, reprinted in *Thirty Years of Treason: Excerpts from Hearings Before the House Committee on Un-American Activities, 1938–1968*, edited by Eric Bentley (London: Thames and Hudson, 1972), pp. 700–708.

13. Erik Barnouw, *Tube of Plenty: The Evolution of American Television* (New York: Oxford University Press, 1975), pp. 218–22.

14. Stephen J. Whitfield, *The Culture of the Cold War* (Baltimore: Johns Hopkins University Press, 1991), pp. 168–69; David Caute, *The Great Fear: The Anti-Communist Purge Under Truman and Eisenhower* (New York: Simon and Schuster, 1978), p. 21.

15. Whitfield, *Culture of the Cold War*, p. 28.

16. Victor S. Navasky, *Naming Names* (New York: Penguin Books, 1981), pp. xvii–xxiii. This book proved a treasure trove of information and ideas on which I have drawn in this chapter.

17. Ibid., p. 23.

18. Ibid., pp. 12, 40.

19. Larry Ceplair and Steven Englund, *The Inquisition in Hollywood: Politics in the Film Community, 1930–1960* (Berkeley: University of California Press, 1983), pp. 65–66; Clayton R. Koppes and Gregory D. Black, *Hollywood Goes to War: How Politics, Profits and Propaganda Shaped World War II Movies* (New York: Free Press, 1987), pp. 185–221.

20. Caute, *Great Fear*, p. 318.

21. Ibid., p. 85; Navasky, *Naming Names*, p. 22.

22. Navasky, *Naming Names*, pp. 247–48, 316–19.

23. Caute, *Great Fear*, p. 120.

24. Bentley, ed., *Thirty Years of Treason*, pp. 785–89.

25. Marty Jezer, *Abbie Hoffman, American Rebel* (New Brunswick, N.J.: Rutgers University Press, 1992), pp. 38–40.

26. Bentley, ed., *Thirty Years of Treason*, pp. 865–67; Whitfield, *Culture of the Cold War*, p. 125; Jezer, *Abbie Hoffman*, pp. 185–86.

27. Michael Barson, *"Better Dead Than Red!" A Nostalgic Look at the*

Golden Years of Russiaphobia, Red-Baiting, and Other Commie Madness (New York: Hyperion, 1992).

28. Ceplair and Englund, *Inquisition in Hollywood*, p. 52; Navasky, *Naming Names*, p. 333; Donner, *Age of Surveillance*, p. 179. Donner gives an estimate of 1,500 informers in the Party in 1956.

29. Caute, *Great Fear*, pp. 310, 454, for the purge in the universities, see Ellen W. Schrecker, *No Ivory Tower: McCarthyism and the Universities* (New York: Oxford University Press, 1986); in the unions, see George Lipsitz, *Class and Culture in Cold War America: "A Rainbow at Midnight"* (New York: Praeger, 1981).

30. Maria Reidelbach, *Completely MAD: A History of the Comic Book and Magazine* (Boston: Little, Brown, 1992), pp. 122, 132–35; John Le Carré, *The Spy Who Came in from the Cold* (New York: Bantam Books, 1975), p. 156.

THE HAUNTING OF CHILDHOOD

1. David Nasaw, *Going Out: The Rise and Fall of Public Amusements* (New York: Basic Books, 1993), pp. 174–75, 184–85; Simon Frith, *Sound Effects: Youth, Leisure, and the Politics of Rock 'n' Roll* (New York: Pantheon Books, 1981), pp. 244–45; Neil Leonard, "The Reactions to Ragtime," in *Ragtime: Its History, Composers, and Music*, edited by John Edward Hasse (New York: Schirmer Books, 1985), pp. 106–8.

2. William H. Chafe, *The Unfinished Journey: America Since World War II* (New York: Oxford University Press, 1986), p. 112; Dwight MacDonald, "Profiles: A Caste, A Culture, A Market," *New Yorker* (November 22, 1958): 60, 73–74.

3. James Gilbert, *A Cycle of Outrage: America's Reaction to the Juvenile Delinquent in the 1950s* (New York: Oxford University Press, 1986), p. 155. I've relied heavily on Gilbert's splendid study in this chapter; Marty Jezer, *The Dark Ages: Life in the United States, 1945–1960* (Boston: South End Press, 1982), p. 240.

4. Frederick Wertham, *Seduction of the Innocent* (New York: Rinehart, 1954), pp. 150–51.

5. Linda Martin and Kerry Segrave, *Anti-Rock: The Opposition to Rock 'n' Roll* (New York: Da Capo Press, 1993), p. 52.

6. Nelson George, *The Death of Rhythm & Blues* (New York: Dutton, 1989), p. 62; Jezer, *Dark Ages*, p. 280; Martin and Segrave, *Anti-Rock*, pp. 59 ff.; for a provocative discussion of the place of the juvenile delinquent in American consciousness and of the postwar rediscovery of poverty, see Barbara Ehrenreich, *Fear of Falling: The Inner Life of the Middle Class* (New York: Pantheon Books, 1989).

7. George, *Death of Rhythm & Blues*, pp. 52, 64–66; George's fine book, far more wide-ranging and daring than its title indicates, was especially useful on these racial border crossings.

8. Gilbert, *Cycle of Outrage*, pp. 71–73.
9. William W. Savage, Jr., *Comic Books and America, 1945–54* (Norman: University of Oklahoma Press, 1990), p. 12; Maria Reidelbach, *Completely MAD: A History of the Comic Book and Magazine* (Boston: Little, Brown, 1991), p. 22.
10. Mike Benton, *Horror Comics: The Ilustrated History* (Dallas: Taylor, 1991), p. 39; Gilbert, *Cycle of Outrage*, p. 101; Reidelbach, *Completely MAD*, p. 26.
11. Reidelbach, *Completely MAD*, pp. 26–28; see also Martin Barker, *A Haunt of Fears: The Strange History of the British Horror Comics Campaign* (London: Pluto Press, 1984), for the British version of the hysteria over comics; Benton, *Horror Comics*, pp. 51–54.
12. George Lipsitz, *Class and Culture in Cold War America: "A Rainbow at Midnight"* (New York: Praeger, 1981), p. 26; Gilbert, *Cycle of Outrage*, pp. 22–23; Ehrenreich, *Fear of Falling*, p. 96.
13. Editil Evans Asbury, "Rock 'n' Roll Teen-Agers Tie Up the Times Square Area," *New York Times*, February 23, 1957, pp. 1, 12. I thank Simon Frith for pointing me toward this article.
14. Macdonald, "A Caste, A Culture," pp. 57 ff.; Gilbert, *Cycle of Outrage*, pp. 205–10.
15. Charlie Gillett, *The Sound of the City: The Rise of Rock and Roll*, rev. ed. (New York: Pantheon Books, 1983), p. 13; Jezer, *Dark Ages*, pp. 275, 278–79; Martin and Segrave, *Anti-Rock*, p. 95.
16. Gillett, *Sound of the City*, pp. 41, 69.
17. Erik Barnouw, *Tube of Plenty: The Evolution of American Television* (New York: Oxford University Press, 1975), pp. 145–46, 206; George, *Death of Rhythm & Blues*, pp. 40–42, 49–50.
18. Martin and Segrave, *Anti-Rock*, pp. 94–96.
19. Gillett, *Sound of the City*, p. 64.
20. Jezer, *Dark Ages*, pp. 281, 289.
21. Douglas Gomery, "If You've Seen One, You've Seen the Mall," in *Seeing Through Movies*, edited by Mark Crispin Miller (New York: Pantheon Books, 1990), pp. 64–67.
22. Thomas Doherty, *Teenagers and Teenpics: The Juvenilization of American Movies in the 1950s* (Boston: Unwin Hyman, 1988), p. 241. Doherty's book includes a smart history of the development of a teenage market and of early media marketing strategies aimed at teens.
23. Gilbert, *Cycle of Outrage*, pp. 162–95.
24. "Rocketing Births: Business Bonanza," *Life* (June 16, 1958): 83.
25. Barnouw, *Tube of Plenty*, pp. 157–63, 166; David Marc, *Comic Visions: Television Comedy and American Culture* (New York, Routledge, 1992), p. 66.
26. See Gary Grossman, *Saturday Morning TV* (New York: Dell, 1980).
27. Critics, scholars, and citizen groups addressing television's threatening nature invariably chew over the (generally unfathomable) ways in which twenty-four-hour-a-day home entertainment affects our mental makeup and world view, while the unprecedented strangeness of TV's

beachhead in the home remains largely unnoted. The developing system for recording and selling more and more closely "seen" parts of the audience should instead be treated as a major aspect of television history—not just what was on the screen, but what those behind the screen saw through it, with those ghostly Neilsen families as its fictional characters. From material provided by the Neilsen Media Research Company.

28. J. Fred MacDonald, *Who Shot the Sheriff? The Rise and Fall of the Television Western* (New York: Praeger, 1987), pp. 16–17, 21–22, 39–43.

29. Cy Schneider, *Children's Television: The Art, the Business, and How It Works* (Lincolnwood, Ill.: NTC Business Books, 1987), pp. 19–22, 26.

30. Grossman, *Saturday Morning TV*, pp. 18–20; J. Fred MacDonald, *Television and the Red Menace: The Video Road to Vietnam* (New York: Praeger, 1985), pp. 121–22.

31. Grossman, *Saturday Morning TV*, p. 20; Barnouw, *Tube of Plenty*, pp. 263–64.

32. Todd Gitlin, *Inside Prime Time* (New York: Pantheon Books, 1983), p. 182; Marc, *Comic Visions*, p. 35.

33. Barnouw, *Tube of Plenty*, pp. 164–65; William Shatner, *Star Trek Memories* (New York: HarperCollins, 1993), pp. 282–86; Martin and Segrave, *Anti-Rock*, pp. 106–8.

34. Martin and Segrave, *Anti-Rock*, pp. 62–63, 97.

35. Marc, *Comic Visions*, pp. 45, 71–72.

36. For the adult western, see MacDonald, *Who Shot the Sheriff?*, pp. 47 ff.

37. Although I have seen all the *Twilight Zone* episodes quoted except the premier, I also relied on Marc Scott Zicree, *The Twilight Zone Companion*, 2nd ed. (Los Angeles: Silman-James Press, 1992), pp. 15, 22–23, 96.

38. Michael McClintock, *Instruments of Statecraft: U.S. Guerrilla Warfare, Counter-insurgency, and Counter-terrorism, 1940–1990* (New York: Pantheon Books, 1992), p. 174.

ENTERING THE TWILIGHT ZONE

1. Geoffrey Perret, *A Country Made by War: From the Revolution to Vietnam—the Story of America's Rise to Power* (New York: Vintage Books, 1990), pp. 471, 481–87; Fred Kaplan, *The Wizards of Armageddon* (New York: Torchstone/Simon and Schuster, 1984), p. 44.

2. "Can Russia Deliver the Bomb?," *Life* (October 10, 1949): 45; H. W. Brands, *The Devil We Know: Americans and the Cold War* (New York: Oxford University Press, 1993), p. 65; Kaplan, *Wizards*, p. 289.

3. Perret, *Country Made by War*, p. 482; Walter LaFeber, *America, Russia, and the Cold War, 1945–1980*, 4th ed. (New York: Wiley, 1980), p. 226.

4. Melvyn P. Leffler, *A Preponderance of Power: National Security, the*

Truman Administration, and the Cold War (Stanford: Stanford University Press, 1992), pp. 398–99.

5. Marilyn Young, *The Vietnam Wars, 1945–1990* (New York: Harper-Collins, 1991), p. 33.

6. David Halberstam, *The Best and the Brightest* (New York: Random House, 1972), p. 45.

7. Paul Boyer, *By the Bomb's Early Light: American Thought and Culture at the Dawn of the Atomic Age* (New York: Pantheon Books, 1985), p. 359.

8. Kaplan, *Wizards*, pp. 174–75.

9. Maxwell D. Taylor, *The Uncertain Trumpet* (New York: Harper, 1960), pp. 146, 173.

10. Kaplan, *Wizards*, pp. 197–99.

11. The phrases are John F. Kennedy's, from Kaplan, *Wizards*, p. 249; Mao Zedong, *Comrade Mao Tse-tung on "Imperialism and All Reactionaries Are Paper Tigers"* (Beijing: Foreign Language Press, 1958), pp. 17–18; "All Reactionaries Are Paper Tigers," in *Selected Works of Mao Zedong*, vol. 5 (Beijing: Foreign Languages Press, 1977), p. 517.

12. Jonathan Schell, *The Time of Illusion* (New York: Vintage Books, 1976), pp. 342, 337–87. There is no cannier analysis of the politics of credibility and the meaning of limited war than Schell's in this book, and I have relied heavily on it.

13. Charles Maechling, Jr., "Counterinsurgency: The First Ordeal by Fire," in *Low-Intensity Warfare: Counterinsurgency, Proinsurgency, and Antiterrorism in the Eighties* (New York: Pantheon Books, 1988), p. 21; Stephen E. Ambrose, *Rise to Globalism: American Foreign Policy, 1938–1976*, rev. ed. (New York: Penguin Books, 1976), p. 274; Michael McClintock, *Instruments of Statecraft: U.S. Guerrilla Warfare, Counter-insurgency, and Counter-terrorism, 1940–1990* (New York: Pantheon Books, 1992), p. 165.

14. McClintock, *Instruments of Statecraft*, pp. 179–81.

15. John Hellmann, *American Myth and the Legacy of Vietnam* (New York: Columbia University Press, 1986), pp. 45–47.

16. "John F. Kennedy Inaugural Address," in *Great Issues in American History: From Reconstruction to the Present Day, 1864–1981*, edited by Richard Hofstadter and Beatrice K. Hofstadter, rev. ed. (New York: Vintage Books, 1982), pp. 545–49.

17. Karen Schwartz, *What You Can Do for Your Country: An Oral History of the Peace Corps* (New York: William Morrow, 1991), pp. 17, 32–33; Stephen J. Whitfield, *The Culture of the Cold War* (Baltimore: Johns Hopkins University Press, 1991), p. 211.

18. Schwartz, *What You Can Do*, p. 49.

19. Maechling, *Low-Intensity Warfare*, p. 22.

20. Martin Luther King, Jr., "Letter from a Birmingham Jail," in *A History of Our Time: Readings on Postwar America*, 2nd ed., edited by William H. Chafe and Harvard Sitkoff (New York: Oxford University Press, 1987), pp. 181–91.

21. Massimo Teodori, ed., *The New Left: A Documentary History* (Indianapolis: Bobbs-Merrill, 1969), pp. 97–102.

22. James Miller, *"Democracy Is in the Streets": From Port Huron to the Siege of Chicago* (New York: Torchstone/Simon and Schuster, 1987), pp. 329–74.

23. Halberstam, *Best and the Brightest*, pp. 75–76.

24. Michael Klare and Peter Kornbluh, "The New Interventionism: Low-Intensity Warfare in the 1980s and Beyond," in *Low-Intensity Warfare*, p. 11.

THE ERA OF REVERSALS

1. *Star Spangled War Stories*, no. 131 (February–March 1967).

2. Ira H. Gallen, *Television Toys: A Video Series*, vol. 1 (New York: Video Resources NY, 1990); Cy Schneider, *Children's Television: The Art, the Business, and How It Works* (Lincolnwood, Ill.: NTC Business Books, 1987), p. 26.

3. Sydney Ladensohn Stern and Ted Schoenhaus, *Toyland: The High-Stakes Game of the Toy Industry* (Chicago: Contemporary Books, 1990), pp. 112–13; Katharine Whittemore, "Confessions of an Action Figure," *New England Monthly* (December 1987): 76–77; Carol Markowski and Bill Sikora, *Tomart's Price Guide to Action Figure Collectibles* (Dayton, Ohio: Tomart, 1991), pp. 106–7.

4. Whittemore, "Confessions," p. 77; Markowski and Sikora, *Action Figure Collectibles*, p. 107.

5. Michael Uslan, ed., *America at War: The Best of DC War Comics* (New York: Simon and Schuster, 1979), pp. 205–21.

6. Frances Fitzgerald, *America Revised: History Schoolbooks in the Twentieth Century* (Boston: Atlantic-Little, Brown, 1979), pp. 110–11, 129.

7. David Wise and Thomas B. Ross, *The Invisible Government* (New York: Random House, 1964), pp. 3–5, 351.

8. Erik Barnouw, *Tube of Plenty: The Evolution of American Television* (New York: Oxford University Press, 1975), pp. 332–40.

9. *The Warren Commission Report: Report of the President's Commission on the Assassination of President John F. Kennedy* (New York: St. Martin's Press, undated), pp. 21–22, 244, 255.

10. Edward J. Epstein, "Shots in the Dark," *New Yorker* (November 30, 1992): 55.

11. Daniel Ellsberg, *Papers on the War* (New York: Simon and Schuster, 1972), p. 16 n. 8.

12. Walter LaFeber, *America, Russia, and the Cold War, 1945–1980*, 4th ed. (New York: Wiley, 1980), p. 228.

13. Morley Safer, *Flashbacks: On Returning to Vietnam* (New York: St.

Martin's Press, 1990), pp. 138–39; David Halberstam, *The Powers That Be* (New York: Knopf, 1979), pp. 487–91.

14. Daniel C. Hallin, *The "Uncensored War": The Media and Vietnam* (Berkeley: University of California Press, 1989), p. 132. In addition to relying on his book—the best analysis of the media and Vietnam—I thank Dan Hallin for sharing with me tapes of news reportage from that time.

15. Safer, *Flashbacks*, pp. 44–45; Halberstam, *Powers That Be*, pp. 488, 510.

16. Michael Arlen, *Living-Room War* (New York: Viking Press, 1969), p. xi.

17. Safer, *Flashbacks*, p. 141; Wallace Terry, *Bloods: An Oral History of the Vietnam War by Black Veterans*, rev. ed. (New York: Ballantine, 1992), pp. 3–5.

18. Safer, *Flashbacks*, pp. 145–46, 150; Halberstam, *Powers That Be*, p. 490; J. Fred MacDonald, *Television and the Red Menace: The Video Road to Vietnam* (New York: Praeger, 1985), p. 236.

19. See Michael S. Sherry's striking account of these fire raids in his *The Rise of American Air Power: The Creation of Armageddon* (New Haven: Yale University Press, 1987), pp. 273–92; for the use of fire in Korea, see Geoffrey Perret, *A Country Made by War: From the Revolution to Vietnam—the Story of America's Rise to Power* (New York: Vintage Books, 1990), pp. 464–67.

20. Arlen, *Living-Room War*, p. 113. From draft-card burning and the phrase "Burn, baby, burn" to Quaker war protester Norman Morrison's self-immolation and the hundreds of protests aimed at the Dow Chemical Company for producing napalm, fire as a contested symbol was never far from consciousness in the Vietnam era.

21. Larry Engelmann, *Tears Before the Rain: An Oral History of the Fall of South Vietnam* (New York: Oxford University Press, 1990), p. 4; see also Alan Dawson, *55 Days: The Fall of South Vietnam* (Englewood Cliffs, N.J.: Prentice-Hall, 1977); and for the abandonment of America's Vietnamese intelligence network, see Frank Snepp, *Decent Interval: An Insider's Account of Saigon's Indecent End Told by the CIA's Chief Strategy Analyst in Vietnam* (New York: Random House, 1977).

22. Jonathan Schell, *The Time of Illusion* (New York: Vintage Books, 1976), pp. 137–38, 277; Frances Fitzgerald, *Fire in the Lake: The Vietnamese and the Americans in Vietnam* (New York: Vintage Books, 1973), p. 623 n. 16; James William Gibson, *The Perfect War: The War We Couldn't Lose and How We Did* (New York: Vintage Books, 1988), pp. 201–2; Robert Jay Lifton, *Home from the War: Vietnam Veterans, Neither Victims Nor Executioners*, rev. ed. (New York: Basic Books, 1985), p. 36.

23. Neil Sheehan, *A Bright Shining Lie: John Paul Vann and America in Vietnam* (New York: Vintage Books, 1989), p. 683; Larry Berman, *Lyndon Johnson's War: The Road to Stalemate in Vietnam* (New York: Norton, 1989), p. 37.

24. Schell, *Time of Illusion*, p. 356; Douglas Kinnard, *The War Managers:*

American Generals Reflect on Vietnam, rev. ed. (New York: Da Capo Press, 1991), p. 19.

25. James C. Thomson, Jr., "How Could Vietnam Happen? An Autopsy," *Atlantic Monthly* (April 1968): 47–53; Arlen, *Living-Room War*, p. 105.

26. Seymour M. Hersh, *The Price of Power: Kissinger in the Nixon White House* (New York: Summit Books, 1983), pp. 569, 617; Kinnard, *War Managers*, p. 115.

27. Ellsberg, *Papers*, pp. 47–52; Ross Y. Koen, *The China Lobby in American Politics* (New York: Harper & Row, 1974), p. 152.

28. Clark Clifford, *Counsel to the President* (New York: Random House, 1991), p. 410; Ellsberg, *Papers*, p. 50; Hallin, "Uncensored War," p. 170; Kinnard, *War Managers*, p. 25.

29. Todd Gitlin, *The Sixties: Years of Hope, Days of Rage* (New York: Bantam Books, 1987), p. 310. No book captures the feel of the 1960s better than Gitlin's wonderful work. Hersh, *Price of Power*, p. 597.

30. Gitlin, *Sixties*, p. 400.

31. Ibid., p. 302; Berman, *Lyndon Johnson's War*, p. 99; Sheehan, *Bright Shining Lie*, p. 735.

32. Marilyn B. Young, *The Vietnam Wars, 1945–1990* (New York: Harper-Collins, 1991), p. 237, the canniest one-volume history of the war(s). Berman, *Lyndon Johnson's War*, p. 154.

33. Hersh, *Price of Power*, pp. 52–53, 188; Roger Morris, *Uncertain Greatness: Henry Kissinger and American Foreign Policy* (New York: Harper & Row, 1977), pp. 146–48; Walter Isaacson, *Kissinger: A Biography* (New York: Simon and Schuster, 1992), pp. 145, 164, 259, 263.

34. Clifford, *Counsel to the President*, p. 466; Berman, *Lyndon Johnson's War*, p. 143; Kinnard, *War Managers*, p. 78.

35. Stanley Karnow, *Vietnam: A History* (New York: Viking Press, 1983), p. 526; David Hunt, "Remembering the Tet Offensive," in *Vietnam and America: A Documented History*, edited by Marvin E. Gettleman, Jane Franklin, Marilyn Young, H. Bruce Franklin (New York: Grove Press, 1985), pp. 359–65.

36. Berman, *Lyndon Johnson's War*, pp. 114 ff.; Karnow, *Vietnam*, p. 512.

37. Hersh, *Price of Power*, pp. 126, 622.

38. Richard M. Nixon, in Gettleman et al., eds., *Vietnam and America*, pp. 438–39.

39. *Report of the National Advisory Commission on Civil Disorders* (New York: Bantam Books, 1968), p. 135; Thomas A. Johnson, "Worse Racial Strife Than Riots Feared by Some Analysts," *New York Times*, October 22, 1968, p. 1; Gettleman et al., eds., *Vietnam and America*, pp. 336–37, 371.

40. Berman, *Lyndon Johnson's War*, p. 183; Kinnard, *War Managers*, p. 133; see pp. 124–35 for Kinnard's fascinating discussion of military antagonism toward the media. The claim that the United States had actually "won" the military part of the war in Vietnam found its most sophisticated expression in Colonel Harry G. Summers, Jr.'s post-Vietnam book *On Strategy*, but was a commonplace among war makers and war supporters at the time.

41. Kinnard, *War Managers*, pp. 69–70, 107; Sheehan, *Bright Shining Lie*, p. 696; Gibson, *Perfect War*, pp. 113, 305–7. No one has dealt with the American war as a production process organized on a management-labor model with its quotas of and bonuses for death the way James William Gibson has in this brilliant book. I have relied heavily on it in this section.

42. Gibson, *Perfect War*, p. 141; Richard Hammer, *The Court-Martial of Lt. Calley* (New York: Coward, McCann & Geoghegan, 1971), pp. 258–59.

43. Gibson, *Perfect War*, p. 113; Gloria Emerson, *Winners and Losers: Battles, Retreats, Gains, Losses and Ruins from a Long War* (New York: Random House, 1976), p. 65.

44. *The Pentagon Papers*, as published by the *New York Times* (New York: Bantam Books, 1971), pp. 542–44.

45. Seymour M. Hersh, *Cover-Up: The Army's Secret Investigation of the Massacre at My Lai 4* (New York: Random House, 1972), p. 83.

46. Young, *Vietnam Wars*, p. 213; Karnow, *Vietnam*, p. 602.

47. *Pentagon Papers*, pp. 372, 567–68.

48. Jonathan Schell, *The Real War* (New York: Pantheon Books, 1987), pp. 199–201.

49. Mary Rowlandson, "A Narrative of the Captivity and Restoration of Mrs. Mary Rowlandson," in *So Dreadful a Judgment: Puritan Responses to King Philip's War, 1676–1677*, edited by Richard Slotkin and James K. Folsom (Middletown, Conn.: Wesleyan University Press, 1978), pp. 323–25.

50. "Son My Mothers Call for Vengeance," *Viet Nam Courier*, May 27, 1968, in *Crimes of War*, edited by Richard A. Falk, Gabriel Kolko, and Robert Jay Lifton (New York: Vintage Books, 1971), pp. 360–62.

51. Hersh, *Cover-Up*, p. 10.

52. Ibid., pp. 74–77; Hammer, *Court-Martial*, pp. 244–45, 367; "The Massacre at My Lai," *Life* (December 5, 1969): 39.

53. For the various cover-ups, see Hersh, *Cover-Up*.

54. Peter Braestrup, *Big Story: How the American Press and Television Reported and Interpreted the Crisis of Tet 1968 in Vietnam and Washington* (New York: Anchor/Doubleday, 1978), pp. 251–52.

55. Seymour M. Hersh, *My Lai 4: A Report on the Massacre and Its Aftermath* (New York: Random House, 1970), pp. 105, 109; Hammer, *Court-Martial*, pp. 23–25.

56. Hersh, *My Lai 4*, pp. 134–35; see also Hersh, "The Story Everyone Ignored," *Columbia Journalism Review* (Winter 1969–70): 55–58.

57. "The Massacre at My Lai," pp. 37–39.

58. Hersh, *My Lai 4*, p. 121.

59. "The Massacre at My Lai," pp. 37–43; "My Lai: An American Tragedy," *Time* (December 5, 1969): 23, 25.

60. Harold Jacobs, ed., *Weatherman* (n.p.: Ramparts Press, 1970), p. 347; Hersh, *Cover-Up*, p. 117.

61. Hersh, *Cover-Up*, p. 14; Hammer, *Court-Martial*, p. 47.

62. Vietnam Veterans Against the War, *The Winter Soldier Investigation:*

An Inquiry Into American War Crimes (Boston: Beacon Press, 1972), pp. 11, 22; Terry, *Bloods*, pp. 29–30; Gibson, *Perfect War*, p. 202.

63. Safer, *Flashbacks*, p. 128.

64. Sheehan, *Bright Shining Lie*, p. 524.

65. James Miller, *"Democracy Is in the Streets": From Port Huron to the Siege of Chicago* (New York: Simon and Schuster, 1987), p. 318.

66. Hersh, "The Story Everyone Ignored," p. 57; *My Lai 4*, pp. 159–60.

67. Fitzgerald, *Fire in the Lake*, p. 494; Hammer, *Court-Martial*, p. 366.

68. Edward M. Opton, Jr., and Robert Duckles, "It Didn't Happen and Besides, They Deserved It," in Falk, Kolko, and Lifton, eds., *Crimes of War*, p. 441; Hammer, *Court-Martial*, pp. 374–377.

69. "Americans Speak Out on the Massacre at Mylai," *Life* (December 19, 1969): 47; Hersh, *My Lai 4*, pp. 151, 156; Hugh Sidey, "In the Shadow of Mylai," *Life* (December 12, 1969): 4.

70. Richard Nixon (statement), in Falk, Kolko, and Lifton, eds., *Crimes of War*, pp. 220–21; Hersh, *My Lai 4*, p. 159.

71. Telford Taylor, *Nuremberg and Vietnam: An American Tragedy* (Chicago: Quadrangle Books, 1970), p. 12; "The Massacre at My Lai," p. 42; "The My Lai Massacre," *Time* (November 28, 1969): 19.

72. Hammer, *Court-Martial*, pp. 37–38.

73. Miller, *"Democracy Is in the Streets,"* pp. 284, 298; Elinor Langer's wonderful description of the moment is in "Notes for Next Time: A Memoir of the 1960s," *Working Papers* (Fall 1973): 68; see Gitlin, *Sixties*, p. 471, for a small correction of her description.

74. Schell, *Time of Illusion*, pp. 97–98.

75. Peter Schrag, *Test of Loyalty: Daniel Ellsberg and the Rituals of Secret Government* (New York: Simon and Schuster, 1974), pp. 35–36.

76. Ellsberg, *Papers*, pp. 15, 286; Sheehan, *Bright Shining Lie*, pp. 591–92.

77. Schrag, *Test of Loyalty*, pp. 24–25; Ellsberg, *Papers*, pp. 251, 297, 304.

78. Ellsberg, *Papers*, p. 28; Schrag, *Test of Loyalty*, p. 33.

79. Ellsberg, *Papers*, pp. 28, 38–39, 101, 247, 305.

80. Neil Sheehan, "Should We Have War Crimes Trials?," *New York Times Book Review* (March 28, 1971): 1; Young, *Vietnam Wars*, pp. 259–60.

81. Hersh, *Price of Power*, p. 385; Morris, *Uncertain Greatness*, p. 250.

82. Schrag, *Test of Loyalty*, pp. 105–6, 109.

83. Ellsberg, *Papers*, pp. 39, 277, 281, 294, 305. I would also like to thank David Rudenstine for sharing with me a draft of his chapter on Ellsberg for his forthcoming book on the Pentagon Papers case.

84. See, for instance, James B. Reston, Jr., "Is Nuremberg Coming Back to Haunt Us?," *Saturday Review* (July 18, 1970), and Sheehan, "Should We Have War Crimes Trials?"

85. Emerson, *Winners and Losers*, pp. 329–30.

86. Vietnam Veterans Against the War, *Winter Soldiers*, p. xiv.

87. John Hellmann, *American Myth and the Legacy of Vietnam* (New York: Columbia University Press, 1986), pp. 91–92.

88. Hersh, *Price of Power*, pp. 608–9.

89. See Jeanine Basinger, *The World War II Combat Film: Anatomy of a*

Genre (New York: Columbia University Press, 1986), pp. 202–12, for an interesting discussion of the development of the "dirty" war movie.

90. See Richard Slotkin, *Gunfighter Nation: The Myth of the Frontier in Twentieth Century America* (New York: Atheneum, 1992), pp. 591–613, for a brilliant analysis of the ways *The Wild Bunch* and the war were intertwined.

91. Todd Gitlin, *Inside Prime Time* (New York: Pantheon Books, 1985), p. 227.

92. Clarence R. Wyatt, *Paper Soldiers: The American Press and the Vietnam War* (New York: Norton, 1993), pp. 151–56.

93. Hallin, *"Uncensored War,"* pp. 155–58.

94. Harold R. Isaacs, *Images of Asia: American Views of China and India* (New York: Harper & Row, 1972), p. 167 n. 84; "War Against Women and Children," no. 22 (n.p.: International Chewing Gum, 1938).

95. Michael Klein, "Historical Memory, Film, and the Vietnam Era," and David James, "Documenting the Vietnam War," in *From Hanoi to Hollywood: The Vietnam War in American Film,* edited by Linda Dittmar and Gene Michaud (Brunswick, N.J.: Rutgers University Press, 1990), pp. 36–38, 246–53; MacDonald, *Television and the Red Menace,* pp. 239–40.

96. Braestrup, *Big Story,* pp. 156, 161. Braestrup (unlike Hallin) believes that the inability to see the enemy led the media to give that enemy a major propaganda coup in Tet Offensive reportage.

97. Slotkin, *Gunfighter Nation,* p. 627.

98. *Pentagon Papers,* pp. 432, 438.

99. Berman, *Lyndon Johnson's War,* p. 59.

100. Halberstam, *Powers That Be,* pp. 430 ff.; MacDonald, *Television and the Red Menace,* pp. 202–5.

101. Hallin, *"Uncensored War,"* pp. 103, 108; Halberstam, *Powers That Be,* pp. 428, 514.

102. Jacobs, *Weatherman,* p. 70.

103. Gitlin, *Sixties,* p. 356; Jacobs, *Weatherman,* pp. 184–86, 450, 510.

104. Gitlin, *Sixties,* p. 264.

105. Frank Donner, *The Age of Surveillance: The Aims and Methods of America's Political Intelligence System* (New York: Knopf, 1980), pp. 259–63; Todd Gitlin, *The Whole World Is Watching: Mass Media in the Making and Unmaking of the New Left* (Berkeley: University of California Press, 1980), pp. 188–89.

106. Christian G. Appy, *Working-Class War: American Combat Soldiers and Vietnam* (Chapel Hill: University of North Carolina Press, 1993), pp. 112, 245, 283–85, 302; Lifton, *Home from the War,* pp. 168, 220, 223; Gibson, *Perfect War,* p. 199; Colonel Robert D. Heinl, Jr., "The Collapse of the Armed Forces," in Gettleman et al., eds., *Vietnam and America,* pp. 322–31.

107. Heinl, "Collapse," pp. 325–27; see Appy, *Working-Class War,* pp. 298 ff., for a discussion of class resentment and envy in the Vietnam War.

108. Lisa Hsiao, "Project 100,000: The Great Society's Answer to Military Manpower Needs in Vietnam," and William King, "'Our Men in Viet-

nam': Black Media as a Source of the Afro-American Experience in Southeast Asia," in "A White Man's War: Race Issues and Vietnam," *Vietnam Generation* (Spring 1989): 14, 22–23, 30, 110; Appy, *Working-Class War*, p. 22; Terry, *Bloods*, pp. 305, 312. On blacks picking up the gun (and white fears of "slaughter"), the place to start is with NAACP branch chairman Robert Williams's account of self-defense against the Klan in Monroe County, North Carolina, in 1961, *Negroes with Guns* (Chicago: Third World Press, 1973).

109. Young, *Vietnam Wars*, p. 240.

110. Kirkpatrick Sale, *SDS* (New York: Vintage Books, 1974), pp. 303–4; this book is a mine of material on the period and should not be out of print.

111. Bruce Oudes, ed., *From: The President, Richard Nixon's Secret Files* (New York: Harper & Row, 1989), pp. 129–34; Young, *Vietnam Wars*, pp. 249–51.

112. Sale, *SDS*, pp. 383–84.

113. Clifford, *Counsel to the President*, p. 566.

114. Schell, *Time of Illusion*, pp. 55, 131–32, 202, 278; Oudes, *From: The President*, p. 136; Stanley I. Kutler, *The Wars of Watergate: The Last Crisis of Richard Nixon* (New York: Knopf, 1990), p. 104.

115. New York Times, *The White House Transcripts* (New York: Bantam Books, 1974), pp. 5, 135–38; Hersh, *Price of Power*, p. 319.

116. I have relied on Seymour Hersh's superb political biography of Henry Kissinger, *The Price of Power*, for the details of White House taping, tapping, and spying (as for much else); see esp. pp. 316, 321–25, 379–80, 397–401, 465–71, 519. See also Hersh, "Nixon's Last Cover-Up," *New Yorker* (December 14, 1992): pp. 76 ff.

117. Isaacson, *Kissinger*, p. 400; Hersh, *Price of Power*, pp. 441, 489.

118. Times, *White House Transcripts*, pp. 141, 152.

119. For these figures, see Young, *Vietnam Wars*, pp. 301–2; Noam Chomsky, "Visions of Righteousness," in *Unwinding the Vietnam War: From War Into Peace*, edited by Reese Williams (Seattle: Real Comet Press, 1987), pp. 296–97.

120. Young, *Vietnam Wars*, p. 324; *Report on Civil Disorders*, p. 107.

121. "Text of the President's Address on U.S. Policies in Vietnam," *New York Times*, April 8, 1965, p. 16; Young, *Vietnam Wars*, p. 153.

122. "Text of President's Address," p. 16; Karnow, *Vietnam*, pp. 414, 419.

123. Max Frankel, "Johnson's Speech Viewed as Bid to World Opinion," *New York Times*, April 8, 1965, p. 1; Charles Mohr, "President Makes Offer to Start Vietnam Talks Unconditionally; Proposes $1 Billion Aid for Asia," *New York Times*, April 8, 1965, p. 1.

124. Gettleman et al., *Vietnam and America*, pp. 477, 487–89. Nixon's letter was not made public until the Carter administration took office in 1977. On Kissinger's avoidance of the word *reparations*, see Isaacson, *Kissinger*, p. 450.

125. Young, *Vietnam Wars*, pp. 301–3.

126. Richard Nixon, *The Real War*, 2nd ed. (New York: Touchstone/Simon and Schuster, 1990), p. 114.

AFTERLIFE

1. For all information on Lucas's life, I relied on Dale Pollock, *Skywalk-ing: The Life and Films of George Lucas* (London: Elm Tree Books, 1983), pp. 38–39, 142–85; see also Peter Biskind, "The Last Crusade," in *Seeing Through Movies*, edited by Mark Crispin Miller (New York: Pan-theon Books, 1990).

2. For information on Hagelstein, I relied on William J. Broad, *Star War-riors: A Penetrating Look into the Lives of the Young Scientists Behind Our Space Age Weaponry* (New York: Simon and Schuster, 1985), pp. 29, 105–27; see also Charles A. Robinson, Jr., "Advance Made on High-Energy Laser," *Aviation Week and Space Technology* (February 23, 1981): 25; E. P. Thompson, ed., *Star Wars* (New York: Pantheon Books, 1985), pp. 17–18.

3. Biskind, "The Last Crsade," pp. 116–17; Pollock, *Skywalking*, pp. 153–55.

4. Stephen J. Sansweet, *Star Wars: From Concept to Screen to Collectible* (San Francisco: Chronicle Books, 1992), pp. 13, 71; interview with Bernard Loomis, March 31, 1993.

5. Tom Engelhardt, "The Shortcake Strategy," in *Watching Television*, edited by Todd Gitlin (New York: Pantheon Books, 1986), pp. 87–94.

6. Bob Woodward, *The Commanders* (New York: Simon and Schuster, 1991), p. 347.

7. Paul Boyer, *By the Bomb's Early Light: American Thought and Culture at the Dawn of the Atomic Age* (New York: Pantheon Books, 1985), pp. 361–64; Edward Tabor Linenthal, *Symbolic Defense: The Cultural Sig-nificance of the Strategic Defense Initiative* (Urbana: University of Illi-nois Press, 1989), pp. xv, 10. This is a fascinating, if overlooked, cul-tural study.

8. "President's Speech on Military Spending and a New Defense," *New York Times*, March 24, 1983, p. A20; Tim Weiner, "Lies and Rigged 'Star Wars' Test Fooled the Kremlin, and Congress," *New York Times*, August 18, 1993, p. A15.

9. Linenthal, *Symbolic Defense*, pp. 14–15; Lou Cannon, *President Rea-gan: The Role of a Lifetime* (New York: Touchstone/Simon and Schus-ter, 1991), p. 293; Garry Wills, *Reagan's America: Innocents at Home* (Garden City: Doubleday, 1987), p. 358; Michael Rogin, *Ronald Reagan: The Movie and Other Episodes in Political Demonology* (Berkeley: University of California Press, 1987), pp. 2–3.

10. Linenthal, *Symbolic Defense*, pp. 6–7, 108–12; Rogin, *Ronald Reagan*, pp. 1–3.

11. Jacqueline Sharkey, *Under Fire: U.S. Military Restrictions on the Media from Grenada to the Persian Gulf* (Washington, D.C.: Center for Public Integrity, 1991), pp. 62–63, 65–66; see also Michael Arlen, "The Falklands, Vietnam, and Our Collective Memory," *New Yorker* (August 16, 1982): 70–75.

12. June Namias, *White Captives: Gender and Ethnicity on the American Frontier* (Chapel Hill: University of North Carolina Press, 1993), pp. 36–46; Woodward, *Commanders*, p. 339. For past uses, see, for instance, General Maxwell Taylor's reference to "military polemists . . . [who] can only belabor the folly of having accepted the [Korean] conflict on such restricted terms. This, they say, was fighting a war *with one arm tied behind our back*"; or President Lyndon Johnson's Vietnam plaint, "[S]ome people say stop the bombing, but I can't tie General Westmoreland's right arm behind his back right now." Maxwell Taylor, *The Uncertain Trumpet* (New York: Harper, 1960), p. 14; Larry Berman, *Lyndon Johnson's War: The Road to Stalemate in Vietnam* (New York: Norton, 1989), p. 183.

13. H. Bruce Franklin, *M.I.A. or Mythmaking in America* (Chicago: Lawrence Hill Books, 1992), pp. 58, 70–71, 74.

14. Ibid., pp. 135–36; for a good, brief history of the changing image of the vet on screen, see Rick Berg, "Losing Vietnam: Covering the War in an Age of Technology," in *The Vietnam War and American Culture*, edited by John Carlos Rowe and Rick Berg (New York: Columbia University Press, 1991), pp. 132–40.

15. Pat Aufderheide, "Good Soldiers," in *Seeing Through Movies*, edited by Mark Crispin Miller (New York: Pantheon Books, 1990), pp. 87–88, 95, 111; it was in this fine essay that I first found the term "noble grunt" films.

16. Cannon, *President Reagan*, pp. 485–91.

17. Richard Nixon, *The Real War*, 2nd ed. (New York: Touchstone/Simon and Schuster, 1990), p. 115; Sharkey, *Under Fire*, p. 78; Mark Hertsgaard, *On Bended Knee: The Press and the Reagan Presidency*, 2nd ed. (New York: Schocken Books, 1989), p. 213.

18. Interview with H. Kirk Bozigian, September 17, 1991.

19. Interview with Larry Hama, October 4, 1991; *The G.I. Joe Order of Battle* (New York: Marvel Entertainment Group, 1985), p. 47. In the 1960s, the Louis Marx toy company sold its "Warriors of the World" figures ("handpainted by artists") in individual boxes; each historical fighting figure from Roman legionnaires to World War II combat soldiers was given a fictitious name and a printed card "showing a colored drawing on one side and a detailed, fantasized story about that particular personage on the other." Thomas P. Terry, ed., *Plastic Figures and Playset Collector*, special collector edition (Lacrosse, Wis.: Specialty Publishing Company, 1994), pp. 19ff.

20. "Turning the Past into the Future at Hasbro," *Collecting Toys* (February 1993): 47; see also Engelhardt, "Shortcake Strategy," p. 47.

21. Bozigian interview.

22. Sharkey, *Under Fire*, p. 28.

23. ABC News, "War in the Gulf: Answering Children's Questions," transcript, January 26, 1991, p. 2; Inga Saffron, "Imaginations Run Wild About War," *Times Herald Record*, January 25, 1991; "When Little Children Have Big Worries," *Newsweek* (January 28, 1991): 40; Fred

Rogers with Hedda Bluestone Sharapan, "Helping Parents, Teachers, and Caregivers Deal with Children's Concerns About War" (Family Communications, n.d.); Dr. Joyce Brothers, "Helping Children Overcome Fallout from War," *Los Angeles Times*, March 19, 1991, p. E2; Patricia Reilly Giff, *The War Began at Supper: Letters to Miss Loria* (New York: Dell/Yearling, 1991), p. 48.

24. "How to Talk to Your Child About the War" (Boston: Work/Family Directions, 1991); "Suggestions for Helping Young Children Respond to WAR" (Philadelphia: Please Touch Museum, 1991); William H. Tuttle, Jr., *"Daddy's Gone to War": The Second World War in the Lives of America's Children* (New York: Oxford University Press, 1993), p. 149.

25. The *Washington Post's* Henry Allen quoted in Jay Rosen, "Politics, Vision, and the Press: Toward a Public Agenda for Journalism," in Jay Rosen and Paul Taylor, *The New News v. the Old News: The Press and Politics in the 1990s* (Twentieth Century Fund, 1992), pp. 22–23. Thanks to Jay Rosen, who first made this general point to me. Sharkey, *Under Fire*, p. 129.

26. Sharkey, *Under Fire*, p. 145; Malcolm W. Browne, "The Military vs. the Press," *New York Times Magazine* (March 3, 1991): 29.

27. Carolyn Wakeman, ed., *The Media and the Gulf: A Closer Look* (Berkeley: Graduate School of Journalism, University of California, 1991), p. 29.

28. Woodward, *Commanders*, p. 376.

29. On generals and publicists in World War II, see Paul Fussell, *Wartime* (New York: Oxford University Press, 1989), pp. 160–61; Phillip Knightley, *The First Casualty* (New York: Harcourt Brace Jovanovich, 1975), pp. 279–82; on military vetting practices, see "Spin Control Through Censorship: The Pentagon Manages the News," *Extra!* (special issue) 4, no. 3 (May 1991): 15.

30. John J. Fialka, *Hotel Warriors: Covering the Gulf War* (Baltimore: Johns Hopkins University Press, 1991), p. 55. Fialka's figures are on the high end of estimates of journalists in the Gulf. The Pentagon estimated 800–1,600 journalists in Saudi Arabia. Sharkey, *Under Fire*, p. 128.

31. John R. MacArthur, *Second Front: Censorship and Propaganda in the Gulf War* (New York: Hill and Wang, 1992), p. 94.

32. Douglas Kinnard, *The War Managers: American Generals Reflect on Vietnam*, rev. ed. (New York: Da Capo Press, 1991), pp. 129, 132–33.

33. See Fialka, *Hotel Warriors*, esp. pp. 25–31, for evidence that where, as in the case of the Marine Corps, reporters were aided and encouraged rather than shunted aside and treated as the enemy, coverage was more effusive and fuller without being faintly more investigative or oppositional.

34. Michael R. Gordon, "Schwarzkopf Says 'Hawks' Pressed for Early Land War," *New York Times*, September 20, 1992, p. 1.

35. John Balzar, *Manchester Guardian Weekly* (March 3, 1991): 10. See also Balzar's account in Wakeman, *Media and the Gulf*, p. 74.

36. "Heroes at Work," *Newsday*, special parade section, June 10, 1991, p. 12.

37. See Marilyn Young, "This Is Not a Pipe, This Is Not Vietnam," *Middle East Report* (July–August 1991): 21–24, for the best essay so far written on the Vietnam-Iraq analogy; R. W. Apple, Jr., "Baghdad Rejects U.N. Police Force to Protect Kurds, *New York Times*, May 10, 1991, p. 1.

38. On the problem of forgetting the bomb, see Jonathan Schell, *The Abolition* (New York: Knopf, 1984).

ACKNOWLEDGMENTS

As an editor for fifteen years, my job was, in part, to wait for other people sitting alone in rooms to finish and deliver their manuscripts to me. Sometimes we would talk by phone or meet, and I would discuss, cajole, or encourage in one fashion or another, always aware of what a cooperative effort would be involved in producing their books, always aware of the larger cast of characters—editor, copyeditor, designer, compositor, production manager, salespeople, and finally, reader—who would be called upon. Now, having been alone in a room myself for several years, I turn to these acknowledgments even more aware of how many friends, colleagues, and workmates filled the "solitary" time when this book was written, and of what a strange, labor-intensive activity writing (hence reading) turns out to be.

You could say I began this book in the 1950s simply by becoming conscious. But like so many of my peers, who dreamed of escaping that Eisenhower-era world of abundance and fear, when I felt I had done so, I seldom looked back. So writing this book involved a journey to a long ignored childhood land, to a time when it was possible to map the "Chinese invasion" of America, and then to those years in the later 1960s when I first became aware that something was distinctly awry with the screen story of America so familiar to me.

In returning to those decades, I also revisited a pop-culture landscape that I sometimes find horrifying exactly because its artifacts continue to affect me so deeply. I still, in fact, possess a small assortment of my favorite toy soldiers, and on the rare occasions that I unpack them from two small boxes stored in the upper reaches of a closet, I still feel an unparalleled fondness for them. As I graze the late-night hours on cable

TV, I still get a chill down my spine when, sabers drawn and bugle blowing, the cavalry charges. Tears still well up when that young second lieutenant reads the letter John Wayne (just killed by a Japanese sniper) meant for his son in *The Sands of Iwo Jima*, or when at any war movie's end the enemy fall by the score and GIs advance to the strains of some military tune. I felt moved recently simply to find a used copy of Quentin Reynolds's children's book *Custer's Last Stand*, and to see, so many years later, the familiar illustration of the sole survivor of Custer's command, Myles Keogh's horse Comanche, proud head bowed, being led away by a soldier. In the flyleaf of my present copy is the penciled comment, dated 1956–57 in a young hand, "One of the deep moving books, I thoroughly enjoyed"; and in another, even younger hand, simply "I LOVE AUTIE" (Custer's nickname). My sentiments of the time exactly.

My suspicion is that you can't grasp the changes the war story was undergoing in the 1950s without first admitting to the deep ways in which it thrilled you. The code organizing that cultural moment, already dissolving then, is now gone. When shown World War II films or old cowboy movies, my children or those of my friends, are often puzzled by them. Those films were such highly coded forms that without the right surroundings, without a specific sort of childhood, without the overarching story, there is no way to get them. There is, in a sense, nothing to get. In this book, I have endeavored to hide neither my love for and attraction to, nor my dislike for and disgust at what I've attempted to map out. Those were for me the best of play times and, often, the worst of actual moments.

I began the writing process that led to this book with an article, "Ambush at Kamikaze Pass," first published in the journal of an organization I had helped to found, *The Bulletin of Concerned Asian Scholars*. It was a piece on the treatment of the Third World in American films and I did much of my research in the summer of 1969 by randomly flipping the channels of a broken-down television set with a pair of pliers until I intersected with any of the hundreds of war, adventure, or western movies then (as now) cycling through TV's off hours. There was something about watching those bodies falling so innocently on screen, while simultaneously knowing about, and furious about, disturbed and unnerved by, and fearful of the real bodies, Asian and American, falling without grace and not bloodlessly in Indochina, that broke down certain boundaries in me—and began a line of thought that led, a quarter-century later, to *The End of Victory Culture*.

I continued to prepare for this book, without being faintly aware of it, as an editor at Pantheon Books, sharing the developing thoughts of others about American society. So I must first express my debt of gratitude to those like Paul Boyer, Ariel Dorfman, and Pat Aufderheide, who had no idea that they were helping me while I was helping them. I must also thank Todd Gitlin, who started me writing again in 1983 by convincing me that there was something more to do with TV shows than simply watch them.

Perhaps I would never actually have written this book if my wife, Nancy Garrity, had not helped organize me into it. She lived with a certain patience and dignity through the sometimes difficult fallout from my journey elsewhere. To her, I cannot begin to express my appreciation and love. To my children, Maggie and Will, I must also express a special appreciation. Without their very existences I would never have turned to child culture and so would have missed a crucial component of this book. Over the years, they have expressed their curiosity about this project with delicacy and affection.

My greatest advantage as a writer undoubtedly lay in having, from my years in publishing, such a plethora of wonderful, professional editors to call upon in what they may have experienced as my (too) many hours of need. This book simply would not have happened were it not for five editors:

Peter Dimock, whose keen editorial eye and critical encouragement buoyed me from the earliest moments, and whenever I doubted myself or my work thereafter;

Jim Peck, thoughtful old friend, who went through the book from first to last so many times, sharing and criticizing in a way that always drove me toward the next stage;

Jonathan Cobb, on whom I've relied for so long, whose bracing commentary and perfect editorial touch must be experienced to be believed;

Sara Bershtel, whose encouragement and sage advice at crucial moments in this book's development meant the world to me;

and Steve Fraser, who saved my book's life and whose incisive critical commentary forced me back to the computer for the final months necessary to make this the book it is.

No list of editors would be complete without my indispensable phone editor, Beverly Gologorsky, whose criticism and advice were made all the more valuable by the experience of the sixties that we shared; and without the wonderful Wendy Wolf, whose support was ever appreciated.

I feel grateful to a number of generous friends (or friends of friends) who were willing to read through all or part of the manuscript at various stages of development, offering criticism and help of every sort. First and foremost was Marilyn Young, who shared her work, her thoughts, and her materials with me, offering criticism, companionship, and encouragement; then there was John Dower, who took time from a particularly busy schedule to help me reorganize the early parts of the book. I also thank George Blecher, Millie Hawk Daniels, Simon Frith, Todd Gitlin, and Orville Schell for their helpful comments.

Others who offered me their time, their thoughts, or in some cases directed me to, loaned me, or gave me articles, books, comics, tapes, or other materials from the period I was studying include Michael Barson, H. Kirk Bozigian, Nancy Carlsson-Paige and Diane Levin, Leslie Clark, Haruko and Ted Cook, Bruce Cumings, Dan Hallin, Larry Hama, Mike Klare, Elinor Langer, Ed Linenthal, J. Fred MacDonald, David Rudenstein, and Art Spiegelman. I thank them all.

Being neither an archivist nor a professional scholar myself, I relied heavily on the distinguished scholarship of others. I hope I have acknowledged that debt in my notes, but there are always those authors whose deeper influence on one's thoughts simply cannot be traced through references. I owe special intellectual debts to Richard Slotkin, whose three-volume work on the creation and elaboration of frontier myths in American society was indispensable to my work, as it must be to anyone now considering American culture; Jonathan Schell, whose Vietnam reportage, writings on nuclear issues, and remarkable book *The Time of Illusion* helped shape my thoughts on the post–World War II decades; and James William Gibson, whose *The Perfect War*, perhaps the most original postwar book on Vietnam, had a particularly strong influence on my reconsideration of the war years. Finally, I feel deeply indebted to the thoughts and work of the late Nathan Huggins, whose new introduction to his book *Black Odyssey* so powerfully affected my views on the American narrative and whose greatest work, sadly, still lay ahead.

I offer my heartfelt thanks to Elaine Markson, my literary agent, who saw me through all those years with such good grace and optimism.

I would also like to express my appreciation to the John Simon Guggenheim Foundation for granting me a year of support to do a book on the business of childhood which, except for the effect the Persian Gulf War had on me, I might indeed have done (and will perhaps someday do). Certainly, their designating me as one of their fellows helped make this book possible.

Sharon Cohen and Debbie Taybron of the Bank Street College of Education library never complained no matter how many times I appeared with yet another request for an interlibrary loan. Special thanks is due to them, and also to the street booksellers (especially Larry Kaplan) on the blocks approaching Columbia University from whose displays I reconstituted a long discarded library of 1960s books, found forgotten magazines of the 1940s, 1950s, and 1960s, and often discovered works that sent me in unexpected directions. In a world in which publishing backlists are being decimated, they, like New York's used-book institution, the Strand, provided me with materials unavailable in any bookstore (not to speak of endless hours of pleasurable browsing).

At Basic Books, I appreciated the care that Joan Bosi, Ellen Levine, Justin McShea, and Gay Salisbury took either with my manuscript or with me. No one there was more patient or more helpful than Matthew Shine in the face of my many worries. I thank him especially.

Among newspaper and magazine editors, I would like to thank Doug Foster of *Mother Jones*, Antonin Liehm and Frank Berberich of *Lettre Internationale*, Oyvind Pharo of *Samtiden*, Arne Ruth of *Dagens Nyheter*, Micah Sifrey of *The Nation*, and Karen Syberg of *Information*.

I also extend a fond thanks to Sylvia Warren, who coexisted with me every day while this book was being written, and to Nancy S. Spaniel with whom I shared so many lunches.

Finally, I offer a special bow to Jim Blatt, who lived through so much of this with me the first time around.

INDEX